DOSTOEVSKY
BEYOND
DOSTOEVSKY

SCIENCE,
RELIGION,
PHILOSOPHY

ARS ROSSICA

SERIES EDITOR – **David Bethea**
(University of Wisconsin–Madison)

DOSTOEVSKY BEYOND DOSTOEVSKY

SCIENCE, RELIGION, PHILOSOPHY

Edited by
SVETLANA EVDOKIMOVA
VLADIMIR GOLSTEIN

BOSTON
2016

Library of Congress Cataloging-in-Publication Data:
A catalog record for this book is available from the Library of Congress.
© 2016 Academic Studies Press

ISBN 978-1-64469-028-4
ISBN 978-1-61811-527-0 (electronic)

Cover design by Ivan Grave
Book design by Kryon Publishing
www.kryonpublishing.com

Published by Academic Studies Press in 2016
28 Montfern Avenue
Brighton, MA 02135, USA
press@academicstudiespress.com
www. academicstudiespress.com

Table of Contents

ACKNOWLEDGMENTS

We would like to extend the most heartfelt gratitude to our stellar contributors, both for their thought-provoking essays and for the patience, which they brought to the editorial process. We would like to acknowledge the generous support of Brown University, which provided funds both for the Dostoevsky conference that we organized at Brown in 2014, and for the production of this volume. Special thanks to Chris Carr, the Slavic Department graduate student— now the holder of freshly minted Ph.D.—for his readiness to interrupt his research and help us with proofreading and streamlining the collection.

This is a high time to highlight the superb editorial work of the Academic Studies Press team. Blending patience with outstanding expertise, erudition, and exactitude, Scott Barker III proved to be an ideal copy editor; Kira Nemirovsky provided invaluable help and support at the moments of exasperation and frustration that necessarily accompany any editorial endeavor. Let us also use this opportunity to express our sincere gratitude to all our colleagues, family members, and friends for giving practical advice, helpful information, and their untiring interest and encouragement throughout the process. Very special thanks go to Robert Louis Jackson for inspiring us with his groundbreaking Dostoevsky scholarship and for his passion for Russian literature that continues to serve as a model of scholarly vocation for his numerous students and colleagues.

Introduction:
Fiction beyond Fiction:
Dostoevsky's Quest
for Realism

Svetlana Evdokimova and Vladimir Golstein

Discussing historical processes leading to the development of nations, Ivan Pavlovich Shatov, a character in Dostoevsky's novel *The Devils*, expresses his profound skepticism about modern science and rationalism:

> There is no nation that set itself up on the foundations of science and reason; there has never been an example of it, unless for a second only, out of stupidity . . . Science and reason have, from the beginning of time, played a secondary and subordinate part in the life of nations; so it will be till the end of time. Nations are formed and moved by another force which orders and rules them, the origin of which is unknown and inexplicable . . . It's the spirit of life, as the Scriptures call it . . . It's the aesthetic principle, as the philosophers call it; they also identify it as the ethical principle. "The seeking of God," as I call it more simply . . . God is the synthetic personality of the whole people, taken from its beginning to its end . . . Reason has never been able to define good and evil or even to distinguish good from evil even approximately. On the contrary, it has always confused them, shamefully and pathetically; science, in its turn, provided only fist-enforced solutions. Half-science, unknown to humanity till our century has excelled at that in particular, being the most dreadful scourge of humanity, worse than plagues, famine, and war. Half-science is the despot, of a kind that has never been imposed upon humanity before. This despot has its priests and slaves, before

this despot everyone bows with love or superstition hereto unimaginable;
the science itself trembles before it, while shamefully condoning it.[1]

Although the question of national formation and nationalism is not the focus of
the present volume, the connection between science, religion, philosophy, and
aesthetics is. Shatov's voice is not Dostoevsky's own. However, the way Shatov
identifies "the spirit of life" (*dukh zhizni*) with aesthetics (*nachalo esteticheskoe*),
moral philosophy (*nachalo nravstvennoe*), and with theology (*iskanie Boga*) as
the history-shaping forces, is indicative of Dostoevsky's awareness of the intense
interaction between diverse spheres of knowledge and modes of inquiry. Shatov
does not simply dismiss rationalism and empiricism for their inadequacy in
resolving moral questions. Instead, he targets science's "fist-enforced solutions"
(*razresheniia kulachnye*), that is, the doctrinaire imposition of scientific truths
as absolute and final truths, and criticizes the blind application of scientific
principles to all aspects of human life, or the practice referred to by Shatov as
"half-science" (*polunauka*). The ascending power of scientism was a serious
intellectual threat that Dostoevsky—along with his numerous contemporaries—had to confront. Dostoevsky's art and his search for "realism in a higher
sense,"[2] represent his response to the pressures and challenges of this despo-
tism. By aspiring to provide a counterpart to merely scientific and rational
inquiry, Dostoevsky's "realism," therefore, assumed an extraliterary task. In this
sense, Dostoevsky went a step even further than such nineteenth-century lumi-
naries as Pushkin, Gogol, and Tolstoy, all of whom strove to transcend the
boundaries of fictionality and were therefore perceived as more than "authors,"
more than mere fiction writers.[3]

It might be a risky proposition to claim that Russian literature is inherently
more intergeneric and interdisciplinary than its Western counterparts, that it is

---

1 F. M. Dostoevsky, *Polnoe sobranie sochinenii v tridtsati tomakh* [*PSS*], ed. V. G. Bazanov et al.
   (Leningrad: Nauka, 1972–1990), 10:198–99; hereafter cited as *PSS* by volume and page. All
   translations are ours unless otherwise specified.
2 *PSS*, 27:65.
3 Russian writers' stubborn denial of generic indebtedness, their insistence on their ability to
   transcend and transform the inherited Western literary patterns, was typical of Russian
   culture in general, and of its literature in particular. It is not surprising then that Russian
   readers routinely perceived the great classic authors of Russian literature as thinkers and
   visionaries, philosophers and gurus who shaped Russian national and cultural identity.

more deeply involved with other areas of human knowledge than literary traditions of other countries, or even that it has created distinctly new forms of literature. It is of paramount importance, however, to explore how the writings of such powerhouses of Russian cultural development as Dostoevsky are interconnected with other domains of human knowledge and discourse. What is there in Dostoevsky's fiction that is "more" than fiction or that goes "beyond" fiction? Dostoevsky's ambition to create realism "in a higher sense" should be considered precisely in the context of his struggle to transcend the boundaries of fictionality and to respond to the pressures and challenges posed by modern science. In line with Russian cultural tradition, Dostoevsky was relentless in his drive to go "beyond" fiction by engaging not only with major contemporary issues (including questions of social justice, philosophical, and theological debates) but also with various methods of inquiry. Indeed, Dostoevsky's oeuvre with its wide-ranging interests and active engagement with philosophical, religious, political, economic, and scientific discourses of his time represents a particularly important case for the study of cross-fertilization among disciplines. The primary goal of this volume is, therefore, to consider Dostoevsky's real or imagined dialogues with the aesthetic, philosophic, and scientific thoughts of his predecessors, contemporaries, and heirs. Such issues as the interaction between scientific and social discourses, the positivistic and idealist components of intellectual history and aesthetics, and philosophical and theological contexts of his oeuvre form the core of the intellectual framework of the volume.

Dostoevsky's "fantastic realism" or "realism in a higher sense" was deeply rooted, as this volume aspires to suggest, in the scientific and philosophical thought of his time. In his frequently cited letter to N. D. Fonvizina (1854), Dostoevsky announced, "I can tell you about myself that I am a child of this century."[4] Many readers acknowledged Dostoevsky's enduring ability to be engaged with modernity, but what exactly did Dostoevsky mean when he referred to himself as "a child of his century"? The way he grappled with the most pressing challenges presented by the science, philosophy, religion, and aesthetics of his time tells us a great deal about his sense of modernity. Referring to doubt as the prevailing attitude toward religion ("a child of doubt and disbelief"), Dostoevsky reveals that his religious hesitance may have been

---

4 *PSS*, 28(1):176.

formed under the impact of the ascending power of scientific discourses. Dostoevsky's doubt, however, extended both to the power of science and to the validity of religion.

Although Dostoevsky, in his later years, in particular, consistently rebelled against the exaggerated trust in the efficacy of the natural sciences' methods as applied to all areas of knowledge, he nevertheless took the challenge of science seriously. Moreover, some of his contemporaries even observed Dostoevsky's almost "chemical" method of characterization. Commenting on *The Double*, V. N. Maikov emphasizes Dostoevsky's "scientific" approach to his character's mental state and compares it to "an inquisitive person penetrating the chemical composition of matter": "What could be more positivistic, so it seems, than a chemical view of reality? And yet, the picture of the world illuminated by this view always appears to us as if bathed in some kind mystical light."[5] Indeed, the science of the period had acquired a heretofore unknown prestige. Richard G. Olson, among others, scrutinized this phenomenon, observing in his *Science and Scientism in Nineteenth-Century Europe* that "social theorists and those literary and artistic figures who molded the larger public culture continued through the nineteenth century to borrow heavily from development in the natural sciences in formulating their understanding of humans and their societies."[6] Exploring the issue from the Russian perspective, Diane Denning Thompson commented that "scientific ideas and methods spread into areas of thought where they had hitherto been absent: into biblical scholarship, history, philosophy and social and political theory."[7] As a "child of his century," Dostoevsky himself was to a certain degree a man of science. Let's not forget that Dostoevsky's father was a doctor, and Dostoevsky himself was an engineer by education, facts that are frequently glossed over. He received a good scientific education, including a solid grounding in mathematics and geometry. It is not a coincidence that his rebellion against knowledge offered by science frequently takes the form of a mathematical rebellion. But Dostoevsky's Underground Man hardly makes his notorious attack on "twice two is four" out of ignorance or

---

5   V. N. Maikov, "Nechto o russkoi literature v 1846-om godu," in *Literaturnaia kritika: Stat'i, retsenzii* (Leningrad: Khudozhestvennaia literatura, 1985), 182.

6   Richard G. Olson, *Science and Scientism in Nineteenth-Century Europe* (Champaign: University of Illinois Press, 2008), 2.

7   Dianne Denning Thompson, "Dostoevsky and Science," in *The Cambridge Companion to Dostoevskii*, ed. W. J. Leatherbarrow (Cambridge: Cambridge University Press, 2002), 192.

stubborn irrationalism.[8] Without trying to dismiss all scientific knowledge, Dostoevsky vehemently argues against *simplifications* (one of his favorite terms), suggesting that a particular brand of science cannot and should not usurp absolute and complete dominance over other fields of intellectual exploration. Dostoevsky had a particular distaste for axioms of all sorts, be they mathematical or ethical ones. In this respect he took a stance very different from that of his famous older French contemporary, Victor Hugo, a writer whom he otherwise greatly admired. Deploying the notion of "twice two is four" not to subvert rationalism but, on the contrary, to mock people's predilection for rewriting simple equations and questioning the axioms of Euclid's geometry, Hugo asserted that the notions of good and evil are also "axioms" of sorts. In *Napoléon le Petit* (1852) he writes,

> Here are some axioms of which you have probably an idea. Two and two make four. Between two given points the straight line is the shortest. The part is less than the whole. Now, get seven million five hundred thousand votes to declare that two and two make five, that the straight line is the longest road, that the whole is less than its part; get it declared by eight millions, by ten millions, by a hundred millions of votes, you will not have advanced a step . . . There are axioms in probity, in honesty, in justice, as there are axioms in geometry; and the truth of morality are no more at the mercy of a vote than are the truths of algebra.[9]

Dostoevsky would disagree. For him, the truths of morality are not at the mercy of a vote, but they are not axioms either. Hugo's sense of moral certainty might appear a bit strange in a Romantic, but Hugo was also an heir to the venerable rationalist tradition; he clearly owed his certainties to the moral authority of science and logic, articulated with unprecedented boldness by one of his

---

8   *PSS*, 5:119. "Twice two makes four seems to me simply a piece of insolence. Twice two makes four is a pert coxcomb who stands with arms akimbo barring your path and spitting. I admit that twice two makes four is an excellent thing, but if we are to give everything its due, twice two makes five is sometimes a very charming thing too" (ibid.). Dostoevsky, for sure, wasn't the first, nor was he the last, to play with the idea of "two times two may be five." The notion that two and two could somehow become five was already mentioned by George Gordon, Lord Byron, who states in his 1813 letter to his fiancée, Annabella Milbanke: "I know that two and two make four—and should be glad to prove it too if I could—though I must say if by any sort of process I could convert 2 & 2 into *five* it would give me much greater pleasure." Lord Byron, *Selected Letters and Journals*, ed. Leslie A. Marchand (Cambridge, MA: Harvard University Press, 1982), 340. Undoubtedly, this Romantic concept appealed to Dostoevsky.

9   Victor Hugo, *Napoleon the Little* (London: Vizetelli and Company, 1852), 185.

countrymen, Pierre-Simon Laplace, who in the preface to his 1814 "Philosophical Essay on Probabilities" penned this vivid, and supposedly the first,
articulation of scientific determinism:

> We may regard the present state of the universe as the effect of its past and
> the cause of its future. An intellect which at a certain moment would know
> all forces that set nature in motion, and all positions of all items of which
> nature is composed, if this intellect were also vast enough to submit these
> data to analysis, it would embrace in a single formula the movements of the
> greatest bodies of the universe and those of the tiniest atom; for such an
> intellect nothing would be uncertain and the future just like the past would
> be present before its eyes.[10]

Dostoevsky, however, didn't share this confidence in scientific, mathematical,
and moral axioms and their explanatory power. In part, his suspicion of "axioms"
may have been nourished by his exposure to Russia's scientific climate of the
time. We recall that the Underground Man's rebellion against "twice two is
four" goes hand in hand with his rebellion against Euclidian geometry.[11] His
protest, however, is not against arithmetic per se. Rather, he suggests that
self-evident ideas, such as two plus two equals four, comforting as they are, may,
in fact, have no reality outside the mind. Dostoevsky's interest in non-Euclidean
geometry highlights the fact that he must have been well aware that some
Euclidean proofs might very well be—in the words of Russian mathematician
and geometer Nikolai Lobachevky—"merely explanations and were not mathematical proofs in the true sense."[12] Lobachevsky produced geometry that he
called "imaginary," and this concept might have been more congenial to Dostoevsky's notion of "realism in a higher sense" than its Euclidean counterpart.
Curiously, the connection between a scientific outlook and a corresponding
type of realism would be later elucidated by Albert Einstein, who drew on the
non-Euclidean geometry and its further development in the theory of complex
numbers, the theory of vectors, and the theory of relativity. In his "Remarks on

---

10 Pierre-Simon Laplace, *A Philosophical Essay on Probabilities* (New York: Dover, 1951), 4.
11 For Dostoevsky's interest in non-Euclidean geometry, see Dianne Denning Thompson,
    "Dostoevsky and Science," 205–7. See also "Dostoyevsky & Science: The Brothers Karam-
    azov," *Cambridge Forecast Group Blog*, November 3, 2007, https://cambridgeforecast.
    wordpress.com/2007/11/03/dostoyevsky-science-the-brothers-karamzov/.
12 Quoted in Jason Socrates Bardi, *The Fifth Postulate: How Unraveling a Two-Thousand-Year-Old
    Mystery Unraveled the Universe* (Hoboken, NJ: John Wiley and Sons, 2009), 142.

Bertrand Russell's Theory of Knowledge," Einstein makes a distinction between an "aristocratic illusion" concerning the power of pure thought to gain the knowledge about the "objective world" and the "plebeian illusion of naïve realism," based solely on sense perception:

> During philosophy's childhood it was rather generally believed that it is possible to find everything which can be known by means of mere reflection. It was an illusion which anyone can easily understand if, for a moment, he dismisses what he has learned from later philosophy and from natural science; he will not be surprised to find that Plato ascribed a higher reality to "ideas" than to empirically experienceable things. Even in Spinoza and as late as in Hegel this prejudice was the vitalizing force which seems still to have played a major role.

The more aristocratic illusion concerning the unlimited penetrative power of thought has as its counterpart the more plebeian illusion of naïve realism, according to which things "are" as they are perceived by us through our senses. This illusion dominates the daily life of men and of animals; it is also the point of departure in all of the sciences, especially of the natural sciences.[13]

Dostoevsky's realism definitely was not an example of what Einstein viewed as "plebeian illusion of naïve realism," nor was it a purely "aristocratic" one. Dostoevsky defended his "higher realism" specifically against naïve realism, stressing the fundamental need to go beyond empirical comprehension into the realm of spiritual apprehension as the only way of grasping the very essence of reality: "I have my own view of reality (in art), and what most people regard as fantastic and exceptional is sometimes for me the very essence of reality. Everyday trivialities and conventional view of them, in my opinion, not only fall short of realism but are even contrary to it."[14]

Dostoevsky proposes here his version of "imaginary realism," or realism that reaches beyond the surface rather than blindly embracing *a priori* concepts, sensory experiences, and conventional views. Without denying the importance of sensory experiences and "real facts," Dostoevsky suggests a more integrative approach, including both observation of empirically

---

13   Albert Einstein, "Remarks on Bertrand Russell's Theory of Knowledge," in *The Philosophy of Bertrand Russell, ed.* P. A. Schlipp (New York: Tudor, 1944), 281.
14   Dostoevsky, Letter to N. N. Strakhov, February 26, 1869, *PSS*, 29(1):19.

experienced things and penetration into the realm of "ideas."[15] In his letter to A. N. Maikov (December 11, 1868), he writes, "I have entirely different notions of reality and realism from those of our realists and critics . . . With their kind of realism you cannot explain so much as a hundredth part of the real facts which have actually occurred. But with our idealism we have even prophesied facts."[16] Dostoevsky, therefore, links realism to epistemology. His realism, rooted as it was in both sensory experiences and Platonic idealism, was shaped, at least in part, under the impact of new trends in science. Dostoevsky focused on the epistemological doubts (it is in this sense also, that he viewed himself as "a child of doubt and disbelief"), on skepticism connected with the empirical sciences' ability to capture the dynamic nature of reality, on science's dependence on ever-changing scientific paradigms, each overturning the "absolute foundations" of the previous one. As he puts is in his Notebooks for *A Raw Youth*:

> Facts. They pass before us. No one notices them . . . I cannot tear myself away, and all the cries of the critics to the effects that I do not depict real life have not disenchanted me. There are no bases to our society . . . One colossal quake and the whole lot will come to an end, collapse and be negated as though it had never existed. And this is not just outwardly true, as in the West, but inwardly, morally so. Our talented writers, people like Tolstoy and Goncharov, who with great artistry depict life in upper-middle-class circles, think that they are depicting the life of the majority. In my view they have depicted only the life of the exceptions, but the life which I portray is the life that is the general rule. Future generations, more objective in their view, will see that this is so. The truth is on my side, I am convinced of that.[17]

What Dostoevsky suggests here is that conventional realist writers, such as Tolstoy and Goncharov, while trying to depict reality, have barely touched on the real itself, having not being fully aware that our inquiries into the nature of reality result in dynamic and perpetual state of flux. His "imaginary realism"

---

15 Malcolm Jones provides an important insight in Dostoevsky's integrative approach to realism by ascertaining that his fantastic realism "is about the intersubjective experience of reality and the elusiveness of a much sought-after, universal Truth." Jones, *Dostoevsky after Bakhtin: Readings in Dostoevsky's Fantastic Realism* (Cambridge: Cambridge University Press, 1990), 30.

16 *PSS*, 28(2):329.

17 *PSS*, 16:329.

stubbornly juxtaposes the "reality" of empirical facts to the "reality" of "essences." In *Diary of a Writer*, he presents his philosophical view of realism in clear opposition to the prevailing literary one: "'One must depict reality as it is,' they say, whereas such reality does not exist and has never even existed on earth, because the essence of things is inaccessible to man who perceives nature as it is reflected in his ideas, after passing through his senses; therefore one has to give more room to the idea and not to be afraid of the ideal."[18] We see how in Dostoevsky a "pure thought" claims its epistemological validity "independently of sense perception." Here Dostoevsky seems to be closer to Einstein's awareness of the "gulf" that logically separates the concrete world of material objects, on the one hand, from the abstract world of ideas, on the other.[19]

Along with some other "realist" Russian writers, who inherited the Romantic ethos of the "age of wonder," such as Tolstoy, for example, Dostoevsky exhibits profound suspicion of science as absolute truth and therefore engages in creating alternative narrative structures, highlighting the limits of deterministic, logical, predictable, that is, "scientific" unfolding of both a

---

18 *PSS*, 21:75. Curiously, in Dostoevsky's thought, the personal truth of an individual consciousness is often presented in its juxtaposition to empirical facts, whether this personal truth takes the form of acceptance of a higher ideal of Christ or of earthly axioms of Euclid's geometry. Although Ivan Karamazov draws on the authority of geometry, his ideas and conclusions belong to the domain of "personal truth": "Even if parallel lines do meet and I see it myself, I shall see it and say that they've met, but I still won't accept it" (*PSS*, 14:214). In an almost complete reversal of this argument, Dostoevsky insists in his aforementioned letter to Fonvizina that "if someone proved to me that Christ is outside the truth, and that in reality the truth were outside Christ, then I should prefer to remain with Christ rather than with the truth" (*PSS*, 28[1]:176). What is remarkable about these quotations is that while the speakers' visions of truth are radically different (belief in Euclid's "earthly" truth versus belief in Christ), the structure of the argument remains the same. The acceptance of God and acceptance of Euclid's geometry become ultimately a matter of faith, of personal preference, and commitment. What Dostoevsky suggests here is that he prefers to accept Christ as something that goes beyond and transcends empirical reality and established scientific facts. By the same token, Ivan Karamazov refuses to accept the "truth" of non-Euclidean geometry (which postulates that the parallel lines might meet) even if it is proven to him empirically, preferring to stick to his belief in Euclidean geometry. In other words, in both cases the argument is made in favor of a personal conviction, based on some deep-seated intuition or insight, against the "reality" or "truth" proven through traditional scientific methods or arguments.

19 Einstein writes, "We have the habit of combining certain concepts and conceptual relations (propositions) so definitely with certain sense experiences that we do not become conscious of the gulf—logically unbridgeable—which separates the world of sensory experiences from the world of concepts and propositions" (Einstein, "Remarks," 287).

character and a plot (similar to Tolstoy's attempt to delineate the limits of historiography). Dostoevsky's concept of the individual was formed in clear opposition to both the philosophy of the Enlightenment, with its belief in progress and cumulative organic growth, and to nineteenth-century realism and naturalism, preoccupied with the effects of heredity and environment upon the individual, presenting an individual character as the sum of causal and deterministic unfolding of his traits. Dostoevsky's characters, by contrast, affirm their radical freedom by evolving through sudden leaps and turns that defy the predictability of behavior. To some extent, this fascination with the eccentric can also be attributed to the Romantic ferment of science that swept across Europe at the end of eighteenth century but reached Russia somewhat later. Discussing a sudden series of breakthroughs in the fields of astronomy and chemistry that may have influenced the Romantic age and the Romantic taste for poetic inspiration coupled with "intense, even reckless, personal commitment to discovery," Richard Holmes writes,

> Romantic science would seek to identify such moments of singular, almost mystical vision in its own history. One of its first and most influential examples was to become the story of the solitary brooding Newton in his orchard, seeing an apple fall and "suddenly" having his vision of universal gravity. This story was never told by Newton at the time, but only began to emerge in the mid-18th century, in a series of memoirs and reminiscences.[20]

Much has been made of Dostoevsky's particular taste for "sudden" changes taking place in his novels, including mystical illuminations, personal epiphanies, and transformation, and for the overall prominence of such concept as "suddenly" in his poetics. It might be fruitful to link those elements of his poetics to the Romantic "ethos" of "sudden" discovery and to the very scientific climate that have shaped this ethos.[21] While Dostoevsky, similar to his famous

---

20 Richard Holmes, *The Age of Wonder: How the Romantic Generation Discovered the Beauty and Terror of Science* (New York: Pantheon, 2008), xvii.

21 Dostoevsky scholarship has long paid attention to on overwhelming prominence of the words "sudden" and "suddenly" in Dostoevsky's poetics. Cf. V. N. Toporov, "O strukture romana Dostoevskogo v sviazi s arkhaichnymi skhemami mifologicheskogo myshleniia. (Prestuplenie i nakazanie), in *Structure of Texts and Semiotics of Culture*, ed. Jan van der Eng (The Hague: Mouton, 1973). Toporov observes that the word "suddenly" occurs 560 times in *Crime and Punishment* and concludes: "The maximum frequency in the use of this word

Russian and Western European contemporaries, such as George Eliot, was striving to create adequate forms of literary realism, their respective versions were shaped by the different ways each of them responded to scientific theories of their time. A "breeding ground" for Dostoevsky's aesthetics and his religious and philosophical views included the thought and works of not only Darwin but also of Lobachevsky and such scientists as Mechnikov, Mendeleev, and Pavlov. Rather than merely modifying and reaffirming the claims of the histori-cally received scientific discoveries, these scientists articulated a new paradigm and, therefore, attracted Dostoevsky's scrutiny, even though he frequently disagreed with the specific conclusions or implications of their research. These nineteenth-century scientists generated "scientific revolutions,"[22] to use Thomas S. Kuhn's term, or, in Alain Badiou's terms, created an "event," that is, they discovered a rupture in the appearance of normality and opened a space to rethink reality. In this volume, two of those scientists, Darwin and Pavlov, receive particular attention.

Even though great examples of the two- or three-way exchange between science, literature, and then back to science can be found throughout this volume, the first part of this collection specifically addresses Dostoevsky's engagement with the challenges posed by the works of Darwin, Pavlov, and other scientists whose biological discoveries paved the way toward the recon-ceptualization of social, cultural, political, artistic, and psychological categories. This process of reconceptualization provoked Dostoevsky to his own ground-breaking literary discoveries and reconceptualizations.

David Bethea and Victoria Thorstensson's "Darwin, Dostoevsky, and Russia's Radical Youth" gets the ball rolling in chapter 1 as they concentrate on the very lively polemics within Russian fiction and journalism on the issues of uses and abuses of Darwin's theories. The chapter presents Darwin's reception in the writings of Russian radical intellectuals, such as Nikolai Chernyshevsky, Dmitry Pisarev, and Varfolomei Zaitsev, their ambitious and frequently groundless claims about the promise of science, and their consequent dismissal

---

occurs at such narrative steps, which coincide with transitions or depiction of emotional changes. In Russian literature, there are no other examples (with the exception of other texts of Dostoevsky) that would even remotely come close to *Crime and Punishment* in terms of their saturation with this word" ("O strukture romana Dostoevskogo," 234, 266–71).

22 Thomas S. Kuhn, *The Structure of Scientific Revolutions* (Chicago: University of Chicago Press, 1962).

of idealism and metaphysics, resulting in the radical reinterpretation of basic categories of society, art, and religion. These young radicals' highly partisan reading of Darwin was bound to produce reaction both in the journalism of the period and in fictional writings, including the major texts of Dostoevsky. Bethea and Thorstensson suggest that Darwin is present in Dostoevsky's oeuvre in various mediated forms, as a person, as a scientist, but even more importantly as an exaggerated figure conjured up by the imagination of his Russian epigones and their ideological opponents, be it the journalists Nikolai Strakhov and Mikhail Katkov or conservative writers, such as Nikolai Leskov and Alexander Diakov. Bethea and Thorstensson's discussion of these authors provides a very concrete and helpful background to Dostoevsky's thinking on the subject of science and biology, in particular. The overextension of science's claims, carried out by Dostoevsky's radical contemporaries, and their embrace of the caricatured vision of Social Darwinism clearly took educated Russians by storm, leaving its mark on their perception of science and philosophy, materialism and religion. Such spectacular misreading could not but trouble Dostoevsky, who was ready to challenge their assumptions and conclusions, moving boldly to "anti-empiricist, anti-positivist, anti-'mechanico-chemical' thought." Dostoevsky's skepticism toward all worldly truths, which are separated from the dynamic and open-ended approach that he associated with Christ, had put him on alert when Darwin's insights were mechanically and slavishly applied to the study of human development.

Darwin's thought, however, influenced not only the natural and social sciences but also the development of literary narratives. As Gillian Beer argues in her study *Darwin's Plots: Evolutionary Narrative in Darwin, George Eliot, and Nineteenth-Century Fiction*, Darwinian ideas insinuated themselves into the very texture and structure of the nineteenth-century English novel so that Darwinian notions of time, inheritance, variation, and selection permeated its very structure. As Beer explains, such novels as *Middlemarch* deal explicitly with the "web of affinities" determining relations within a specific time and space: "The web exists not only as an interconnection in space but as succession in time. This was the aspect of the image emphasized by Darwin in his genealogical ordering."[23] Taking Beer's argument as a point of departure, Liza Knapp,

---

23   Gillian Beer, *Darwin's Plots: Evolutionary Narrative in Darwin, George Eliot, and Nineteenth-Century Fiction* (Cambridge: Cambridge University Press, 1984), 157.

in chapter 2, "Darwin's Plots, Malthus's Mighty Feast, Lamennais's Motherless Fledglings, and Dostoevsky's Lost Sheep," offers a compelling argument about how Dostoevsky's response to Darwin penetrated deep into the aesthetic level of his works, pervading the very plots of Dostoevsky's narratives. Yet Knapp demonstrates that, as opposed to his English counterparts who were also influenced by the Malthus-inspired social Darwinism, Dostoevsky, resistant as he was to Social Darwinism, processed Darwin's plots differently from English novelists. Even in his early novels, such as *Netochka Nezvanova*, Dostoevsky counters Darwin's plots of the survival of the fittest with his Christian plots, novelizing the struggle for Netochka, the poor and unfortunate one, to be given a place at nature's "mighty feast." Knapp also points to the example of *The Idiot*, which clearly reveals Dostoevsky's subversion of Malthusian-Darwinian scenarios in his defiance of the "realistic" triumph of Malthusian "truths." Although, as Knapp insightfully concludes, "the consumptive and the lost sheep perish and the epileptic ends as an idiot," the novel as a whole "sustains its spirit of metaphysical rebellion."

Moreover, one could add that in his search for "realism in a higher sense," Dostoevsky strove to combine the plots based on the "low truths" of Darwinian struggle with cases and situations that seemed to defy probability ("fantastic and exceptional"), but which, nevertheless, convey "the very essence of reality." In opposition to the English novel, which is grounded in causality and predictability, Dostoevsky developed a particular taste for narrative and ideological surpluses, for the overabundance of characters, situations, causes and ideas, for broken continuity, for eruptions, epiphanies and all kinds of sudden changes; these narrative strategies disrupt the predetermined, "evolutionary" plot structure and overburden it with excess and schematic violations. Dostoevsky seeks for alternatives on the level of plot, theme, and characterization, and he tends to create characters marked as "oddballs," as eccentrics who are not immediately recognized as typical or average.[24] Such are his Alyosha

---

24 Dostoevsky was clearly sensitive to the statistical fashion of deterministic scientific studies. Cf. the discussion of the impact on his work of statistical studies by Adolphe Quetelet in Irina Paperno's *Suicide as a Cultural Institution in Dostoevsky's Russia* (Ithaca, NY: Cornell University Press, 1997), 19–45. Several studies in our volume discuss the role of oddballs in Dostoevsky's poetics, be it Kalganov in *The Brothers Karamazov*, or Porfiry Petrovich, the highly eccentric detective in *Crime and Punishment*.

Karamazov, or Prince Myskhin from *The Idiot*, or the Ridiculous Man from "The Dream of a Ridiculous Man."

Anna Berman's "'Viper will eat viper': Dostoevsky, Darwin, and the Possibility of Brotherhood" (chapter 3) foregrounds this complexity and ambiguity in Dostoevsky's approach to Darwin. Grappling with the subject of Darwin, Berman takes as a point of departure Daniel Todes's pioneering work on Darwin's reception in Russia. In his study, Todes explores and articulates the dominant line of thinking of both Russian scientists and philosophers, who were vehement on the subject of keeping Malthus and Darwin apart. Consequently, many Russians proved to be extremely hesitant, if not resistant, toward applying some radical ramification of Darwinian thought to the domain of social relationships. At the same time in Europe, such applications fell on rather fertile grounds, to the great dismay of such diverse Russian thinkers as Ilya Mechnickov, Peter Kropotkin, Andrei Beketov, Nikolai Danilevsky, and, of course, Dostoevsky. It is clear that the idea of cooperation as the powerful force within the unfolding biological drama was very dear to Russian thinkers. Dostoevsky mocked the facile reading of Darwin through his scathing portrayal of Andrei Semyonovich Lebezyatnikov, a character in *Crime and Punishment* who exemplified these "new ideas": "In England compassion is forbidden, giving way to political economy."[25] However, as Berman shows, Dostoevsky, true to his character, loved to play devil's advocate. When Beketov finds faults with Darwin's theory on the basis of his inability to imagine violent and bloody struggle between father and son over the last sip of water, Dostoevsky, in his last novel, demonstrates precisely the opposite. For Berman, Dostoevsky's view of the family hardly remains static, unfolding from seeing family as a tightly knit knot of mutual commitments in *Crime and Punishment* to the family of *The Brothers Karamazov*, where the Karamazovs are based on accidental and random relationships, and therefore exposed to the pitfalls of Darwinian struggle. In her meticulous and creative reading of Darwin's impact on Dostoevsky's last novel, Berman views Ivan's psyche as split between the two opposite stances concerning the familial relationships: love and sacrifice versus Darwinian struggle and competition to the bitter end.

---

25   *PSS*, 6:14.

Berman's insight into the complexity of the very issue of brotherhood takes us to the heart of Dostoevsky's view of man and reality: while it is easy to imagine that strangers are governed by the Malthusian relationship based on the "dog-eat-dog" principle, it is much more difficult to do so in the case of the sibling relationships. Yet, the presence of family hardly guarantees suprahuman love, devotion, and sacrifice. Dostoevsky appears to be very consistent here with his integrative approach, exploring the minute details of actions dictated by necessity and science, but at the same time introducing actions that stress mysterious, unexplainable, and illogical causality, much more akin to spiritual impact. Despite all of the Karamazov brothers' proclamations to the opposite, none of them seem to accept the brotherhood of Smerdyakov. The tension between easily proclaimed principles of abstract religious love and the concrete reality of loving one's unattractive neighbor, or brother, are foregrounded and problematized. It is clear that we are dealing here with an issue that is more serious than biological brotherhood or fatherhood. One's interpretation of the novel clearly depends on how one views the family and the mutual responsibilities of its members. Do the religious and moral teachings on such responsibilities enter into the conflict with those dictated by Darwin and biological science? Berman's reading of the text highlights the fact that the two approaches and outlooks should not be viewed as engaged in all-out conflict, but rather in a dynamic, unpredictable, yet mutually informed interaction.

Dostoevsky's grappling with the scientific thought of his time becomes further illuminated in Daniel Todes's chapter 4, in which he explores the interaction between Dostoevsky and two of his younger readers and admirers, the illustrious physiologist Ivan Pavlov and his committed Christian Orthodox wife, Serafima Karchevskaya. Todes's careful and attentive reading of the epistolary exchange between these three participants provides a fascinating example of how complex and dynamic one's views on science and religion can be. Despite his explicit embrace of atheism, Pavlov consistently stressed the dialectics of necessity and freedom, highlighting the complex manifestation of freedom within the laws of nature, while trying to avoid the simplification of pseudoscientific determinism at all costs. On a personal level, one can't help but admire Pavlov's acumen, his tolerance, and his open-mindedness; being an atheist himself, he welcomed his religious wife and equally religious Dostoevsky and wondered "how science might reconcile the seemingly contradictory truths that humans were subject to the determinism of natural law but remained responsible for their actions and to some extent, free." Later in life, he expressed his strong opposition to the Soviet attempts to suppress religion. Serafima's letters and descriptions provide curious anecdotes that reveal that Dostoevsky could not always raise himself above essentialism, above ethnic determinism, and the debilitating rationality of his own prejudices. Yet it also becomes obvious that in his communications with Pavlov and his wife, Dostoevsky found great support for his views of science as a field that is unpredictable and dynamic, whose trajectory involves sudden jumps and curves, rather than deterministic linearity. Todes's creative portrait of these three remarkable individuals, and of the environment in which they functioned, is illuminating, vivid, and gripping in its contradictions. The new and original material that Todes brings into the scholarly discourse on Dostoevsky confirms that science—be it in the form of biology, physiology, and psychology—while firmly grounded in empirical reality, frequently thrives through nonlinear, and therefore seemingly unscientific moments of shift, expansion, and indeterminacy.

Dostoevsky's skepticism toward positivist science combined with his profound interest in scientific discoveries of his time informed both his aesthetic sensibility and his moral philosophy. Even though Dostoevsky's contributions to the development of Russian religious thought and Western philosophy, and also to psychology and psychoanalysis, are frequently acknowledged, they are rarely analyzed in detail. Several authors, including Steven Cassedy, David Cunningham, Charles Larmore, and Sergei Kibalnik in Part II, discuss Dostoevsky's philosophical outlook and his implicit or explicit dialogue with various philosophical schools and traditions, bringing Dostoevsky's sophisticated dialectical thought to the surface.

In his provocative chapter 5, "Dostoevsky and the Meaning of 'the Meaning of Life,'" Cassedy revisits the question of "meaning" by outlining the history of the concept and considering the historical and intellectual circumstances that led to its emergence. While tracing its origins back to German Romantic philosophy and all the way forward to the existentialism of Camus, Cassedy suggests that the "word 'meaning' surfaces, when conventional forms of belief are under assault and European intellectuals are fishing around for a vocabulary that they can press into service in order to characterize from outside religion what's happening inside religion." In other words, the meaning of life (rendered by several Russians terms, such as *smysl, tsel', znachenie*) tends to be connected with religious questions, or, to be more precise, with situations "when conventional faith is under challenge." Indeed, the believers among Dostoevsky's characters seem to have an understanding of the meaning of life, even though they rarely articulate it, as opposed to those who, having lost their faith and what Dostoevsky calls "higher meaning," embark on the road of despair and even suicide. Cassedy suggests that the "meaning" clearly depends on the position of the observer, whether he is a believer or not, highlighting the irony of the situation, in which "meaning of life lacks meaning" and the very quest for meaning signifies the loss of faith and, consequently, of meaning. Cassedy brings Dostoevsky's shifting, evolving, and circuitous thought to the foreground. Paradoxically, for Dostoevsky to find the meaning of life, one has to lose it.

It may also be useful to recall Dostoevsky's particular fascination with the book of Job and the Jobean quest for meaning. The question of "meaning" dissolves only when one is ready to accept its limitations, trust the meaningless, and embrace faith, which for Dostoevsky involves, first and foremost, the work of active love directed toward others. Consequently, the process of meaning-discovery consists in giving up on one's search and acquiring the position from which one no longer interrogates the meaning of life, but embarks on life through faith and active love.[26] We may recall Zosima's advice to "a lady of little faith": "Strive to love your neighbor actively and incessantly. And when you are able to utterly forget yourself in your love . . . you'll believe without doubts . . . active love involves work, commitment, and for some—it is a complete science."[27]

---

26 Cf. St. Augustine's position that clearly foreshadows Dostoevsky's thought: "Understanding is the reward of faith. Therefore, seek not to understand that you may believe, but believe that you may understand" (*Tractates on the Gospel of John*, tractate 29).

27 *PSS*, 14:52–54. Dostoevsky suggests that the abstract search for meaning, the search that is based not on the living experience of faith and love, is bound to result in futile intellectual wonderings, similar to the Underground Man's vicious circle of reasoning. The dangers of this type of circuitous reasoning were mocked already by Milton in his comments on the philosophically minded devils, trapped in their search for meaning:
Others . . . reason'd high
Of Providence, Foreknowledge, Will and Fate,
Fixt Fate, free will, foreknowledge absolute,
And found no end, in wandring mazes lost.
(*Paradise Lost*, 2.558–61)

As has been observed by readers, Dostoevsky's work abounds in intellectual paradoxes. It is to the paradox of a Christian who constructs the strongest possible case for atheism, as well as the paradox of an atheist who cannot take God off his mind, that David Cunningham devotes his chapter 6, "Dostoevsky and Nietzsche: The Hazards of Writing Oneself into (or out of) Belief." Drawing on René Girard's observation that Dostoevsky was writing "ahead of his faith," Cunningham offers a useful dichotomy of "writing ahead of one's faith" and "writing behind one's faith." In the latter type of writing, the author expresses his religious position, which is already set, acting more or less like a social scientist articulating the latest findings of his field. In the former, the process of writing constitutes an open-ended search, an inner quest, the dialectics of pro and contra. As Cunningham argues, in contrast with Nietzsche's writing *behind* his faith or rather "behind his *unfaith*," Dostoevsky writes *ahead* of his faith in a sense that he writes without knowing in advance where the story will end and explores the questions as broadly as possible without trying to resolve the mysteries of the universe, man, and religion. Cunningham discusses the issue using the opposition between *Historie* and *Geschichte* ("the things that happened" versus "the story of the things that happened"). The latter refers to the stories that the Church told about Jesus, while the former relates to what actually occurred in his life. The method of writing "behind one's faith" was associated with new "scientific" trends in historiography (Cunningham links this trend to the emerging Life-of-Jesus researchers intent to produce "serious scholarship about faith"), which aspired to determine and describe only irrefutable facts. Dostoevsky clearly finds himself in the opposite camp from this approach, openly favoring *Geschichte*. "That is, in fact, what the Gospels are; and, in a very different sense, it is also what Dostoevsky's novels are," concludes Cunningham. This fruitful opposition points toward the very core of Dostoevsky's creative process, in which nothing is set in stone, the world keeps unfolding and remains open-ended. Cunningham appropriately quotes René Girard, who observed that "for Dostoevsky, writing is a means of knowing, an instrument of exploration; it is thus beyond the author himself, ahead of his intelligence and faith."

In chapter 7, "Dostoevsky as Moral Philosopher," Charles Larmore links the question of Dostoevsky's skeptical attitude toward the exclusive authority of empirical evidence to his moral philosophy. Revisiting the well-trodden territory of Dostoevsky's view of theodicy and the tensions between Ivan's and the Grand Inquisitor's "showing by argument" versus Christ's and Alyosha's "showing by deed," Larmore suggests that the confrontation between the Grand Inquisitor and Christ implies the two opposing ideas of human freedom.[28] These two notions of freedom involve the "radical freedom" to rise above our own sphere of concerns (or the *freedom of conscience*) and the *instrumental freedom* of being able to get what one wants. The latter kind of freedom fits in with our experience of how the world works, whereas the former is based on something that goes beyond such evidence. The best proof of radical freedom is our capacity to exercise it ourselves. Christ's and Alyosha's "showing by deed" demonstrates the limitations of any view of mankind's possibilities constructed on the evidence of what human beings usually think or do. Furthermore, Larmore offers an insightful interpretation of Dostoevsky's contribution to moral philosophy by identifying inner contradictions and inconsistencies within Ivan's arguments, that is, his "devotion to justice and his determination to stick to evidence." Ivan's very assumption that there is no God because the world is filled with the unjust and unjustifiable suffering of innocent children presupposes a sense of justice and a moral view that Ivan is trying to deny. In other words, Ivan relies on moral principles as he tries to explain his lack of faith in God and, therefore, in morality. Exposing the contradictions within Ivan's "two principal commitments," Larmore concludes that "his zeal for justice *shows by what it is* the error in his other, that is, in his determination to base his view of humanity on the way the world generally goes." The crucial moral truth, as Dostoevsky views it, is that "in our concern for the good of others we demonstrate the freedom we have to transcend what the evidence would otherwise prove to be the character of human motivation."

While Larmore discerns the inner logical contradictions in Ivan's conclusion that if there is no God, then "everything is permitted," Sergei Kibalnik, in

---

28 Dostoevsky's privileging the "showing by deed" over "showing by argument" is indeed a feature ubiquitous in his oeuvre. Many complex philosophical discussions find their resolution in Dostoevsky through nonverbal acts of human kindness. Consider, for example, *The Brothers Karamazov*'s parable of an onion, which focuses on the series of acts of giving and sharing; and the memorable story of a pound of nuts presented to Dmitry when he was a child, a story that merges in his mind with philosophical and theological issues of the Trinity. Consider also the significance of a pillow put under Dmitry's head by an unknown benefactor and its role in Dmitry's spiritual transformation.

chapter 8, "'If there's no immortality of the soul . . . everything is lawful': On the Philosophical Basis of Ivan Karamazov's Idea," focuses on the famous sentence's sources and philosophical contexts. Kibalnik places Dostoevsky's and his characters' musings on atheism and morality in the context of European philosophical thought, Ludwig Feuerbach's and Max Stirner's in particular. For Dostoevsky, as Kibalnik sees it, "the complicated dialectics of faith and morality, disbelief and Man-godhood, love for a neighbor and love for mankind in *Brothers Karamazov* cannot be understood without taking into account their interdependence with contemporary philosophical discourses." The philosophical basis of Ivan's reasoning might be, in part, based on the popularization of Max Stirner's ideas of "ego" and "self-enjoyment," which refuses to recognize any limits. Stirner's declaration of individualism and immoralism, in turn, stems directly from Feuerbach's concept of religion as an "objectification" of human consciousness. As Kibalnik reminds us, Nikolai Speshnev, a member of the Petrashevsky circle, was one of the early champions of these ideas (Speshnev became later a prototype for the character of Stavrogin in Dostoevsky's *The Devils*) and insisted that Feuerbach's anthropotheism was the first step for "science" to secure "complete and unconditional denial of religion." It is important to recognize Dostoevsky's polemic with contemporary philosophical discourses (which are instrumental in understanding Ivan's metaphysical rebellion) and his insistence on the interdependence between morality and the belief in the immortality of soul. Relying on Robert Louis Jackson's reading of Ivan's predicament, Kibalnik maintains that Dostoevsky's solution to the philosophical impasse of Ivan was the conviction that "acts of love produce faith." Both Jackson and Kibalnik emphasize that Dostoevsky believed that the scandalous and seemingly convincing logic of "if there is no God, everything is allowed" could be transcended only through concrete actions, through active love. Thus, despite differences in perspectives, Jackson, Kibalnik, and Larmore seem to agree that "showing by deed," and therefore changing the terms of the polemics, appears to be Dostoevsky's main strategy in challenging contemporary philosophical, theological, and scientific discourses. Undoubtedly, this is the strategy that Dostoevsky deploys consistently in his fiction, a point argued by other contributors to this volume, including Gary Saul Morson, Carol Apollonio, Deborah Martinsen, and Olga Meerson.

The questions of "showing by deed" and "showing by arguments" inevitably lead us to the problem of representation and, therefore, aesthetics. The
three chapters in Part III in this volume address Dostoevsky's aesthetic
concerns. Dostoevsky's religious and philosophical views, tensions between
atheism and faith are reflected in what Robert Louis Jackson calls Dostoevsky's
"quest for form," that is, his aesthetics.[29] How does one negotiate between the
so-called natural truth and artistic truth, between empirical data and intellectual or spiritual categories, between *Historie* and *Geschichte*, to use David
Cunningham's application of hermeneutic categories to Dostoevsky's thought?
Jackson's, Susanne Fusso's and Svetlana Evdokimova's essays deal with various
aspects of Dostoevsky's aesthetics and his polemic with his contemporaries on
the subjects of his art and his understanding of realism.

In his nuanced reading of Dostoevsky's complex, dynamic, and dialectical responses to Hans Holbein's *Dead Body of Christ in the Tomb*, Jackson in
chapter 9 takes us back to the fundamental issues of Dostoevsky's thought and
his views of the tasks of art to portray an image in something that has no image,
to see beauty in ugliness. He further discusses Dostoevsky's belief in art's
ability to convey not only natural or actual truth but also a higher, artistic
truth. Jackson considers Dostoevsky's aesthetics within the context of such
diverse thinkers and artists as St. Augustine, John Keats, and Victor Hugo, all
of whom express an aesthetic-spiritual outlook congenial to Dostoevsky and
are concerned with the problem of beauty and ugliness in artistic representation. Jackson argues that Augustine's notion of "formed formlessness" or
"formless form" is particularly useful for the understanding of the concept of
two kinds of beauty so central in Dostoevsky's aesthetics. Holbein's seemingly
repulsive, albeit well-executed, depiction of Christ's crucified body represents
for Dostoevsky this tension between artistic and natural truth, between two
kinds of beauty. Dostoevsky's interpretation and understanding of Holbein's
painting foregrounds his own concepts of reality and realism as a triumph of
artistic and spiritual truth over natural truth. The pro and contra of Holbein's
Dead Christ in Jackson's interpretation of Dostoevsky's response to it consists
in the painter's power to evoke contradictory reactions from the audience. The

---

29 See Robert Louis Jackson, *Dostoevsky's Quest for Form: A Study of His Philosophy of Art*
(Bloomington, IN: Physsardt, 1978).

viewer's ability to see the form in something that is formless ultimately depends on the degree of his or her prior receptivity and inner preparation. One could either project onto the canvas one's own spiritual crisis, as does Ippolit Terentiev (a character in *The Idiot*, who a priori resists faith) or internally visualize one's ideal aesthetically and spiritually, as does Dostoevsky. "A sense of permanent unrest and unease, and endless imaging of, and striving for, the unattainable ideal—here is where Dostoevsky leaves us," concludes Jackson. Curiously then, Jackson's analysis of Dostoevsky's aesthetics reinforces Cunningham's insights about writing "ahead of one's faith" versus "behind one's faith." Holbein's painting emerges as a work of art executed "ahead" of Holbein's faith. It is for this reason that it evoked such a powerful and dialectical response from Dostoevsky, whose aesthetic sensibility and creative thinking seems to be always ahead of his faith.

Approaching the issue of aesthetics from a biographical and historic perspective, Fusso explores, in chapter 10, Dostoevsky's relationship with his rival publisher and fellow journalist, Mikhail Katkov. Fusso sees Dostoevsky and Katkov as two conservatives sharing many aesthetic positions and agreeing on fundamental issues but engaging nevertheless in a passionate polemic over Russian cultural and political roles, especially the legacy of Pushkin. These dialectics of differences and similarities clearly exaggerated their individual antipathies. As biting and personal as this polemic might have been, it ignited Dostoevsky to write some of his most important aesthetic "manifestoes," including his essay "Mr. –bov and the Problem of Art," in which he defined his concept of art as independent from both the "utilitarian" and "pure artistic" perspectives. Ultimately, the story of the sharp personal attacks and disagreements between these two men had a "happy ending," as Katkov, to Dostoevsky's surprise, agreed to publish what would become *Crime and Punishment*, the first of Dostoevsky's major novels. These aesthetic disputes, which were part of "the bare-knuckled nature of nineteenth-century Russian journalism," undoubtedly sharpened Dostoevsky's own polemical muse.

Fusso's discussion of Dostoevsky and Katkov's literary polemic highlights Dostoevsky's intense preoccupation with the issues of aesthetics. Romantic debates over the utility of art had acquired new poignancy in Dostoevsky's time, as various intellectual movements—scientism, pragmatism, materialism, and nihilism—resumed their attempts to redefine art, provoking Dostoevsky toward new artistic discoveries and insights.

Dostoevsky's preoccupation with the questions of art and representation is considered by Evdokimova from the point of view of his concern with the crisis of Platonic aesthetics. In chapter 11, "Dostoevsky's Postmodernists and the Aesthetics of Incarnation," Evdokimova discusses Fyodor Karamazov as a performing artist who anticipates the anti-Platonic turn in modern philosophy described, among others, by Deleuze and Baudrillard, theoreticians investigating postmodern sensitivity. In contrast to Dostoevsky's religious aesthetics, based on the Platonic (and Neoplatonic) representation and captured in his notion of "realism in a higher sense," Fyodor Karamazov (along with Ivan Karamazov's devil and several other characters who represent modern aesthetic trends) emerges as a prophet of postmodernism, a representative of the poetics of phantasmatic simulacra, of the destabilization of meaning, and aleatory verbal defilement. Reading Fyodor's notorious blasphemy and buffoonery as the manifestation of his rejection of Platonic representation and the embrace of the aesthetic existence of simulacrum, Evdokimova argues that Fyodor's use of distorted quotations, his references to the nonexistent originals, his deconstruction of cultural intertext, and his hypertextuality link his performance-driven activity to postmodern aesthetics. Dostoevsky sensed the pending crisis in the aesthetic and religious consciousness of modernity, and he was therefore concerned, as Evdokimova argues, with the rupture between the modern aesthetic and its foundation in Platonic tradition. Trying to defend his "realism in a higher sense," Dostoevsky was critical of both the naturalistic understanding of realism, which, in his opinion, was limiting itself to exterior similarity and superficial depiction, and of the emerging aesthetic sensibility that separated the image from the proto-image. In response, Dostoevsky offered what Evdokimova calls the "aesthetics of incarnation," that is, aesthetics based on the assumption of continuity between the ideal form and the empirical world.

Being the "child of his century," Dostoevsky grappled not only with new aesthetic trends but also with the new trends in psychology. How do modern scientific and philosophical views refract themselves in the way we conceive of human personality, identity, selfhood, and consciousness? Dostoevsky's notion of "realism in a higher sense" is clearly tied to his concept of self and of consciousness: "They call me psychologist: that's wrong, I am only a realist in a higher sense, that is, I depict all the depths of human soul."[30] A cluster of authors address the issues of selfhood in Dostoevsky's oeuvre in Part IV, exploring his fascination with peculiar kinds of literary characters, such as doubles, shadows, "angels," men "without qualities," catalysts, and other indeterminate and ambiguous personalities.

In chapter 12, "What Is It Like to Be Bats?," Gary-Saul Morson draws a sharp line that separates Dostoevsky from writers who approach human consciousness from the perspective of scientific materialism. For Morson, the line that divides the two groups is connected with their respective views on the mystery of consciousness, the existence of which always presupposes a point of view. According to Morson, Dostoevsky was convinced that "a purely objective, point-of-view-less description of the world could never be complete. The materialists must be wrong precisely because for them that description is complete." One of Dostoevsky's strategies of challenging the Russian intelligentsia's materialistic point of view on human consciousness shaped by the scientism's rejection of its mystery was to populate the pages of his fiction with doubles, replicas, shadows, and other ambiguous and amorphous characters whose presence foregrounded the tensions between similarity, identity, and consciousness. How can a likeness end in identity if identity implies a point of view? Morson places the cultural anthropology of doubling characters within the debates on materialism, religion, and subjectivity by Dostoevsky, on the one hand, and by the radical Russian intelligentsia, on the other. He links the phenomenon of the simultaneous fear of doubles and entrapment in doubling to the crisis of personhood understood as consciousness. The only way out of this crisis, Morson emphasizes, is suggested by the moments of "genuine sympathy for others that allow one to escape the logic of doubling, of leaving one's own shadow behind."

Other scholars also discuss Dostoevsky's interest in doubles and the implication of this category for his concept of self. Yuri Corrigan, in chapter 13, "Interiority and Intersubjectivity in Dostoevsky: The Vasia Shumkov Paradigm," focuses on Dostoevsky's conception of personality, of solipsism, and of doubles as issues located at the cross-section of psychology, sociology, philosophy, and religion. Corrigan contrasts the neo-Romantic "expressivist" conception of a deep mysterious soul (drawing on Charles Taylor's taxonomy) with the notion of self as located in the "intersubjective dialogical space"

---

30 *PSS*, 27:65.

(Bakhtinian paradigm). Exploring the tension between what he calls "indwelling" and relational models of selfhood in early Dostoevsky's story, "A Weak Heart," Corrigan identifies the complexity of Dostoevsky's construction of self in the tension between interiority and intersubjectvity. He concludes that the self in Dostoevsky is thought of "on the one hand, as an *essence*, a bottomless depth, encompassing the entire universe, and on the other, as an *activity, event*, or *point of view* that constitutes itself outwardly through relationships." In contrast to scholars who locate Dostoevsky's concept of personality entirely in human relationships, Corrigan maintains that only the self that partakes of both domains has a chance of proper development; for "without the positioning of an essential interiority principle within the self, human beings will consume each other . . . thus the need of the reconstitution of the interior realm from its dispersal into adjacent convulsively embracing, selves." This turn to some "essential interiority," similar to Morson's emphasis on uniqueness of subjectivity and "point-of-viewness," suggests that despite their seemingly successful banishment by the positivism of science, the Romantic concepts of the soul and of the mysterious self managed to recover their place in Dostoevsky's thought and art.

Focusing on one of Dostoevsky's marginal characters, Kalganov, from *The Brothers Karamazov*, Michal Oklot, like Morson and Corrigan, returns to the question of subjectivity and the crisis of personhood in Dostoevsky in chapter 14, "Dostoevsky's Angel—Still an Idiot, Still beyond the Story: The Case of Kalganov." Oklot's central metaphor, the angel, defines Dostoevsky's concept of personality through its "latent openness," or "the surplus negating a possibility of finding [its] own identity." Drawing from theological and poetic writings, Oklot sees an angel as a liminal creature *par excellence* that "stands for everything that is different in us and, yet, is not different, at the same time," since "to put it oxymoronically," he writes, "its identity is in its impossibility." In other words, the marginal-"angelic" characters are important figures for understanding Dostoevsky's anthropology of no-identity, of which major concepts are incompleteness and surplus. For Oklot, angelic incompleteness exemplified by Dostoevsky's marginal characters is related not so much to dialogic openness or the intersubjective aspect of selfhood (also questioned by Corrigan) as to its subjective and ontological dimension. In Dostoevsky's anthropology, our implied incompleteness gives us ontological hope for immortality, for that which is not complete cannot die, concludes Oklot, revoking Ernst Bloch's philosophy of hope. The "angelic" Kalganov, in Oklot's reading, is a figure of incompleteness and as such could point to spiritual resurrection, but, continues Oklot, this "kernel of existence" remains in Dostoevsky uncovered and unrealized.

Vladimir Golstein approaches the problem of the personality's latent openness in Dostoevsky through the prism of characters-catalysts who serve as facilitators in the process of recovering one's identity. In chapter 15, "The Detective as a Midwife: Porfiry Petrovich in *Crime and Punishment*," Golstein's exploration of Socratic subtext focuses on the complex and contradictory function of the novel's detective. Porfiry's role is different from a usual, fully emplotted fictional character—he is this "liminal creature," to use Oklot terminology, that serves as a dialogical catalyst for Raskolnikov's self, enabling it to unfold into its full identity by the end of the novel. Porfiry Petrovich is not merely a detective whom Raskolnikov tries to avoid or outsmart. Porfiry is a facilitator who strives to apprehend and help to bring forth Raskolnikov's conscience, his better self that needs time and effort to be delivered. Porfiry's role as a "midwife," is not dissimilar from that of a novelist as Dostoevsky envisioned it, namely, "under the conditions of total realism to find a human being within a human being."[31] In other words, in their role as "midwives," Socrates, Porfiry, and ultimately Dostoevsky, fully grasp the thoughts, actions, and motives of their interlocutors, yet manage to go beyond the surface, uncover, and deliver that inner man, that core of goodness that is not immediately detected by experimental methods. They serve as catalysts, as spiritual midwives capable of detecting and encouraging the rebirth and the restoration of the fallen self.

Several scholars further discuss the relational nature of the self in Dostoevsky by focusing not on his strategy of deploying doubles or catalysts in his narratives, but on the predicament of isolation and alienation, a predicament that highlights the relationship of the self to others. As we acknowledge Dostoevsky's fascination with various kinds of disturbed personalities, be it those who experience the anxiety of doubling, or those who, similar to the underground man, are engrossed in the solipsism of their hyporationalizing selves, the question of "Why is the I the way it is?" becomes especially pertinent. It is this question that Carol Apollonio raises in chapter 16, "Metaphors for Solitary

---

31 *PSS*, 27:65.

Confinement in *Notes from Underground* and *Notes from the House of the Dead.*"
Focusing on Dostoevsky's use of the special metaphor of solitary confinement
and on the immediate effects of imprisonment on Dostoevsky's characters,
Apollonio delves into Dostoevsky's notion of selfhood by considering the
impact of isolation on human consciousness. Citing examples from biologists
who observed apes in solitary cages, from psychologists who analyzed the
psychological development of orphans, and from modern sociologists who
examined the effects of solitary confinement, Apollonio reveals that Dostoevsky's insights into the detrimental results of isolation, which become a
modern condition, are corroborated by the experiments conducted by modern
social science and psychology. However, Dostoevsky's conclusions in Apollonio's thoughtful reading are paradoxical and contradictory: conditions of
solitude might be salutary for an individual's spiritual and moral development
but "compulsory communal cohabitation" as experienced by Dostoevsky's
narrator Gorianchikov in his *Notes from the House of the Dead* could cause his
greatest suffering. It is this "solitary confinement within a crowd," that is, the
predicament of an ego separated from the community and failing to resolve the
dual challenge of freedom and solipsism that Dostoevsky investigates in his
postimprisonment texts. Thus, Apollonio's analysis of the paradox of solitary
confinement within a crowd reinforces Corrigan's assertion of the importance
of balance between interiority and exteriority in Dostoevsky's notion of self.
Dostoevsky's underground man, as Apollonio aptly observes, diagnoses himself
as "a creature of acute self-consciousness, in other words, a product of modern
secular science." His solitude is a condition shared by all modern humanity. The
way to overcome this painful isolation for the Underground Man is, once again,
through drawing on the relational aspect of self—in his case the act of writing
and addressing his text to the reader, or, as we could say, through entering the
Bakhtinian interpersonal dialogical space.

Apollonio's discussion of solitary confinement in relation to Dostoevsky's
concept of self dovetails with Deborah Martinsen's chapter 17, "Moral Emotions
in Dostoevsky's 'Dream of a Ridiculous Man,'" which focuses on the spiritual
awakening of the story's protagonist, caused by his need for "the other." The
question of self is connected here with an acute human need to break out of
"this circle of self" by engaging with and responding to the needs of others.
Utilizing the concept of moral emotions developed by modern psychology and

sociology (Gabriele Taylor, Jesse Prinz, J. David Velleman), Martinsen explores the moral development of the story's protagonist and highlights his need to transcend the limits of his isolated self. It is precisely the intricate and complex balance between the inevitability of human alienation and the never-ending striving to regain the lost human community and metaphysical unity that constitutes the trajectory of moral development in Martinsen's probing reading of Dostoevsky. Focusing on the emotional trajectory experienced by the protagonist of "The Dream of the Ridiculous Man," Martinsen explores the tensions and oscillations between the rational model of behavior based on the principles of the Enlightenment and the conversion-driven, unpredictable, mysterious ways of healing the divided self by connecting it with others, or, as Martinsen labels it, between the models of Voltaire's philosophical "Micromegas" and Dickens's *Christmas Carol*. Love and pity as "other-directed emotions," in contrast with shame, a "self-directed emotion," heal the Ridiculous Man's divided self and help him to overcome his metaphysical alienation. The Ridiculous Man's moral emotions repair the social bond and establish connection to all living things. In line with other contributors' observations that only genuine connection with others allows Dostoevsky's characters to escape the logic of doubling, of alienation, and of solipsism, Martinsen concludes that "for Dostoevsky, belief in something greater than self, something that links all living beings, is essential to morality."

An important way to think about the way human beings connect to each other and, therefore, overcome the danger and pain of isolated consciousness is through education. If, as Bakhtin insists, personality in Dostoevsky is located entirely within human relationships, then considering education as a form of human relationship that may help to strengthen that sense of self through belonging to a wider cultural community acquires a particular significance. One could say that Dostoevsky's view of the nation as self is "relational," similar to his view of personhood. As seen from the opening quote to this Introduction, some of Dostoevsky's characters even conceive of God as the "synthetic personality of the whole people," that is, in terms of collective interpersonal relations. Dostoevsky's concept of nation becomes an extension of his concept of self if we consider his insistence that a nation (for him, Russia) acquires identity through responding to the other (to the world). For Dostoevsky, to become a true Russian is to become universal. Education then is an important way of connectivity, a way of establishing a dialogical bond between an isolated self and the "interiority" of the nation and the world. Dostoevsky's interest in pedagogical philosophies and the goals of education are, therefore, closely connected with his concept of self and of national identity. In chapter 18, on Dostoevsky's messianic pedagogy, Inessa Medzhibovskaya explicates Dostoevsky's thinking on education as an integral process that involves the interaction between an individual and a nation, and by extension between a nation and the world. Dostoevsky imagined true Russian education as the process of restoring "the brotherhood and integrity of the human being who is giving the education in the image of Christ."[32] The writer's commitment to the ideology of the soil (*pochvennichestvo*) implies a project of combining Russian native spirituality with the achievements of European civilization. His educational project, however, becomes distinctly messianic in his emphasis on the uniquely Russian ability for synthesis and "translation." As Medzhibovskaya aptly observes, "Dostoevsky's constant recourse to Hegel's principle of *Aufhebund* ("sublation"), or the dialectical lifting of contradictions (*sniatie protivorechii*) is remarkable in its intended messianic sense." By exploring the roots of Dostoevsky's messianic educational vision, from classical Greece to Enlightenment Germany, and tracing Dostoevsky's theories through time (going not only back in time but also forward), Medzhibovskaya shows how some of his ideas result in positions that he himself might have found questionable. Placing Dostoevsky's thinking on education in the context of such diverse twentieth-century authors as Durkheim, Lyotard, Foucault, and Deleuze, Medzhibovskaya points out that "Dostoevsky's messianic pursuit of 'All-Knowledge' through constant re-authoring 'with a difference' of what is borrowed is misappropriated in the intellectual mainstream of the West. Deleuze and other Western postmodernists take Dostoevsky's message as a warning against 'overfull understanding,' as means to protect one's subjectivity from *knowing all* and *knowing like all*."

The final three studies in the volume in Part V shed light on the relationship of the self to the other in Dostoevsky through the prism of intercultural connections. Donna Orwin, Olga Meerson, and Marina Kostalevsky examine Homeric, biblical, and Koranic motifs in Dostoevsky's novels as a way to locate both the self and the nation in the intersubjective dialogical space and time.

---

32 *PSS*, 14:284.

Donna Orwin in her "Achilles in *Crime and Punishment*" focuses on Dosto-evsky's self-conscious engagement with the *Iliad*, but she addresses a set of issues that goes beyond literary subtext, as she explores Dostoevsky's reading of the Greek poet, and Dostoevsky's poetics in general. Taking its cue from Dosto-evsky's essay "Mr. –bov and the Question of Art," Orwin delineates Dostoevsky's dynamic and interactive view of art as something that captures and reflects the age while simultaneously giving it its shape. Dostoevsky, as Orwin points out, makes fun of the positivist writers' rejection of the great classics of past civiliza-tions as irrelevant in the present day and especially of their "application of materialist standards to determine its value." Dostoevsky, by contrast, finds great affinities between Homeric times and those of the Great Reforms in Russia as the peak moments in the national lives of their respective people. Orwin's discussion concentrates on comparing and contrasting Raskolnikov and Svidrigailov in terms of their associations with Achilles; she then utilizes the contrast to further elucidate Dostoevsky's artistic strategies. Raskolnikov manages to transform his "classical Achilles rage" into an act fitting "a great-souled man" as he embarks on the path of Christian penance and humility. In contrast, Svidrigailov's encounter with a fireman wearing an Achilles-like helmet provides only "a debased, ironic form" of strength associated with Homer's hero. The most powerful symbols of the past—whether Greek, Old Testament, Ottoman, or Roman—are either invested with, or divested of, meaning, depending on the character's (or writer's) ability to see continuity and appreciate "the lessons of bygone eras." By saturating his imagery with clas-sical references, from Homer in particular, Dostoevsky reveals his view of art as an interactive process.

Olga Meerson, in chapter 20, on the symbolism of Isaac Binding in *Crime and Punishment*, merges her study well with Orwin's discussion of Homer as she considers another important "symbol of the past"—the Old Testament. While acknowledging Dostoevsky's uneasy attitude toward Jews and his alleged everyday anti-Semitism, Meerson focuses on Dostoevsky's paradoxical identifi-cation with Judaism, seeing it as artistically productive and "morally and theologically significant." Meerson provides a fresh reading of *Crime and Punish-ment*'s epilogue, where, as she suggests, Raskolnikov is compared to Isaac to be sacrificed by his father. Textual similarities between this scene in Genesis 22:1–13 and *Crime and Punishment*'s epilogue serve as a clue to Raskolnikov's otherwise inexplicable transformation. Dostoevsky's own experience of being condemned to death and having his sentence commuted, Meerson argues, had to put the binding of Isaac squarely into his subconsciousness, if not consciousness. By situating Raskolnikov in the position of Isaac, Dostoevsky foregrounds his repentance as an emotional experience rather than a rational argument or logical conclusion, for "no rational argument would liberate the character from his own prison of ideological labyrinths." This allusion emphasizes the experiential nature of Raskolnikov's repentance and establishes the analogy with the biblical experiences of repentance. "This analogy tells by showing, not by proving or arguing," concludes Meerson, reaffirming, therefore, Dostoevsky's preferred strategy of refuting rational arguments by the deeds of love (*Notes from the Underground*, *The Brothers Karamazov*), as was discussed in several other chapters of this volume. The intercultural and interreligious aspect of Dostoevsky's thought and his poetics is conveyed through his use of Old Testament allusions. Raskolnikov's need for exteriority is achieved through his "subjective and unconscious experience of the Aqedah" that "takes him outside this-worldly time and space."

Finally, considering Dostoevsky's concept of time not only in the context of Judeo-Christian tradition but also against the background of a Koranic vision of time, Marina Kostalevsky in chapter 21 identifies a particular form of time that mediates between the this-worldly and other-worldly notions of temporality, which she calls "epileptic time" in reference to the sense of time experienced in moments before an epileptic fit. This particular sense of time, made famous by the Prophet Muhammad, was also experienced both by Dostoevsky and by his character Prince Myshkin. As Kostalevsky demonstrates, Dostoevsky describes Prince Myshkin's epileptic fit with a Koranic reference to the Prophet's vision of paradise when the jug of water that he overturned continues spilling. Kostalevsky utilizes Dostoevsky's own image of the time of Muhammad to discuss issues pertinent to the novelistic genre itself—its form, shape, and structure, and its mysterious unfolding, which embraces both stasis, when nothing seems to change and everything returns to the previous, and simultaneous dynamism, when a great deal occurs during a moment of revelation. As Kostalevsky puts it, "physiological dysfunction becomes a literary form." Both Dostoevsky and his characters privilege these moments of revelation, of the time understood as *kairos*, those moments when they get a glimpse into a higher reality and knowledge about themselves and their fellow human beings. We could say that in the moments of revelation, Dostoevsky's characters reach out beyond the confines of self, reach beyond surface reality in an epistemological impulse similar to their author's attempt to go beyond realism and beyond fiction.

In his *The Island of Knowledge*, a very popular book on the inherent mysteries of science, physicist Marcelo Gleiser underscores the tension between an "island of knowledge" and the ocean of the unknowable: "We strive toward knowledge, always more knowledge, but must understand that we are, and will remain, surrounded by mystery. . . . It is the flirting with this mystery, the urge to go beyond the boundaries of the known, that feeds our creative impulse, that makes us want to know more."[33] In this urge to go "beyond," science, philosophy, religion, and fiction meet. Dostoevsky, probably more than any other Russian writer, strove to go beyond all boundaries, all "mind-forged manacles," to use Blake's phrase, thus expanding the island of fiction.

---

33 Marcelo Gleiser, *The Island of Knowledge: The Limits of Science and the Search for Meaning* (New York: Basic Books, 2014), xiv.

PART 1

Encounters with Science

I

....

Darwin, Dostoevsky, and Russia's Radical Youth

David Bethea and Victoria Thorstensson

The period of the 1860s was one of the most volatile in the history of Russian culture. Normally cited as chief flashpoints of the turmoil are the Reform Manifesto of 1861 liberating the serfs and the heated debate generated in the periodic press by the new legislation's less-than-perfect implementation. On a practical level, the most pressing issue of the day was how to combine freedom for the serfs (*krest'iane*), including a path to eventual ownership of the land they worked, with economic sustainability for the nobility (*dvorianstvo*), including sources of cheap labor needed to run their estates in the future. At the same time, the ideological orientations at the center of much discussion showed a larger thrust and counterthrust, one aimed at capturing the correct notion of "progress"— with all that word entailed—of Russian history at this turning point. It is this second, more capacious discursive arc that permeates the cluster of classic literary texts defining the decade, from Turgenev's traditional liberal viewpoint in *Fathers and Children* (*Ottsy i deti*, 1862), to Chernyshevsky's radical reposing of the youth movement's character and aspirations in *What Is to Be Done?* (*Chto delat'?*, 1863), to Dostoevsky's deconstruction of Chernyshevsky's utilitarianism and "rational egoism" (*razumnyi egoizm*) in *Notes from Underground* (*Zapiski iz podpol'ia*, 1864) and *Crime and Punishment* (*Prestuplenie i nakazanie*, 1866).

The idea of progress, or the right way forward, written into these texts thematically was also mapped onto the plot of generational transition. Correspondingly, each of these works produced controversial characters whose stories epitomize this struggle: Turgenev's Bazarov, the nihilist doctor who dissects frogs to learn how people, with their origins in the animal world, think and feel; Chernyshevsky's "ordinary" threesome of liberated woman Vera Pavlovna, medical student (and savior-cum-fictitious husband of Vera) Lopukhov, and classmate of Lopukhov (and eventual true love of Vera) Kirsanov, along with his "extraordinary" new man Rakhmetov; and Dostoevsky's Underground Man, who prefers to stay in the "cellar" from which Lopukhov has freed Vera—that cellar (*podval*) now having morphed from a cage of externally imposed social conditions into something intentionally spiteful and self-created (*podpol'e*). In Dostoevsky the role of Vera's viciously manipulative mother is taken over by the Underground Man himself, while the medical-scientific training said to "explain" the social behavior of a Bazarov or Lopukhov collides with the irrationality of the Underground Man's perverse ("I am a sick man") affection for his own toothache.

At the center of the radical youth's early 1860s flurry of journalistic and creative activity stand several, mutually interlocking epistemological frames, all of which reduce ultimately to the notion of the rational, the measurable, the statistically normative. As Alexander Vucinich writes in his classic *Darwin in Russian Thought*, "[Nihilism] represented a unique combination of materialism, espoused by Büchner and Moleschott, and positivism, a philosophical legacy of Auguste Comte and his followers.... Both [materialism and positivism] viewed Darwinism as a generally successful effort to enhance the power of science in the unceasing war against mysticism, irrationalism and supernaturalism."[1] Our presentation here focuses on the Darwinian frame and on Dostoevsky's response to that frame as he embarks on his major period. We devote particular attention to *Notes from Underground* and *The Demons* (*Besy*, 1871–72) as texts (and contexts) reacting to the appearance first of Darwin's *On the Origin of Species* (1859) and then of his *The Descent of Man* (1871). Perhaps more than any others, these two works by Darwin, along with T. H. Huxley's *The Place of Man in Nature* (1863), set the tone for debate in the 1860s and 1870s. With typical Russian cultural impatience, the battle lines are drawn between those wanting to hurry the process of natural selection along up the

---

1 Alexander Vucinich, *Darwin in Russian Thought* (Berkeley: University of California Press, 1988), 26.

zoological ladder and interpret "survival of the fittest"[2] in new democratic terms and those insisting that human instinct hides the basis for morality and that altruism is neither rational nor empirically probative. In short, the elegant unpacking of finches' beaks as differing foraging tools depending on an island's locale and topography in the Galapagos becomes the broad brush of Social Darwinism. In Dostoevsky's and his interlocutors' (both friendly and adversarial) telling, this shift is a contested one for the idea of "progress."

For the record, by the time Dostoevsky enters the fray with *Notes*, a lively exchange on the meaning of Darwin's epochal discoveries has already been taking place among leading scientists and cultural critics, including A. N. Beketov, Dzh. G. L'iuis (George Henry Lewes), N. N. Strakhov, S. A. Rachinsky, K. A. Timiryazev, and M. A. Antonovich. For example, the distinguished botanist Andrei Beketov argues in the *Russian Messenger* (*Russkii vestnik*) as early as 1860, without mentioning Darwin, that organic nature is defined more by harmonious balance than disruptive struggle and by a parts-to-whole and whole-to-parts proto-awareness more suggestive of Lamarck (and before him Aristotle's entelechy). By the same token, Nikolai Strakhov, who began as a physics and math teacher and went on to defend a master's thesis on the bone structure of the mammalian wrist, writes in Dostoevsky's *Time* (*Vremia*) already in 1862, in his review of different translations of *On the Origin of Species*, about the latent dangers—or as he terms it "bad signs" (*durnye priznaki*)—of applying the scientific method to other disciplines, a trend that will expand in subsequent years into full-blown Social Darwinism, while the soon-to-be-eminent plant physiologist Kliment Timiryazev becomes the Russian version of "Darwin's Bulldog" in his 1863–64 comments in *Fatherland Notes* (*Otechestvennye zapiski*), arguing strongly in favor of organic transformation and in so doing adding his impeccable imprimatur to the sociocultural links between Darwinism and nihilism. It is against this heated background that the Chernyshevsky-versus-Dostoevsky polemic takes center stage.

From the "Anthropological Principle" and *What Is to Be Done?* to *Notes from Underground*

A cornerstone of the nihilists' program was the idea that progress must be presented in a manner devoid of metaphysics—1840s Hegelian explanations for how an abstract spirit expressed itself in history through a process of dialectic

---

2   The phrase was initially Herbert Spencer's.

winnowing needed to be replaced by a scientific episteme that explained concrete examples of actual organic life through the physiological and the empirically measurable. Natural science provided what appeared to be an indisputable means of organizing the material of life in a manner that applied to all; it was meaningful in that it made sense, and it was democratic in that it only recognized its own authority, not that of church, state, or traditional metaphysics.

The premises underlying Chernyshevsky's scientific program were laid out for all to see in his "Anthropological Principle in Philosophy" (*Antropologicheskii printsip v filosofii*), which appeared in the *Contemporary* (*Sovremennik*) in 1860.[3] This rambling stroll through current ideas about the natural world had one overarching purpose: to build by analogy logical bridges from the, by now accepted, "tight" knowledge that science had produced about such phenomena as the chemical reactions involved in metallurgy to the still disputed, "looser" speculation about causality versus free will in human behavior. Chernyshevsky's tone throughout is confident, almost breezy, as he moves from the realm of the inorganic to the organic, from social classes to nations to humanity in general. The ideas that he advances are crucial to all subsequent discussions of the role of Darwinian evolution in Russian social life:[4]

1   Because of his practical life experience and working-class background, the European "common man" (*prostoliudin*) is better able to understand how the real world works than someone from the privileged classes, but what he needs now is access to scientific knowledge.[5]

---

3 Nos. 4–5 of vol. 80: http://az.lib.ru/c/chernyshewskij_n_g/text_0430.shtml. "Anthropological Principle" begins as an overview of P. L. Lavrov's *Ocherki voprosov prakticheskoi filosofii* (1860) but soon launches into Chernyshevsky's own arguments as to how the methods of the natural sciences can (and should) be applied when studying any aspect of the living world, including human history and social behavior.

4 To be sure, Chernyshevsky does not cite Darwin anywhere directly in his essay, as the English naturalist's ideas were just making their way to Russia at this time, but his formulations are pervaded throughout by the scientific logic then being championed by Darwin and his followers, especially the idea that human nature and animal nature are one. Later in his career Chernyshevsky would disagree with aspects of popular Darwinism, including its emphasis on competition ("survival of the fittest") at the expense of cooperation (socialism).

5 "Благодаря своей здоровой натуре, своей суровой житейской опытности, западноевропейский простолюдин в сущности понимает вещи несравненно лучше, вернее и глубже, чем люди более счастливых классов. Но до него не дошли еще те научные понятия, которые

2 Human nature is unified (coterminous with the animal world) and not dual (body vs. soul).[6]

3 The difference between inorganic and organic nature is one of degree, not kind.[7]

4 Yes, there are still lacunae in our knowledge left by the study of the natural sciences, but those gaps will be filled in the future by the already existing structure of the scientific method, not by metaphysical speculation.[8]

5 Moreover, the inexact or "soft" sciences (history, moral philosophy, psychology) have taken in recent times to applying methods from the exact sciences (mathematics, physics, astronomy, chemistry), so that progressive thinkers have begun to find "exact" solutions to moral questions.[9]

6 The phenomena we identify as originating in the "moral" (seemingly non- physical) realm happen as a result of causality (*prichinnost'*) and not as an expression of free will (*volia*); this process always begins externally and only then moves to a mental plane; example: the person who gets up in the morning and decides to step on one foot as opposed to the other does so either because it is more convenient or

---

наиболее соответствуют его положению, наклонностям, потребностям и (как нам кажется, наиболее соответствуют истине, а во всяком случае) сообразны с нынешним положением знаний."

6 "Принципом философского воззрения на человеческую жизнь со всеми ее феноменами служит выработанная естественными науками идея о единстве человеческого организма; наблюдениями физиологов, зоологов и медиков отстранена всякая мысль о дуализме человека."

7 "Словом сказать, разница, между царством неорганической природы и растительным царством подобна различию между маленькою травкою и огромным деревом—это разница по количеству, по интенсивности, по многосложности, а не по основным свойствам явления."

8 "Говорят: естественные науки еще не достигли такого развития, чтобы удовлетворительно объяснить все важные явления природы. Это—совершенная правда; но противники научного направления в философии делают из этой правды вывод вовсе не логический, когда говорят, что пробелы, остающиеся в научном объяснении натуральных явлений, допускают сохранение каких-нибудь остатков фантастического миросозерцания."

9 "Естественные науки уже развились настолько, что дают много материалов для точного решения нравственных вопросов. Из мыслителей, занимающихся нравственными науками, все передовые люди стали разработывать их при помощи точных приемов, подобных тем, по каким разработываются естественные науки."

comfortable, or because he consciously challenges himself in an opposite manner to show his will, but even this last move is conditioned by previous experience—thus, the idea of the will as "free" is itself an illusion.[10]

7   A person wishes to do what is pleasant to himself and to avoid what is unpleasant; a person is considered good by society when he obtains the pleasant for himself by doing the pleasant for others, and a person is considered evil by society when in the effort to gain the pleasant for himself he inflicts the unpleasant on others.[11]

8   Physiology and medicine tell us that the human organism is a combination of many chemical elements involved in a complex chemical process called life; the relationship of physiology to chemistry can be compared to the relationship of national history to universal history.[12]

9   Actions that seem altruistic are on closer inspection personally beneficial (from *pol'za*).[13]

---

10 "Положительно известно, например, что все явления нравственного мира проистекают одно из другого и из внешних обстоятельств по закону причинности, и на этом основании признано фальшивым всякое предположение о возникновении какого-нибудь явления, не произведенного предыдущими явлениями и внешними обстоятельствами. ... Самым обыкновенным примером действий, ни на чем не основанных, кроме нашей воли, представляется такой факт: я встаю с постели; на какую ногу я встану? захочу—на левую, захочу— на правую. Но это только так представляется поверхностному взгляду. На самом деле факты и впечатления производят то, на какую ногу встанет человек. Если нет никаких особенных обстоятельств и мыслей, он встает на ту ногу, на которую удобнее ему встать по анатомическому положению его тела на постели. Если явятся особенные побуждения, превосходящие своею силою это физиологическое удобство, результат изменится сообразно перемене обстоятельств."

11 "Человек любит приятное и не любит неприятного—это, кажется, не подлежит сомнению. ... Добр тот, кто делает хорошее для других, зол—кто делает дурное для других,—кажется, это также просто и ясно. Соединим теперь эти простые истины и в выводе получим: добрым человек бывает тогда, когда для получения приятного себе он должен делать приятное другим; злым бывает он тогда, когда принужден извлекать приятность себе из нанесения неприятности другим."

12 "Физиология и медицина находят, что человеческий организм есть очень многосложная химическая комбинация, находящаяся в очень многосложном химическом процессе, называемом жизнью. ... Отношение физиологии к химии можно сравнить с отношением отечественной истории к всеобщей истории."

13 "Вообще надобно бывает только всмотреться попристальнее в поступок или чувство, представляющиеся бескорыстными, и мы увидим, что в основе их все-таки лежит та же

10   Only what is acknowledged by science as useful or beneficial (*poleznoe, vygodnoe*) on a general, rather than individual, human level is what can be considered the true good (*dobro*).[14]

Next, what Chernyshevsky achieved in *What Is to Be Done?* was the merging, now in story form, of the utilitarian principle of "the best for the most" with the Darwinian principle of survival of the fittest, so that the younger generation portrayed in the novel, those who act nobly by acting out of self-interest, are also the ones whose future it is to, literally, inherit the earth. But in borrowing heavily from John Stuart Mill and Henry Thomas Buckle, Chernyshevsky performs his most improbable intellectual somersault: he places the prime mover of human evolution in his famous formula of "rational egoism" (*razumnyi egoizm*), which conjoins people's preference in life for *what is pleasurable on an individual basis* to the forward march of *what is useful or beneficial for the group*. And the proof of Chernyshevsky's attempt, aided by the incredible circumstances in which he composed his text, was in, so to speak, the charismatic pudding: he was a martyr for writing such an inspiring story while in prison; it was a miracle that this story passed the bungling censors and got published; and the writer-thinker-agitator's special talent for applying a scientific paradigm *holistically* was a landmark event that captured the imagination of the radical youth.

Varfolomei Zaitsev

An important intermediate link between Chernyshevsky, who as leader of the radical youth is the primary target in *Notes* and *Crime and Punishment*, and the same Dostoevsky who takes on Russia's chief social ills, such as drunkenness, prostitution, and violent crime, in his postexile turn to the people is Varfolomei Zaitsev.[15] Zaitsev's case is representative in various ways that lead directly into

---

мысль о собственной личной пользе, личном удовольствии, личном благе, лежит чувство, называемое эгоизмом."

14 "Наука говорит о народе, а не об отдельных индивидуумах, о человеке, а не французе или англичанине, не купце или бюрократе. Только то, что составляет натуру человека, признается в науке за истину; только то, что полезно для человека вообще, признается за истинное добро."

15 Zaitsev was born into the family of a clerk; in this respect he was neither the offspring of nobility, like Pisarev, nor the son of a priest, like Chernyshevsky. He studied jurisprudence for one year (1858–59) at St. Petersburg University and medicine for two to three years at Moscow University. After he passed his *polulekarskii ekzamen*, he left the university to

the thematics and argumentation of *Notes* and *Crime and Punishment*. As a young critic with radical leanings, Zaitsev begins as a reviewer at the *Russian Word* (*Russkoe slovo*) and then writes in 1863, contemporaneously with the appearance of *What Is to Be Done?*, a long piece retelling the ideas of Adolphe Quetelet titled "Natural Science and Justice" (*Estestvoznanie i iustitsiia*).[16] This work both builds off Chernyshevsky and at the same time departs from him in a manner suggestive of future dangers for the radical movement. One of the aspects of Zaitsev's work that shows up especially vividly is the wholesale and often reckless colonization of other disciplines under the banner of science, in general, and Darwin, in particular.

In "Natural Science and Justice," Zaitsev sets out to prove that if we follow the scientific method, we have to come to the conclusion that moral values are relative, and normal behavior and criminal, aberrant behavior are ultimately indistinguishable. If in China it is permissible to kill female offspring because they are perceived to be less useful societally, then why should infanticide (*detoubiistvo*) be judged so harshly by European standards? Aren't an ancient Assyrian and a modern-day Englishman as different, in terms of speciation, as a wolf and a dog?[17] Looked at this way, the metaphysical construct of free will is a "childish self-delusion" (*detskoe samoobol'shchenie*) and human nature is animal nature: "A human being is nothing other than an animal organism, and an animal organism depends on a thousand physical conditions in itself as well as in the surrounding environment. It follows that a human being is the slave of his body and of external nature."[18]

As of yet, continues Zaitsev, we cannot say precisely what part of our physical existence is affected when we make decisions that we call "moral" or "spiritual,"

---

support his family (mother and sister). In 1863, he took some additional coursework at the Petersburg Medical-Surgical Academy but never finished his degree. From the early 1860s, he was already involved with the nihilist circles. From 1863 on we find Zaitsev working full-time at the *Russian Word*. This pattern of catching on with a journal as a fledgling reviewer and then, with experience, proceeding to represent the journal's ideological leanings through longer essays and "thought" pieces was followed by many of the young radicals of the day, including Zaitsev, Chernyshevsky, Pisarev, Antonovich, and Dobroliubov.

16 Zaitsev, *Russkoe slovo* 7 (1863): 98–127.

17 V. A. Zaitsev, *Izbrannye sochineniia v dvukh tomakh* (Moscow: Izd-vo Vses. ob-va politkatorzhan i ssyl'no-poselentsev, 1934), 1:73. This logic as to the grey area between species and subspecies/variety will be used in Zaitsev's subsequent article "Edinstvo roda chelovecheskogo" (see below).

18 Ibid., 1:72: "Человек есть не что иное, как животный организм; животный же организм зависит от тысячи физических условий как в самом себе, так и в окружающей среде; следовательно, человек—раб своего тела и внешней природы."

but what we can say is that any reasonable hypothesis on this issue must start with only two possible premises: the physical (physiological) and/or the chemical. Organic chemistry tells us, furthermore, that all organisms, "from a human being to a lichen," change "under qualitative and quantitative" modulations, like the ratio of water to carbon, or, if carbon is substituted for nitrogen, the ratio of water to nitrogen. Based on this analogy, because we are dealing with degrees and not kinds, we can also say that any change in the quantity or quality of the component parts constituting the human brain, circulatory system, and nervous system will translate into a corresponding deviation from the normal condition in a person's "spiritual and moral world," his "will, worldview, ideas, antipathies and sympathies."[19]

Zaitsev's logic forces him into several corners. First, by asserting there is no firm basis in the physiochemical makeup of *Homo sapiens* for morality (a statement that certainly appears true prima facie!) he prepares the ground for what Dostoevsky would eventually present as the dangers of "all is permitted" (*vse pozvoleno*): that is, no morality means that survival of the fittest can be taken completely literally, as in who is the strongest can take for himself whatever he wants (cf. Svidrigailov). This is clearly a serious "dumbing down" of Darwin's theory of natural selection, which pivots not on the principle of brute strength, but on that of which trait, passed down passively (hence *selected by nature*) over time, allows the marked group a better chance at survival. Second, feeling more at home in the world of scientific classification than perhaps he should given his rudimentary training,[20] Zaitsev plays into the hands of obscurantists and bigots waiting in the wings for the scraps from his table by arguing *against* Darwin in a second,

19 Ibid., 1:73: "В духовном и нравственном мире человека, в его воле, миросозерцании, понятиях, антипатиях и симпатиях."
20 Strakhov, whose scientific education was superior to Zaitsev's, mounted a comprehensive critique of the nihilist obsession with pseudoscience (*polunauka*) in his journalistic work published throughout 1860s and 1870s. He saw semi-education (*poluobrazovanie*) and pseudoscience as typically Russian phenomena, but he held radical journals particularly responsible for breeding and propagating this tendency through their practice of "destroying authority figures" from the scientific community straight from the shoulder; see, e.g., "Pis'mo k redaktoru 'Vremeni,'" *Vremia* (May 1861): 21. Strakhov felt that the popular scientific articles filling the pages of Russia's "thick journals" did the sciences a disservice by making them appear easy, sensational, and accessible to all:

    [Our age] has gone crazy about the popularization of knowledge, about transmitting already arrived-at results, "the latest words" of science. It invents less thorough and simplified ways of teaching, as if the labor of thought, the serious work of the mind, is the most pernicious thing in the world, as if the whole purpose of education is to prepare as many of those light-minded chatterboxes who repeat the trendiest scientific terms but

contemporaneous piece entitled "The Unity of the Human Race."[21] Now the unpredictable critic turned naturalist asserts with a kind of wild intensity that human races are as different among themselves as other animal species (i.e., they are not subspecies or varieties but actually *different species*), which then leads him to the conclusion—one that Darwin used his considerable faculties to find reasons to reject during his Beagle voyage—that people of color *should be* enslaved by the white race because that is a "kinder" form of domination. For Zaitsev this is a not insignificant issue because its solution could help avoid bloodshed in the United States. Furthermore, insists Zaitsev, one cannot find a single European scientist of note who would not agree that "the colored tribes/races [*plemena*] stand lower [i.e., on the evolutionary ladder] than white ones by their very organic conditioning [*po samym usloviiam svoego organizma*].[22] Thus, Zaitsev breezily rejects Darwin and comes out for polygenism (the human races have different origins) versus monogenism: "While Darwin's theory is at variance with polygenism when the latter is based on the idea of a species as permanent, one cannot deny the fact that at the present time the human races represent species as distinct as the horse and the ass/donkey."[23]

Zaitsev's scandalous statements form a fitting prelude to Dostoevsky's positions, as expressed through his "character-ideas" in *Notes* and *Crime and Punishment*: (1) the critic's emphasis on crime and prostitution, which he discusses at length and explains exclusively in terms of statistics and environmental factors; (2) his strained attempts to debunk examples of black heroism (Shakespeare calls Othello a Moor, but he was actually white-skinned(!), hence

---

who are alien to the true scientific spirit as possible. (*Iz istorii literaturnogo nigilizma, 1861–1865: Pis'ma N. Kositsy, Zametki Letopistsa i pr.,* 102)

Strakhov thus concluded that the people popularizing and simplifying science for their impressionable young audience were themselves just boys, ignorant students, young and immature people whose wisdom did not "constitute anything important, deep or complicated" (ibid., 194–95). Dostoevsky clearly shared Strakhov's sentiments.

21 In 1864, Zaitsev published another book review entitled "'Edinstvo roda chelovecheskogo' (Jean Louis Armand de Quatrefages de Bréau)," *Russkoe slovo* 8 (1864): 93–100 (signed V. Z.). Quatrefages had a dual degree in medicine and science and held one or more university chairs. This book is actually an edition of his lecture course that apparently came out in 1861 and was translated in 1864 into Russian (by a certain A. D. Mikh——n).

22 Zaitsev, *Izbrannye sochineniia,* 1:228.

23 Ibid., 1:230: "Хотя теория Дарвина противоречит полигенизму, когда он основывается на постоянстве вида, но нельзя отрицать того, что в настоящее время человеческие расы представляют столь же отличные виды, как, например, лошадь и осел."

the character's success as a general); (3) his jibe aimed at Strakhov, Dostoevsky's main critic on these topics at *Epoch* (*Epokha*), who Zaitsev predicts will now claim that he, Zaitsev, "is maligning Shakespeare." But Dostoevsky and Strakhov must have both enjoyed the delicious irony in this case, since Zaitsev's arguments caused a furor among the radicals, whose normal position, represented by Antonovich (the "outsider satirist" or *postoronnii satirik*) at *The Contemporary*, was to promote cooperation among the oppressed.

Notes and *Crime and Punishment*

As we move from the contextual sphere out of which Dostoevsky created his novels into the textual sphere proper in which he engaged the ideas of his time, how prominent a place does Darwinian thinking occupy in our own analysis? How important *is* Darwin, broadly conceived, to Dostoevsky's artistic world?

To answer this question, the modern reader needs to rethink the issue of influence (and intertextuality) and consider the Darwinian episteme more in terms of "infection" (a communicable virus spreading on its own) than in terms of straightforward, one-to-one influence. Darwin's personhood (*lichnost'*) is present in Dostoevsky's texts, but its power is in the chain reaction it unleashes, not in the normal hide-and-seek game played by literary critics looking for intertextual traces of their quarry. Thus, Darwin is both more present and less present than virtually any other contemporary interlocutor in *Notes*, since it is his airtight logic, borrowed not from philosophy but from science proper, that is everywhere challenged, everywhere scorned. As the Underground Man seethes early on (chap. 3, pt. 1):

> I calmly continue about people with strong nerves, who do not understand a certain refinement of pleasure. In the face of some mishaps, for example, these gentlemen may bellow like bulls, and let's suppose this brings them the greatest honor, but still, as I've already said, they instantly resign themselves before impossibility. Impossibility—meaning a stone wall? What stone wall? Well, of course, the laws of nature, the conclusions of natural science, mathematics. Once it's proved to you, for example, that you are descended from an ape, there is no making a wry face, just take it for what it is. Once it is proved to you that, essentially speaking, one little drop of your own fat should be dearer to you than a hundred thousand of your fellow men, and that in this result all so-called virtues and obligations and other ravings will be finally resolved, go ahead and accept it, there is nothing to be done, because two times two is—mathematics. Try objecting to that.

> "For pity's sake," they'll shout at you, "you can't rebel: it's two times two is four! Nature doesn't ask your permission; it doesn't care about your wishes, or whether you like its laws or not. You're obliged to accept it as it is, and consequently all its results as well. And so a wall is indeed a wall … etc., etc." My God, but what do I care about the laws of nature and arithmetic if for some reason these laws and two time two is four are not to my liking?[24]

Now, in this passage, familiar to all students of Dostoevsky, we see both Darwin (through Huxley: "you are descended from an ape") and the other authority figures fueling the ideas of Chernyshevsky and Zaitsev. The moral, the altruistic ("so-called virtues and obligations and other ravings") is raised up as something no longer existing in its own right because "natural science" (Darwin) and "mathematics" (Buckle) have made them categories determined by chemistry, the measurable, "two times two." "Darwin" becomes the name (although not identified as such here) of the inevitable, the immovable, a stone wall. But that is not really what Darwin is (remember that in *On the Origin of Species* he does not specifically take up human behavior—that would be Huxley's gambit in *Man's Place*); Darwin is more tentative, more aware of what it is possible to say at a certain point, not only in the evolution of man, but also in the *evolution of scientific discourse*. This passage, then, is much more about the virus that has been injected into the body politic by Chernyshevsky and Zaitsev than about a polemical battle with a celebrated English naturalist.

Note also that Dostoevsky goes precisely to where the radical youth go to counter their "discoveries": nerves, the nervous system, how senses and feelings become thoughts, become cognized, become consciousness. For this is the place *to which Darwin would not yet go*, but Chernyshevsky, Zaitsev, Pisarev, and others are only too happy to: if our animal nature is one, if our bodies and minds are one, then we should be able to move logically, objectively, from chemistry to our mental worlds and to the actions emanating therefrom. The Underground Man does not possess "strong nerves," since such a well-adjusted person has no problem accepting the "impossibility" of challenging natural laws. But what he does possess in the extreme is "heightened consciousness" (*usilennoe*

---

24   Fyodor Dostoevsky, *Notes from Underground*, trans. Richard Pevear and Larissa Volokhonsky (New York: Vintage, 1994), 13; F. M. Dostoevskii, *Polnoe sobranie sochinenii v tridtsati tomakh* [*PSS*], ed. V. G. Bazanov et al. (Leningrad: Nauka, 1972–90), 5:105; hereafter cited as *PSS* by volume and page.

soznanie), which will not allow him to accept the law of "rational egoism," of doing good by acting in his own interest ("profit," or *vygoda*) and helping others by seeking his own pleasure. Instead he chooses to revel in his toothache, to enjoy visiting the unpleasant on others if he happens to be indisposed. If Chernyshevsky can explain why a man chooses to step on one foot rather than the other while getting out of bed in the morning, then the Underground Man will not close the circuit between "instinct" (something programmed, hard-wired) and "consciousness" (something learned, something belonging to culture, something added after the initial programming). This is the "most prof-itable profit" (*samaia vygodnaia vygoda*) the Underground Man raves about and gives to his enemy-friends and to his prostitute in part 2.

Crime and Punishment extends the dialogue of *Notes* into a sprawling plot involving real crime, more extensive social problems, and a consciousness (Raskolnikov's) that is tragically divided against itself and its own motivations (i.e., decidedly not the radicals' one body/one mind construct). Space does not permit extensive discussion here, but suffice it to say that Sonya embodies conscience (without seeming to have much of a body herself) and the very anti-thesis of *vygoda* ("profit"); Lebezyatnikov is a perfect example of the audience, well-meaning but easily duped, for Chernyshevsky's and Zaitsev's tracts; Luzhin represents the individual who serves what is profitable to himself but in so doing hurts others (and when he slanders Sonya by planting the money on her, he tries to explain her alleged thievery by social conditions); and of course Svidrigailov, whom literary critics tend to define as a proto-Nietzschean Übermensch "beyond good and evil," but who could just as accurately be charac-terized as the "fittest" member of a new subspecies of humans who acts as pure "sensualist" (he cannot *feel* morality) and has no problem (until the end) with the one body/one mind principle. The virus contracted by the Chernyshevskys and Zaitsevs is set to grow into a generational pandemic, which is precisely what Raskolnikov dreams—the "new strain of trichinae," the "microscopic creatures parasitic in men's bodies"—in the second epilogue during his final illness and prior to his Eastertime redemption and ultimate bonding with Sonya. The fact that these microscopic organisms, which though deriving from chemistry and biology become agents of pure "intelligence and will" (i.e., cate-gories of consciousness), turn on their hosts to create an apocalyptic scenario of universal carnage and death suggests to what extent the radicals' insistence on their own rectitude and "right thinking" is ready to enter another, more dangerous stage—Social Darwinism writ large. The younger generation has no *self*-awareness, they do not question their premises, hence the metaphor of being carried away by disease. The desire for the pleasant that Chernyshevsky places at the root of all causality (*prichinnost'*) in human activity has become mindless suffering.

Before moving on, however, we should mention another prominent figure from the radical generation, Dmitry Pisarev, who takes up the topic of Darwin just as Dostoevsky is publishing *Notes* but before he begins work on the new novel that would become *Crime and Punishment*. The long essay entitled "Progress in the World of Animals and Plants," which was serialized in the *Russian Word* over several issues in 1864, is a landmark of its kind for several reasons.[25] First, it does a brilliant job of distilling and popularizing Darwin's principal findings in *On the Origin of Species* and laying the foundation for the subsequent interweaving in the educated public's mind of scientific method, nihilistic pragmatism, and democratic appeal, and it does so completely straightforwardly, without wandering off on ideological rants. Pisarev chides his reader for not challenging the epistemological grey area around the word "instinct." This is a welcome departure from the cognitive lurchings of Zaitsev, who is apt to elide the unconscious and the conscious in organic life without knowing it and who picks and chooses his examples, unlike Darwin himself, without "connecting the dots" between them. In "Progress in the World of Animals and Plants," by contrast, Pisarev emerges as a legitimate dialogic partner to Darwin, as he marshals the latter's evidence to pose questions as to where instinct may stop and learned behavior, the first glimmerings of consciousness, may start in the organic world.

To take one example, the critic asks about the reproductive habits of the American versus the European cuckoo: Why does the European cuckoo place her eggs in other birds' nests, while the American species does not?[26] Since the European cuckoo lays eggs over different time periods (a several days' lapse), it must be certain the earlier eggs are being sat upon by other birds so that the older chicks, once hatched, do not interfere with the growth and hatching of younger ones. Yet the American variety has an analogous egg-laying cycle and does not perform the act of

---

25 Dmitrii Pisarev, "Progress v mire zhivotnykh i rastenii," *Russkoe slovo* (*Russian Word*) (1864): no. 4, 1–52; no. 5, 43–70; no. 6, 233–74; no. 7, 1–46.

26 Ibid., 1–9.

deception. How does instinct work in this case? What is individual learning and experience that the cuckoo then applies to its next pregnancy and what is hard-wired, as we might say today, or as Pisarev terms it, what is like the street organ (*sharmanka*), that is, something involving no conscious decision-making? Alternatively, there is the case of the American ostrich (*straus*), whose females form a group and take turns sitting on each others' eggs after building a nest together. Pisarev wants to know how these birds know what to do, but he does not press forward recklessly, collapsing distinctions, linking lichens and human behavior. Moving more inductively, he does not explain every "here" from the "there" of blind determinism, as Dostoevsky and Strakhov might suppose of a member of his generation and leanings. Thus, Diderot's famous organ stop/piano key (*fortep'iannaia klavisha* [*sic*]) of predetermined thought upon which the Underground Man refuses to be played becomes for Pisarev—whether by chance or by intertextual echo we cannot say—the *sharmanka* metaphor:

> When we observe, on the part of some animal, a series of acts directed at a certain goal and then with complete success achieving that goal, then we usually, in accordance with our all-embracing wisdom, assert off the cuff that the animal does not know to what precisely its actions are leading, and that it is acting completely unconsciously, just as a street organ emits one note after the other without having the slightest possibility of following the melody. Perhaps this comparison of an animal to a street organ is fairly accurate in certain instances; perhaps in fact the comparison can be applied aptly to certain actions of a human being. For example, sexual attraction leads to propagation of the species. At the same time, a youth in love thinks least of all about a father's future obligations: his every action, every word, every thought is striving constantly toward one inevitable denouement, and all the while the denouement itself, with its significant increase in cares and hard-to-handle expenses, even frightens him. Here it seems the young man indeed can be portrayed as a street organ. But the young woman who senses the end of her term and tries to prepare diapers and baby clothes for her future child—no one would say that she is acting unconsciously, according to some unknown impulse. Perhaps the life of the cuckoo bird presents us with similar occurrences, in part street organ-like, in part un-street organ-like. But which occurrence/happening [*iavlenie*] can we relegate to one category, which to the other? This seems to me an exceedingly complicated question, and even one that is not always solvable.[27]

---

27 Ibid., 5: "Когда мы видим, со стороны какого-нибудь животного, ряд поступков, направленных к известной цели, и вполне достигающих этой цели, то мы обыкновенно, по нашей всеобъемлющей мудрости, утверждаем сплеча, что животное не знает, к чему

This passage, both metaphorically rich (the extended simile of the *sharmanka*) and logically nuanced, should be placed into the Underground Man's "monologic dialogue" with the radicals, because only then can we as modern readers see these two powerful minds coming at each other from different directions. The juxtaposition of cuckoo bird and human mating habits is handled tentatively, yet perceptively; we do not feel that Pisarev is trying to say what cannot yet be legitimately said. We can almost hear him, the anti-Strakhov and anti-Dostoevsky, polemicizing with the Underground Man at every turn. Pisarev's final intellectual sally in "Progress" is a kind of look into the future with ramifications perhaps more pertinent today than at the time the piece was originally penned. Rather than rejecting art altogether à la Bazarov, he suggests, proleptically, that art will become its true self when it sees the "poetry" in Darwin and Lyell's thinking:

> When readers acquaint themselves with Darwin's ideas, even as the latter are presented in my weak and pale essay, then I will ask them whether we acted well or poorly when we rejected metaphysics, scorned our poetry, and expressed utter contempt for our official aesthetics. Darwin, Lyell and other like thinkers—these are the philosophers, these are the poets, these are the aestheticians of our time.[28]

именно клонятся его поступки, что оно действует совершенно бессознательно, подобно тому, как шарманка выпускает из себя одну ноту за другою, не имея ни малейшей возможности следить за развитием мелодии. Может быть, это сравнение животного с шарманкою в некоторых случаях довольно верно; может быть даже, это сравнение прилагается также удачно к некоторым действиям человека. Например, половое влечение клонится к размножению породы; а между тем, влюбленный юноша всего менее думает о предстоящих обязанностях отца; каждый его поступок, каждое слово, каждое помышление ежеминутно стремится к этой неизбежной развязке, а в то же время, самая развязка, быть может, даже пугает его, как значительное приращение забот и непосильных расходов. Здесь человек, очевидно, изображает собою шарманку. Но молодая женщина, чувствуя приближение срока своей беременности, старается приготовить для будущего ребенка пеленки и рубашечки, тогда никто не скажет, что она поступает бессознательно, по неизвестному ей импульсу. Может быть, жизнь кукушки представляет нам такие явления, отчасти шарманочные, отчасти нешарманочные. Но какое явление отнести к одной категории, какое—к другой?—это, мне кажется, вопрос чрезвычайно затруднительный, и даже не всегда разрешимый."

28 Ibid., 9: "Когда читатели познакомятся с идеями Дарвина, даже по моему слабому и бледному очерку, тогда я спрошу у них, хорошо или дурно мы поступали, отрицая метафизику, осмеивая нашу поэзию и выражая полное презрение к нашей казенной эстетике. Дарвин, Ляйель и подобные им мыслители—вот философы, вот поэты, вот эстетики нашего времени."

Demons: From Darwinism to Social Darwinism

By November 1871, a reviewer in the *Russian Messenger* was already reporting that Darwin's *Descent of Man* had appeared in three translations earlier that year.[29] The backdrop for this heightened interest now included, in the sphere of politics and criminal law, the sinister appearance on the public scene of Dmitry Karakozov, Nikolai Ishutin, Sergei Nechaev, and their prototerrorist organizations, all of which managed to adapt a peculiar version of Darwinist principles to their nihilist program for the violent overthrow of the social system in the name of love for humankind. The virtually concurrent serialization of Dostoevsky's *Demons*, Leskov's *At Daggers Drawn* (*Na nozhakh*, 1870–71), Goncharov's *The Precipice* (*Obryv*, 1871), Krestovsky's *Panurge's Herd* (*Panurgovo stado*, 1869), and Pisemsky's *In the Whirlpool* (*V vodovorote*, 1871) constituted another crucial, though almost exclusively critical, context for the reception of Darwin's new book on Russian soil. All these novels portrayed in vivid images the transformation of the radical youth of the 1860s into bloodthirsty, criminal-minded fighters in the "struggle for existence," for whom the pleasure principle (personal "benefit") had replaced traditional moral values.

One of the most influential voices in the campaign against Social Darwinism (and, by extension, against Darwinism proper) was Mikhail Katkov, whose journal the *Russian Messenger* provided the venue for the serialization of three of the five novels mentioned above. Throughout 1871, the *Russian Messenger* returned repeatedly to the subject of Darwin's new book. Lengthy and consistently unfavorable reviews of *Descent of Man* were published, while interspersed among the reviews were new installments of *Demons*, *At Daggers Drawn*, Aleksei Tolstoy's polemical poems directed against the nihilists, and reports from the meetings and activities of the (First) International. In order to understand the animus fueling the *Russian Messenger*'s attacks on Darwin, the modern reader needs to bear in mind how the true target of this polemical edge—the peculiar Russian brand of Social Darwinism—almost completely eclipsed scientific Darwinism, both in the minds of the Russian nihilists and of their ideological opponents. As suggested previously, the unfortunate substitution of Social Darwinism for Darwinism proper in nihilist circles was a result of many factors, but, most importantly, it

---

29 Anon., "Po povodu novoi teorii Darvina," *Russkii vestnik* 96 (November 1871): 321–60.

was due to the younger generation's search for a holistic scientific vision of the world, and to their misjudgment of how much proper scientific training is needed in order to navigate contemporary science and its methods.

During the *Russian Messenger*'s anti-Darwinist campaign of 1871–72, the intensity of the journal's condemnation of Social Darwinist practices indicates to what extent the conflation of Darwinism and Social Darwinism had reached new levels. Thus, in his review of *Descent of Man* in May 1871, a critic ("D.") from the journal states that Darwin "applies his theory on the origin of species to man," but that in this instance the naturalist's study "does not represent anything new in a strict scientific sense."[30] Moreover, the potential evil that can come from the book's dissemination significantly outweighs its benefit for science, since it "provides rich food for the sort of flippancy that has nothing in common with freedom of thought—a flippancy [*legkomyslie*] in need of basic scientific knowledge yet demanding science's final word," with the result that "it becomes an argument in the hands of those propagandizing the pernicious philosophy that rejects morality at its foundation."[31] Darwinism's conclusion that humans "have no other immortality and no other spiritual life than animals" could make morality and conscience lose their position of highest authority and cease being the "restraining force" humanity needs to survive (cf. Raskolnikov's final dream of the microscopic, trichinae-like organisms).[32]

In fiction, the radical generation's obsession with natural sciences, from the very beginning, was translated into a symbolic association of nihilists with certain animal imagery. After Bazarov, the dissection of frogs and experiments on their nervous system became a cliché in fictional representations of nihilists. In the nihilist discourse, the nervous system was perceived to be the seat of what was previously known as "a soul and a heart," and the location of all perceptions and feelings. Not surprisingly, Dostoevsky saw the seeds of degeneration of

---

30 D., "Angliiskie kritiki o novoi knige Darvina (Proiskhozhdenie cheloveka i polovoi podbor)," *Russkii vestnik* 93 (May 1871): 372–85: "[Дарвин] применяет свою теорию о происхождении видов к человеку"; "[книга] не представля[ет] чего-либо нового в строго-научном смысле" (372).

31 Ibid., 372: "Новое сочинение Дарвина может дать обильную пищу легкомыслию, не имеющему ничего общего со свободой мысли, нуждающемуся в азбуке науки, но требующего непременно ее 'последнего слова,' … [книга] может сделаться … аргументом в руках пропагандистов пагубной философии отрицающей нравственность в ее основах."

32 Ibid, 384. "[Трудно … по теории Дарвина] приписать человеку другое бессмертие или другое духовное бытие кроме того каким одарены скоты."

nihilists' ideas in this early obsession with frogs. In his humorous poem, "The Nihilism's Fight with Honesty (The Officer and the Nihilist Girl)," which he composed during this period (1864–73), the nihilist girl declares to the officer that, as a starting point of their future romance, they "will collect a sack of frogs."[33] By the late 1860s, however, no new scientific breakthroughs in the understanding of the human nervous system had occurred, and a materialistic solution to the body–soul dichotomy had still not been found in frog anatomy. Consequently, at this time the dissection of frogs ceased to provide a sense of righteousness and firm direction, and the nihilist spirit soured. Thus, the nihilist girl Vanskok in Leskov's *At Daggers Drawn* moans, "I worked on Buckle earlier, I experimented on the frog, and now … I can't do anything else: give me something to work on, give me something to experiment on,"[34] while the "old nihilist" Forov carries a golden charm in the shape of a frog in memory of the first nihilist generation and its ideals.[35] As the nihilists of the late 1860s start to employ more radical means for realizing their social and political goals (i.e., as they move from dissecting frogs to cutting people's throats), their scientific ideas become more firmly associated with Social Darwinism, while their portrayals in fiction move from cold-blooded amphibians to hot-blooded large predators.

To situate the trend in Darwinian terms, the animalistic portrayals of nihilists in literature begin to move up the evolutionary ladder, from more primitive forms to images of "higher" species. As an "expert" on evolution, Fedka, the convict in *Demons*, compares Pyotr Verkhovensky to a "stupid dog" (*glupaia sobachonka*) next to Stavrogin, who in turn stands higher on the ladder ("*pred toboi kak na lestnitse stoit*") and, therefore, cannot be bothered even to "spit" on him.[36] Fedka's insult has much in common with the language of 1860s journalistic broadside, which did not spare words and doubtless supplied ample fodder to

---

33 F. M. Dostoevskii, "Bor'ba nigilizma s chestnost'iu (Ofitser i nigilistka)," *PSS*, 17:15–23, 18. "Мы первым делом натаскаем // Мешок лягушек со всех мест" (18).

34 N. S. Leskov, *Na nozhakh*, in *Sobranie sochinenii* (Moscow: AO Ekran, 1993), 2:1, 165–66: "Я прежде работала над Боклем, демонстрировала над лягушкой, а теперь … я ничего другого не умею: дайте же мне над кем работать, дайте мне над чем демонстрировать." Hereafter this edition is referred to as "*SS* (1993)."

35 Ibid., 54. "[П]о жилету у него виден часовой ремешок, на котором висит в виде брелока тяжелая, массивная золотая лягушка с изумрудными глазами и рубиновыми лапками. На гладком брюшке лягушки мелкою, искусною вязью выгравировано: 'Нигилисту Форову от Бодростиной.'"

36 Dostoevsky, *PSS*, 10:429.

nihilists' critics. The imagery that is part and parcel of such language is present even in the descriptions of left-leaning journalists: Saltykov-Shchedrin, for example, famously called the younger generation "lop-eared holy fools" (*visloukhie i iurodstvuiushchie*).[37] Leskov, on the other hand, as someone who feared the worst, bemoaned the fact that he could not distinguish the "real nihilists" from the "rabid curs [*shal'nye shavki*] who [kept] calling themselves nihilists."[38] Indeed, two such "rabid curs" figure in Leskov's 1864 novel *No Way Out* (*Nekuda*). The author's alter ego, Doctor Rozanov, is shocked when he meets Russian "revolutionaries" Arapov and Bychkov, two blood-thirsty nihilists whose appearance is reminiscent of hunting dogs. Bychkov's facial expression "reminded one, with repulsive faithfulness, of the muzzle of a borzoi who is licking the blood-stained mouth of a young fallow deer."[39] Arapov swears in a frenzy "with foam at his mouth, clenched fists and sparks of implacable hatred in his eyes"; his colleague promises "to flood Russia with blood, to knife everything that has pockets sown unto its pants," and does not cringe when proposing "to slaughter five million so that fifty-five million will live and be happy."[40]

As the imagery presenting nihilists becomes more extreme, moving from associations with small creatures to dogs, monkeys, wolves, and eventually to the "apocalyptic" beasts in *Demons* and *At Daggers Drawn*, the (Social) Darwinist principles that govern the radicals' lives become more articulated and explicit. Alongside the "struggle for survival" and "survival of the fittest," now accepted as standard social-political calculus, we also begin to find new

37   Recall that Zaitsev's surname is a version of "rabbit." M. E. Saltykov-Shchedrin, "X. Mart 1864 goda," in *Sobranie sochinenii v 20 tomakh* (Moscow: Khudozhestvennaia literatura, 1965), 6:290–329.

38   N. S. Leskov, "Nikolai Gavrilovich Chernyshevskii v ego romane *Chto delat'* (Pis'mo k izdateliu *Severnoi pchely*)," in *Sobranie sochinenii v 11 tomakh* (Moscow: Gos. izd-vo khud. lit-ry, 1958), 10:21. Hereafter this edition is referred to as "*SS* (1958)."

39   N. S. Leskov, *Nekuda*, in ibid, 2:257 and 2:307–8. "Арапов ругался яростно, с пеною у рта, с сжатыми кулаками и с искрами неумолимой мести в глазах, наливавшихся кровью …" "Выражение его рыжей физиономии до отвращения верно напоминало морду борзой собаки, лижущей в окровавленные уста молодую лань, загнанную и загрызенную ради бесчеловечной человеческой потехи."

40   Ibid., 301: "Залить кровью Россию, перерезать все, что к штанам карман пришило. Ну, пятьсот тысяч, ну миллион, ну, пять миллионов … Пять миллионов вырезать, зато пятьдесят пять останется и будут счастливы." Leskov's obsession with separating the "rabid curs" from true nihilists will continue. In *At Daggers Drawn*, for example, he draws a tortured distinction between the "genuine nihilists" Forov and Vanskok and the groupies of the "bad" nihilist Pavel Gordanov, who is a "wolf in sheep's clothing."

versions (caricatures) of the "sexual selection" formula meant to govern erotic interactions between men and women. Gordanov in *At Daggers Drawn* becomes the leader and principal ideologue of "no nonsense nihilism" (*negilizm*), the doctrine that refers to conventional morality and "tender feelings" as "nonsense" (*gil'*) and proclaims that the main purpose in life is to win the battle for survival and to become rich by employing "Jesuitism" (including "cunning and trickery" [*khitrost' i lukavstvo*]).[41] Likewise, when the chronicler of *Demons* portrays Verkhovensky, he does so in terms of the Darwinian cliché, only now that struggle has become *too conscious*, too manipulated, not about survival alone but something else: "Of course, there is the struggle for existence in everything, and there is no other principle, everybody knows that, but still . . ."[42] In these fictions, therefore, the proliferation of graphic metaphorical representations of nihilists as animals goes hand in hand with representations of Social Darwinist principles as realized metaphors. *"Homo homini lupus est"* now becomes "survival of the fittest" in the human realm. Wolves (intelligence plus predatory behavior) continue to play a prominent role in literary depictions of nihilists throughout the decade, to the point where the image becomes overused, ultimately exhausting itself in the figure of Nerodovich from Orlovsky's (Golovin's) *Out of the Rut* (Vne kolei, 1882) and the "Wolf" from Markevich's *The Abyss* (Bezdna, 1883–84). At the height of this process, however, nihilists often appear in fiction as an amalgam of various animals. Hence Mark Volokhov, the nihilist antihero from Goncharov's *The Precipice* has serpent-like attributes (the habit of stealing apples from the matriarch's garden and tempting Vera, the young heroine, with them) and almost spectral qualities (he enters and exits through windows), while he is also persistently characterized as a (stray) dog and a wolf, into whose clutches Vera eventually falls. By the same token, Dostoevsky's Verkhovensky has serpent-like qualities, with a tongue that is "unusually long and thin, terribly red, and with an extremely sharp, constantly and involuntarily wriggling tip."[43] At another time,

---

41 Leskov, *SS* (1993), 2(1):162.

42 Fyodor Dostoevsky, *Demons*, trans. Richard Pevear and Larissa Volokhonsky (New York: Vintage, 1994), 551; Dostoevskii, *PSS*, 10:421: "Конечно, во всем борьба за существование, и другого принципа нет, это всем известно, но ведь все-таки."

43 Dostoevsky, *Demons*, 180: "[Я]зык у него во рту, должно быть, какой-нибудь особенной формы, какой-нибудь необыкновенно длинный и тонкий, ужасно красный и с

however, he appears as that most Darwinian of animals: Stavrogin "laughs at his monkey" when Verkhovensky slavishly copies ("apes") him.[44]

Obviously there is a powerful *reductio ad absurdum* at work in portraying the younger generation of radicals as animal-like. This tendency is not only motivated by the law of caricature, however; something else is happening here as well. What Dostoevsky, Leskov, and the others are gesturing toward is how the purity and integrity of serious science is being used against itself. Although the radicals' uncritical absorption of Darwinist ideas and their desire to apply them to themselves and the world around them was a manifestation of the central place that the idea of progress played in their worldview, the resulting Social Darwinism undermined that idea and, actually, resulted in its complete reversal. If progress in nature is accompanied by a continuous "struggle for existence" in which only "the fittest" survive, then what exactly does that mean when applied to human society? Who defines fitness and how can it be separated from the perverseness of consciousness? At what point does the survival instinct in nature (the borzoi taking down the young fallow deer) acquire a moral regulator? What if the borzoi wants more deer meat than it needs to live? By engaging with these images from the animal world, the polemical fiction of the 1860s and 1870s highlighted how the idea of progress could morph into a reality of regress and degeneration.

It is significant that the anti-Darwinist critique in the *Russian Messenger* followed a pattern similar to the one we have been observing in antinihilist fiction: comparisons between humans and representatives of smaller animal species seem harmless and even scientifically useful, but once we reach the realm of larger animals with attributes suggesting advanced mammalian or primate behavior (such as speech, consciousness, human feelings) comparisons become more sinister. Thus, as the critic "D." remarks, "when Darwin gets to the subject of language, to articulate speech, his quick-wittedness stops"; his theory reveals a weakness "in its desire to demean the distinctively human qualities of self-consciousness, individuality, capacity for the abstract and for the creation of general notions."[45] In particular, he claims that the great naturalist's arguments appear vulnerable in "everything that has to do with the development of moral and

---

чрезвычайно вострым, беспрерывно н невольно вертящимся кончиком." Dostoevskii, *PSS*, 10:144.

44 Dostoevsky, *PSS*, 10:405.

45 D., "Angliiskie kritiki": "Когда Дарвин доходит до языка, до членораздельной речи, то его остроумие падает" (374); "[С]лабость в старании унизить отличительные человеческие

intellectual abilities and strivings by means of evolution and natural selection."[46] Even though Darwinists might claim that human religion developed from a feeling analogous to "a dog's devotion to its master," no one will ever be able to "derive religion from a dog or Christianity from a cat."[47] Moreover, although Darwin reportedly "believes it is highly likely" that any animal that develops social instincts and intelligence to a human level will also inevitably acquire a "moral feeling," this, according to the *Russian Messenger*'s critic, has never happened and will never happen because "moral feeling is an exclusively human quality."[48] In a different article, the reviewer in the *Russian Messenger* states that Darwin's theory cannot explain these two exclusively human actions of "the nervous system": "self-consciousness" and "intelligence."[49] Unlike people, no animals "know themselves and know themselves knowing."[50] They do not possess "an understanding of the distinction between truth and lies,"[51] nor can they exhibit genuine free will.[52] Unlike Darwin, who wrote of "a missing link" in the evolutionary history of man, the *Russian Messenger* defended the idea of a complete "rupture" between the human and the animal world. And this alone could explain the fact that human culture remains on the same level as it has always been: "no poetry can be higher than Homer's, no religious feeling can be more sublime than the one expressed in Genesis."[53]

The criticism of Darwin's *Descent of Man* in the *Russian Messenger* boiled down to the core concern about a moral apocalypse, but the key discussion in the book centered on the role of sexual selection in evolution. Likewise, the idea of the progress in sexual relations lay at the core of the nihilist sexual revolution; political, social, or scientific concerns in the nihilist episteme were

---

способности самосознания, индивидуальности, отвлечения, образования общих идей" (375).

46 Ibid., 375: "[В]о всем, что касается развития эволюционным путем или естественным подбором нравственных и интеллектуальных способностей и движений."

47 Ibid.: "Ни один человек никогда не разовьет религию из собаки или христианство из кошки."

48 Ibid.

49 "Po povodu novoi teorii Darvina," 337.

50 Ibid., 338: "[З]нали что они знают, или знали себя познающими."

51 Ibid., 339: "[Н]и самосознания, ни понимания различия между истиной и ложью, правдой и неправдой."

52 Ibid., 345.

53 "Angliiskie kritiki o novoi knige Darvina," 383: "Никакая поэзия не превосходит Гомера; нет религиозного чувства более возвышенного чем в книге Бытия."

secondary and contingent upon finding a successful solution to the "Woman Question." Essentially, the birth of nihilism coincided with Bazarov's failure to persuade Mme Odintsova to hand over her body to his "anatomical theater" and thus to preserve the health of his "nerves." Not much later, Vera Pavlovna succeeded in proving to all perspicacious readers that, through the consistent application of Chernyshevsky-style logic to all realms of human existence, from political economy to the organization of domestic space, the exercise of free love can become a path for personal and universal happiness, fulfillment, and prosperity. It was not accidental that Chernyshevsky's famous novel about sexual liberation became the chief target for all attacks on nihilism, from the start of the polemic in Dostoevsky's *Notes* to the late 1870s, when the last nails in the coffin of nihilism were struck by Katkov's "pleiad": B. M. Markevich and K. Orlovsky (K. F. Golovin), A. Nezlobin (A. A. Dyakov) and P. P. Tsitovich. Stripping the veil of Chernyshevsky's logic from the new people's solution to the "Woman Question," these writers reduced the nihilist version of free love to a banal vaudeville at best, and, at worst, to a horrifying picture of allegedly widespread sexual abuse and exploitation of naïve nihilist women by unscrupulous male predators who practiced Darwinian principles of "sexual selection."

Out of Katkov's pleiad, Alexander Dyakov's (Nezlobin's) literary output engages most consistently with the anti-Darwinian theme and contains the most pointed attack on "sexual selection" practices, which were allegedly dominating the life of Russian nihilist circles in Europe. A renegade, whose tergiversation followed essentially the same route as Dostoevsky's (for Dyakov, from a fervent participation in radical circles in the 1860s to the complete denunciation of his former self and a spiritual rebirth as a staunch conservative in the 1870s), Dyakov obtained his "forgiveness" by striking a deal with Katkov and publishing in 1876–1880 a scandalous cycle of novellas entitled *The Circle Culture* (*Kruzhkovshchina*) in the *Russian Messenger*.[54] Not surprisingly, a copy of this book was in Dostoevsky's library.[55] In the preface to a separate edition of the cycle, Pyotr Tsitovich, a professor of law and Dyakov's editor and publisher, employs the principles of

---

54 Dyakov's immunity from persecution (after a very mild sentence) was granted through Katkov's personal intercession on grounds of the immense benefit (*pol'za*) that his literary activity brings to the "unmasking of the true goals of Russian revolutionaries abroad." See "D'iakov," in *Russkie pisateli: 1800–1917: Biograficheskii slovar'* (Moscow: Bol'shaia Rossiiskaia entsiklopediia, 1992), 2:203–4.

55 *Biblioteka F. M. Dostoevskogo: Opyt rekonstruktsii: Nauchnoe opisanie* (St. Petersburg: Nauka, 2005), 56.

the anti-Darwinist critique as a frame for the interpretation of Dyakov's novellas. He places the "degraded" nihilists on a lower step of the evolutionary ladder; for him, their portrayals by Dyakov constitute "a well-marked atlas" and "a collection of zoological sketches, drawn from nature either in the zoological garden itself or from memory," and the picture presented is one of "intellectual and moral savagery (*odichanie*)."[56] And true enough, the nihilist characters in Dyakov's novellas do present an astonishing picture of pervasive savagery. Thus, a radical by the name of Okhlynnikov, "who was obsessed with everything unclean and filthy," finds pleasure in insulting people's sensibilities by "putting crumbled cigarette butts in the soup." Not satisfied with this, however, he then "tosses a handful of sand [into the bowl], turns over an inkwell, catches a fly and drowns it in the plate, shreds some stearin and, if he is really on a roll, blows his nose into the plate, and gobbling it all up, exclaims 'Let the strong devour the weak!'"[57]

According to Dyakov, then, the struggle for existence as mantra of the young radicals is an ever more sinister misapplication of Darwinian laws to human society. In his essay "Nihilism and Literary Development" ("*Nigilizm i literaturnoe razvitie*") that accompanied his novellas in the second edition of the cycle, Dyakov observes that "Darwin's law does not say that the *best* species survive, only those that are best *adapted* to circumstances," meaning that no positive values are attached to such a survival.[58] Such a survival therefore is

---

56 [P. Tsitovich], "Ot izdatelia," in A. Nezlobin, *Kruzhkovshchina: "Nashi luchshie liudi—gordost' natsii"* (Odessa: V tipografii G. Ul'rikha, 1879), vyp. 1:i.: "Рассказы А. Незлобина—своего рода коллекция зоологических рисунков, сделанная с натуры в самом зверинце или по свежей памяти."

57 A. Nezlobin, *Kruzhkovshchina*, vyp. 1:39–40: "Так, например, был радикал Охлынников, полупомешанный на нечистом и поганом: зовут ли его обедать, или чай пить, он непременно сделает какую-нибудь гадость, особенно если в обществе окажется новый человек, незнакомый еще с его замашками: в суп накрошит папиросных окурков, бросит горсть песку, чернильницу опрокинет, поймает муху и живьем утопит в тарелке, накрошит стеарину, а если уж очень в ударе, то даже и высморкается в тарелку, и все это съест, словно выжжет, приговаривая:

—Да пожрет сильный слабого! Когда его останавливали, уговаривали пощадить аппетит соседей, он вскакивал, словно раненый зверь и начинал беситься.

—Вы дураки!—кричал он, ударяя кулачищами по столу,—не можете понять, что в природе нет чистого и поганого, а есть непреложный закон: 'борьба за существование,' а потому да пожрет сильный слабого."

58 A. Nezlobin, "Nigilizm i literaturnoe razvitie," in *Kruzhkovshchina*, vyp. 3:17: "Дарвиновский закон не говорит, что выживают **лучшие** виды; напротив, выживают более **приспособленные** к обстоятельствам. Дарвин приводит массу примеров, где приспособление достигается хитростью, сноровкой, подделкой, ложью, обманом, т. е. такими качествами, которые в человеческой личности имеют совершенно

often achieved by employing the tricks of "cunning, dexterity, fraud, lies, deception," which, people, unlike animals, normally consider to be immoral, "lowly and vile."[59] The leaders of the nihilist circles, however, allegedly persuade their followers that "people are animals" and, therefore, they should "acknowledge and 'respect' the entire sphere of bestial desires," to eat and think "with one and the same organ: the stomach" (after all, Chernyshevsky taught in *What Is to Be Done?*—"Do what is pleasant for you").[60]

The good reader can see where the ultimate distortion of Darwin's ideas is going. Consciousness, whether pure nervous system or existing in a space where morality is eventually born in higher-level subjects, cannot be accessed through the stomach or the sex drive alone. The variables are too many and the logical bridges from the nerve endings (the "neuronal pathways," as we would say today) to a decision about social interaction and political destiny were not yet "load-bearing" in the 1860s and 1870s, and Dostoevsky, Strakhov, Katkov, and others responded to that attempt at false construction. By the end of the 1870s, writers like Dyakov were revisiting the Darwinian episteme and showing vividly how it cannot be applied "before its time." Thus, Marina, the *femme fatale* from the novella *To the People* (*V Narod*), is initiated into the world of (Social Darwinian) nihilism when she starts to follow their logic of "anything goes":

> The literature of women's emancipation impressed her with its great charm. At that time, ethical questions were decided mainly by the adaptation of man to bestiality and brutishness. … Every idiot … howled to "good and bright female readers" that this is how it's done by the animals, and so it follows that these "good and bright" readers should follow their example. … Darwin was then trendy and, when she had read him, she prepared to apply

---

отрицательное значение, и даже прямо называются низостью, подлостью,—хотя в животном они безразличны. И вот едва человек задумался над этой разностью между скотами и людьми, ему дают книгу о 'происхождении человека,'—с единственной целью, чтобы он проникся **убеждением**, что он тоже животное и даже не особенно высокого порядка,—может быть, три-четыре рода от обезьяны. А раз он животное,— значит и поступать в жизни должен по закону 'борьбы за существование.'"

59 Ibid.

60 Ibid.: "[Т]олько **по-видимому** нигилизм отрицал все. … на самом деле признавал и 'уважал' всю область животных вожделений, служил ей и поклонялся, из нее … выработал общественный тип не нигилиста, а хищника"(5); "оба эти процесса совершались брюхом" (22).

the "struggle for existence" to the struggle for pleasure, without regard for the means.[61]

In the novella *Fatal Sacrifice* (*Fatal'naia zhertva*), the amoral revolutionary Trutnev "develops" Olga Brovskaya by persuading her to leave her fiancé. The latter, by "enslaving" her in a "legal marriage," would never let her "exploit her body" as a free woman—that is, one who wants to satisfy "the normal needs of a human body"—should.[62] After Olga leaves her fiancé and joins the circle, Trutnev sells her for sex to a wealthy groupie to raise funds for the circle. Although Olga's sacrifice brings benefit (*pol'za*) to the circle, she is left with no personal happiness or "benefit" (Chernyshevsky-style) and eventually commits suicide.

To follow the heated dialogue in the Russian press that produced a Marina, an Olga, and a Trutnev on the one hand and an Underground Man on the other is to track perhaps *the* existential question of Dostoevsky's time and, for that matter, ours. Needless to say, "Darwin" was used and misused in these debates, and his words and thoughts were often made to say things in the Russian context he most certainly would not have agreed with at the Linnaean Society of London. By the mid-1880s, and especially by the 1890s, the Russian version of the Darwinian argument was sounded out in different voice zones. Vladimir Solovyev, for example, was a central figure in the Moscow Psychological Society, whose neo-idealist synergies were fed by works like eminent jurist and political philosopher Boris Checherin's *Science and Religion* (*Nauka i religiia*, 1879), with its questioning of Darwin's too passive, too mechanistic concept of adaptation, and famed geochemist and "noosphere" discoverer Vladimir Vernadsky's "On the Scientific Worldview ("*O nauchnom mirovozzrenii*," 1902), with its

---

61 Nezlobin, *Kruzhkovshchina*, vyp. 2:206–7: "Литература женской эмансипации повлияла на нее обаятельно. Тогда этические вопросы решались преимущественно приспособлением человека к зверству и скотству. Каждый дурак … вопил 'хорошим и умным читательницам' о том, как это делается у животных, а потому да последуют 'умные и хорошие' их естественному примеру. … Дарвин тогда был в моде и она прочитала его, и 'борьбу за существование' готовилась применить к борьбе за наслаждение, без выбора средств."

62 Nezlobin, *Kruzhkovshchina*, vyp. 1:117: "Эксплуатируйте свою красоту. Вы скажете, это разврат … Вздор! Самое чистое самопожертвование в пользу дела … неужели бы вы не пожертвовали бы собой, своей красотой, своей молодостью, если бы знали, что эта жертва нужна для пользы, для спасения миллионов людей."

acceptance of the provisional status of the scientific episteme.[63] Thus, in the brilliant exchange of ideas that was to become the symposium and eventual volume *Problems of Idealism* (*Problemy idealizma*, 1902), Solovyev's charismatic presence and unique spiritual integrity are everywhere felt, but he died before the volume could be published. The philosopher's long essay entitled "Beauty in Nature" ("*Krasota v prirode*," 1889), which examines the emergence of the beautiful (symmetry, coloration, euphony, etc.) in different species, all the while parsing meticulously Darwin's texts, appears simultaneously with the Society's early flowering and is a perfect example of the sort of disciplinary boundary "chasteness" the group wanted to observe.[64] Solovyev and Vasily Rozanov, who also wrote on Darwin in a lively response to Solovyev, became direct inheritors of the "Dostoevskian line" of antiempiricist, antipositivist, and, ultimately, anti-"mechanico-chemical" (i.e., early classical Darwinist) thought. Science and philosophy were moving to positions where the disciplinary boundaries of each were pushed and extended, but in responsible, deliberate, respectful ways.

Militant atheism, intelligent design, epigenetics, the selfish gene: the debate goes on today, on different terms, but with equal animation and often vituperation.[65] How to close the gap? Do we say it can't be closed and dismiss further attempts? Is it possible for some "Deep Blue" of the future not only to defeat Garry Kasparov but, "knowing" beforehand all of our experiences, thoughts, and feelings, to predict how we are going to act—which foot we are going to step on, to return to Chernyshevsky? We want to believe we are moving forward, but are we not retelling the same narrative with different characters, different facts, different data sets? Enter the Underground Man.

---

63 See Dana Dragunoiu, *Vladimir Nabokov and the Poetics of Liberalism* (Evanston, IL: Northwestern University Press, 2011), 49–53.

64 "Solov'ev i Darvin: mezhdu Sofiei i 'vyzhivaniem sil'neishikh'" ("Solov'ev and Darwin: Between Sophia and 'Survival of the Fittest'"), *Lotmanovskii sbornik*, ed. L. Kiseleva and T. Stepanishcheva (Moscow: OGI, 2014), 394–406.

65 Of course, Richard Dawkins, brilliant and prolific science writer, dogmatic atheist, and author of the famous *The Selfish Gene* (1976), is perhaps the leading figure internationally in these debates. But other writings and points of view are nowadays almost ubiquitously present. See, e.g., Deepak Chopra and Leonard Mlodinow, *War of Worldviews: Science vs. Spirituality* (New York: Harmony, 2011), Nick Lane, *The Vital Question: Why Is Life the Way It Is?* (New York: Norton, 2015), or Gary Gutting, "The Stone" ("Opinionator"), *New York Times*, March 12, 2013, and July 8, 2014: "Mary and the Zombies: Can Science Explain Consciousness?" and "Does Evolution Explain Religious Beliefs?"

II

....

Darwin's Plots, Malthus's Mighty Feast, Lamennais's Motherless Fledglings, and Dostoevsky's Lost Sheep

Liza Knapp

Dostoevsky and Darwin

Against the background of work by Gillian Beer, George Levine, and others on Darwin's plots and evolutionary narrative in the English novel, what follows explores the relationship of Darwin's plots to Dostoevsky's.[1] The concern is not with how Dostoevsky responded to Darwin *as a scientist*, for, in fact, as others have documented, Dostoevsky was receptive to Darwin's science.[2] Evolution as such was not a stumbling block. As Dostoevsky saw it, all that mattered was the breath of God—whether we come from a lump of clay, Adam's rib, or monkeys was immaterial. What mattered was the freedom and responsibility instilled with that breath, given the possibility that, in Dostoevsky's words, "through his sins,

---

1 Gillian Beer, *Darwin's Plots: Evolutionary Narrative in Darwin, George Eliot and Nineteenth-Century Fiction* (Cambridge: Cambridge University Press, 1983); George Levine, *Darwin and the Novelists: Patterns of Science in Victorian Fiction* (Cambridge, MA: Harvard University Press, 1988).

2 B. E. Lewis, "Darwin and Dostoevsky," *Melbourne Slavonic Studies* 11 (1976): 23–32; Michael Katz, "Dostoevsky and Natural Science," *Dostoevsky Studies* 9 (1988): 63–76; Irene Zohrab, "Darwin in the Pages of *The Citizen* during Dostoevsky's Editorship and Echoes of Darwinian Fortuitousness in *The Brothers Karamazov*," *Dostoevsky Journal: An Independent Review* 10–11 (2009–10): 83–103.

man could again turn into a beast,"[3] as seems to threaten those gathered in Skotoprigonevsk. The plural "sins" reminds us that Dostoevsky was not thinking of original sin but rather the sins that we ourselves commit.[4]

Dostoevsky took exception to what could be subsumed under the label of "Social Darwinism," the application of the "struggle for survival" that rules the animal kingdom to human society. His journal *Time* (Время/*Vremia*) published a review of George Henry Lewes's *Physiology of Common Life*, and it praised Lewes for warning against using the laws of natural science to explain or model human life.[5] Dostoevsky believed that human beings were made in the image and likeness of God and thus should not just do what comes naturally, either in accordance with the laws of nature or in imitation of beasts. Views among interpreters of Darwin varied: at one end of the spectrum were those who believed that his discoveries only confirmed suspicions that the natural world was "red in tooth and claw" and, at the other end, those who believed that they suggested that cooperation and mutual aid were vital to survival and natural behavior. But for Dostoevsky, whether doing what comes naturally amounts to what one of his heroes calls the way of the tigers and the crocodiles (*Idiot*, pt. 2, ch. 10; *PSS* 8:245) or whether it means extending mutual aid was beside the point. What mattered was not "natural" behavior but imitation of the divine. Thus, as Dostoevsky was fond of reminding his readers, often graphically, mutual aid that is not given in the name of God or mutual aid that is offered out of self-interest or in expectation of a "reward" or "honorarium" is on shaky foundation and can lead to cold-blooded murder or

---

3 Dostoevsky's works and letters are cited from F. M. Dostoevskii, *Polnoe sobranie sochinenii v tridtsati tomakh* [*PSS*], ed. V. G. Bazanov et al. (Leningrad: Nauka, 1972–90); hereafter cited as PSS by volume (and book number, when relevant) and page.

4 Letter of June 7, 1876, to V. A. Alekseev, #619, PSS 29(2):85. Below is the Russian original: "Кстати: вспомните о нынешних теориях Дарвина и других о происхождении человека от обезьяны. Не вдаваясь ни в какие теории, Христос прямо объявляет о том, что в человеке, кроме мира животного, есть и духовный. Ну и что же—пусть откуда угодно произошел человек (в Библии вовсе не объяснено, как Бог лепил его из глины, взял от земли), но зато Бог **вдунул в него дыхание жизни** (но скверно, что грехами человек может обратиться опять в скота)."

5 "'Fiziologiia obydennoi zhizni.' Soch. G. G. L'iuisa. Perev. S. A. Rachinskogo i Ia. A. Borzenkova, vol. 1, 1861," *Vremia* 11 (1861): 50–63. V. S. Nechaeva, author of monographs on the journals of the Dostoevsky brothers, could not determine the author of this unsigned review. V. S. Nechaeva, *Zhurnal M. M. i F. M. Dostoevskikh "Vremia" (1861–1863)* (Moscow: Nauka, 1972), 181.

worse (*Idiot*, pt. 3, ch. 4; *PSS* 8:312; notebook entry on "Socialism and Christianity" of 1864, *PSS* 20:190–91).

"Bad Omens" or, the Gospel of Darwin according to Mlle Clémence-Auguste Royer

Dostoevsky was exposed to the practice of using Darwin's discoveries as prescriptions about how human society should work and how human beings should treat each other in the introduction to the French translation of Darwin's *On the Origin of Species* by Clémence-Auguste Royer.[6] Royer's introduction was the subject of Nikolai Strakhov's article "Bad Omens" in *Time* in 1862 (no. 11). Declaring Darwin's theory of evolution to be "a huge step in the development of the natural sciences," Strakhov railed against the rabid views expressed by Royer in her introduction, especially her advocacy of what would come to be known as Social Darwinism—Royer was taken with how, in her view, Darwin's discoveries ratified what she called the "law of Malthus." In his "Essay on the Principle of Population" (1798), Thomas Robert Malthus argued that as population grows (exponentially, if unchecked), it is inevitable that some will suffer and perish. As Malthus put it (in figurative language that would resonate in Dostoevsky's novelistic imagination), "nature's mighty feast" has only a limited number of places. According to Malthus, efforts on the part of "compassionate guests" (those fortunate enough to have a place at the feast) to make room for desperate unfortunates would only wreak havoc and bring misery for all; Mother Nature thus acted "humanely" in refusing "to admit fresh comers when her table was already full."[7] In his *Origin of Species*, Darwin wrote that "as more individuals are produced than can possibly survive, there must in every case be a struggle for existence, either one individual with another of the same species, or with the individuals of distinct species, or with the physical conditions of life."[8] He concluded: "It is the doctrine of Malthus applied with manifold force to the

---

6 "Préface du traducteur," *De l'Origine des espèces ou des lois du progrès chez les êtres organisés, par Ch. Darwin*, traduit en français sur la troisième Èdition avec l'autorisation de l'Auteur par Mlle Clémence-Auguste Royer, avec un préface et des notes du traducteur (Paris: Guillaumin, 1862), http://babel.hathitrust.org/cgi/pt?id=ucm.5324240904;view=1up;seq=9.

7 T. R. Malthus, *An Essay on Population*, ed. Donald Winch (Cambridge: Cambridge University Press, 1992), 249.

8 Charles Darwin, *On the Origin of Species by Means of Natural Selection, or the Preservation of Favoured Races in the Struggle for Life* (London: John Murray, 1859), ch. 3, 63.

whole animal and vegetable kingdoms."[9] Royer, however, was not really interested in what Darwin's discoveries meant to the animal and vegetable kingdoms; rather, her praise was for the "humanistic/humanitarian" and "moral" implications and applications of Darwin's theory: "It is above all in its humanitarian consequences, in its moral consequences, that Mr. Darwin's theory is fruitful" ("Préface," lxii). As she understood it, Darwin's discoveries showed that the exclusion of the unfortunate from nature's mighty feast was proof of benign providence at work in the universe. Strakhov writes of the spin that Royer puts on Darwin's appropriation of Malthus:

> Indeed, what amazing discoveries! What science means! When a family has many children and there is nothing to eat, Malthus simple-heartedly took this to be a misfortune, whereas now we see that the more children, the better, for the beneficial law of natural selection is able to operate even more forcefully. The weak perish and only the naturally selected, the best and most privileged members survive the struggle and, as a result, progress is achieved: the betterment of the whole race.[10]

To put this in terms that would haunt Dostoevsky's work, Royer uses Darwin to justify building the health and happiness of the human race on the blood of innocent children.

Royer greets Darwin as the author of a new covenant that, in her view, put an end to an era of compassion and pity in the name of Christ or in the name of other dreamy creeds of brotherhood and equality. In accordance with Darwin's teachings (as [mis]understood by Royer), we should stop trying to feed the hungry, shelter the homeless, or comfort the sick. Royer writes,

> The law of natural selection, when applied to humanity, shows, surprisingly, to what extent up until now our political and social laws have been false—as has been our religious ethic. It will suffice to expose here one of the minor vices, namely, the exaggeration of that pity, that charity, that brotherhood, in which our Christian era has always placed the ideal of social virtue; it is the exaggeration of self-sacrifice, which consists of always and in all sacrificing what is strong to what is weak, the good to the bad, the beings that are well endowed in mind and body to beings that are defective and weak. And what results from this exclusive and unintelligent protection provided to the weak, the infirm, the incurables, even the wicked,

---

9 Ibid.
10 Nikolai Strakhov, "Durnye priznaki," *Vremia* 11 (1862): 169.

to all those disgraced by nature? The result is that the afflictions with which they are tainted tend to be perpetuated and multiplied indefinitely; it is that evil increases instead of diminishing and that it grows at the expense of the good. How many of these beings exist that are incapable of living on their own, that burden with all their weight those with able arms, and that in the society in which they languish, at great cost to themselves and others, take up for each of themselves three times as much space under the sun as a healthy individual! ... Has no one seriously thought about this? (Royer, "Préface," lvi)

For the record, Darwin himself complained that Royer had bastardized his views.[11] Dostoevsky makes clear in his fiction that Royer's attitudes were anathema to him, perhaps nowhere more profoundly than in *The Idiot*, a novel that shows at work the kind of Christ-like compassion that Darwin, as Royer presents it, had done away with.

If Royer in her attack on Christianity strikes us as Nietzschean *avant la lettre*, we might trace the genealogy as follows: (1) Myshkin, Dostoevsky's Christ-like hero, was his answer to (as Lebedev would say) not just social Darwinism but, if you will, the whole tendency, of which Mlle Royer is, so to speak, a perfect representative; (2) even as Nietzsche repudiated Christian values in *Der Antichrist* (1895), he, in the words of Walter Kaufman, "conceived of Jesus in the image of Dostoevsky's *Idiot*."[12] At this point, when Nietzsche wanted to know why Christian love had not succeeded in making the world a better place and when he proposed tougher love as a solution, we might see Nietzsche as Royer's ideological godson. Although Nietzsche disagreed on various points with Darwin and Spencer, his solutions were a far cry from the radical form of compassion, tender mercy, and self-sacrifice embodied by Myshkin, qualities often regarded as atavism or anathema in the age of Darwin (as heralded by Clémence-Auguste Royer).

---

11 Of Royer, Darwin wrote to Asa Gray that she "is [an] ardent Deist & hates Christianity, & declares that natural selection & the struggle for life will explain all morality, nature of man, politicks &c &c!!!" (June 10–20, 1862; http://www.darwinproject.ac.uk/entry-3595). In a letter to J. D. Hooker, Darwin complained, "Almost everywhere in Origin, when I express great doubt, she appends a note explaining the difficulty or saying that there is none whatever!!" (September 11, 1862; http://www.darwinproject.ac.uk/entry-3721).

12 Walter Kaufman, *Nietzsche: Philosopher, Psychologist, Antichrist*, 3rd ed. (New York: Vintage, 1968), 339.

Darwin's Plot on the Island of England and on Russian Novelistic Sod

Dostoevsky processed Darwin's *plots* differently from English novelists. Many novels of Dostoevsky's Victorian counterparts were ruled by a genealogical imperative, whereby the thrust of the plot is to reveal how everyone is related.[13] As Catherine Gallagher and Stephen Greenblatt argue in *Practicing New Historicism*, this is true of Dickens at least up until *Great Expectations* (1861). Plots often turned on discovering "genealogical identity," unraveling a mystery of origins, and reclaiming rightful inheritance.[14] The question "What connection can there be?" was seldom left rhetorical. Thus, as George Levine writes, for Dickens, Darwin made "literal" "the metaphorical, Christian view that we are all one [family] and deny our brotherhood at our peril."[15] Dickens, according to Levine, often "strains his plotlines" to prove this point.

The elaborately constructed multiplot novels of Dostoevsky's English counterparts have often been presented as entangled banks, the novelistic equivalent of Darwin's vision in the finale of the *Origin of Species*.[16] Beer has

---

13   Gillian Beer (in *Darwin's Plots*) argues that Darwin's scientific works reflect the hopes and fears of his age—as he wrote, he was inspired by and drew from the narratives in play in his cultural milieu, ideas that were already in the air, and novelistic plots already in print. (Thus, for example, he was an attentive reader of Dickens.) This aspect of Darwin's work helps explain why, to post-Darwinian readers, English plots that predate the publication of *On the Origin of Species* in 1859 often feel "Darwinian."

14   Catherine Gallagher and Stephen Greenblatt, *Practicing New Historicism* (Chicago: University of Chicago Press, 2000), 178. Novels such as *Bleak House* and *Oliver Twist* are about unraveling a mystery of origins.

15   Levine, *Darwin and the Novelists*, 149.

16   Darwin writes (*Origin of Species*, ch. 14, 489–90), "It is interesting to contemplate an entangled bank, clothed with many plants of many kinds, with birds singing on the bushes, with various insects flitting about, and with worms crawling through the damp earth, and to reflect that these elaborately constructed forms, so different from each other, and dependent on each other in so complex a manner, have all been produced by laws acting around us. These laws, taken in the largest sense, being Growth with Reproduction; inheritance which is almost implied by reproduction; Variability from the indirect and direct action of the external conditions of life, and from use and disuse; a Ratio of Increase so high as to lead to a Struggle for Life, and as a consequence to Natural Selection, entailing Divergence of Character and the Extinction of less-improved forms. Thus, from the war of nature, from famine and death, the most exalted object which we are capable of conceiving, namely, the production of the higher animals, directly follows. There is grandeur in this view of life, with its several powers, having been originally breathed into a few forms or into one; and that, whilst this planet has gone cycling on according to the fixed law of gravity, from so simple a beginning endless forms most beautiful and most wonderful have been, and are being, evolved."

suggested a form of cross-fertilization such that Darwin's reading of Dickens and others fed his scientific imagination. Thus, these novels exhibit traits such as variation, relatedness, and diversity.[17] But the fact that critics often refer to these novels as being "*over*populated" should give us pause. They suggest that, in fact, Malthus casts a shadow over English multiplot novels. Criticism of these English novels often presents characters or plotlines vying—competing—for their place at the feast of the narrative where, as it turns out, space is limited so that only certain select plots matter and certain select characters achieve the status of novelistic heroes.[18]

These "overpopulated" narratives keep reminding us that everyone has "an equivalent center of self" and has a right to narrative "franchise." Thus, in *Middlemarch*, when asking, "But why always Dorothea?," George Eliot's narrator intercedes to "protest against all our interest, all our effort at understanding being given to the young skins that look blooming in spite of trouble" and to browbeat readers into recognizing that Casaubon has rights, too (ch. 29; 278).[19] But even as the narrator reminds us of Casaubon's "intense consciousness," the plot thrust of *Middlemarch* is still to have him die off so that Dorothea can marry Ladislaw and multiply.[20] After all, it is rumored in *Middlemarch* that Casaubon's blood, examined "under a magnifying glass," was revealed to be "all semicolons and parentheses" (ch. 8, 71). In contrast, Will Ladislaw is red-blooded and offers genetic diversity.

The novels of George Eliot, Charles Dickens, and others have often given the impression to readers and critics that their characters vie for the narrator's attention or that plotlines compete for space that is limited. It would seem that "the doctrine of Malthus has been applied" here, too, "with manifold force."[21] According to this model, it is assumed that only a limited number of characters

---

17 See Beer, *Darwin's Plots.*

18 On characters "compet[ing] for attention in the narrative web" of *Middlemarch* and other novels, see Alex Woloch, *The One vs. the Many: Minor Characters and the Space of the Protagonist in the Novel* (Princeton, NJ: Princeton University Press, 2003), 31 et passim. Although Woloch does not discuss Darwin directly, his descriptions of plotlines vying for attention, and of heroes competing for a limited number of "major" roles, evoke Darwin's plots.

19 The edition I use is George Eliot, *Middlemarch*, ed. Rosemary Ashton (London: Penguin, 1994).

20 Darwin warns that "the vigorous, the healthy, and the happy survive and multiply" while others die.

21 These phrases belong to Darwin in *Origin of Species*, ch. 3.

will emerge as "major," with others relegated to being "minor." The specter of competition looms in George Eliot's multiplot novels, even if she modifies Darwin's plots to fit the version of Darwinism that she shared with George Lewes. According to them, Darwinism did not mean what Dostoevsky called "the way of the tiger and the crocodile," or what Tolstoy called "monkey sex,"[22] but rather a belief that more evolved creatures conquered the sex instinct and behaved altruistically, thus contributing to a reduction in misery for all. Eliot's work is imbued with what Gallagher calls "moral-restraint Malthusianism."[23] Thus, for all its apparent compassion for the down and out—for those who, according to Malthus, should be denied a place at nature's mighty feast—Eliot's world bears the traces of this English belief in progress and poetic justice.[24] And this is played out in her plots.

How do Dostoevsky's novelistic worlds differ? To English readers like Virginia Woolf, Dostoevsky's novels felt generically different from their English counterparts. Woolf believed that the distinctiveness of Russian novels had something to do with the novelistic sod from which they sprang.[25] In "The

---

22 Dostoevsky's Lebedev refers to the "way of the tiger and the crocodile" in *The Idiot* (pt. 2, ch.10; *PSS* 8:245). Tolstoy uses this term in reference to the Parisians in "Kreutzer Sonata" (ch. 11).

23 Catherine Gallagher, *The Body Economic: Life, Death, and Sensation in Political Economy in the Victorian Novel* (Princeton, NJ: Princeton University Press, 2008), 174

24 Although George Eliot does not figure obviously in the rich pantheon of Dostoevsky's influences among contemporary novelists, her work was so popular in literary circles in Russia that it is reasonable to presume that he knew Eliot's work. Dostoevsky's Skotoprigonevsk is a far cry from Middlemarch, but it is possible to see *Middlemarch* as a novel that hovered in the reaches of Dostoevsky's novelistic imagination as he wrote *The Brothers Karamazov*. The episode involving Alyosha's visit to the Snegiryov hut can be read as a Dostoevskian appropriation and subversion of Brooke's visit to the Dagley cottage after his son has stolen a leveret: both episodes involve a young boy transgressing against a "master" and the boy's drunken father standing up to the "master," who the father thinks has come to demand that his son be punished. Dostoevsky, like Eliot, uses the episode to show the humiliated and insulted struggling to maintain dignity.

25 In her attention to how environment affects the artifacts of culture, Virginia Woolf may be following in her father's footsteps. Leslie Stephen (Woolf's father) wrote that "history depends upon the relation between the organism & the environment." This particular line from Leslie Stephen was recorded by Thomas Hardy in his notebook. Hardy wrestled with the hold of (Social) Darwinian and Malthusian thought in his fiction, most notably *Jude the Obscure* (1895). See Angelique Richardson, "Biology in the Victorian Novel," in *A Concise Companion to the Victorian Novel*, ed. Francis O'Gorman (Malden, MA: Blackwell, 2005), 203–4.

Russian Point of View," she famously contrasted novels produced in a culture ruled by the teapot (Victorian and Edwardian novels) to those by Dostoevsky and others that were produced in a culture ruled by the samovar. Whereas in the teapot-ruled English novels, "spaced is crowded" and "time limited" and "pressure" was greater to sort out the classes (and thereby privilege what Peter Walsh in *Mrs. Dalloway* calls "the ruling class"), the Russian novel and its plots seemed to Woolf to be more open and the Russian novelist more prone to compassion.[26] Thus, under the influence of the Russian point of view, Woolf in *Mrs. Dalloway* questions her culture: when the shell-shocked veteran of the Great War, Septimus Warren Smith, throws himself out of the window, Woolf invites us to see this act as somehow being related to his being denied a place at Mrs. Dalloway's party, which might be seen as a novelistic recreation of Malthus's "mighty feast" with its limited number of guests. As Woolf tells it, Septimus Warren Smith has been in some way forced out of the window by the "ruling class" so that their world, which he fought to preserve, could continue. Woolf thus rehearses but profoundly challenges the Malthusian-Darwinian plots that prevailed in her culture. By contrast, when the title character in Dostoevsky's "Meek One" jumps out of the window holding an icon of the Mother of God to her breast, we have a very different plot. Or, to cite one more searing illustration of the hold of Darwin's (and Malthus's) plots on the English novel: in Thomas Hardy's *Jude the Obscure*, when Jude's boy murders his siblings before hanging himself, he leaves a one-line suicide note, "Done because we are too menny [*sic*]." In Dostoevsky's world, by contrast, when a child commits suicide, she does it because she feels that she has "killed God"—this unspeakable despair results from being violated by Stavrogin (*PSS*, 11:18). Each child's rationale for suicide reflects the ultimate concerns of the novelist in question.

The Parable of the Lost Sheep on Russian Soil: Dostoevsky's Answer to Darwin's Plots

I take *The Idiot* to be Dostoevsky's ultimate answer to Darwin's plots as adapted by his English contemporaries: Dostoevsky takes his inspiration from the master plot of the lost sheep. In the original Gospel parable, we are asked what

---

26 Virginia Woolf, "The Russian Point of View," *The Common Reader*, ed. Andrew McNeillie, (New York: Harcourt Brace, 1984), 180.

man of us, having a hundred sheep and having lost one, does not leave the ninety-nine in the wilderness and go after the lost one until he finds it. Having found it, the man places it on his shoulders rejoicing and, coming home, calls to his neighbors and friends, asking them to rejoice with him because he has found his sheep that was lost. The parable ends with the assertion that there is more joy over this one sheep—or repentant sinner—than over the ninety-nine sheep. This parable, evoked in a host of different ways in *The Idiot*, is remarkable for how it defies economic and Malthusian sense. It reminds us that these doctrines hold no sway in the kingdom of God. Why would the shepherd abandon in the wilderness ninety-nine good, upright, deserving sheep to go after a stray, whose wayward ways possibly signal that this lost sheep has a penchant for vice? Wouldn't it be common sense (an English construct!) for the shepherd just to let this one go? As Royer (who, in the words of Darwin, "hates Christianity") argues, wasting resources on lost causes—who each already take up "three times as much space under the sun" as one fit (upright) person—does a disservice to all (Royer, "Préface," lvi).

In Dostoevsky's novels, in contrast to the Gospel parable, not all lost sheep are found. As criticism of *The Idiot* attests, readers have asked Royeresque and Nietzschean questions in the face of Nastasya Filippovna's corpse or Myshkin's apparent idiocy at the very end. Was anything gained by his compassion? Was Myshkin a failure? Or should he simply have recognized that there are only a certain number of places at "the mighty feast"? Was Myshkin wasting resources on those who, in Royer's view, take up far more than their share of space under the sun? Did his attempt to restore Nastasya Filippovna result in misery for all? To be sure, we all want good to prevail in life and poetic justice in novels. And we wish that Myshkin's efforts to restore the lost sheep Nastasya Filippovna Barashkova had saved her life and restored her to the community. Perhaps we even wanted a double wedding at the end, with Aglaya married to Myshkin and Nastasya Filippovna to Rogozhin.

Does the fact that our desires for a happy ending are not satisfied (or the fact that there is no poetic justice) still mean that the compassion of Myshkin has been for naught? We may think of what will become of Kolya Ivolgin, who draws close to his mother and "may perhaps become a truly good human being" (*Idiot*, pt. 4, ch. 12; *PSS* 8:508). And, also, as Myshkin shows compassion for the murderer Rogozhin and strokes his cheek, the narrator dismisses him as an idiot, or worse, and remarks critically that there was nothing more that Myshkin could do. And many readers and critics have agreed that Myshkin fails here. But I see it differently. After all, in Dostoevsky's samovar-ruled world, we are challenged to look beyond the bottom line. At the very least, we must extend that bottom line beyond the boundaries of the plot. Thus, we are left to ask whether Myshkin's compassion for the murderer Rogozhin does not, in fact, have an effect on Rogozhin. Myshkin is sowing in Rogozhin's heart seeds of his future repentance, which could bear fruit for Rogozhin in prison camp in Siberia. This is the pattern Dostoevsky set up in *Crime and Punishment,* where it appears that the boundless compassion of Sonya Marmeladov—or the act of charity of the mother and daughter who give Raskolnikov a coin in the name of Christ only to have him throw it into the Neva—enters the murderer Raskolnikov's heart and prepares it for the "gradual rebirth" that he will undergo in Siberia (*PSS* 6:422).

Dostoevsky and Darwin's Plots: Excluding Malthus from the Feast of the Мать-сыра земля ("Moist Mother Earth")

Dostoevsky's faith—or the choice of Christ over economic, scientific, and other forms of truth that he expressed in his letter to Fonvizina after prison camp in Siberia—might explain why he responded so differently to Darwin's plots, preferring the master plot of the parable of the lost sheep, at least until *Brothers Karamazov.* As a child of his century, Dostoevsky had to reckon with Darwin like everybody else. But he did so in an intellectual, cultural, and literary milieu that had declared itself hostile to Malthus. As Daniel Todes has argued, whereas "for Darwin and other leading British evolutionists, the expression 'struggle for existence' appealed to common sense, and its Malthusian associations posed no problem," this was not true for Russian evolutionists, who wanted their Darwin without Malthus and, further, substituted "mutual aid" for "struggle for existence."[27] Todes invites us to consider that the spin that these Russian evolutionists put on Darwin—their emphasis on mutual aid rather than struggle—stemmed from what they, as young naturalists, observed in

---

27   Daniel Todes, *Darwin without Malthus: The Struggle for Existence in Russian Evolutionary Thought* (Oxford: Oxford University Press, 1989), 3. See further (inspired by Todes's work) Stephen Jay Gould, "Kropotkin Was No Crackpot," in *Bully for Brontosaurus: Reflections in Natural History* (New York: Norton, 1991), 325–39.

their more sparsely populated expanses of the Russian Empire—in Siberia and elsewhere. By contrast, as Todes explains, Darwin and other Darwinists did their scientific work in the tropics, crowded with species, but they also had as their social point of reference the relatively more overpopulated British Isles.

Dostoevsky's response to Darwin is thus quintessentially Russian (according to Todes's scheme) insofar as Dostoevsky rails against the Malthusian line and the metaphor of competition. The work of Peter Kropotkin and other Russian evolutionists promoting "mutual aid" was published after Dostoevsky's time, and Dostoevsky did not live to read his fellow member of the Petrashevsky circle Danilevsky's 1885 exposé of Social Darwinism (and Darwinism). But, as Todes has argued, already in his 1869 *Russia and Europe*, Danilevsky rehearses the argument of this later work when he presents Darwinism as the natural expression in scientific form of Englishness. To support this view, Danilevsky notes that individualism, struggle, and competition are bred into the English, whether in debate societies or boxing matches.[28] Dostoevsky had similar intuitions about the English, which he had expressed most dramatically in the description of London in his 1863 *Winter Notes on Summer Impressions*, when he writes of "the millions of people, abandoned and chased from the human feast, jostling and throttling each other in the underground darkness, into which they have been thrust by their older brothers, groping their way and knocking at gates and seeking outlet, so as not to smother in a dark basement"—this is Dostoevsky's vision of the English incarnation of Darwin's "entangled bank" crossed with Malthus's "mighty feast" that excludes the poor and downtrodden.

Malthus's Mighty Feast and Lamennais's Orphaned Fledglings in Dostoevsky's Plots

Whereas Victorian novelists—and scientists—had sucked in Malthus's doctrine with their mother's milk, Dostoevsky cut his teeth as a novelist in St. Petersburg in a milieu that was already very wary of Malthus. Malthus's *Essay on the Principle of Population As It Affects the Future Improvement of Society* (1798) did not appear in full Russian translation until around the time of Darwin's *Origin of Species*, but its essence and key metaphors were certainly known to Dostoevsky in the 1840s.

---

28   Todes, *Darwin Without Malthus*, 41.

His fellow member of the Petrashevsky circle, Ivan-Ferdinand Iastrzhembsky, who taught political economy at the Technological Institute in Petersburg, spoke on this subject at Petrashevsky's Fridays on occasions when Dostoevsky was present. Iastrzhembsky is reported to have found Malthus's measures for keeping population down "inhuman."[29] Dostoevsky was also familiar with Vladimir Odoevsky's harangue in *Russian Nights* (1844) against "the absurd reasoning of the English economist" Malthus. Odoevsky drew attention to the fact that Malthus made revisions to his essay in attempt to appease "so-called moral people" with their illusions of "English decency." But, Odoevsky maintains, this did not really change much. Among Malthus's excisions was the infamous passage in which he declared that nature's mighty feast has a finite number of places and that it just does not make sense to give way to compassion and allow the poor to come to the table. Better to let them starve and keep down population. This notion of calculatingly denying segments of the population—the poor, the unfit—a place at the table so shocked Vasily Zhukovsky that in his translation of Byron's "Prisoner of Chillon," he worked in a gratuitous reference to it: "Without a place at the earthly feast / I would be a superfluous guest at it" ("Без места на пиру земном / Я был бы лишний гость на нем").[30]

Antipathy to Malthus's doctrine, made overt in Dostoevsky's later works, was palpable in his works from the start of his career (before Darwin had revealed that "the doctrine of Malthus" is "applied with manifold force to the whole animal and vegetable kingdoms" in his 1859 *Origin of Species*). The young Dostoevsky's very act of making "poor folk" his novelistic subject in 1846 can be seen, in the context of the acute awareness of Malthus among Russian intellectuals at the time, as an expression of defiance against Malthus's dismissal of poor folk from the mighty feast.

In *Netochka Nezvanova* (1849), which Dostoevsky hoped would be his first full-fledged novel, we see Dostoevsky writing in defiance of Malthus and, in the process, inoculating his plots against the ethos that would be associated with Darwin from the 1860s on. The heroine's evocative name—the nickname

---

29 My information on Dostoevsky's exposure to Malthus comes from the commentary on references to Malthus in *The Idiot* (*PSS*, 9:448–49, 452). Dostoevsky would also have been familiar with V. A. Miliutin, "Mal'tus i ego protivniki," *Sovremennik*, nos. 8 and 9 (1847) (*PSS*, 9:449).

30 This addition to Zhukovsky's translation of Byron is noted in the commentary (*PSS*, 9:432).

contains the Russian word for "no," we never learn her patronymic, and her last name is the negative past passive participle of the verb meaning "to name, to call, or to invite"—designates her as one who is denied a place at the mighty feast. There are numerous of Russian proverbs about uninvited guests *not* having a place at the table, such as "На незваного гостя не припасена и ложка" ("For the uninvited guest, there is not even a spoon"); "Кто ходит незваный, редко уходит негнаный" ("He who arrives uninvited seldom leaves without being driven away"); "Незваный гость хуже татарина" ("The uninvited guest is worse than a Tatar"). After living in abject poverty in Petersburg with her mother and stepfather, Netochka Nezvanova was left in the gutter after her mother died of consumption and her stepfather abandoned her (and died). Yet this sickly and desperate child, denied a place at the mighty feast, survived because she was taken in by Prince Kh., who lived in a house with red velvet curtains that Netochka had admired and dreamed of. Prince Kh. intends to "bring her up with his children."

The plot, at least at this turn, runs counter to scenarios envisioned by Malthus. Indeed, Prince Kh., identified by Dostoevsky scholars as a precursor to Prince Myshkin, is inspired by Christian charity and Marian compassion. Though Dostoevsky on some level was inspired by the Russian Orthodox piety of his childhood, the characterization of Prince Kh. was also influenced by strains of Christianity that Dostoevsky was attracted to during this period, specifically those associated with French Christian socialism that Konstantin Leont'ev would later denigrate by calling "rosy." The plot motif of the adopted orphan appears in Félicité Lamennais's *Paroles d'un croyant* (1834), which was among the works that Dostoevsky and others of the Palm-Durov circle wanted to print on the lithograph machine they had procured. (Whereas the larger Petrashevsky circle was engaged in talk, Dostoevsky and other members of this smaller group had started to take action in the hope of disseminating texts that would raise consciousness in Russia.) Dostoevsky's friend Alexander Miliukov, who had translated this work of Lamennais, reported that Dostoevsky praised his translation. Lamennais's *Paroles* was anticlerical and critical of the social order, but even so it was fervently Christian as it sought to inculcate an ideal of charity and fraternity that is as antithetical to Malthus's doctrine and to Darwin's law of natural selection (as understood by Royer). Lamennais includes the following episode: Two fathers each have many children and they worry about what will become of their families should they die. One day the two fathers notice nests of birds in the shrubs, each with a mother bird tending to her young. Suddenly a bird of prey swoops down on one of the mother birds just as she is passing a worm into the mouth of one of her young. The two men assume that her now-orphaned young will die. However, they come back in a few days only to find that the orphaned baby birds have survived. How? To their surprise, the other mother is feeding them along with her own young and making "no distinction." At this point, one father says to the other: "You see, why should we worry? God never abandons his own. If I die before you, you will be the father of my children, and vice versa; and if we both die, they will have as father their Father in heaven."[31] Elsewhere in Lamennais's *Paroles*, God counsels humankind: "Help each other, for there are among you some who are stronger and some who are weaker, some who are infirm and some who are hearty; and yet all must live. And if you do thus, all will live because I will reward the pity you have for your brothers and I will make your sweat fruitful."[32]

Dostoevsky is likely to have taken Lamennais's tale of mutual aid among birds as a master plot that provides an alternative to those at work in Malthus's dog-eat-dog world. Lamennais's tale about orphaned fledglings being fed by another mother, coupled with his admonition to "help one another" (with emphasis on the fit helping the unfit), is a French Christian socialist variant of the "mutual aid" that Russian evolutionists like Peter Kropotkin later documented at work in the world of nature. And, certainly, intimations of this mutual aid had been reported earlier. Thus, as Kropotkin relates in *Mutual Aid: A Factor in Evolution* (1890–1906), back in 1827 Goethe had become excited when the Eckermann told him that "two little wren-fledglings, which had run away from him, were found by him next day in the nest of robin redbreasts, which fed the little ones together with their own youngsters." Goethe thought that "if it be true that this feeding of a stranger goes through all Nature ... as a general law," then it "confirmed his pantheistic views."[33] Dostoevsky was not a wannabe naturalist in the fashion of Goethe. In this respect, he was able to separate facts of

---

31 Félicité Lamennais, *Paroles d'un croyant* (Paris: Librairie de la Bibliothèque Nationale, 1897), 52–54.

32 Ibid., 24.

33 P. Kropotkin, *Mutual Aid: A Factor of Evolution*, 2nd ed. (New York: McClure Phillips, 1904), xi.

science from faith. Thus, for him, any tales of orphaned fledglings being fed would remain parables to inspire human beings to prepare for the kingdom of God while still living on earth.

Dostoevsky's Novel of the Accidental Family and Darwin's Plots

Although it incorporates elements of rosy Christian plots, the "real world" depicted in *Netochka Nezvanova* also displays characteristics of Malthus's mighty feast. Whereas Prince Kh. acts on Christian charity, his wife operates according to different principles: all that matters to her is the preservation of members of her own family, whom she regards, in proto-Darwinian form, as "favored" "in the struggle for life."[34] Her realm of privilege, of patrimony, and of tradition (all of which Netochka lacks) guarantees her and her progeny a place at the feast. This family life looks ahead to what Dostoevsky would refer to in the 1870s as the "genealogical family" and present Leo Tolstoy as its novelist par excellence. Dostoevsky contrasted the genealogical family with the accidental family, indirectly presenting himself as the novelist of a new form of family novel, one governed by its own rules. Whereas the genealogical gentry families depicted by Tolstoy managed to survive and flourish, protected and favored as they were, Dostoevsky saw his mission as novelist of the accidental family as becoming ever more important as more and more families were becoming "accidental."[35] And this mission started to emerge even before Tolstoy's novels presented a metric for Dostoevsky to deviate from. This mission emerged as he wrote *Netochka Nezvanova*.

In *Netochka Nezvanova*, Princess Kh. is concerned first and foremost with the welfare and success of her own children. As far as Princess Kh. is concerned, her husband should have let Netochka die in the gutter in a fashion consistent with the Malthusian (and eventually Social Darwinian) scenario whereby those who are not "vigorous, healthy, and happy" die off, ceding the way to the select

---

34 The second part of Darwin's book title is … *the Preservation of Favoured Races in the Struggle for Life.*

35 Irene Zohrab ("Darwin in the Pages of *The Citizen*," 94) suggested that Dostoevsky "uses Darwinian terminology" in this vision in the 1870s of a family created by "accident" or "chance." At the same time, the essence of Dostoevsky's vision of this accidental family—and of the *novel of the accidental* family—is found before Darwin in *Netochka Nezvanova*.

and fit.[36] One episode in particular shows the princess monomaniacally bent on the preservation of her biological offspring. We are told that the princess loved nobody except perhaps her own children—and a ferocious bulldog, which tyrannized the household and stole food from the orphan. Initially, however, the princess had no love in her heart for this dog, a sickly stray picked up on the street and brought home by her husband. On her order, the dog was kept outside. But one day this unfavored bulldog saved Sasha, the young heir, from drowning in the Neva. After doing so, the bulldog gained the princess's favor. She changed his name from "Friks" to "Falstaff," brought him into the house, and vowed to feed and keep him despite his nasty disposition. The princess honored and welcomed Falstaff because he played a role in the preservation of her species, whereas she wanted Netochka (another stray her husband brought home out of charity) banished.

In keeping with her proto-Darwinian approach to life, Princess Kh. concludes that having Netochka is a threat to the preservation of her family: what Netochka refers to as a romance develops between her and Katya, the daughter of the prince and princess. The girls slip into each other's beds at night; during the day they kiss "at least a hundred times," according to Netochka's estimate. Katya seems to be moved by Netochka's plight: Katya calls Netochka her "little orphan" and her "lamb." However, this "happiness," as Netochka put it, was not destined to last long. Via the French governess, word of the romance between the two girls reaches Princess Kh. She acts quickly to banish Netochka. Why? Netochka is a threat to the princess's genealogical imperatives—to her daughter Katya's marriage prospects. That is to say, Katya's love for Netochka interferes with the process of natural selection. The two girls are separated when Princess Kh. takes her children to Moscow, which also happens to be better for the health of the son. Although it might seem that this proto-Darwinian plot prevails in part 2, it has been fractured in profound ways that anticipate Dostoevsky's later defiance of Darwin's plots. There are hints that Katya and Netochka will be reunited in the future. In the meanwhile, Prince Kh. places Netochka with Alexandra Mikhailovna, his stepdaughter. Alexandra Mikhailovna loves Netochka as her own, in a triumph over biology. When the work ends (abruptly, because of Dostoevsky's arrest), Alexandra

---

36   Darwin, *Origin of Species*, ch. 3, 79.

Mikhailovna, on her deathbed, entrusts her own children to Netochka rather than to her husband, thus suggesting a model of mutual aid that, like Netochka's rescue from the gutter by Prince Kh., defies Malthusian-Darwinian scenarios.

Lamennais's parable of the motherless birds being fed was among Dostoevsky's sources, but in key moments Dostoevsky invokes Christian plots with a less rosy coloring. Netochka's plot unfolds in the zone of icons of the Mother of God. The master plot at the heart of *Netochka Nezvanova* also has a Marian aura and harks back to the Gospel of John 19:26–27: Jesus from the cross sees his mother and his beloved disciple and tells her to behold her son and tells the beloved disciple to behold his mother, with the denouement of this plot, in the last half of 19:27, that from this time on the disciple took her unto his own home.

From the early—anti-Malthusian, pre-Darwinian—stages of Dostoevsky's career as a novelist, Dostoevsky began the process of subverting Darwin's plots. As he novelized the struggle for Netochka Nezvanova, that uninvited guest, to be given a place at the mighty feast, he makes her the foremother of future heroes, including Myshkin and Ippolit. In *The Idiot*, written in a time of developing concern about Social Darwinism (and its apparent application "with manifold force" of "the doctrine of Malthus" to the human kingdom), Dostoevsky has both Ippolit and Myshkin depict themselves as unfortunates denied a place at nature's mighty feast.[37] In his "Necessary Explanation," which he reads at Myshkin's birthday party, Ippolit refers to the "feast and chorus" of nature, at which everyone else has and knows his place, but he is a "stillborn fetus" (*Idiot*, pt. 3, ch. 7; *PSS*, 8:343). Then, as Myshkin awaits his dawn rendezvous with Aglaya on the green bench, he recalls what Ippolit had said about not having a place at the feast and acknowledges that he, too, had shared this feeling of being denied a place and of feeling like a "stillborn fetus" (*Idiot*, pt. 3, ch. 7; *PSS*, 8:351). (The epileptic Myshkin, like the consumptive Ippolit, is handicapped in the struggle for survival, for, as Darwin pronounced, "the vigorous, the healthy, and the happy survive and multiply," and others die.) In fact, one might suggest that, had it not been for Ippolit's plight taking over Myshkin's consciousness at this pivotal moment and had his heart not been pierced by Nastasya Filippovna's suffering, the novel might have run a different course toward a happier ending, one more characteristic of the English novel. (Thus, Myshkin

---

37   A reference to Malthus, according to the commentary in *PSS* (9:452).

might have pursued his personal happiness with Aglaya; together they might have survived and multiplied.) According to Malthus-inspired Social Darwinian theory, the consumptive Ippolit should simply be written off, as should be that lost lamb Nastasya Filippovna Barashkova, not to mention the murderer Rogozhin. But Dostoevsky pierces Myshkin's heart with their suffering, which had as its consequence that he cannot marry, multiply, and survive. In *The Idiot*, the consumptive and the lost sheep perish and the epileptic ends as an idiot, but what distinguishes Dostoevsky's novel from most English variations on Darwin's plots is how it sustains its spirit of metaphysical rebellion.[38]

---

38 Joseph Frank characterizes Ippolit as a "metaphysical rebel" in *Dostoevsky: The Miraculous Years, 1865–1871* (Priceton, NJ: Priceton University Press, 1995), 331.

III

"Viper will eat viper": Dostoevsky, Darwin, and the Possibility of Brotherhood

Anna A. Berman

As Darwinian thought took root across Europe and Russia in the 1860s after the publication of *On the Origin of Species* (1859), intellectuals wrestled with the troubling implications the "struggle for existence" held for human harmony and love. How could people be expected to "love their neighbors" if that love ran counter to science? Was that love even commendable if it counteracted the perfection of the human race through the process of natural selection? And if Darwinian struggle was supposed to be most intense among those who were closest and had the most shared resources to compete for, what hope did this hold for the family?

Darwin's Russian contemporaries were particularly averse the idea that members of the same species were in competition. As Daniel Todes, James Rogers, and Alexander Vucinich have argued, Russian thinkers attempted to reject the Malthusian side of Darwin's theory.[1] Situated in the harsh, vast expanses of Russia, rather than on the crowded, verdant British Isles, they

---

1 Daniel Todes, *Darwin without Malthus: The Struggle for Existence in Russian Evolutionary Thought* (Oxford: Oxford University Press, 1989); James Allen Rogers, "The Russian Populists' Response to Darwin," *Slavic Review* 22, no. 3 (1963): 456–68; Alexander Vucinich, *Darwin in Russian Thought* (Berkeley: University of California Press, 1988).

argued that of the three struggles Darwin included under the umbrella of "struggle for existence"—(1) with the environment, (2) with other species, and (3) within a species—climate and other species were the true adversaries.[2] For example, in "Neskol'ko slov o sovremennoi teorii proiskhozhdeniia vidov," which Ilya Mechnikov (1845–1916) submitted to Dostoevsky's journal, *Vremia* in 1863, Mechnikov argued that Darwin's idea that struggle is most intense between closely related organisms violated common sense: "As everyone knows shared dangers and obstacles do not stimulate struggle between the individuals subject to them, but, on the contrary, impel them to unite together in one society and to resist these obstacles with joint, more reliable forces."[3]

Similarly, the botanist Andrei Beketov (1825–1902)—a friend and former roommate of Dostoevsky's—argued in an 1873 article that if one were to follow the Malthusian logic in Darwin's theory,

> members of a family [would] have incomparably more antagonism between them than members of the community [*obshchina*], village, city, or state … It [would] unalterably follow that members of the family consuming part of what they are given, a fixed amount of food and other physical necessities, [would] take away the same part of this necessary material from all the rest. Parents [would] struggle with their children, brothers and sisters [would] struggle among themselves, etc.[4]

Beketov used the image of a starving father and his beloved son in a bloody struggle for a sip of water as proof of the absurdity of this logic. The very idea that father and son would destroy each other for survival seemed so impossible to him that he believed this image alone was enough to prove Darwin's theory flawed.[5]

---

2 Todes, *Darwin without Malthus*, 3, 8–9, 21, 33.

3 "Neskol'ko slov o sovremennoi teorii proiskozhdeniia vidov" (1863), quoted in Todes, *Darwin without Malthus*, 88.

4 A. N. Beketov, "O bor'be za sushchestvovanie v organicheskov mire," *Vestnik Evropy* 10 (1873): 588.

5 Instead, he argued the "struggle" was really an interaction of forces that helped bring about balance, not destruction. Beketov went on to argue that the principle of Christian love derived from this "struggle," evolving over thousands of years (Beketov, "O bor'be za sushchestvovanie," 592–93). Dostoevsky would not be convinced by this kind of logic. He saw nothing innate in the love of one's neighbors, but instead a very different kind of struggle that relied on faith.

Dostoevsky's final novel clearly challenges this assurance. In *The Brothers Karamazov*, brothers and father are locked in a deadly struggle that Dostoevsky linked to the threats of "Darwinism" by labeling the conflict with the Darwinian metaphor "viper will eat viper" (*odin gad s'est druguiu gadinu*).[6] In his novels, Dostoevsky tested "Darwinian" ideas in his portrayals of family struggle.[7] In *Crime and Punishment* (1866), Dostoevsky, like Beketov, relied on the family to *dis*prove the sinister implications of Social Darwinism. However, by the time of *Brothers Karamazov*, his conception of family had become fully "accidental," and blood ties alone were not enough to stave off the "struggle for existence" or of "sexual selection" within the family. I believe that in *Brothers Karamazov*, Dostoevsky used the threat of Darwinian struggle entering the family to prove the need for "active kinship," like his idea of "active love." Familial duty can hold out against instinctive passions of rivalry and hatred only when the characters recognize family as a social construct that must be *created* through their own actions. For Dostoevsky, family bonds must be actively bestowed, not actively earned or passively accepted as birthright.

In *Crime and Punishment*, the ties of family are, if anything, *too* strong and family members *too* ready to make sacrifices for each other.[8] Dunya and Rodya are one of Dostoevsky's only sibling pairs to have shared a warm childhood

---

6 For the expression "viper will eat viper," Dostoevsky chose the word *gad*, as opposed to *zmei*, limiting the biblical significance. While the serpent that tempts Eve is a *zmei*, *gad* appears in the synodal translation of the Bible as a more neutral term, referring to reptiles as a category (alongside birds and beasts of the land [*zveri zemnye*]).

7 Dostoevsky never engaged with the details of Darwin's writings, and it is not entirely clear how much of Darwin's work he read himself and how much he simply read about in the Russian press. For the purposes of this chapter, I am using "Darwinism" to denote the popular conception of Darwin's theory held by Dostoevsky and other contemporary Russians, rather than the theories as Darwin himself wrote and understood them.

8 The devotion of Raskolnikov's mother and sister weighs on him like a burden. This is expressed more explicitly in the drafts: "His mother's caresses are a burden" (*PSS*, 7:136). All references to Dostoevsky are to *Polnoe sobranie sochinenii v tridtsati tomakh* [*PSS*], ed. V. G. Bazanov et al. (Leningrad: Nauka, 1972–90); hereafter cited as *PSS* by volume and page. For *Crime and Punishment* and *Brothers Karamazov*, I have relied on the English translations of Pevear and Volokhonsky: *The Brothers Karamazov*, trans. Richard Pevear and Larissa Volokhonsky (London: Vintage, 2004); *Crime and Punishment*, trans. Richard Pevear and Larissa Volokhonsky (London: Vintage, 2007). The English page number follows the Russian. All other translations are my own. For a psychoanalytic interpretation of the burdens placed by family love, see W. D. Snodgrass, "Crime for Punishment," *Hudson Review* 13, no. 2 (1960): 217–18.

together in a loving home, and concern for each other is one of their primary motivators. Early in the novel, just after receiving his mother's painful letter about Dunya's impending marriage, Raskolnikov attempts to save a drunken girl on the street from a preying lecher, an action clearly prompted by concerns for saving his own sister. After giving money to a kindly policeman for a cab to take the girl home, Raskolnikov has a sudden change of heart, turns back, and tells the policeman to give the girl to the lecher. He thinks, "Let them gobble each other alive—what is it to me?" (*PSS*, 6:24; 50).[9] Diane Thompson has rightly noted the Darwinian note in this phrase.[10] Raskolnikov imagines the girl's inevitable descent and early death and muses, "Every year they say, a certain percentage has to go … somewhere … to the devil, it must be, so as to freshen up the rest and not interfere with them. A percentage! Nice little words they have, really, so reassuring, so scientific."

But this "scientific," Social Darwinian outlook comes up against a major stumbling block in Raskolnikov's thought—his sister: "And what if Dunechka somehow gets into the percentage!" (*PSS*, 6:43; 50). Like Beketov in his later article, Raskolnikov finds the falseness of this scientific thought self-evident when applied to the family.[11] Darwin may be acceptable for "them," thinking in the abstract about "percentages," but not for his real and beloved sister. In this, Raskolnikov is aligned with the Russian populists of the 1860s, who rejected the idea of the struggle for existence taking place among people and instead emphasized the "necessity of cooperation among individuals of the same species."[12] Resources are shared among the Raskolnikovs selflessly. In this unhappy, but nonaccidental, family there is an innate, unquestioned feeling of connection. Raskolnikov's moments of loathing for his mother and sister stem precisely from the depth of his love for them, which exacerbates his horrible guilt.

In *Crime and Punishment*, Dostoevsky leaves Darwinism at the doorstep, never bringing its threatening implications into the home. But fourteen years

---

9 Pevear and Volokhonsky translate *"pust' ikh pereglotaiut drug druga"* as "let them all gobble each other," but I removed the word "all" for accuracy.

10 Diane Thompson, "Dostoevskii and Science," in *The Cambridge Companion to Dostoevskii*, ed. W. J. Leatherbarrow (Cambridge: Cambridge University Press, 2002), 202.

11 James P. Scanlan argues that Dostoevsky's fictional creations serve as humanistic equivalents of theoretical models in the sciences; see Scanlan, *Dostoevsky the Thinker* (Ithaca, NY: Cornell University Press, 2002), 4. By this logic, the family is a testing ground for scientific theories in *Crime and Punishment*.

12 Rogers, "Russian Populists' Response to Darwin," 460.

later, in *Brothers Karamazov* (1880), he would do just that. In his final novel, the rivalry for resources—money and women—takes place within the family. Father and son are ready to kill each other for the attentions of Grushenka, brothers compete for the heart of the proud Katerina Ivanovna, and an inheritance lies waiting to be divided among the legitimate offspring of a greedy, hoarding father who would prefer not to share. After Ivan defends his father from a physical attack by their brother Dmitri, he tells Alyosha, "Viper will eat viper and it would serve them both right!" (*PSS*, 14:129; 141). This Darwinian language (which echoes Raskolnikov's "let them gobble each other alive") becomes a symbol of family rivalry.[13] Ivan assures Alyosha in this moment that he would never allow Dmitri to kill their father, but later in the courtyard he returns to his words about "two vipers eating each other up," making it clear to Alyosha that he holds this wish, though he will not act upon it (*PSS*, 14:131; 143).

Two kinds of Darwinian struggle become encoded in Ivan's phrase about the vipers, which appears five times over the course of the novel. The first is the "struggle for existence" of natural selection, made famous—and famously unpopular in Russia—in *On the Origin of Species*. The second is the struggle of sexual selection that Darwin elaborated in 1871 in *The Descent of Man and Selection in Relation to Sex*.[14] Within a year of its English publication, there were already three Russian translations, and the book was quickly taken up by the press in Russia.[15] Therefore, although Dostoevsky never made a direct reference to *Descent of Man*, he must have been familiar with the key ideas, thereby expanding his conception of "Darwinism" from the time of *Crime and Punishment* to the time of writing *Brothers Karamazov*.

Natural selection is based on survival, but sexual selection is based on reproduction—controlled by both female choice and male combat.[16] The

---

13 Diane Thompson also links this phrase with Darwin ("Dostoevskii and Science," 202). Darwin never actually made such a statement, but the phrase clearly draws on common conceptions of Darwin's ideas.

14 Darwin described sexual selection briefly in *Origin of Species* and then explained this theory in much greater depth in *Descent of Man*, where he drew out the parallel between animals and humans.

15 For the publication history, see Vucinich, *Darwin in Russian Thought*, 50–51.

16 Darwin believed sexual selection could explain aesthetic phenomena—bright plumage, mating rituals, extravagant nests—not explicable through natural selection alone. The idea of female "choice" was controversial among Darwin's contemporaries because it suggested

rivalry between Dmitri and Fyodor Karamazov embodies Darwin's theory of sexual selection: "Two males fighting for the possession of the female," with Fyodor's envelope of money tied with a ribbon an equivalent to "male birds displaying their gorgeous plumage, and performing strange antics before an assembled body of females."[17] Each man is trying to lure his mate away from the other males.

Alyosha realizes that Ivan's view of Dmitri as a "viper" is related to the struggle of sexual selection between the brothers and to Dmitri's struggle with their father. Entering Katerina Ivanovna's drawing room the day after Dmitri's attack, Alyosha thinks of the rivalry between his brothers and remembers Ivan's phrase: "'Viper will eat viper,' his brother Ivan had said yesterday, speaking with irritation about their father and Dmitri. So in his eyes their brother Dmitri was a viper, and perhaps had long been a viper? Perhaps since Ivan had first met Katerina Ivanovna?" (*PSS*, 14:170; 187). Alyosha realizes that Dmitri became a "viper" to Ivan when he became a rival for the female (Katerina) and part of this second Darwinian struggle. Recognizing these "new pretexts for hatred and enmity in their family," Alyosha does not know what to do with his "active love." *This* is the struggle that interested Dostoevsky: how "Darwinian" antagonism could be overcome.

Linking the struggles within the Karamazov family to Darwinism served an ideological function for Dostoevsky, raising the stakes of the conflicts from individual rivalries to a question about the roots of human actions. "Viper will eat viper" relegates human behavior to instinct, taking away free will and abnegating moral responsibility. The idea that science could explain and "justify" human actions was troubling to many thinkers in the nineteenth century, not just to Dostoevsky.[18] One of the most controversial and upsetting features of Darwin's theory for his contemporaries was the idea that man was

---

animals had greater rational powers than people were ready to concede. For a concise over-view of the reception of Darwin's theory of sexual selection in the nineteenth century, see Erika Lorraine Milam, *Looking for a Few Good Males: Female Choice in Evolutionary Biology* (Baltimore: Johns Hopkins University Press, 2010), 1–28.

17   Charles Darwin, *The Descent of Man and Selection in Relation to Sex* (New York and London: D. Appleton and Company, 1922), 214.

18   For example, in a series of articles in the late 1880s and 1890s, Tolstoy argued that people were using science to justify the existing social order and the exploitation of the lower class; see Lev Tolstoy, "O naznachenii nauki i iskusstva" (1887), "Nauka i iskusstvo" (1890–91), and "O nauke i iskusstve" (1891–93).

just another animal, descended from the same ancestor as the apes, an idea that threatened the sense of man as a moral and rational actor governed by conscience and will. While Darwin's theory emphasized the animal side of man's nature, Dostoevsky's vision of man included the earthly but gave priority to man's spiritual side.[19]

Dostoevsky explained this vision in an 1876 letter to Vasily Alekseev. After analyzing the first temptation of Christ (turning stones into bread), Dostoevsky turned to Darwin: "By the way, recall the current theories of Darwin and others about the descent of man from monkeys. Not going into any theories, Christ declares directly that besides the animal world, man has the spiritual" (*PSS*, 29[2]:85). Dostoevsky went on to explain that it did not matter where man came from (the Bible did not explain how he was molded from clay): "But God blew life into him (but it is bad that through sins, man can return again to beast [*skota*])." From this comment it is evident that what mattered to Dostoevsky was not man's descent (looking back) but the presence of a spiritual life that divided him from animals (how he moves forward). For Dostoevsky, only man had heard Christ's teachings and could chose to act against the animal side of his nature and to heed this moral calling. As James Scanlan has argued, "For Dostoevsky there is no altruism in man's purely material makeup; love of others is a spiritual ability that enters human nature only through its participation in the divine."[20]

Darwin actually held a similar belief, though this nuance to his views did not receive great attention in Russia. And the Russians may be forgiven for this lapse, because Darwin literally relegated it to a footnote. According to Darwin's theory, the social instincts were bred into man through the process of natural selection, just as they were in all other social animals. As he explained in *Descent of Man*,

> As man is a social animal, it is almost certain that he would inherit a tendency to be faithful to his comrades, and obedient to the leader of his tribe; for these qualities are common to most social animals. He would consequently possess some capacity for self-command. He would from an inherited tendency be willing to defend, in concert with others, his fellow-men; and

---

19 James Scanlan has illustrated this beautifully in the first chapter, "Matter and Spirit," of *Dostoevsky the Thinker*.
20 Ibid., 84.

would be ready to aid them in any way, which did not too greatly interfere with his own welfare or his own strong desires.[21]

And when this aid *did* interfere with his strong desires, Darwin argued that some instinctive desires were stronger than others and that the social instincts could become stronger than any other instinct.[22] Darwin defined a moral being as "one who is capable of comparing his past and future actions or motives, and of approving or disapproving of them," and he acknowledged that man alone can be "ranked as a moral being."[23] In his discussion, he focused mainly on instances when people risk their lives for strangers, but he added an intriguing note: "The wish for another man's property is perhaps as persistent a desire as any that can be named; but even in this case the satisfaction of actual possession is generally a weaker feeling than the desire: many a thief, if not a habitual one, after success has wondered why he stole some article."[24] Raskolnikov—of course a much more complicated case—would be forced to agree.

Tucked into this section about the social instincts, Darwin included the following footnote that Dostoevsky would have whole-heartedly endorsed:

> Enmity or hatred seems also to be a highly persistent feeling, perhaps more so than any other than can be named ... Dogs are very apt to hate both strange men and strange dogs, especially if they live near at hand, but do not belong to the same family, tribe, or clan; this feeling would thus seem to be innate, and is certainly a most persistent one. It seems to be the complement and converse of the true social instinct. From what we hear of savages, it would appear that something of the same kind holds good with them. If this be so, it would be a small step in any one to transfer such feelings to any member of the same tribe if he had done him an injury and had become his

---

21 Darwin, *Descent of Man*, 110. Dostoevsky made similar points about people's instincts to help others in his response to part 8 of *Anna Karenina* in his *Diary of a Writer* (PSS, 25:218–23). He believed taking action is natural when an unknown innocent is in danger. But this is a question of saving a life, not *loving* the person. Dostoevsky did not think we can love without the soul getting involved.

22 Darwin, *Descent of Man*, 112.

23 Ibid., 113.

24 Ibid., 114. For the influence of Kant and Hume on Darwin's moral thought, see Michael Ruse, *Charles Darwin* (Malden, MA: Blackwell, 2008), 215–19.

enemy. Nor is it probable that the primitive conscience would reproach a man for injuring his enemy; rather it would reproach him, if he had not revenged himself. To do good in return for evil, to love your enemy, is a height of morality to which it may be doubted whether the social instincts would, by themselves, have ever led us. It is necessary that these instincts, together with sympathy, should have been highly cultivated and extended by the aid of reason, instruction, and the love or fear of God, before any such golden rule would ever be thought of and obeyed.[25]

So for Darwin, like Dostoevsky, enmity and hatred were persistent feelings that must be overcome, and it would take more than the "social instincts" to achieve this. Darwin's final point—the need for "the love or fear of God" to arrive at "love thy enemy"—was almost exactly the argument Dostoevsky made (though for Darwin one could question whether God Himself need exist, or only the "love or fear" in humans who believe in Him). However, this spiritual side of Darwin was absent from the way Dostoevsky invoked him.

In *Brothers Karamazov*, Dostoevsky placed the Darwinian, animal view of human behavior in opposition to the Christian idea of man as a moral being with a duty to honor his family. In the tavern meeting before Ivan's "rebellion," Alyosha asks Ivan if he is really about to leave town and then asks: "What about Dmitri and father? How will it end between them?" (*PSS*, 14:211; 231). This question refers back to their first "viper" conversation, but here Ivan answers not with Darwin, but with an inverted biblical reference: "Am I my brother Dmitri's keeper or something? ... Cain's answer to God about his murdered brother, eh? Maybe that's what you're thinking at the moment? But, devil take it, I can't really stay on here as their keeper!" (*PSS*, 14:211; 231–32). In the biblical formulation, defending Fyodor Pavlovich would be a moral duty, while in the Darwinian formulation (as construed by Ivan), it means interfering in the natural order of things. Dostoevsky pits these two opposing stances on familial duty and love against each other in Ivan's psyche, making the tension between the two the moral heart of the novel.

Ivan's attitude toward his family's struggle is directly related to his feelings about God. Early in the novel, Zosima tells Ivan that the question of his faith has not yet been decided and that "even if it cannot be resolved in a

---

25 Darwin, *Descent of Man*, 114n27.

positive way, it will never be resolved in the negative way either" (*PSS*, 14:65; 70). Even though Ivan may *wish* for his father's death, he will never *act* against God in that way. When Ivan decides to "return his ticket" to God's world (*PSS*, 15:223; 245), he is not rejecting God (he is explicit about this). Instead he rejects "Euclidean gibberish," as he puts it: the scientific view of the world as necessarily what it is. Science—the side Darwin would be on (though Ivan does not mention Darwin here)—reinforces and justifies the existing order. When Ivan focuses on the suffering of innocent children, he cannot accept this order. When he focuses on his vile father and shameful brother and "viper eating viper," he seems ready to accept the existing order ... almost.

As Ivan wrestles with his moral culpability after the murder, he returns again and again to the vipers. Two weeks after his first postmurder visit to Smerdyakov, he encounters Alyosha in the street and suddenly brings up their conversation when he had "reserved the right to wish" for his father's death. "But didn't you also think then that I was precisely wishing for 'viper to eat viper'—that is, precisely for Dmitri to kill father, and the sooner the better ... that I myself would not even mind helping him along?" he asks Alyosha (*PSS*, 15:49; 611). Alyosha is pained to admit this is true, and Ivan, even more troubled, returns to Smerdyakov for a second visit. He again comes away convinced of Dmitri's guilt, and returns to viewing Dmitri as a viper, even instilling this idea in Katerina Ivanovna. On the night before the trial, after a series of talks with Ivan, Katerina Ivanovna tells Alyosha and Ivan: "Just an hour ago I was thinking how afraid I am to touch that monster ... like a viper ... but no, he's still a human being for me!" (*PSS*, 15:37; 599). The opposition she draws between viper and human is linked to the opposition between man following animal instincts (Darwin) versus man as a moral, spiritual being (Christianity). She then turns to Ivan and tells him she has been to see Smerdyakov, adding: "It was you [*ty*], you who convinced me that he is a parricide" (*PSS*, 15:37; 599).[26] Clearly Katerina Ivanovnva's formulation has been shaped by Ivan's inner struggle. Ivan's use of Darwinian ideas

---

26 Alyosha is startled that she is using *ty*. Drawing attention to this intimacy again brings back the struggle between the two men for Katerina's affections.

causes her to question the very humanity of a man she had considered to be her fiancé.

Ivan, in turn, realizes he has come to "hate" Dmitri "not because of Katya's 'reversions' to him, but precisely *because he had killed their father!*" (*PSS*, 15:56; 619).[27] It is not Darwinian rivalry of sexual selection, then, but revulsion at the idea of parricide that divides Ivan from Dmitri. In other words, Ivan's *respect* for the family is what threatens his brotherly love. And indeed, he ultimately discovers Dmitri *is* worthy of this love because he did *not* kill their father. This truth comes to Ivan in the third and final meeting with Smerdyakov. After Smerdyakov echoes Alyosha's prophetic words, "*it was not you that killed him*," Ivan furiously seizes Smerdyakov by the shoulders and commands: "Tell all, viper! Tell all!" (*PSS*, 15:59; 623). This is the first time the word "viper" (*gad*) appears in the novel not in reference to Dmitri. Ivan is beginning to understand where the true guilt lies.

This link between Smerdyakov and the viper is reinforced moments later when Smerdyakov asks Ivan to open the bundle he has pulled out of his stocking, and Ivan recoils "as if he had touched some loathsome, horrible viper" (*PSS*, 15:60; 624). With Smerdyakov, not Dmitri, as viper, struggle has not fully penetrated the family, as Smerdyakov is not an acknowledged relation. However, Ivan recoils from the evidence because he sees himself as a viper, too, by association. He wished for his father's death and left town, renouncing his family duty.

Ivan does not want to allow this failing twice. On the stand in the trial the next day, succumbing to brain fever, he hands over Smerdyakov's money and announces: "It was he who killed father, not my brother. He killed him, and killed him on my instructions ... Who doesn't wish for his father's death?" This is supposed to be a noble act of self-sacrifice to save his brother. Increasingly, incoherently lost in his inner dialogue, Ivan exclaims: "Everyone wants his

---

27 As I have discussed elsewhere, the narrator skews our impression of Ivan and Dmitri's relationship, never showing any of the conversations between them and emphasizing Ivan's repugnance for his brother; see Anna A. Berman, "Siblings in *The Brothers Karamazov*," *The Russian Review* 68 (2009): 275. Consequently, I do not take the "hatred" the narrator refers to as a given.

father dead. Viper devours viper." He now uses this Darwinian logic as an abnegation of moral or familial duty (*PSS*, 15:117; 686).

Ivan believes he is guilty because he wished for his father's death, but this is not where his guilt lies.[28] True, he maintained the "right to wish," but he, like Dmitri, did not act on this wish. Dostoevsky does not go so far as to allow acknowledged kin to shed each other's blood in Darwinian struggle. Instead, Ivan and the other legitimate Karamazov brothers are guilty of rejecting Smerdyakov's brotherhood. They never allowed him into the socially constructed bonds of family that could have bound him to moral action, despite the fact that Fyodor Pavlovich's paternity is acknowledged during the trial. Ivan's claim—"it was he who killed father, not my brother"—denies the fact that Smerdyakov is as much a brother to him as Dmitri (both share a father but are of different mothers).[29] And this claim is echoed by Alyosha: "The lackey killed him, my brother is innocent" (*PSS*, 15:189; 768).

By the time of *Brothers Karamazov*, Dostoevsky had embraced his idea of the "accidental family." Dmitri, Ivan, and Alyosha are not united by warm childhood memories in a shared home (or even by two shared parents), as are Raskolnikov and Dunya. Their initial emotional and social connection scarcely differs from that of a random group of people. Consequently, for these brothers the thought of a sibling is no longer enough to topple the impulse to "let them gobble each other alive." "Accidental family" for Dostoevsky is more than blood ties—it is the *construction* of family through "active kinship," through the acknowledgment of familial bonds that may have no shared associations and memories to support them.

Smerdyakov is omitted from even this basic acknowledgment. Like the tortured children Ivan describes in his rebellion, Smerdyakov has been left out in the cold, but he is no longer five years old, so it is little wonder he has given up begging "dear God" (*bozhen'ka*) to protect him and has turned from God

---

28 Freud, building on Darwin's ideas in *Descent of Man*, argues in *Totem and Taboo* that we all have these murderous wishes about our father; see Sigmund Freud, *Totem and Taboo*, in *The Standard Edition of the Complete Psychological Works of Sigmund Freud* (London: Hogarth, 1958), 13:146.

29 Olga Meerson also points out this denial; see Meerson, *Dostoevsky's Taboos* (Dresden: Dresden University Press, 1998), 197.

altogether. Although no custom or nineteenth-century law mandated his legitimation in the eyes of his brothers, his exclusion and crime in *Brothers Karamazov* highlight the need for a stronger, more inclusive understanding of the family bond.[30] In Dostoevsky's world, people cannot rely on their pasts to foster these bonds—they must be actively bestowed.[31] Only this "active kinship," and the faith underlying it, has any chance of turning vipers into men who do not kill their fathers, but only "retain the right to wish."

---

30 Here I am in agreement with Liza Knapp's interpretation of "accidental family" in her study of *The Adolescent*: "In a state of 'chaos' and 'decomposition,' but ripe for rebirth in a more loving form"; see Liza Knapp, "Dostoevsky and the Novel of Adultery: *The Adolescent*," *Dostoevsky Studies* 17 (2013): 43–44. In *Brothers Karamazov*, the family is not reborn in this "more loving form," but Dostoevsky continues to express the need for such rebirth.

31 The counterview is expressed by Dmitri's defense attorney, who suggests that to be a real father one must not only beget a child but *care* for that child. This "adulterer of thought" (as Dostoevsky labels him) argues that "love for a father that is not justified by the father is an absurdity, an impossibility. Love cannot be created out of nothing: only God creates out of nothing" (*PSS*, 15:169; 744). Rakitin, another discredited character, makes a similar claim/demand to Alyosha and Grushenka: "What's there to love you for? ... One loves for some reason, and what has either of you done for me?" (*PSS*, 14:319–20; 353).

IV

Encounters with the Prophet: Ivan Pavlov, Serafima Karchevskaia, and "Our Dostoevsky"

Daniel P. Todes

In his biography of Dostoevsky, Joseph Frank suggests that the writer's distinctive talent resided in his integration of larger ideological and cultural issues into the lives of his protagonists without reducing his stories to mere allegories or his characters to simple stereotypes. For Frank, this quality of "felt thought" lent a distinctive quality to Dostoevsky's fiction.[1]

This was certainly true for the two protagonists of my story, who identified closely with characters in Dostoevsky's novels and grappled by way of those characters, both through their engagement with the author as writer, person, and symbol; and through their own lives, self-definition, and relationship. One was a man, one a woman; one an atheist, the other a fervent believer. Both were carried by the tides of their time to St. Petersburg, where they married, and one of them, physiologist Ivan Pavlov, became famous (so the other, Serafima

---

This article is based on materials in Daniel P. Todes, *Ivan Pavlov: A Russian Life in Science* (Oxford: Oxford University Press, 2014). © 2014 Oxford University Press. Used by permission.

1 Joseph Frank, *Dostoevsky: A Writer in His Time* (Princeton, NJ: Princeton University Press, 2010), xv, 477.

Karchevskaia, destroyed most of her papers to preserve her privacy *from* posterity).

Dostoevsky spoke deliberately to people like Ivan and Serafima, advocating passionately for religious faith (which he insisted was the only basis for a reliable morality), the wisdom of the folk, and Russia's unique historical mission—and so against the secularism and scientism of the "people of the 1860s" (*shestidesiatniki*). His attitude toward the populists of the 1870s was more complex, but, to the degree they shared the *shestidesiatniki's* values, also quite critical. In the second half of the 1870s he acquired the reputation of a principled and profoundly Russian moralist, a prophet, in disorienting times— and many people of various political hues (particularly, it seems, women) corresponded with him about their personal travails, even appearing at his apartment seeking spiritual counsel.[2]

Let me set the stage for our protagonists' interaction with Dostoevsky by sketching the life trajectories that brought each to his door.

Ivan Pavlov was born in Riazan in 1849, the eldest son of a priest in a family whose clerical service (along both paternal and maternal lines) stretched back four generations to the time of Peter the Great. He imbibed Eastern Orthodoxy at home, in his father's church, and at the local seminary. There he learned a routinized approach to life in order to balance body and spirit, along with the certainties of faith and the moral personality of one who governed himself and approached God through conscience and the quest for virtue. As the seminary curriculum put it, conscience was the "expression of [God's] moral law, written upon our hearts"; and the conscientious Christian enacted "the moral nature of man, his special moral virtues and obligations [*dostoinstvo*] and calling." At the seminary, in the only formal course Pavlov ever took on psychology, this doctrine was explicated through the anatomical, physiological, and ultimately mysterious relations between body and spirit.[3]

---

2 On Dostoevsky's visitors, see, for example, Igor Volgin, *Poslednii god Dostoevskogo: Istoricheskie zapiski*, 4th ed. (Moscow: ACT Zebra E., 2010), 393.

3 On Pavlov's early years, see Daniel P. Todes, *Ivan Pavlov: A Russian Life in Science* (Oxford: Oxford University Press, 2014), 17–29. For seminary doctrine on conscience and psychology, see the published text and detailed course notes of Pavlov's instructor: N. F. Glebov, *Psikhologiia* (Riazan: Tip. Gub. Pravl., 1863), and Gosurdarstvennyi Arkhiv Riazanskoi Oblasti, *fond* 1280 *opis'* 1 *delo* 412 (unpaginated file).

Like many youth of his generation, Pavlov was influenced by the profound changes in Russian society in the 1860s and by the essays of the *shestidesiatniki*, particularly his favorite author, Dmitrii Pisarev, to reject religion for science and modernization. Breaking bitterly with his father, he quit the seminary and headed for the sparkling center of Russian science, St. Petersburg University. There he studied physiology with the brilliant and politically reactionary experimental physiologist Il'ia Tsion. In an unforeseeable calamity for Pavlov, however, student demonstrators brought Tsion's career to an abrupt end in 1875, casting his protégé into the professional wilderness. He is struggling, mentor-less, with his doctoral research when our story begins in 1879.[4]

The values of one's early years are not easily—and perhaps never completely—cast off, and Pavlov's letters of the time show him struggling earnestly to replace religious sources of certainty with those of his new secular faith. He sought to replace the omniscience and wisdom of God with a knowledge of equally deterministic natural law, and the soul's aspiration to godliness—and God's inevitable judgment after death—with a firm and systematic secular sense of virtue, of *dostoinstvo* ("moral obligations"). Two other lifelong keywords, the negative *sluchainost'* ("chance, randomness") and the positive *pravil'nost'* ("regularity, lawfulness"), captured that struggle—the horror of chance and the unforeseen and his quest to overcome them with the certainties of personal morality, a highly structured daily schedule, and scientific law.

Six years younger than Pavlov, Serafima Karchevskaia grew up in a close, devoutly religious family in the Crimean port city of Berdiansk. Her adored father, a naval officer, died when she was young, and in his memory she thereafter had intimates address her as he had, as "Sara." The swiftly changing cultural currents of reform-era Russia influenced her very differently than they had Ivan. Serafima came of age after Karakozov's fateful shot at the tsar and after the suppression of Ivan's favorite journals, when Lavrov and Mikhailovsky were expounding the populist doctrines that would dominate the 1870s. The populists, too, believed in science and positive knowledge—materialism and anticlericalism remained in vogue among the vanguard youth—but they emphasized the importance of individual conscience and rejected as elitist the *shestidesiatniki*'s single-minded scientism. Privileged, educated youth in an

4 Todes, *Pavlov*, 30–58.

impoverished country, they insisted, must discharge their moral debt to the folk by helping to enlighten the peasantry and relieve their suffering.

Like many of her peers, Serafima never warmed to Pisarev, and she remained deeply religious. Progressive youth of her generation shared with Ivan's a commitment to women's liberation, and, against her mother's wishes, she traveled to St. Petersburg in the fall of 1877 to enroll in the pedagogical courses at the city's first women's gymnasium. Lacking intellectual self-confidence and possessed of decidedly moderate instincts, she never rejected the traditional model of womanhood exemplified by her mother, but she also wanted to live life on a larger canvas and to discharge her moral debt by teaching peasants how to read. In St. Petersburg's student circles, her relative cultural conservatism set her apart. Offended by the young men's "very crude attitudes toward us young girls," she was puzzled when one medical student referred to the girls as "common property" and was repelled when a sophisticate explained what that meant. Most difficult and isolating was the atheism of many of her fellow students. "I fell into a whirlpool of nonbelievers," she later recalled, and, considering herself less intelligent than many of them, she sought reassurance in prayer at St. Petersburg's Kazan Cathedral.

Among those aggressive atheists was Ivan Pavlov, whom she met in 1878 through a mutual friend. Shortly thereafter, their circles merged into a "Society of Cheap Apartments" that enjoyed the city's beauty and cultural offerings as best they could on a tight budget. Ivan wooed her awkwardly but ardently. By March 1880 the couple could not avoid contemplating their future, since Serafima would soon be completing her studies and returning home.[5]

Dostoevsky was at this time intervening forcefully in the pressing ideolog-ical, political, and spiritual issues of the day in his *Diary of a Writer* and his novels *The Adolescent* and, especially, *The Brothers Karamazov*, which Ivan and Serafima read and discussed when it was serialized in *Russkii vestnik*. "Our Dostoevsky," as Pavlov referred to him, provided a mutually respected point of reference as they grappled with their feelings and beliefs about a set of related, sensitive subjects that was very important for them as a couple headed, perhaps,

---

5 For Serafima's early years, see Todes, *Pavlov*, 72–74; on their courtship, ibid., 74–81. The citation concerning the "whirlpool" is from her manuscript autobiography: S. V. Pavlova, *Vospominaniia*, at the St. Petersburg filial of the Russian Archive of Sciences (ARAN), *fond* 259 opis' 1 *delo* 169, *list* 396. Such archival locations are given below as ARAN 259.1.169: 96.

for marriage—faith and religion, reason and science, intimacy and morality. For Serafima, Dostoevsky provided a touchstone, an authoritative and reputable source of support for her as an intimidated believer. For Ivan, he provided both a powerful expression of the emotional and intellectual issues with which he was grappling and also the terms in which he needed to justify himself to Serafima as a reliably good man.[6]

We cannot know when they first discussed Dostoevsky, but it was apparently the deep personal resonance for both of them of *The Adolescent* that brought him to the center of their emotional lives. Ivan first referred to that novel in the "journal" with which he courted Serafima from afar during the summer of 1879. In one of his essays for it, "The Critical Period in the Life of a Rational Person," he self-confidently preached the gospel of systematic scientific work as a bridge across the treacherous waters of the "critical period" between youth and adulthood, as a means of preserving youthful intellectual pleasures and passions in a mature form that facilitated continued intellectual development while contributing meaningfully to knowledge and society. A shorter second essay provided an implicit counterpoint to "The Critical Period," revealing himself to Serafima as introspective and chronically uncertain. She had apparently shared her own self-doubts in earlier letters, and he now confided that he, too, was a *samoed*—"a person who consumes himself." "One part of him eats, the other is eaten." He had just finished Dostoevsky's *The Adolescent*, an "enormous work" featuring just such a protagonist. Generalizing freely from his own experience (as he would throughout his life), Ivan explained that in the *samoed*, thoughts and wishes constantly opposed one another, every idea elicited a contrary one, every joy the realization that this result of mere chance (*sluchainost'*) would inevitably be followed by equally random misfortune. When the *samoed* dared to believe something—in his work, about people, or life—he immediately began reflexively to undermine that belief through counterarguments and a compulsive recognition of the paucity of his knowledge: "He devours his happiness, weakens his working idea."

"What creates such people?" he wondered. "Nature, organization? Perhaps." But those were the province of some future physiology and psychology.

---

6 Pavlov refers to "our Dostoevsky" in a letter of [February] 3, [1881], published in A. D. Nozdrachev, E. L. Poliakov, K. N. Zelenin et al., eds., *I. P. Pavlov: Pervyi nobelevskii laureat Rossii* (St. Petersburg: Gumanistika, 2004), 2:161.

Clearly, though, the *samoed*'s plight was rooted in the hypocrisy of contemporary life, in which children were taught to read and listen carefully and to love wisdom, but then were chastened for speaking "an unacceptable truth." Similar experiences throughout life reinforced the torturous inner world of the adult *samoed*, "undermining his every joy, his every idea."[7]

In March 1880, Serafima helped organize a literary evening in which Turgenev and Dostoevsky were featured to raise money for needy students. Dostoevsky read a passage from *The Adolescent* in which the mother of an adolescent girl, Olya, describes their travails as pious new arrivals of meager means in St. Petersburg and the callous, offensive, and exploitative encounters that led to her sensitive daughter's suicide. Serafima later recalled that when "The Prophet" spoke, "his face was completely transformed, his eyes flashed with lightning, which burned the hearts of people, and his face shined with the inspiration of a Higher power!" Identifying with Olya and so deeply moved by the writer's powerful, empathetic portrayal of her own emotional turmoil, she determined to confide in him.[8]

Serafima would always refer to the encounters that followed as "the most important moment in my religious life."[9] She told the story this way in her manuscript autobiography:

Shortly after the literary evening, she and two other deputies visited Dostoevsky's apartment to thank him. The author greeted them warmly and, to mark the occasion, gave each his photograph, which he inscribed in common Russian fashion with the recipient's first name and patronymic. When Serafima's turn came and she supplied the name by which her intimates addressed her, however, the author turned cold. "He looked at me unkindly" and wrote, not the expected "To Sara Vasil'evna," but rather the curt "To Miss Karchevskaia."[10]

---

7 Ivan Pavlov, *Popalsia: Ezhenedel'noe izdanie sluchainogo proiskhozhdeniia, neopredelennogo napravleniia, s trudno predvidimoiu budushchnostiiu* [1879], in ARAN 259.2.1299: 29–31.

8 On this event, see *Letopis' zhizni i tvorchestva F. M. Dostoevskogo 1821–1881* (St. Petersburg: Akademicheskii Proekt, 1995), 3:392. Serafima's various accounts of these encounters differ slightly. I am using here the autobiographical drafts in S. V. Pavlova, *Detskie rasskazy, skazki, fragmenty*, ARAN 259.1.171: 250–251, 261–267. For the passage that so moved her, see Fyodor Dostoevsky, *The Adolescent*, trans. Richard Pevear and Larissa Volokhonsky (New York: Alfred A. Knopf, 2003), 171–77 (pt. 1, chap. 9, sec. 5).

9 Draft letter from Serafima Pavlova to [Evgeniia Sikorskaia], ARAN 259.1.171: 254.

10 This inscribed photograph remains among her papers at the Memorial'nyi Muzei-Kvartira akademika I. P. Pavlova in St. Petersburg.

Mystified by the bad impression she had somehow made, but determined to consult him about her spiritual struggles, she mustered her courage and returned to his apartment. He again rebuffed her coldly. Returning yet again, she was ushered to his study, where the writer "politely but dryly invited me to sit." Launching into a confession of her crisis of faith, she discovered the reason for his hostility: "When I said that I had been raised in a religious, Eastern Orthodox family, Fyodor Mikhailovich exclaimed, 'Eastern Orthodox? Then why are you named Sara?'" When she explained, he sprang from his seat "grabbed me by both hands and said: 'How could you exchange such a marvelous, pure Orthodox name for a Yid name!' After this clarification his face was transformed and his attitude toward me became gentle and attentive."

Relieved to be on the right side of The Prophet's anti-Semitism, she poured her heart out and "for the first time in my life understood my own religious beliefs." She confessed her dislike of the Old Testament—"the history of a foreign and unlikable people [and its] … cruel, vengeful God"; explained her belief in "Jesus Christ for himself … for his complete gentleness and humility, full of the fire of truth [and] unlimited love"; and then raised her main problem: Was she guilty of excessive pride? Was she right to insist upon her religious faith in the face of so many intelligent critics?

This, as she surely knew, was music to Dostoevsky's ears. He encouraged her to stand her ground and assured her that, although she might waver temporarily amid life's confusions, she would "always walk the radiant road of faith." Complimenting her on her "truly Russian" attitude toward the Bible, he invited her to return. During their final meeting, he explained that uncertainty was necessary to true faith; thereafter, she writes, "I ceased fearing my doubts."[11]

So goes the narrative in her autobiography. A very private person, she apparently shared little of the content of these sessions even with her intimates (including Pavlov). Responding decades later to a query from her sister, she added a detail that, perhaps—to whatever extent we can read between the lines of a long-distant memory—reveals another dimension of that encounter:

> As for "The Grand Inquisitor," I lived through an entire drama while seated across from F. M. and hungrily catching his words; only then did I understand the great significance for divine faith of the struggle with doubts. Many who believe in the power of the intellect often fall into errors, making

---

11 Pavlova, *Detskie rasskazy*, 261–67.

compromises with their conscience, and only a few exceptional people who believe only in reason and the power of science remain exalted people; and the purity of their life resembles that of the sons of God, and God will take them to Himself, since, despite their lack of faith, by their deeds they were creations of His will! It is truly so.[12]

Serafima seems here to allude to a question she posed to Dostoevsky, not about her own crisis of faith, but about that of her ardent suitor, Ivan Pavlov. She attributed her own vacillations to a lack of self-confidence and intelligence, not to any great belief in reason and science; nor would she have identified with the corrosive, sophisticated logic of Dostoevsky's Grand Inquisitor. That, rather, was the language of Ivan Pavlov. So, she may be alluding here to another very personal question that she posed to Dostoevsky, or simply reflected upon in his presence: If, as he insisted, faith in God and immortality was necessary to a reliable morality, could a young atheist prove dependably good and moral—a suitable life companion for an Orthodox believer? If so, Dostoevsky's affirmative response would have proven profoundly reassuring and memorable.

The couple became engaged shortly thereafter, but they postponed their marriage for a year so he could complete his doctoral thesis, while she taught peasants in the countryside. In an intense correspondence during their separation, they discussed the issues of faith, reason, science, morality, and intimacy in the context of Dostoevsky's work, especially *The Brothers Karamazov*. (Since Serafima destroyed her half of the correspondence after her husband's death, we have only the faint echo of her voice in his replies.)

In several letters, Pavlov confessed to identifying uncomfortably with Ivan Karamazov, whose harsh rationality and inability to make a religious leap of faith condemned him to nihilism, spiritual disintegration, and mental breakdown. (In at least two of her replies, Serafima clearly encouraged him to elaborate on this theme.) Ivan confided: "The more I read, the more uneasy my heart became. He bears a great resemblance to your tender and loving admirer." Karamazov's "basic nature, or at least his given state, is the same as mine. Obviously, this is a man of the intellect .... The mind, the mind alone has overthrown everything, reconstructed everything. ... And the person was left wooden-headed, with a terrible coldness in the heart, with the sensation of a strange emptiness in his being." Reason brought Karamazov its rich satisfactions—"recall the Great

---

12 Pavlova, draft letter to [Sikorskaia], 254rev.

Inquisitor and such great flights of moral thought"—"yet what a [sorry] life" he led.[13] Pavlov described his own plight by citing Karamazov's confession that he would gladly surrender the pleasures of reason for the comforts of faith: "I would give away all this superstellar life, all the ranks and honors, simply to be transformed into the soul of a merchant's wife weighing eighteen stone and set candles at God's shrine." Yet, as for Karamazov, a combination of his nature and life experiences rendered this impossible.[14]

Pavlov implicitly disagreed with Dostoevsky's view that the basic problem was "the triumph of reason." It resided, rather, in "our very nature" and so raised an important challenge that was unfortunately beyond the limitations of currently "paltry science"—understanding "the human type."[15] Human psychology constituted "one of the last secrets of life, the secret of the manner in which nature, developing by strict, unchangeable laws, came in the form of man to be conscious of itself"—and, to some extent, free.[16] Returning to this subject a few weeks later in another reflection about *Brothers Karamazov*, he added: "Where is the science of human life? Not even a trace of it exists. It will, of course, but not soon, not soon."[17]

In the same spirit, he took up throughout his letters Dostoevsky's notion that no reliable morality was possible without religious faith. "I myself do not believe in god,"[18] he reminded Serafima, but the religious language of his letters both captured his own struggle for secular replacements and reassured her that he shared her basic values and goals. "Unshrinking rationality and a commitment to truth," he wrote, was the basis of his struggle for personal virtue, for *dostoinstvo* ("moral obligations"). "It is for me a kind of God, before whom I reveal everything, before whom I discard wretched worldly vanity."[19] A disciplined approach to scientific research could provide both spiritual satisfaction and (Dostoevsky

---

13 Ivan Pavlov to Serafima Karchevskaia [October] 7, [1880], in ARAN 259.2.1300/1 [unpaginated file].

14 Ivan Pavlov to Serafima Karchevskaia, [September] 17, [1880], and [September] 13, [1880], in ARAN 259.2.1300/1. In the novel, not Karamazov himself but his creation, the "gentleman visitor" (the devil), makes this statement.

15 Ivan Pavlov to Serafima Karchevskaia, [October] 7, [1880], in ARAN 259.2.1300/1.

16 Ivan Pavlov to Serafima Karchevskaia, [September] 28, [1880], in ARAN 259.2.1300/1.

17 Ivan Pavlov to Serafima Karchevskaia, [October] 7, [1880], in ARAN 259.2.1300/1.

18 Ivan Pavlov to Serafima Karchevskaia, Wednesday, [September] 11, [1880], in Nozdrachev et al., *I. P. Pavlov*, 116.

19 Ivan Pavlov to Serafima Karchevskaia, Saturday, [September] 20, [1880], in ARAN 259.2.1300/1.

notwithstanding) a robust, ethical connection to other people. One must work by a strict schedule with a definite plan and constantly struggle, as did a believer, "with circumstances and with one's own weaknesses." The usefulness of scientific research, and its interest to others, guaranteed that it was "vital"—that is, it joined the researcher to a community and served humanity. Thus, it was both moral and a proof against nihilism.[20]

When Dostoevsky died in January 1881, Pavlov hurried to his apartment to pay his respects, and he returned the next morning to join the mourners who accompanied the writer's coffin to the Alexander-Nevskii Lavra. Describing all this to Serafima, he observed that Dostoevsky's spiritual exemplar, Aleksei Karamazov, had become a model for youth. A few days later he reported on the eulogies, dwelling upon Suvorin's surprising revelation that Dostoevsky had planned a sequel to *Brothers Karamazov* in which Aleksei becomes, as Pavlov put it, a "Russian socialist," a revolutionary of a new type, drawing upon uniquely Russian traditions: "Did you think, my dear, that our Dostoevsky could become such a socialist, a radical!" He concluded that "so many people at his grave decided, pledged, to be better, to resemble him. As have we, my dear Sara!"[21]

Serafima's inner life thereafter is largely hidden from us, but she invoked Dostoevsky frequently over the next six decades as a reassuring touchstone. When her first child died, she blamed her wavering faith and drew comfort from the writer's prophecy that she would thereafter walk the true path. His photo adorned her wall alongside those of her children, and his wisdom played a central role in the autobiographical narrative she composed from the 1920s through the 1940s. Few of her letters survive, but among them is this passage to close friends during Easter 1931: "Christ has Arisen. For me, in these words resides our entire Orthodox faith, which became infinitely dear to me after my instructive conversations with Dostoevsky .... How he understood the human soul and penetrated the dark, unconscious depths."[22]

---

20 Ivan Pavlov to Serafima Karchevskaia, Wednesday, 8 a.m., [September] 17, [1880], and Friday, [October] 3, [1880], in ARAN 259.2.1300/1.

21 Ivan Pavlov to Serafima Karchevskaia, [January] 31, [February] 1, and [February] 3, 1881, in Nozdrachev et al., *I. P. Pavlov*, 156–61 ("Russian socialist" on 160; "As have we" on 161). Volgin devotes much of his *Poslednii god Dostoevskogo* to a discussion of Dostoevsky's attitudes that makes Suvorin's revelation quite plausible.

22 Serafima Pavlova to Boris Babkin, March 29 [1931?], in 390/22/3/8, Osler Library Archive Collections, McGill University, Montreal.

Pavlov struggled throughout his adult life—both in and outside the laboratory—with the issues highlighted in his encounter with Dostoevsky. His research on conditional reflexes, much misunderstood in the West, was an attempt to understand, not mere behaviors, but rather, as he put it, the mysteries of "the human type," of "our consciousness and its torments." For more than thirty years (1903–36) he sought to develop that "science of human life" that had seemed so necessary and so distant when he corresponded with Serafima in 1880—to understand the emotional and intellectual life of animals and humans, the sources and dynamics of personality and human nature. And, as he had in those same letters, he wondered how science might reconcile the seemingly contradictory truths that humans were subject to the determinism of natural law but remained responsible for their actions and, to some extent, free.[23] His attitude toward religion evolved over time. He remained always an atheist, but the militant anticlericalism of the young ex-seminarian gave way to an increasing appreciation of the cultural role of religion as an adaptive "defensive reflex" that protected humans from the harshness and uncertainty of life. He denounced the Bolshevik suppression of religion and even subsidized the local church near his science village at Koltushi.

His final days during the winter of 1935–36 found him grappling with the same set of issues as he had during his encounter with Dostoevsky more than a half century earlier. In an unfinished essay, he addressed the relationship of reason and science to religion and faith, of the grand issues concerning science and religion to personal morality, certainty, and the life well led. He even suggested tentatively and hopefully—in a distant echo of Suvorin's reference to Aleksei's transformation into a "Russian socialist" in Dostoevsky's projected sequel to *Brothers Karamazov*—that, despite its grave crimes and blunders, a Bolshevism made more reasonable and humane by the growth of Russian scientific culture might become a genuine Russian contribution to Christianity's "greatest of all human truths, the truth of the equality of all people."[24]

---

23 On the content and methodology of Pavlov's scientific quest, see Todes, *Ivan Pavlov*, 287–302; on his view of free will, ibid., 526–27, 790–91n50.

24 ARAN 259.1a.39: 30. For a discussion of this essay, see Todes, *Ivan Pavlov*, 717–22.

PART

2

Engagements with Philosophy

V

Dostoevsky and the Meaning of "the Meaning of Life"

Steven Cassedy

It appears innocent enough. In the conversation leading up to the famous meta-physical challenges in the "Rebellion" chapter of *The Brothers Karamazov*, Ivan responds to his brother Alyosha's assertion that we must all love life. "Love life more than its meaning [*smysl ee*]?" Ivan asks. "Certainly," Alyosha answers, "love it before logic, as you say. Certainly it has to be before logic, and only then will I understand the meaning [*smysl poimu*]."[1] Today we take no notice of the English phrase "meaning of life," or its Russian equivalent (*smysl zhizni*), so widespread has its use been for so long, and we're unlikely to think a Russian author in the 1870s was doing anything unusual when he used it, just as we're unlikely to pause, when we read it, to wonder what it means.

But what *does* it mean here, in this dialogue? Ivan is distinguishing *life* itself from *the meaning of life*, apparently insisting that to love one is not the same as to love the other. He understands his brother to be placing a higher value on loving life itself than on loving the meaning of life, suggesting that the meaning of life—or at least a concern for it—somehow falls short of just plain life—and

---

1 Dostoevsky, *Polnoe sobranie sochinenii v tridtsati tomakh* [*PSS*], ed. V. G. Bazanov et al. (Leningrad: Nauka, 1972–90), 14:210; abbreviated hereafter as Dostoevsky, *PSS*. All translations in this chapter are my own.

a concern for *it*. And we know that Ivan has a whole list of images that he himself appears to associate with just plain life (sticky leaves in the spring, for example), and that those images somehow correspond to the less cerebral and less rational Ivan, the Ivan who unthinkingly loves children. Is the meaning of life the thing you get once you come to *understand* life? Almost certainly not, unless Alyosha is choosing his words carelessly, for what he speaks of understanding is not life but life's *meaning*. Is each brother using the word *meaning* and, by implication, the phrase "meaning of life," in a different sense? Will *meaning* have a purely scientific-materialist definition for Ivan, so that loving life itself, rather than its (scientific) meaning, is a refusal of the scientific-materialist point of view? Alyosha appears to be steering his older brother away from such an under-standing when he urges him to love life before *logic*, only outside of which, he thinks, one can find meaning.

The full phrase "meaning of life" (*smysl zhizni*) shows up a few pages later. Right before announcing that he doesn't accept God's world, Ivan offers his surprising list of concessions: "And so, I accept God and not only willingly but, what's more, I accept his wisdom too and his purpose [*tsel'*]— completely unknown to us—I believe in order, in the meaning of life, I believe in the eternal harmony in which we will apparently merge together, I believe in the Word toward which the universe is tending and that 'was with God' and that is God, and so on and so on, etc., to infinity" (Dostoevsky, PSS, 14:214). The "meaning of life" thus shows up on a list of what Ivan, always a sort of orthodox Kantian, would consider metaphysical ideas "unknown to us."

But what does it mean? There are no further references to it in *Brothers Karamazov*, so we would look in vain for an additional context that might help us discover what Ivan has in mind (or, to be more precise, what Dostoevsky might have had in mind for Ivan to have in mind). Does "the meaning of life" in this passage mean the same thing it meant in the previous chapter? Does Ivan use the phrase casually and carelessly, as it has been used so often in everyday conversation and popular writing in more modern times? But that would suggest that, in the late 1870s, the phrase *smysl zhizni* had been around in everyday conversation and popular writing in Russia for long enough that real people similar to the fictional Ivan could use it casually and carelessly, betting that no one would press them to define their terms.

As best I can tell, it hadn't. The phrase in its Russian incarnation had emerged recently. As always in cultural matters, Russia lagged behind the West, but the equivalent phrases in other European languages were also of relatively recent vintage. The use of the phrase "meaning of life" and its equivalents in other languages was a modern phenomenon, dating back no farther than the end of the eighteenth century. The *frequent*, casual, and uncritical use of it outside Russia, by the time Dostoevsky wrote *Brothers Karamazov*, was a very modern phenomenon indeed, dating back no more than a generation or so.

So, where did Dostoevsky get it, and how does he want us to construe it?

Neither question is easy to answer in any simple or definitive way, but we can take a look at the evolution of the phrase in its non-Russian contexts, its emergence in Russian writing, and Dostoevsky's own use of it before *Brothers Karamazov*.

The Non-Russian Contexts

There's a whole academic cottage industry that might be called "meaning of life studies." Many of the books and articles produced in this industry are *about* "the meaning of life." With one or two exceptions, these are of no help to us whatever, as most of the authors either never bother to define *meaning* as they're using it or define it in such a way as to leave us no farther along than we were without the definition. A group of German scholars has taken on the task of studying the *history* of the phrase *der Sinn des Lebens* ("the meaning of life") and its equivalents in various European languages. The editors of an anthology titled *Der Sinn des Lebens* have written an introduction that includes a short historical subsection titled "'Sinn des Lebens'—seit wann?" ("'The meaning of life'— since when?"), much of it drawn from the work of a historian of "the meaning of life," Volker Gerhardt of Humboldt University.[2] The editors cite a lengthy work by the late German philosopher Hans Blumenberg titled *Die Lesbarkeit der Welt* (1981) (*The Readability of the World*), in which the author historically traces the idea of "reading"—and, by obvious extension, discovering meanings in—the world.

All the evidence suggests that the story of "the meaning of life" begins in German-speaking lands in the late eighteenth century. In *Die Lesbarkeit der Welt*,

---

2 Christoph Fehige, Georg Meggle, and Ulla Wessels, eds., *Der Sinn des Lebens* (Munich: Deutscher Taschenbuch Verlag, 2000), 19–22.

Blumenberg (whose topic was *not* exclusively "the meaning of life") showed that the Romantic era gave rise to a tendency to represent nature and the universe itself as possessed of language, therefore as carrying meaning in the same way that words in a book carry meaning. Among those in the Romantic era who first formulated the conflation of world, book, holy book, and history was Novalis. In one of his mysterious philosophical fragments, dating from 1798, he writes, "Only an artist can guess the meaning of life."[3] A couple of years later, in another fragment, he writes, "The meaning of the world has gone missing. We're left with nothing but the letters [of the alphabet]."[4] The remark occurs in a broader context in which *God, world, poet, symbol, words, hieroglyphs,* and *letters* appear to have mingled so as to become almost indistinguishable.

Novalis, Friedrich Schlegel, and Friedrich Schleiermacher circulated a collection of ideas at the turn of the nineteenth century that constituted an important early contribution to the rise of the phrase *Sinn des Lebens.* Schlegel regarded religion as a synthesis of philosophy and poetry and contemplated a new Bible that would be an "absolute Book," an "ever-becoming Book" in which "the gospel of mankind and culture [*Bildung*] is revealed."[5] In the *Transcendentalphilosophie* (1800–1801), Schlegel calls the world an "allegory," claiming that, for this reason, "every being has only so much reality as it has sense [*Sinn*], meaning [*Bedeutung*], spirit."[6]

Schleiermacher, of course, is the author of *Über die Religion: Reden an die Gebildeten unter ihren Verächtern* (*On Religion: Speeches to Its Cultivated Despisers*, 1799), which to the historian of ideas conveniently serves (with due allowance for simplification) as the work that inaugurated the modern comparative study of religion. That's principally because, despite the intention suggested in the work's title (namely, to *defend* religion), Schleiermacher, by distinguishing between existing religions (plural) and religion (singular) as an overarching concept, and then by characterizing religion (singular) universally as the expression of an essentially human impulse, uncoupled the study of religion from the

---

3 Novalis, *Schriften,* ed. Richard Samuel (Stuttgart: W. Kohlhammer, 1960), 2:562; cited in Fehige et al., *Der Sinn des Lebens,* 22.

4 Ibid., 2:594; cited in Hans Blumenberg, *Die Lesbarkeit der Welt* (Frankfurt am Main: Suhrkamp, 1981), 256.

5 *Kritische Friedrich-Schlegel-Ausgabe,* ed. Ernst Behler (Munich: Ferdinand Schöningh, 1958–2006), 2:265; cited in Blumenberg, *Die Lesbarkeit der Welt,* 269.

6 *Kritische Friedrich-Schlegel-Ausgabe,* 12:40; cited in Blumenberg, *Die Lesbarkeit der Welt,* 273.

particular religious faith of the investigator. The insight that led to Schleier-macher's distinction paved the way for the modern science of hermeneutics and the secular, scholarly study of Scripture in the nineteenth century. The work of David Friedrich Strauss and Ernest Renan (both of whom Dostoevsky despised), each the author of an antimetaphysical *Life of Jesus*, is unthinkable without that distinction.

Schleiermacher was a Romantic thinker, determined, like Novalis and Schlegel, to tear down boundaries. In the collection of writings gathered together under the title *Hermeneutics* (composed between 1805 and 1833), he speaks of merging two seemingly incompatible perspectives: the philological perspective in interpretation, from which we seek to identify individual sections of Scripture with individual authors, and the "dogmatic" perspective, from which we regard Scripture as a single text by a single author, namely, the Holy Spirit. The natural consequence of merging the two is that meaning, which from the first perspective inheres in words, now possibly comes to inhere in the world. Like his fellow Romantics at the turn of the century, Schleiermacher had been thinking about *reading* the world, with the conse-quence that meaning (*Sinn*) emerges in that world. "The artist," he wrote in 1800, "chases after everything that can become sign and symbol of mankind; he rummages through the treasure of languages, he forms the chaos of tones into the world; he seeks secret meaning [*Sinn*] and harmony in the beautiful color play of nature."[7] But note well, the impulse here is artistic creation, not religious faith conventionally construed.

By the time we get to Ludwig Feuerbach in the early 1840s, an author with whose ideas Dostoevsky was all too familiar, *meaning* will have lost any connec-tion with texts, real or metaphorical, but it will have become indispensable to a view that seeks in far more radical terms than we find in Schleiermacher to reduce religious faith to the human. Here quite possibly is a source, if not *the* source, of the concept of "the meaning of life" in Russia—or at least in Dostoevsky. Feuerbach's language, replete with grossly simplified Hegelian terms but also with references to existence, being, and non-being, points ahead to the language of twentieth-century existentialism. Early in *The Essence of Christianity* (1841), Feuerbach is attempting to ground the claim that religion is reducible to human

---

7   Friedrich Schleiermacher, *Schleiermacher Kritische Gesamtausgabe*, ed. Hans-Joachim Birkner et al. (Berlin: Walter de Gruyter, 1980–), 1.3:20.

reason, which he holds to be roughly the same thing as self-consciousness—self-consciousness, of course, being the ultimate human attribute. Here's where he finds himself speaking of meaning (*Sinn*). It's *Unsinn* ("nonsense/nonmeaning"), he suggests, to say that the world does not exist, but in this *Unsinn* you find the true *meaning* (*Sinn*) of the world. Why? "Nothingness, non-being," he writes, "is aimless [*zwecklos*], meaningless [*sinnlos*], understandingless [*verstandlos*]. Only being has an aim [*Zweck*], has a cause [*Grund*] and a meaning [*Sinn*]." Next, *meaning* emerges organically (if not persuasively) from Feuerbach's Hegelian-materialist worldview. Reason, he says, is the self-consciousness of being, and therefore it *is* self-conscious being: "The aim [*Zweck*], the meaning [*Sinn*] of being first reveals itself in Reason." That's because "Reason is being that is objective to itself as an end in itself [*Selbstzweck*]." The clunky Hegelianism of the last sentence aside, what Feuerbach is claiming here at least fits an overarching theme of his book. It all comes down to self-consciousness, seen from a purely materialist perspective. Self-consciousness implies something that understands itself. In a materialist world, that something cannot be spirit; it must be simply *being*. Being (self-consciousness) therefore understands being (the world). To understand is to discover *meaning*, and thus self-consciousness discovers the *meaning of being*, which is the same as the meaning of the world—or of life.[8]

Of course, it would be absurd to claim that Dostoevsky or any other nineteenth-century Russian writer carefully studied *The Essence of Christianity* and culled from it Feuerbach's concept of *the meaning of life/world/being* and then began to use the equivalent Russian phrases with all the nuances I've just described. In fact, it's entirely possible that Feuerbach, never a particularly rigorous thinker, was relatively uncritical in his use of phrases that included the word *Sinn*, suggesting that by the early 1840s these phrases had established themselves in German so solidly that they could be used uncritically. But even if that is so, the context matters. The phrases show up in a discussion of religion at a moment when conventional forms of religious belief (however defined) are under assault and European intellectuals are fishing around for a vocabulary that they can press into service in order to characterize from *outside* religion what's happening *inside* religion (What are all those benighted people searching for?). That's when the word *meaning* surfaces.

---

8 Ludwig Feuerbach, *Sämtliche Werke*, ed. Wilhelm Bolin and Friedrich Jodl (Stuttgart-Bad Cannstatt: Frommann Verlag, 1960), 6:52–53.

Meaning Comes to Russia

In a dictionary article on "Sinn des Lebens," Volker Gerhardt speaks of a shift in the meaning of the German word *Sinn*, which in an earlier era, very much like *sens* in French and the corresponding words in Italian and Spanish, meant "sense" (as in our five senses) or "direction" (*Richtung*; in fact, its most primitive meaning) and only more recently came to mean *meaning* (*Bedeutung*).[9] Shifts in the meaning of a word don't necessarily result in the complete replacement of an older meaning with a newer one, and in the case of *Sinn*, Gerhardt shows, we end up with a nexus of possible meanings: aim (*Ziel*), purpose (*Zweck*), target (*Skopus*), telos (*Telos*), and value (*Wert*). And in German writers, these other words often appear in place of *Sinn* before the words *des Lebens* ("of life") in passages that make it difficult for the reader to determine whether or not the resulting phrases all mean the same thing. In *The Essence of Christianity* alone, Feuerbach uses variously *Zweck des Lebens* ("purpose of life"), *Wert des Lebens* ("value of life"), *Bedeutung des Lebens* ("meaning or significance of life"), not to mention *Sinn der Geschichte* ("meaning of history"), *Sinn des Seins* ("meaning of being"), and *Sinn unseres Wesens* ("meaning of our essence"). It hardly needs to be stated that the English word *meaning* in modern metaphysical contexts, from the popular to the academic, is often indistinguishable from—and often substitutes for—the words *value* and *purpose*.

And this brings us to Tolstoy. The word that will overwhelmingly be used in the Russian phrase corresponding to the German *Sinn des Lebens* (and the English "meaning of life") is, of course, *smysl*. This Russian word has a provenance different from the German *Sinn*. Because of the *mysl* root, it originally has to do with thinking, understanding, reasoning, as in the phrase *zdravyi smysl* ("common sense"—English curiously took its phrase from French). It then comes to denote "meaning"—what words possess. One could perhaps argue that the German word's original association with sense experience and the Russian word's original association with mental life suggest a common association with subjectivity, as in the English *meaning* when it means "intention." But there is less in the Russian word to suggest "direction," "aim," "purpose," "target" than in the German *Sinn*.

---

9 Volker Gerhardt, "Sinn des Lebens," in *Historisches Wörterbuch der Philosophie* (Basel: Schwabe & Co., 1971–2007), 9:815.

And yet these meanings are what the word appears to take on in Tolstoy, once he begins to use the phrase *smysl zhizni*. A diary entry from April 1847, among the earliest writings we have by Dostoevsky's great rival, is filled with instances of the phrase *tsel' zhizni* ("the goal/purpose of life"). The majority of these occur in places where the young university dropout is wondering in the broadest terms about human life. "The purpose of man's life [*tsel' zhizni cheloveka*] is the greatest possible promotion of the most thorough development of all that exists," he writes, for example.[10]

A reference to the meaning of life makes an appearance in a famous letter that a thirty-year-old Tolstoy wrote to his cousin Aleksandra Alekseevna Tolstaya in 1859. He is offering up a *profession de foi*, listing (not for the last time) the stages in his own spiritual-religious development. He had spent ten years living peacefully with logic, in the absence of religion. "Then came a time," he writes, "when everything became open, there were no more mysteries in life, but life itself began to lose its meaning [*smysl*]."[11] Nothing that follows clarifies his use of the word *smysl*.

The phrase *smysl zhizni* then appears in *War and Peace* (1869). In fact, there's a fascinating passage that shows the transition from *smysl* in connection with words and language to *smysl* in connection with life. Pierre has been taken prisoner and has watched the French execute five of his compatriots. He meets an older peasant man named Platon, who is a veritable fount of folksy and therefore truthful sayings. When Pierre asks Platon to repeat something he has just said, Platon can't remember the words, nor, when asked, can he remember the words of his favorite song. He has no comprehension of the words when they're detached from their context. Words in their context (a song) then become an analogy for individual life in *its* context (some unnamed larger whole):

> [The words] *Rodimaya* ["my dear"], *berezan'ka* ["birch tree"], and *toshnen'ko* ["my heart aches"] were all in there, but [when these sentiments were] put into words, no meaning [*smysl*] came out. [Platon] did not understand, nor could he understand, the meanings [*znacheniya*] of the words taken separately from speech. Each word of his and each action was the manifestation of

---

10   Leo Tolstoy, *Polnoe sobranie sochinenii*, ed. Vladimir Chertkov (Moscow: Gosudarstvennoe Izdatel'stvo Khudozhestvennoi Literatury, 1928–58), 46:30–31. Hereafter Tolstoy, *PSS*.

11   L. N. Tolstoy and A. A. Tolstaya, *Perepiska (1857–1903)*, ed. N. I. Azarova et al. (Moscow: Nauka, 2011), 158. Thanks to Irina Paperno for pointing out this passage to me.

a reality unknown to him, which was his life. But his life, as he looked at it, had no meaning [*smysla*] as a separate life. It had meaning [*smysl*] only as a part of a whole, which he constantly felt. His words and actions poured out of him as evenly, necessarily, and immediately as a scent detaches itself from a flower. He could understand neither the value nor the significance [*znachenie*] of a separately considered action or word. (Tolstoy, *PSS*, 12:50–51)

Naturally, the language Tolstoy's narrator uses to convey the outlook of the peasant is language that only someone from Tolstoy's or Pierre's social and educational class could understand, and yet the feeling that the narrator attributes to the humble-yet-admirable peasant requires the use of the word *meaning* as applied to life.

Tolstoy began to use *smysl zhizni* in earnest in *Anna Karenina* and then never quit for the rest of his life. But here is where the meaning of *smysl* begins to become unstable. In many instances, it's difficult to know whether the word *smysl* should be understood as synonymous with *tsel'* ("aim," "goal") or whether it denotes or connotes "meaning," as in the meaning of a word. In the two famous passages from *Anna Karenina* that feature the word *smysl* in connection with life, it's not easy to tell. As in *War and Peace*, there's a peasant named Platon who inspires the use of the word. Konstantin Levin is told by another peasant that Platon "lives for the soul. He remembers God" (Tolstoy, *PSS*, 19:376). These two sentences inspire the ambiguous revelation that leads to the conclusion of the novel. "And I was amazed," Levin thinks to himself, "that, despite the greatest exertion of thought along this path, the meaning of life, the meaning of my motives and aspirations, did not reveal itself to me. But the meaning of my motives [now] is so clear to me that I live constantly according to it, and I was amazed and overjoyed when the peasant expressed it: to live for God, for the soul" (Tolstoy, *PSS*, 19:378). And, of course, the final sentence of the novel is about the meaning of life, but understood in a rather peculiar way: "But my life now, my entire life, independently of what might happen to me, every minute of it not only is not meaningless, as it used to be, but has the indubitable meaning of good, with which I have the power to invest it" (Tolstoy, *PSS*, 19:399). What does "meaning of good" [*smysl dobra*] mean? The meaning that the word "good" carries? A *purpose* that *is* "the good"?

The work by Tolstoy that likely carries the highest concentration of instances of the phrase "meaning of life" (or *meaning* in this meaning) is

Confession, written from 1879 to 1882 and published illegally, in Geneva, in 1884 (it was initially banned by Russian censors). It's every bit as difficult to determine the meaning of *meaning* in this work as it was in the passages from *Anna Karenina*. In an early chapter, the phrase arises in connection with the question, posed by a dying brother, "Why [*zachem*, "for what"] did he live … and why was he dying?" (Tolstoy, *PSS*, 23:8). Tolstoy actually asks the question, "In what does the meaning of my life consist?" Science, he says, answers the question incorrectly by telling him *what he is* (in the world of physics)—"a temporal, accidental cohesion of particles" (Tolstoy, *PSS*, 23:21). Subsequent, more accurate answers to the question don't really say what the meaning *is*; instead they tell us where it is to be found, what things *give* meaning, or what things meaning is associated with. We can find meaning among common people, he discovered. Faith is knowledge of the meaning of life. In order to understand the meaning of life, one must live not parasitically but genuinely.

Then in 1902, Vladimir Chertkov, Tolstoy's editor and most famous hanger-on, published a little book (in Russian) "by" the master, under the title *On the Meaning of Life: Thoughts of Leo Tolstoy,* consisting of diary entries, notebook scribblings, and other unpublished material.[12] Within two years, the book appeared in English, French, and German translation. Many of its gems of wisdom appear without context, but at least here we find numerous instances of sentences beginning "The meaning of life is . . ." Not that these sentences necessarily clarify just what the word *meaning* means to Tolstoy, but they do show that, unlike so many other writers who never *said* what the meaning of life was, Tolstoy did not hesitate to do so. In most instances, the meaning of life is either a purpose (so that one could substitute the word *tsel'* for the word *smysl* without seriously altering the meaning) or some very prized feature of life. Either way, we can read many of the sentences as urging us to *do* something that Tolstoy believes good people should do, rather than helping us to *understand* something about life (discover a meaning in it as we do in a word).

It's also safe to say that, in the majority of instances, the question of "the meaning of life" is posed in a context where conventional religious faith is under challenge. And this seems to be the case for occurrences of the phrase over Tolstoy's career. Through the period of *Confession*, it almost never occurs

---

12   Leo Tolstoy, *O smysle zhizni: Mysli L. N. Tolstogo* (Berlin: G. Shteinitz, 1901).

except in connection with the absence of faith, as if the unbeliever, from outside, had no better phrase for what a believer, from inside, would possess. When Tolstoy begins to write pithy statements about what the meaning of life is, it's largely in response to the possibility of *not* knowing what it is.

Dostoevsky Discovers It—or Its Absence

The notion of the meaning of life—and the phrase *smysl zhizni*—surfaced in Dostoevsky's writing a couple of years before he composed we have *Brothers Karamazov*. It happened in the *Diary of a Writer*, always in connection with three interrelated themes: what Dostoevsky clearly believed to be a veritable epidemic of suicide in Russia, the loss of religious faith that was responsible for that epidemic, and the scientific-materialist worldview that was responsible for the loss of religious faith.[13] The story begins in June 1876, when the author received a letter from a total stranger, who signed himself "N. N." The correspondent details the process by which he lost all religious faith and came to embrace a purely scientific, materialist view of the world. He gives the list of writers who helped inspire the process: Ernest Renan, author of *La Vie de Jésus* (1863); positivist historian Henry Thomas Buckle, who taught him "the meaning of history" (*smysl istorii*); John Stuart Mill; Darwin, thanks to whom he became "a different man"; and Feuerbach. But, as "N. N." writes, the starting point lay in his childhood: "An abominable upbringing and school discipline bore their fruit: flippancy, absence of principles, tasks, incomprehension both of myself and generally of the meaning of life!" (Dostoevsky, *PSS*, 24:472). At the end of the intellectual process, "N. N." wrote, stood *atheism*, which he proclaimed *"the Great Mystery"*: "But the mystery remains a mystery, and it is in just this that the entire meaning of our existence consists, the entire cycle of conditions in which the world stands. You see, it is atheism."[14] At the end of the *entire* process, presumably (we don't know for certain), was the writer's own death, for this letter to Dostoevsky was a suicide note.

---

13 Irina Paperno has told the story of this episode in Dostoevsky's career in her excellent study of suicide in late nineteenth-century Russia; see Paperno, *Suicide as Cultural Institution in Dostoevsky's Russia* (Ithaca, NY: Cornell University Press, 1997), 162–84.
14 Partly quoted in Dostoevsky, *PSS*, 24:472; quoted at greater length, in the original Russian, in Paperno, *Suicide as Cultural Institution*, 294–95.

From October through December of the same year, Dostoevsky returned obsessively in his journal to the theme of suicide, as if it were a true epidemic in Russia. In October, in an article titled "Sentence" (*Prigovor*), he printed what appeared to be a letter to himself from someone identified as "N. N.," just like the author of the extended suicide note, except that this "N. N." and his letter were entirely fictional. In December, in an article titled "Empty Assertions" (*Goloslovnye utverzhdeniia*), he commented on the article "Sentence" (as if in response to "N. N.") and reflected generally on suicide in his era: "Those," he wrote, "who, having taken away from man his faith in his own immortality, want to replace this faith, in the sense of the highest purpose of life [*vysshei tseli zhizni*], 'love for mankind,' those, I say, are the ones who raise their hand against themselves; for, instead of love for mankind they merely plant in the heart of one who has lost his faith the seed of hatred for mankind. . . . And there emerges precisely the opposite, for only with faith in his own immortality can man grasp his entire reasonable purpose on earth. Without conviction in his own immortality, man's ties to the earth are severed, become thinner and rotten, and the loss of the highest meaning of life [*vysshego smysla zhizni*] . . . without doubt brings in its wake suicide." (Dostoevsky, *PSS*, 24:49)

The connection to one of the most quoted sentiments in *Brothers Karamazov* should be obvious, namely, that (according to Ivan) without belief in immortality the moral law disappears and "all is permitted."

Dostoevsky returned repeatedly that December to "the highest meaning of life" (or equivalent phrases) and its connection with scientific materialism and suicide. "The highest meaning of life" is here firmly equated with belief in the immortality of the soul, and the ills of the younger generation—ills that lead even to suicide—are all owing either to a loss of "the highest meaning of life" or to a perversion of it. In an article about today's youth, he laments the number of people who pray from time to time and even go to church but give no thought to—let alone believe in—the immortality of their souls. "And meanwhile," he writes, "it is only from this faith, as I was saying above, that the highest meaning and significance of life [*vysshii smysl i znachenie zhizni*] emerges, that the desire and urge to live emerges. Oh, I repeat, there are many who are avid to live, lacking all ideas and the entire highest meaning of life, to live simply the life of an animal." Many of these even yearn for "the highest purposes and significance of life [*vysshim tseliam i zhacheniiu zhizni*]," he goes on to write, and some will shoot themselves precisely from having yearned for and not found "the highest meaning of life" (Dostoevsky, *PSS*, 24:50).

He returns to the refrain several times in the same December number of *Diary of a Writer*. "Indifferentism" is the name he gives to the malady afflicting today's youth, or, more specifically "indifferentism to the highest purposes of life." The malady has created for the younger generation a crushing burden, namely, to *find* the highest meaning of life. "It is at least clear to the point of complete obviousness," he writes, "that our young generation are condemned to search out for themselves ideals and the highest meaning of life. But this isolation of them, this leaving of them to their own devices is terrible. This is a question that is much, much too significant at the present moment, at the present instant of our life. Our youth is situated in such a way that absolutely nowhere can it find any indication of the highest meaning of life" (Dostoevsky, *PSS*, 24:51).

What to say about a seventeen-year-old girl who committed suicide for no apparent reason? Dostoevsky had written about her in the October issue, and now in December, he responds to a critic: "I expressed the supposition that she died from melancholy [*ot toski*] (much too early melancholy) and from the purposelessness of life—but as a consequence of an upbringing, in her parents' home, perverted by a theory, an upbringing with an erroneous concept of the highest meaning and purposes of life, with the intentional extermination in her soul of its [the soul's] immortality" (Dostoevsky, *PSS*, 24:54). Having a *correct* concept of the highest meaning and purposes of life appears to be practically equivalent to believing in the immortality of the soul.

One additional episode in Dostoevsky's life brought to the fore the question of "the meaning of life." It was the author's correspondence with Arkadii Kovner, the impoverished Russian Jew who in 1875 embezzled a large sum of money from the bank where he was employed, allegedly in order both to strike a political blow against big business and to help provide for his family. It's a priceless story for many reasons having nothing to do with "the meaning of life"—Kovner, as "the Jewish Pisarev" and conscious imitator of Raskolnikov, deserves at least a minor place in nineteenth-century Russian and Russian-Jewish cultural history. After his arrest, Kovner wrote two letters to Dostoevsky from prison, the second one in response to "Empty Assertions." He truly takes a page from the playbook of his addressee in this second letter, for he is a master at adopting and pursuing opposing sides of an argument. He quotes back at Dostoevsky this line from "Empty Assertions": "But there is only one highest idea on earth, namely the idea of the immortality of man's soul, for all the other 'highest' ideas of life by which man might be alive flow only from this one." A Jew and a self-proclaimed atheist, Kovner decides to attack this assertion on logical grounds, correcting it to something that he himself, of course, couldn't possibly believe (at least, if his statements about his own beliefs were sincere). "It seems to me," he writes, "that all the 'highest' ideas of life must flow not from the idea of the immortality of the soul but from the idea of the existence of God, that is, of a being who consciously creates the universe, *consciously* directs and *consciously* takes an interest in *all* the actions of all living things, or at least of people" (Dostoevsky, *PSS*, 29[2]:280). And what could be more Dostoevskian than the following sequence of thoughts?

> Does a God exist who *consciously* directs the universe and who *takes an interest in* … people's actions? As for me, till now I've been convinced of the opposite, especially as regards the last circumstance. I fully acknowledge that there exists some "force" (call it God, if you like) that created the universe, that *eternally* creates and that can *never* be accessible to the human mind. But I cannot countenance the thought that this "force" takes an interest in the life and actions of its creatures and *consciously* directs them, whoever and whatever these creatures might be. (Dostoevsky, *PSS*, 29(2):280)

Kovner then, gleefully goading Dostoevsky, lists all the things that, thanks to science and a materialist worldview, he *knows* to be true, including "Darwin's hypothesis about the origin of species." A few paragraphs later he comes to this: "You observe with complete justice that without the idea of immortality (or, in my opinion, God) there is no meaning or logic in life … and yet in the very existence of the soul, immortality, a God who punishes and rewards (in whatever philosophical interpretation of this you like), there is even less meaning and logic" (Dostoevsky, *PSS*, 29(2):280–81; ellipsis in the original).

As Irina Paperno correctly observes, these thoughts will find their way, with relatively little modification, into *Brothers Karamazov* in book 5, "Pro and Contra" (a phrase, incidentally, that Kovner uses in this second letter).[15] And this brings us back to the beginning. If the articles in *Diary of a Writer* offer any

---

15 Paperno, *Suicide as Cultural Institution*, 202.

clue to what Ivan has in mind when he refers, twice, to the meaning of life in his conversation with Alyosha, then what can we say about the concept? In *Diary of a Writer*, the "highest meaning of life" (or any closely related phrase) appears to be something you seek, find, lose, or misconstrue. We can see, too, that its loss (1) easily comes about through the acceptance of a scientific, materialist world-view and (2) can thereby lead to suicide. Its possession, on the other hand, allows, entails, or is accompanied by belief in the immortality of the soul. But this still leaves us without anything even close to a definition. The word *meaning* appears in connection with "purposes," but this fact tells us very little. In modern English parlance, "meaning of life," "purpose of life," and "meaning and purpose of life" are often indistinguishable. When Dostoevsky writes "concept of the highest meaning and purposes of life," we don't know if he regards "meaning" and "purposes" as synonyms or as distinguishable terms.

What we can say for certain, however, is that in the *Diary of a Writer* articles, "the highest meaning of life" is never presented as something that anyone actually has or has found. It's there as the thing whose absence, along with the absence of belief in immortality, helps explain suicide. Once again, the phrase enters the scene when conventional faith is the object of doubt. So what does "the meaning of life" mean in the conversation between Ivan and Alyosha? It appears likely that Alyosha gets it right: it's what you find after you've abandoned logic—and, presumably, the scientific, materialist worldview. Why not just say "immortality" or "God"? Because we've adopted the perspective of one who has recently denied the existence of both. From the perspective of denial, "the meaning of life" is a kind of secular placeholder for what the denier denies. And then suddenly the phrase shows up in the list of what Ivan now, for the sake of his circuitous argument, claims to believe, as it keeps company with a set of conventional metaphysical ideas: God, God's wisdom and purpose, eternal harmony, and the Word of God. Any other of these terms could easily have appeared on such a list centuries earlier. But "the meaning of life" is clearly a newcomer. Saying you believe in it is almost like announcing dramatically not "I now believe in God," but "I now believe in a transcendent, supernatural entity." It's the outsider's point of view.

Even if Dostoevsky never offered a satisfactory definition of "meaning," as in "the meaning of life," he appears to have left a legacy outside Russia in connection with the concept and phrase. I'll give just one example. Albert Camus, in *The Myth of*

Sisyphus (1942), leads off with the idea, appearing to have borrowed his thoughts directly from his favorite Russian author. "There is only one truly serious philosophical problem," Camus writes in the opening sentence. "It's suicide. To judge that life is or is not worth living is to answer the fundamental question of philosophy." How to determine the truth of this claim? By people's actions, Camus says. No one has ever *died* for any other philosophical argument, including Galileo (who formally renounced his heliocentric hypothesis to escape being burned at the stake). "On the other hand," Camus continues, "I see that many people die because they consider that life is not worth living. I see others who have paradoxically gotten themselves killed for ideas or illusions that give them a reason to live. ... I judge, therefore, that the meaning of life is the most pressing of questions."[16] Then, in a chapter on Kirillov, Camus begins by telling us that all of Dostoevsky's heroes "interrogate themselves on the meaning of life." Suicide in Dostoevsky is an "absurd theme," and Dostoevsky is an "existential novelist."[17]

The idea comes up again nine years later in *L'Homme révolté* (*The Rebel*, in the published English translation). Here the philosophical problem is murder justified by logic. In the introduction, Camus defines the absurd in terms of murder but with recourse to the same terminology he had used in *Myth of Sisyphus*: "The sentiment of the absurd, when one presumes from the outset to infer a rule of action from it, renders murder at the least indifferent and, consequently, possible. If one believes in nothing, if nothing has meaning [*sens*] and if we can affirm no value, then everything is possible and nothing has any importance."[18] As in the earlier work, Dostoevsky furnishes Camus with an illustrative example, in a chapter titled "Le Refus du salut" ("The Rejection of Salvation"). Because the topic is murder, this time Camus chooses Ivan Karamazov (instead of Kirillov) and the consequence of what Camus understands to be Ivan's rejection of immortality: "If he rejects immortality, then what is left for him? Life in its elementary form. The meaning of life having been suppressed, there still remains life. 'I live,' says Ivan, 'in spite of logic'" (*The Rebel*, 77).

Here is not the place to enter into a discussion of these books in their own right. The question is simply whether Camus and Dostoevsky are talking about

---

16   Albert Camus, *Le Mythe de Sisyphe: Essai sur l'absurde* (Paris: Gallimard, 1942), 15–16.
17   Ibid., 140, 145, 148.
18   Albert Camus, *L'Homme révolté* (Paris: Gallimard, 1951), 15.

the same thing when they use the expression "meaning of life" (or a variant of it). This is difficult to say, given that neither author, to my knowledge, ever gave a definition of the expression (*smysl zhizni; sens de la vie*). But the contexts lead me to suspect that Camus was appropriating for his own use words that, seen in their originally setting, do not mean quite the same thing as the corresponding words in Russian. For Camus, *sens* is paired with "value" (*la valeur*) and the question whether life "is worth" (*vaut la peine*) living. If *le sens de la vie* is contrasted with suicide and murder, it's presumably because, when life has *sens*, we elect to continue to live. Like the German *Sinn*, the French *sens* includes a directional concept, thus suggesting a goal or destination.

Dostoevsky's *smysl zhizni*, by contrast, appears to denote a sort of hidden essence within life (like the meaning residing within a word), something that *inquiring* minds can discover so that they might become *believing* minds. If it's connected with suicide (and, for that matter, murder), it's certainly because someone lacking it sees no reason to live (or, in the case of murder, to let a victim live). So, one could say (though Dostoevsky doesn't use this language) that, as in Camus, for such a person life is not *worth* living. But, lacking the directional suggestion of the word *sens*, the Russian word *smysl* suggests something different. In the end, I think the difference boils down to an extra layer or two of irony in Dostoevsky. Speaking (in his own voice in the *Diary of a Writer* articles, in the voice of a character in his fiction) as a believer (which he probably was not all the time), he holds out the idea of a fixed metaphysical essence of which non-doubters are presumably in possession. For someone who started out from the position of belief and never approached belief from the outside, "the meaning of life" would have no, well, meaning. But, adopting the point of view of a doubter, Dostoevsky confers upon the essence what had already, by the 1870s, come to serve the secular mind as a general designation of such an essence: the phrase "the meaning of life."

The history of "the meaning of life," and of its equivalent phrases in various languages, is to a considerable extent the history of the appropriation of the phrase, via translation, for philosophical, religious, and ideological purposes more or less alien to those in the source (whatever the source might be). Both Dostoevsky and Tolstoy, unwittingly and sometimes indirectly, gave nonetheless richly to a number of later intellectual traditions outside Russia, precisely through this phrase and its variants. Perhaps it is not surprising that subsequent writers were just as remiss as the great Russian authors when it came to defining the phrase, let alone explaining why "meaning" is the right word for conveying whatever those writers were seeking to convey. How odd that a phrase whose meaning is almost never given and is almost always obscure should contain precisely the word for what we can't find.

VI

....

Dostoevsky and Nietzsche: The Hazards of Writing Oneself into (or out of) Belief

David S. Cunningham*

For many years I taught an undergraduate course called Atheists and Apologists, usually as an upper-level seminar in a Religious Studies department. Students were assigned ten primary texts—actually, five pairs of texts, each of which brought two approximately contemporaneous figures into conversation with one another. The paired writers were chosen because they displayed quite significantly different views about God, faith, and morality. Nevertheless, in constructing the pairings, I always tried to complicate any easy conclusions about precisely what makes a particular author an "atheist" and what makes another an "apologist" for religious belief. So, for example, the classes were asked to read Descartes in tandem with Pascal; both authors profess to be believers, but students quickly recognize that they offer very different accounts of belief. In fact, Descartes's rationalism can quickly seem to eclipse his profession of faith. Similarly, many students find Hegel's supposed Christian faith to be distant and sterile, whereas Marx's apparently atheistic arguments are filled with theologically charged turns of phrase.

My thanks are due to Svetlana Evdokimova at Brown University for inviting me to the conference on Dostoevsky, where I presented this material in a (much) earlier form. In particular, I am grateful for her hospitality at the conference and for her patience as the revision of this chapter lingered far too long. Thanks also to Rowan Williams, my theological teacher and mentor.

One of our five pairs of authors—indeed, one of the few that I never altered in some twelve iterations of the course—was Nietzsche and Dostoevsky. We would usually read excerpts from *The Gay Science* and *Zarathustra*, and the whole of *The Antichrist*; this was followed by reading *The Brothers Karamazov* in its entirety.

Both authors challenge my classroom participants on a variety of levels. In Dostoevsky's portrayal of Alyosha, the students know they have found a believer, but they don't always find him sympathetic; they also find "Rebellion" and "The Grand Inquisitor" to be among the strongest arguments against faith, and particularly against the Christian faith in its modern form, that they have ever encountered. Similarly, they feel somewhat bludgeoned by Nietzsche's flaming atheistic tirades, particularly in *The Antichrist*; yet they are also puzzled by his apparent inability to let go of God, even as he rails against the very idea. In Dostoevsky, they discover a Christian who has constructed the strongest possible case for atheism; in Nietzsche, they find an atheist who can't get God off his mind.

The students read primary texts exclusively; I offer them very little in the way of historical background. As a result, most of the students are, somewhat accidentally, readers who both affirm and exemplify the literary-theoretical position identified as "the death of the author." They cannot fall into the "intentional fallacy," because they know far too little about either of these men or their intentions. They have to rely almost exclusively on the texts themselves in order to glean any sense of what either author believed. I provide only the scantiest biographical details, and few students bother to learn more about either man on their own. Thus, as indicators of the impact of each author's writing (without reference to his actual intentions and beliefs), the students provide me with a relatively unalloyed reading; they therefore make useful test cases for how one might discern each author's attitude toward religious faith, using only his published texts as a guide.

Mostly, the students find the texts confusing. One student might experience his faith being sorely tested by Ivan's account of cruelty to children, while another finds Zosima enlightening; one quotes a typical insult from *The Antichrist*, while another observes that, as far as she can tell, only the madman seems to understand the earth-shattering impact of the murder of God. My undergraduates are not particularly skilled readers, but I think their instincts are sound—particularly when they express some uncertainty about where both authors stand. Partly as a result of this lack of clarity, most of them don't find either author particularly convincing (though for different reasons). In the case of Dostoevsky, they don't know what he really believes: he seems to argue both for and against belief. In Nietzsche's case, they can't really miss the fact that he thinks belief is a bad idea, but his tirades don't seem to move them. In the latter case, the author fails to persuade; in the former case, the students can't usually decide what it is, exactly, of which the author is trying to persuade them. It is the *difference* between these two perspectives that interests me most, and to which I will return shortly.

Writing to Believe (or to Deny Belief)

It is something of a commonplace to describe both Nietzsche and Dostoevsky as thinkers who employed their skills as writers to provide themselves with an opportunity to work through their views about faith. In both cases, their writing is laced with theological terminology and biblical allusions— they write about God and about the gods, about demons and angels, about characters who are obsessed with theological or atheological claims. At the risk of oversimplifying, we can observe that Nietzsche was constantly trying to write himself *out of* the faith into which he, as the son of a Protestant pastor, had been born; Dostoevsky, on the other hand, was trying to write himself *back into* the faith from which he had become estranged through various political and philosophical experiments. For Dostoevsky and for Nietzsche, the act of writing is a means by which each man tries to make sense of a faith that is in dynamic motion—a faith that is in the process either of dying or of rising again. That Dostoevsky is wrestling with the call of Christ is attested by his seemingly contradictory assertions of unquenchable doubt and unshakable belief. Nietzsche, born into faith and aware of its powers of temptation, is eager to prove to himself that he has rid himself of it. Yet he continues to feel the need to make this case, in practically everything he writes—until, finally, he is able to write no more.

The two authors were thus engaged in a very similar enterprise, even if they were moving in opposite directions. As Janko Lavrin put the matter, many decades ago,

In his passionate wish for religion Dostoevsky had to explore the problem of God from the angle of a believer and an unbeliever. Yet in contrast to the pious young Nietzsche (who, despite his subsequent denial of everything religious and Christian, at first studied theology at Bonn University in order to become a pastor), Dostoevsky's youth was marked by skepticism which tormented him to the end of his life.[1]

The skepticism that Lavrin mentions here, and that haunted Dostoevsky so profoundly, is both well known and well documented—in everything from his political activities to his personal reflections. In a much-cited letter of 1854, Dostoevsky wrote,

> I can tell you about myself that I am a child of this century, a child of doubt and disbelief, I have always been and shall ever be (that I know), until they close the lid of my coffin. What terrible torment this thirst to believe has cost me and is still costing me, and the stronger it becomes in my soul, the stronger are the arguments against it.[2]

This skepticism, however, is deeply complicated by a later passage in the same letter—a passage that seems, to many readers, to suggest quite the opposite of skepticism, a kind of obscurantism or fideism:

> If someone were to prove to me that Christ was outside the truth, and it was really the case that the truth lay outside Christ, then I should choose to stay with Christ rather than with the truth.[3]

Everyone who reads these words—from deeply invested scholars to very occasional readers—tends to come away from them with profound uncertainties about Dostoevsky's faith. In contrast, very few readers have expressed much hesitation in summarizing Nietzsche's position: he is simply an atheist. He may employ a great deal of theological language in his writing, but there seems to be very little question about where he himself stands.

---

1 Janko Lavrin, "A Note on Nietzsche and Dostoevsky," *Russian Review* 28, no. 2 (1969): 163.
2 *Letters of Fyodor Michailovitch Dostoevsky to His Family and Friends*, trans. Colburn Mayne (Chatto and Windus, 1914); cited in Lavrin, "A Note," 164.
3 This translation is from Malcolm Jones, "Dostoevskii and Religion," in *The Cambridge Companion to Dostoevskii*, ed. W. J. Leatherbarrow (Cambridge: Cambridge University Press, 2002), 155–56.

The passages in Dostoevsky's letter (as quoted above) have been subjected to a great deal of critical scrutiny, and have been interpreted in multiple ways. One of the clearest accounts of what they might mean, and of how we might better understand Dostoevsky's faith through them, comes from the pen of Rowan Williams:

> Dostoevsky's confession of 1854, whatever exactly it meant to him at the time of writing, comes to mean something like this. "Truth," as the ensemble of sustainable propositions about the world, does not compel adherence to any one policy of living rather than another; if faith's claims about Christ do not stand within that ensemble of propositions, that is not a problem. It means that they cannot be confused with any worldly power that might assume the right to dictate a policy for living or impose a reconciliation upon unwilling humanity. This does not mean that they are irrational in the sense of contradictory or in the sense of being arbitrarily willed; they represent something that can make possible new notions of moral awareness precisely because they are not generated by the will. ... At this level, response to Christ connects with a "truth" that is more comprehensive than any given ensemble of facts.[4]

Needless to say, this is a complicated position for Dostoevsky to take. But even if it accurately reflects his views (or, at any rate, his views in 1854), can the same views be gleaned simply by reading his published writings? Would readers come to the same conclusion that Williams reaches here, if they had only read Dostoevsky's novels?

My own consideration of this question has led me to argue that, in using one's published writing as a means of wrestling with (and therefore communicating about) one's faith, one undertakes—as my title suggests—a very hazardous practice. This is particularly the case if one hopes to be understood, to *communicate* one's views to others. At the end of this chapter, I will return to the question of whether the hazardous nature of this enterprise might have more to do with the *content* of the writing—the question of faith—than it does with one's particular *method* of writing about it. In the meantime, it is precisely the different *methods* that Dostoevsky and Nietzsche employ which interests me, because it suggests that the hazards involved in their efforts to write about their faith are hazardous *in different ways*. To that difference I now return.

---

4 Rowan Williams, *Dostoevsky: Language, Faith, and Fiction* (Waco, TX: Baylor University Press, 2008), 26.

The Difference (and Why It Makes a Difference)

As I noted above, my students tend to be more confused by Dostoevsky, even though they are not particularly persuaded by Nietzsche. It may be, of course, that readers experience the attempt to *generate* faith through writing as simply more challenging and more complicated than is the attempt to *eliminate* it. Or, to say the same thing another way: writing one's way *into* faith may just be more interesting, and more fraught, than writing one's way *out of* it. Although I'm willing to consider this as a possible reason for the difference, it doesn't strike me as very likely, and I suspect that one could offer some interesting counterexamples in the work of other writers. In any case, I think there may be better explanations.

One such explanation has to do with genre. Dostoevsky wrote fiction, and even the nonfiction that he wrote has such a strong literary quality that many critics find themselves wondering just how fictional some of his letters and diaries may be. For Nietzsche, fiction was clearly not his primary idiom. Admittedly, *Zarathustra* is something like a fable; in essence, however, it is—like many of Nietzsche's works—a set of aphorisms, collected into a loose narrative frame. As Nietzsche himself said, "Whoever writes in blood and aphorisms does not want to be read but to be learned by heart."[5] He tells us exactly what he thinks, and what *we* should think; as a result, his attitudes about God and belief lie somewhat nearer the surface. We can, of course, plumb Nietzsche's aphorisms for a certain kind of "movement" on questions of faith, some of which may lie fairly deeply buried; that, however, is a different kind of enterprise than the reading of a novel, in which multiple characters vie for our attention. In Dostoevsky's fiction, in particular, as Bakhtin famously noted,

> a plurality of independent and unmerged voices and consciousnesses, a genuine polyphony of fully valid voices, is in fact the chief characteristic of Dostoevsky's novels. What unfolds in his works is not a multitude of characters and fates in a single objective world, illuminated by a single authorial consciousness; rather *a plurality of consciousnesses, with equal rights and each with its own world*, combine but are not merged in the unity of the event.[6]

---

5 Friedrich Nietzsche, *Thus Spake Zarathustra*, in *The Portable Nietzsche*, trans. and ed. Walter Kaufmann (New York: Viking, 1954), pt. 1, sec. 7 ("On Reading and Writing"), 152.

6 M. M. Bakhtin, *Problems of Dostoevsky's Poetics*, ed. and trans. Caryl Emerson, with an introduction by Wayne C. Booth (Minneapolis: University of Minnesota Press, 1984), 6. The entire opening part-sentence of this quotation is italicized in the original.

These fully valid voices, distributed widely among the characters, make it very difficult indeed to "read off" the author's genuine beliefs from the actions and words on the page.

Still, we at least learn *something* about various authors' attitudes toward belief by their decisions to write in particular genres. Fiction, it has been argued, is one of the few forms of writing through which we may come to grasp one of the most defining facts about God—which is that God, by definition, cannot be grasped. Indeed, this is one of the factors that make fictional literature such an important vehicle for teaching about religious belief, and, in particular, about belief in God.[7] God's indefinability means that God cannot be spoken of in definitive language, but only in fits and starts—only in full recognition of the brokenness and ultimate impossibility of the enterprise.

In other words, the only way to write or speak about God, as Rowan Williams notes, is "to go on speaking [and] writing about God, allowing the language of faith to encounter fresh trials every day, and also fresh distortions and refusals."[8] Williams observes that fiction may be the most appropriate mode for doing this, because at its best, it refuses to come to closure: "Every morally and religiously serious fiction has to project something beyond [its] ending or otherwise signal a level of incompletion, even in the most minimal and formal mode, indicating an as-yet-untold story."[9] This helps us understand Williams's comment elsewhere that there can be no fundamentalist fiction;[10] if every detail about God is a fundamental truth in propositional form, then an author can never create the all-important lacunae and open structures that mark all great fiction.

In spite of all this, however, my student readers of Dostoevsky are rarely satisfied with the incompleteness and lack of closure that Williams here endorses. They are not comfortable dwelling in the kingdom of the open text and celebrating their accidental embrace of "the death of the author." They want to know where a writer stands on matters of faith, and, if possible, they want to

---

7 David S. Cunningham, *Reading Is Believing: The Christian Faith through Literature and Film* (Grand Rapids, MI: Brazos, 2004), 31–37.

8 Williams, *Dostoevsky*, 46.

9 Ibid.

10 Ibid., 60. Williams also makes similar points in a variety of other writings about the relationship of theology and literature.

figure that out just by using the text that sits in front of them.[11] On this score, Dostoevsky presents the students with a particular challenge—perhaps because, as noted above, he seems to make such strong arguments for various views and positions. They are looking for a functional response to their questions: Does he believe, or doesn't he? Unfortunately for them, however, fiction—and Dostoevsky's fiction in particular—does not provide that response. Williams again:

> Faith and fiction are deeply related—not because faith is a variant of fiction in the trivial sense, but because both are gratuitous linguistic practices standing over against a functional scheme of things. The gratuity of faith arises from its character as response to the freedom of the creator as unexpectedly encountered in the fabric of the world. The gratuity of fiction arises from the conviction that no kind of truth can be told if we speak or act as if history is over, as if the description of what contingently *is* becomes the sole possible account of language. A fiction like Dostoevsky's which tries to show what faith might mean in practice is bound to be both inconclusive in all sorts of ways, and also something that aspires to a realism that is more than descriptive.[12]

Indeed, we may go further. There may actually be something about the process of writing fiction that somehow *opens up the possibility* of belief. In the process of writing fiction, writing about characters whose destinies one does not yet know, one opens up the possibility of the gratuitous reception of a faith that one cannot yet affirm. In "the world of mathematical closure," says Williams, "the future is clear and there are no significant decisions to be made. In the world of the novel, when all this has been said, everything is still to play for."[13]

In addition, I should here point out that I ask my students to read only *one* of Dostoevsky's works (at least within this particular course—and in my experience, few have encountered him elsewhere). This further reduces their vision of the relationship between the author's faith and his published writings—and on this point, the same would be true for their views about Nietzsche. Given that faith was, for both writers, a thing in motion—something that was in the process of

---

11 I did not usually include readings from Kierkegaard in the course, but his frequent use of pseudonyms would have added another layer of mystery (and, I suspect, frustration) to the students' efforts to discern the author's point of view.

12 Williams, *Dostoevsky*, 46.

13 Ibid., 58.

developing or devolving, as the case might be—readers need to be willing to examine the whole of the corpus, rather than rely on the kind of snapshot that will come from too narrow a focus on one particular work or one particular period in the author's life. The fact that my students receive such a minimal picture of each author makes them interestingly innocent, not only of each author's biographical background, but also of his complex development over time.

This suggests that my students might well feel the weight of all of the afore-mentioned complexities yet more strongly were they to trace what René Girard calls Dostoevsky's "spiritual evolution"[14]—starting from the early works, then moving through *The Idiot* and *The Possessed*, and thence to *Brothers Karamazov*. If "evolution" is the correct way to describe it, Dostoevsky's is a particularly lengthy one: decades elapse; thousands of pages are published; the author is sent to prison in Siberia and returns home again. A student who has only read one novel has very little chance to make a well-grounded argument on this subject, and, indeed, a great many professional critics find it difficult to summon the degree of patient attention that would be necessary to offer a thoroughgoing account of the entire evolutionary journey. As Girard puts it:

> Certain critics of Dostoevsky have the tendency to hurry the rhythm of his spiritual evolution, whether because they desire superficially to "Christianize" his work or, to the contrary, because they desire to de-Christianize it for their own convenience. For Dostoevsky, writing is a means of knowing, an instrument of exploration; it is thus always beyond the author himself, ahead of his intelligence and his faith.[15]

I want to emphasize and highlight that last phrase, because I will return to it shortly: Dostoevsky's writing is, Girard says, "ahead of his faith."

In a way, this is simply to repeat the claims that I made above in conversation with Rowan Williams—that is, that it belongs to the nature of fiction to resist closure, to leave uncertainties hanging, to be constantly "on the move." And Girard clearly wants to make this point himself, because he follows his quoted observation with the remark that "to say this is to say again that Dosto-evsky is essentially a novelist."[16] But this point about the genre of Dostoevsky's

---

14 René Girard, *Dostoevsky: Resurrection from the Underground*, ed. and trans. with an introduc-tion by James G. Williams (New York: Crossroad, 1997), 101.

15 Ibid.

16 Ibid.

writing does not exhaust the potential meaning in Girard's metaphorical description of that writing as "always beyond the author"—that it lies "ahead of his intelligence and his faith." In particular, the spatial metaphor of writing that is "beyond" or "ahead of" its author may help us distinguish the different kinds of hazards that Dostoevsky and Nietzsche face as they try to communicate about the nature of belief. That difference may lie not simply in whether one is trying to generate it or trying to stamp it out, nor even in whether one is writing fiction or aphoristic injunctions. Instead, the difference may be in whether one's writing ventures out "ahead of" one's faith, as Girard describes Dostoevsky's, or whether one's writing lags "behind" one's faith. Girard does not mark this contrast explicitly, but in the present context it seems well worth drawing out.

By "those whose writing lags 'behind' their faith," I am referring to those who assume that they have made all the relevant decisions about faith securely, and that they are writing simply to express their already determined views. This path allows the author to settle the questions first—or at least to assume that they have been settled by others—and only *then* to write about them. This can be done either by believers or nonbelievers, and in a variety of genres. A believer such as C. S. Lewis can write novels to promote a Christian world-view, and Philip Pullman can write novels in order to negate that view. A social critic like Christopher Hitchens can argue against belief using the vehicle of nonfiction, whereas a scientist like John Polkinghorne can use the same genre to make the case in favor of faith. In all these instances, however, the writers seem relatively certain of where they stand before they set pen to paper.

In contrast, when I speak of writing that ventures out "ahead of" its author, I am attempting to suggest that the author is writing without the security of definitive knowledge, without having answered all the questions in advance. Such an author has to allow for the possibility that these questions may be answered differently than she or he might have assumed. Such authors may express their own struggles with respect to religious belief, as Dostoevsky does in his letter of 1854, or as Nikos Kazantzakis does in his authorial preface to *The Last Temptation of Christ*.[17] Taking this approach is particularly hazardous, since one's readers may tend to latch onto one particular aspect of one's oeuvre in which either faith or doubt seems to be in the

---

17 Nikos Kazantzakis, *The Last Temptation of Christ*, trans. P. A. Bien (New York: Touchstone, 1960).

forefront, and to use that element alone to determine the author's attitudes toward faith. This helps to explain why readings of Dostoevsky veer so strongly in one direction or another—with some reading him as an atheist and others as a determined believer.

Hazards *historisch* and *geschichtlich*

In order to explore the differing hazards of writing "ahead of" or "behind" one's faith, I want to consider a different distinction entirely: the one offered by the German terms *Historie* and *Geschichte*. Both of these words have a very complex effective-history and therefore cannot be translated straightforwardly; for present purposes, however, let us describe them as "the things that happened" and "the story of the things that happened," respectively. The distinction is similar to that suggested by the Latin phrases *res gestae* ("the things that happened, the totality of events") and *historia rerum gestarum* ("the account of these events").[18] I think that this distinction might prove fruitful, not least because Nietzsche and Dostoevsky were both writing at a time when the difference between these two approaches (and the further differences they imply) was particularly vexed—and nowhere more intensely than in the theological context.

This was the era of what later came to be known as "Life of Jesus" research, which could be characterized as a shift in focus from *Geschichte* to *Historie*. Until the eighteenth century, and including both the Protestant and Catholic branches of the Western church, accounts of Jesus had traditionally been *geschichtlich*—focused on narrative and story, on the biblical texts as shaping a moral and imaginative world, rather than what we would today call a "historical" account. Enthusiasm for *Geschichte* was of course tempered by the work of Leopold von Ranke and everything that happened in his wake, as scholars in all fields found themselves called to set aside narrative and story and to focus on *wie es eigentlich gewesen ist*—"how things actually happened."[19]

---

18 For more on this distinction, particularly as it relates to a wide range of theological and political questions, see Michael Allen Gillespie, *Hegel, Heidegger, and the Ground of History* (Chicago: University of Chicago Press, 1984), 1–23.

19 Leopold von Ranke, *Geschichte der lateinischen und germanischen Völker von 1494 bis 1514*, 3rd ed. (Leipzig: Duncker und Humblot, 1884 [1824]), preface.

In the theological context, this led to a particularly controversial shift, in which scholars began to ask, really for the first time (at least publicly), "What actually happened?" with respect to the Bible in general and the events surrounding the life of Jesus in particular. These writers—including Hermann Samuel Reimarus, David Friedrich Strauss, and Ernest Rénan, as well as many others—sought to shift this conversation ever more strongly in the direction of *Historie*.[20] They were eager to reach back behind the accumulated layers of story and saga that, in their view, had blinded us to the true nature of Jesus. They wanted to bring him into the modern age as a truly historical figure: a human being who walked on the earth, did certain things, said certain things, and acted in a particular way. The picture of Jesus that emerged from this research was often strikingly different from the traditional version portrayed by the narratives of the Gospels. Researchers explained this by pointing out that the churches told *stories* about Jesus, whereas they were following von Ranke's advice of writing history only in terms of "what actually happened."

This, I want to suggest, may have been what Nietzsche was also seeking to do. We might even think of him as a *Leben-Jesu-Forscher*, following the path taken by a writer whose work he knew well: David Friedrich Strauss, of whom Nietzsche wrote in his *Unzeitgemässe Betrachtungen*.[21] That text focuses not on Strauss's entry into the Life of Jesus research (*Das Leben Jesu, kritisch bearbeitet* of 1846) but rather on a much later text, *Der alte und neue Glaube*. Nevertheless, by the time of this later work, Strauss was even more radical in his rejection of traditional Christian claims about Jesus. Nietzsche is, of course, scathing in his critique of Strauss's work, for reasons to which I will return. I mention the connection here because it reinforces my students' perception that, although Nietzsche consistently expresses his rejection of Christian belief, he does not seem to be able to let it go. He returns time and again to theology, and to

---

20 The work of Reimarus was read only by a few close friends during his lifetime. It was published posthumously by Lessing as "Fragments from an Anonymous Writer" in *Zur Geschichte und Literatur* in 1774–78. Strauss's contribution was the most famous, perhaps: *Das Leben Jesu, kritisch bearbeitet* (Tubingen, 1846) was translated into English by George Eliot as *The Life of Jesus, Critically Examined* (London, 1846). Rénan wrote *Vie de Jésus* in 1863.

21 Friedrich Nietzsche, "David Strauss: The Confessor and the Author (1873)," in *Untimely Meditations*, trans. R. J. Hollingdale, with an introduction by J. P. Stern (Cambridge: Cambridge University Press, 1983), 3–55.

theologians such as Strauss, only in order to repeat his claim that they really don't matter.

Because of Nietzsche's complete rejection of Christianity, however, he is not usually listed among the nineteenth-century "researchers into the life of Jesus." In putting him into this category, I am merely suggesting that he was undertaking some of the same kinds of work as those scholars who are more typically given this label. Like them, he was attempting to retrieve the specificity of the life and death of Jesus, and to rescue it from the religious thicket in which that life had been entangled—including the Jewish mind-set from which Jesus came and the Christian dogmatism into which he was absorbed. So we occasionally get Nietzschean asides in the form of mild appreciations for Jesus, including, famously, that "there was only one Christian, and he died on a cross."[22] Of course, Nietzsche had no vested interest in rehabilitating the figure of Jesus per se; if, however, we were to expand slightly the definition of a "Life of Jesus researcher," we might recognize him as belonging to this way of thinking. He desired to reconstruct the Christian faith itself, using the same kind of methodological move as the Life of Jesus scholars, and working in their idiom. He wants us to know who Jesus really was, precisely to make it easier for us to dismiss him—and, more importantly, to dismiss everything that was built upon and around him. Like the *Leben-Jesus-Forscher*, he has settled his own score with that faith and now just wants "to give us the facts"— in the partial hope that we, or at least some of the "higher men" among us, will strike out on a similar path.

Nietzsche's writing therefore lags "behind his faith"—or, rather, behind his *unfaith*—in the same way that Dostoevsky's writing ventures out *ahead* of his faith. Of course, writing "behind" one's religious views would seem to be the safer course, in that it follows the same pattern of other forms of *Wissenschaft*: first, determine the facts; then, describe them in writing. And lest this be thought of as a method only used by critics of religion, it should be observed that a number of theologians of the nineteenth and early twentieth centuries followed precisely the same path. The works of Friedrich Schleiermacher and Adolf Harnack provide us with prime examples of this approach; both were theologians who wanted to make sure that their scholarly work was placed on

---

22 Friedrich Nietzsche, *The Antichrist*, in *The Portable Nietzsche*, sec. 39, p. 612.

the same footing as that of other disciplines, so they made certain to follow the same methodological pattern.[23] But if we were to trace out the effective-history of their work, we would discover that for them, as for the Life of Jesus researchers, this kind of "serious scholarship about faith" has its own set of hazards. And those hazards may be particularly acute in the case of writing about the *Christian* faith.

"Jesus Does Not Stay"

To understand how this is so, we need to take a somewhat closer look at the methodological approach that I have described as "writing behind one's faith," and especially the form it took within Life of Jesus research. I want to focus on that movement's waning years—an era roughly contemporary with the period in which both Nietzsche and Dostoevsky stopped writing.

By the turn of the twentieth century, Life of Jesus research had developed a sufficiently robust status that accounts of its historical sojourn began to appear; it was a scholarly movement that had become, itself, the subject of scholarly investigation. The most thoroughgoing account of the movement is a book by Albert Schweitzer, the English title of which is *The Quest of the Historical Jesus*. His account demonstrates rather convincingly that, every time nineteenth-century historians sought to employ their best scholarly tools in order to discover "the real Jesus," what they actually discovered were portraits of *themselves*. In seeking to write a biography of this man in particular, they found themselves unwittingly writing their own *autobiographies*. To write a life of Jesus was to stare down into the murky depths of a well, straining to see the water at the bottom. As a face gradually appeared to form there, one imagined that one had finally gazed upon the face of Jesus; the face that one saw, of course, was nothing other than the reflection of one's own. As Schweitzer observes:

> There is no historical task which so reveals a man's true self as the writing of a Life of Jesus. No vital force comes into the figure unless a man breathes into it all the hate or all the love of which he is capable. The stronger the love, or the stronger the hate, the more life-like is the figure which is produced. For

---

23 Adolf Harnack, *What Is Christianity?*, trans. Thomas Bailey Saunders, with an introduction by Rudolf Bultmann (New York: Harper and Row, 1957); Friedrich E. D. Schleiermacher, *On Religion: Speeches to Its Cultured Despisers*, trans. Rudolf Otto (New York: Harper and Row, 1958).

hate as well as love can write a Life of Jesus, and the greatest of them are written with hate. … It was not so much hate of the Person of Jesus as of the supernatural nimbus with which it was so easy to surround Him, and with which He had in fact been surrounded. … And their hate sharpened their historical insight.[24]

Anyone who writes in depth about a particular historical figure must surely *care* about that figure, one way or another—be it through love or through hate. But in the case of Jesus, something else is at work. Here we have the founder of, or at least the chief figure in, one of the most significant moral and intellectual systems in the history of the world—a movement with ramifications in all directions (political, economic, artistic, cultural, sociological, psychological, and many more). It would be hard to find a historical figure more influential, or more polarizing, than Jesus of Nazareth. Few individuals have inspired more love (and hate) among those who have written about him.

Nietzsche was not writing as a historian in the traditional mode, but he was a superb genealogist. Thus, although his writing in a work like *The Antichrist* doesn't really resemble works like D. F. Strauss's *Das Leben Jesu, kritisch bearbeitet*, the latter work certainly did influence Nietzsche; in fact, he read it as a theology student in Bonn, and it was one of the books that led to his rejection of the Christian faith.[25] Some commentators have speculated that one of the reasons for the virulence of Nietzsche's later attack on Strauss was that, particularly in Strauss's late work (*Der alte und neue Glaube*), he had come around to a more radical position on faith and religion—one not far, in fact, from that of Nietzsche himself. Nietzsche was always keen to distinguish himself from others who might have arrived at similar conclusions by another way. And thus, when Nietzsche eventually comes to write *The Antichrist*, he writes in a mode not so distant from that of the *Leben Jesu* genre (though in a more radical vein). As many have noted, it is a book in which Nietzsche actually puts himself forward as the proper alternative to Jesus; in this respect, he provides us with the most extreme case of Schweitzer's metaphor. Nietzsche, too, had looked down the well, and had seen the reflection of his own face.

---

24 Albert Schweitzer, *The Quest of the Historical Jesus: A Critical Study of Its Progress from Reimarus to Wrede* (London: SCM Press, 1954), 4.
25 Briefly recounted in J. P. Stern's introduction to Nietzsche, *Untimely Meditations*, xi.

Thus, building on Schweitzer's claim about Life of Jesus researchers—namely, that "their hate sharpened their historical insight"—we can suggest that Nietzsche's hate sharpened his genealogical insight in a similar way. Yet Schweitzer can also help us understand why it might be the case that works like those of Strauss and Nietzsche—attempts to argue one's way out of faith, and to argue *others* out of it—are often not particularly persuasive. Admittedly, if one's faith were based purely on *Historie,* and if certain historical events were then called into question, one's faith might well be tested. But Christianity has never based its claims on *Historie* alone; indeed, until that category was invented in the modern era, few theologians would have suggested that believers should base their faith only on certain actual events that transpired in Palestine around the time of Tiberius Caesar. Most Christian belief is more interested in the *Geschichte* that developed later, in light of these events—including those writings later compiled as the New Testament but also including a huge range of stories, commentary, treatises, polemics, sermons, prayers, and meditations that were never officially canonized but that have had a tremendous influence nonetheless. If one's faith has been deeply formed over decades by such a wide range of material, then that faith seems unlikely to be easily deterred simply because one person has judged all this material to be worthless, and has written about that judgment in a post hoc fashion (having already determined the answers to all the relevant questions).

This returns us to my suggestion, made in passing much earlier in this chapter, that the hazards of this enterprise might best be characterized not as "writing about faith in a certain genre or with a certain method," but as writing about faith *at all.* Or perhaps it has to do with writing about a *particular* faith, about the *Christian* faith, and, in particular, about the God-man, Jesus Christ.[26] This, at any rate, was Schweitzer's conclusion, who felt that any account of the life of Jesus was bound to fail—at least if it were written in the mode of *Historie.* In a famous passage (in the conclusion of his book), Schweitzer wrote,

> The study of the Life of Jesus has followed a remarkable path. It set out in quest of the historical Jesus [*um den historischen Jesus zu finden*], believing that when it had found Him it could bring Him straight into our time as a Teacher and Saviour. It loosed the bands by which He had been riveted for

---

26 Particularly for its connections to Dostoevsky, an essential text is Vladimir Solovyev, *Lectures on Godmanhood,* ed. Peter P. Zouboff (International University Press, 1944).

centuries to the stony rocks of ecclesiastical doctrine, and rejoiced to see life and movement coming into the figure once more, and the historical Jesus advancing, as it seemed, to meet it. But He does not stay [*er blieb nicht stehen*]; He passes by our time and returns to His own. What surprised and dismayed the theology of the last forty years was that, despite all forced and arbitrary interpretations, it could not keep Him in our time, but had to let Him go. He returned to His own time, not owing to the application of any historical ingenuity, but by the same inevitable necessity by which the liberated pendulum returns to its original position.[27]

Er blieb nicht stehen: Jesus does not stay. The very absence of concrete historical data about him makes it impossible to turn him into a "modern man," impossible to treat him as one might treat any other great figure of *Historie*. He returns to his own time.

Some additional insight may be gained from a close look at the original German title of Schweitzer's book. The first part of the title is *Von Reimarus zu Wrede*; this signals that its account begins with the posthumously published reflections of Hermann Samuel Reimarus (who believed he was onto something so scandalous that he never even sought to publish it), and ends with the work of Wilhelm Wrede, who took the thoroughgoing skepticism that marked Life of Jesus research to its logical conclusion—that is, that not only was Jesus not the messiah, but he did not even *claim* to be. But it is the *subtitle* of Schweitzer's work that is particularly worthy of note: *Eine Geschichte der Leben-Jesu-Forschung*. Schweitzer self-consciously writes a *Geschichte* of Life of Jesus research, not a *Historie*—not "the things that actually happened," but *an account* of the things that happened (and indeed, his own account—which he admits is a very partial and interested one).

To understand the significance of Schweitzer's use of *Geschichte* in his title, it is important to remember that he had also been a *participant* in the movement known as Life of Jesus research. He had published his own "sketch" of the life of Jesus in the same year that Wrede's work appeared.[28] That work has fallen into the same kind of obscurity as just about every other *Historie* that Schweitzer cites and reviews in his account of the movement. On the other hand, Schweitzer's *account* of that movement—his *Geschichte*—had quite the

---

27 Schweitzer, *Quest*, 397, translation slightly altered.
28 Albert Schweitzer, *Das Messiantäts- und Leidensgeheimnis: Eine Skizze des Lebens Jesu* (Tübingen: J. C. B. Mohr, 1901).

opposite impact: it continues to be read widely, in many languages. It remains a significant and frequently cited text, not least for its observations about the mirror-imaging of inquiries into the life of Jesus—and for its haunting conclusion, which reminds us that "Jesus does not stay."

About a decade before Schweitzer's account appeared, another German theologian had summarized and criticized the Life of Jesus movement, and had proposed an alternative. This book, written by Martin Kähler, did not provide the kind of close reading and thoroughgoing account of the various Lives of Jesus, as Schweitzer did; instead, he challenged the movement at the methodological level. Kähler argued that no historian would accept the source materials that the scholars of the Life of Jesus school were using to create a biography of Jesus. This leads him to offer a quite remarkable claim: that the "real" Jesus is exactly one who is carried to us by the tradition—complete with all those historical accretions that so distressed those who embarked upon the Life of Jesus quest. Only by including all of this historical accumulation, says Kähler, can we really get a sense of who Jesus was for those who first encountered him—and, therefore, who he may be for us. In the case of Jesus, at least, we have no access to the *res gestae*; our truest portrait comes from a study of the *historia rerum gestarum*.

I have put off providing the title of Kähler's book, because it will take us back to my original claim as to how we might make use of the two German words for "history" as a means of helping us come to understand Dostoevsky's approach to faith. Kähler's title is *Der sogenannte historische Jesus und der geschichtliche, biblische Christus*. The English translation of this book, which was actually not available until 1964, provided a fairly literal rendering, employing the word *historical* for *historisch* and, for *geschichtlich*, the word *historic*—as in, an event of "historic" importance.[29] The significance of Jesus is not so much as a historical figure, which is lost in the sands of time (though Kähler insisted that Christianity does not therefore forfeit its historical basis, for Jesus did really live and walk the earth). Still, the true relevance of Jesus is that he is a *historic* figure—one who has shaped the way that we tell our history (*Geschichte*). In this sense he is comparable to a figure like Socrates, about

---

29 Martin Kähler, *The So-Called Historical Jesus and the Historic, Biblical Christ*, with a foreword by Paul J. Tillich; trans., ed., and introduction by Carl E. Braaten (Philadelphia: Fortress Press, 1964).

whom we know very little (and almost nothing that would be considered wholly reliable by a modern historian); yet, because of the testimony of others about his life and the traditions that bear him on, his impact on the history of the West is undeniable.

One can't write a *Historie* of Socrates or of Jesus; there is simply not enough historical information on which we can rely, not enough material to inform our scholarship at a level that would pass muster among professional historians. But we can write a *Geschichte*; we can offer an account. That is, in fact, what the Gospels are; moreover, it is also what Dostoevsky's novels are (though in a different sense). They are works that are partial and interested, focusing on Jesus not as a mere figure in a long line of historical figures or even "world-historical individuals," but as a phenomenon of "historic" importance—which is to say, important enough to deserve a *Geschichte* and not just a *Historie*.

For or Against; Ahead or Behind; Historical or Historic

Writing about Jesus (and about Christianity) will be more successful, and will have a deeper and more long-lasting impact on its readers, if authors allow their writing to venture out "ahead of their faith," as did Dostoevsky—not always knowing in advance how the story will end. This is hazardous, because one may always be misinterpreted as having "lost" one's faith or, at the very least, as having "settled" the questions (instead of merely disguising or subverting them). But this hazard can be offset somewhat by exploring the questions as broadly as possible, and by acknowledging that good arguments can be made for a variety of answers. This was, in fact, Dostoevsky's approach—and it has given his writings about faith a very long and interesting effective-history. His willingness to write "ahead of his faith" makes his work fascinating and relevant right up to the present day.

On the other hand, those who allow their writing to lag "behind their faith" seem very much a product of their particular age. This is not to say that Nietzsche's writings are not of interest or relevance today; obviously, the opposite is true. But his polemical writings against Christianity are more didactic, more prone to simple refutation, and therefore considerably less interesting than is his writing on other topics. To write "behind one's faith" is to operate with a different sort of hazard: such writing tends to generate an audience that has already come to the same conclusion as has the author. If those who read

Nietzsche's diatribes against Christianity have not already reached the same conclusions, his arguments will tend to fall on deaf ears. And a similar fate awaits those who write in a similar mode, including the Life of Jesus researchers. If a reader were looking for a way of rejecting traditional Christian claims about Jesus, then these works would be welcomed; but then again, they would be unnecessary, because the reader would already have come to the same conclusion without the need for so much research and inquiry. Those who are less certain about rejecting Christianity often find themselves unconvinced by those who have already made a definitive decision in that regard. This helps us understand why the Life of Jesus researchers remain largely unread today—except when encountered through a *Geschichte* like Schweitzer's, which demonstrates just how much their work remains a child of its age.

At the conference at which this chapter was originally presented, flyers and programs were adorned with an image of Hans Holbein's *Body of the Dead Christ in the Tomb*. This painting, which hangs in the Basel Kunstmuseum, had a famously profound impact on Dostoevsky himself; he made use of it in one of his novels, and several conference participants made reference to it during the event. I had not previously considered the relationship between that painting and the issues that I raise in this chapter, but at the conference, it struck me as relevant in an interesting way. In particular, my reflections here may cast some light on Prince Myshkin's claim, in *The Idiot*, that the painting could lead one to lose one's faith. I certainly cannot explore this point in detail here, but I will mention it by way of conclusion—in the hope that others might take up the question in their own work.

Although he predated von Ranke by more than two centuries, Holbein worked at the very cusp of modernity. In his era, painters were beginning to strive toward a degree of realism that contrasted sharply with their medieval inheritance. In a sense, then, Holbein is painting Jesus in (what would later be described as) the mode of *Historie*, rather than that of *Geschichte*. This is, after all, precisely what a dead body would look like: there are no signs of divinity or holiness, and Christ's face is the very opposite of peaceful rest. Consider this painting in contrast to religious art created in a *geschichtlich* mode: such work is more concerned about the story (and thus also about the resurrection that would come) than it is about the details of documentary history. Western medieval painting bears this mark, as does Eastern Orthodox iconography.

As with visual imagery, so also with narrative accounts. Those that focus on the *res gestae*, the things that actually happened, will generate writing that lags behind the faith of its creator, a merely documentary depiction of the way things are. In contrast, those that focus on the *historia rerum gestarum*—the *narrative account* of the things that happened, the *Geschichte*—will encourage writing that advances ahead of the artist's or the author's faith. Such creative works keep the questions open and generate the kind of polyphonic depth for which Dostoevsky's fiction is rightly celebrated. The Christ that Dostoevsky professed he would hold onto, even against the truth, was not Holbein's dead body—not the historical figure of Jesus, about whose corpse definitive historical and scientific judgments could be made (and in fact had already been made). Rather, Dostoevsky's Christ was much closer to the figure that adorns Orthodox iconography: deeply embedded in the narratives of his life and his relationship to God. This Christ is a phenomenon, not of *historical*, but of *historic* significance.

Dostoevsky as Moral Philosopher

Charles Larmore

Introduction

My title refers, of course, to but one, limited aspect of Dostoevsky's enormous literary achievement. Even so, this subject is far too vast and complex for me to imagine that I could do it justice in a single chapter. I shall focus on *The Brothers Karamazov*, Dostoevsky's last great novel, published first serially in 1879–80 and then as a book in 1881.[1] Moreover, I shall be chiefly concerned with a single chapter in that work, namely, the famous chapter (bk. 5, ch. 5) about the Grand Inquisitor. Much has been written at length and insightfully about the diagnosis of the human condition that this chapter presents. I believe, however, that the deep moral truth that Dostoevsky wanted to communicate in it has largely gone unnoticed.

In the novel, the Grand Inquisitor chapter figures as an expression of Ivan Karamazov's thinking, a "poem in prose" (213) as he calls it, which he has composed and now recites to his brother Alyosha. It cannot therefore be regarded

---

1 I shall be relying on the translation by Constance Garnett of *The Brothers Karamazov*, 2nd ed., Norton Critical Edition, revised by Susan McReynolds Oddo (and Ralph Matlaw) (New York: Norton, 2011). Book, chapter, and page references to this edition will appear in the text.

as reproducing without qualification Dostoevsky's own thinking about the themes of good and evil, freedom, and faith that it treats. If any character's outlook comes close to Dostoevsky's own, it is rather Alyosha's. Yet Ivan—certainly in his discussions with Alyosha—appears to have all the arguments on his side, all the good arguments insofar as they involve evidence and reasoning. With this assessment I believe that Dostoevsky himself would agree. Ivan is the intellectual, more skilled in argument than anyone else in the novel and determined like no one else to live in the light of what arguments based on evidence can establish. Ivan, it could be said, embodies Dostoevsky's thinking about what argument alone can achieve in dealing with the great questions of life. We cannot therefore understand Alyosha's special strength, namely, his wholehearted goodness and the way it represents for Dostoevsky our highest possibility as moral beings, until we see Ivan's arguments and how Alyosha does not so much refute them as demonstrate their limitations by what he does. In fact, Dostoevsky depicts the same superiority of showing by deed to showing by argument in the inner conflict in which Ivan himself is trapped.

Ivan and the Problem of Evil

The principal idea Ivan wishes to convey in the encounter he imagines between the Grand Inquisitor and Christ is that man has no desire for the freedom that consists in following one's own conscience, but craves instead submission to authority. I shall have more to say about how his "poem in prose" gives dramatic expression to this conviction. First, however, we need to consider another basic component of his view of the human condition, one which also plays a role in that story. It appears in the two preceding chapters (bk. 5, chs. 3–4), which describe the meeting between Ivan and Alyosha in a restaurant. There Ivan explains how reflection on the problem of evil has led him to the conclusion that atheism is the only intellectually coherent position.

The existence of evil in the world and especially of innocent suffering, as in the case of children, cannot be reconciled, Ivan insists, with the concept of a wise and loving God who is supposedly the ruler of the world. "I took the case of children," he exclaims to Alyosha,

> only to make my case clearer. Of the other tears of humanity with which the earth is soaked from its crust to its center, I will say nothing. ... Men are themselves to blame, I suppose; they were given paradise, they wanted

freedom, and stole fire from heaven, though they knew they would become unhappy, so there is no need to pity them ... But then there are the children, and what am I to do about them? That's the question I can't answer. ... Listen: if everyone must suffer in order to buy eternal harmony with suffering, what do children have to do with it, tell me, please? It's utterly incomprehensible, why should they suffer too, and buy harmony with suffering? Why should they also furnish material to enrich the soil for the harmony of the future? ... When the mother embraces the torturer who threw her child to the dogs, and all three cry aloud with tears, "Thou art just, O Lord!," then, of course, the crown of knowledge will come and everything will be explained. But what pulls me up here is that I can't accept that harmony. And while I am on earth, I hasten to take my own measures. (211–12)

In this passage, Ivan alludes to the central argument that has been given ever since St. Augustine to explain why evil exists in a world that is under God's control. The problem is the problem of *theodicy*, of finding a way to justify God, who is supposedly omniscient, omnipotent, and all-loving, against the charge that he has been unjust, if not indeed cruel, in creating such a world as this. Augustine's solution was to exonerate God by putting the blame for the world's misery upon man: it is we who have brought evil into the world by our own free will in choosing to disobey God, and all the suffering that makes up human history is both the result and the just retribution—the "harmony," as Ivan calls it—that God has arranged for our evil-doing.[2] Yet this justification, Ivan complains, fails abjectly in the face of the suffering of innocent children, who have done no wrong.

It is important to observe that Ivan's complaint against the Augustinian solution consists in holding it to be not theologically or metaphysically but, rather, morally unacceptable. This kind of objection has a long tradition. Its foremost exemplar was Pierre Bayle, who in his great *Dictionnaire critique et historique*, first published in 1697 and one of the founding documents of the Enlightenment, developed a series of counterarguments that are all of the same form as Ivan's.[3] The attempt to relieve God of any blame for the world's evil and

---

2 See, especially, Augustine's treatise *De libero arbitrio*. An English translation is *On the Free Choice of the Will*, trans. Anna S. Benjamin and L. H. Hackstaff (New York: Macmillan, 1964).

3 Pierre Bayle, *Historical and Critical Dictionary*, trans. Richard Popkin (Indianapolis: Bobbs-Merrill, 1965). It is unlikely that Dostoevsky ever read Bayle. But he may well have been acquainted with Leibniz's *Essais de théodicée* (1710), which are an extended reply to

suffering and to place it entirely upon man because of his wrong-doing leads to a conception of God that conflicts with the most elementary principles of morality. The trouble, Bayle saw, stems from the assumption that God must possess all three attributes of omniscience, omnipotence, and infinite benevolence. Any two of them alone without the third—that is, if we supposed that God was not all-knowing, or not all-powerful, or not all-loving—would accord with the way the world is. But, as he put the point with a picturesque example, a mother who allowed her young daughters to go to a dance, certain that they would be seduced there, but contenting herself with exhorting them to be virtuous and threatening to disown them if they returned dishonored, could not be said to love either her daughters or virtue very much. God's refusal to prevent men from misusing their freedom of choice, even though he knows in advance all the terrible consequences that will ensue, would be a gross moral dereliction if any human being were to do something similar. So too if God were to punish for one person's evil action others who did not even exist at the time it was committed. Yet this is precisely what God has supposedly done in making all of Adam's descendants bear the taint of original sin and inherit all the miserable consequences.[4]

Ivan's "Rebellion"—such is the title of chapter 4 in book 5—takes the form of the latter objection. He appears prepared to accept, perhaps only for the sake of argument, that those who have done evil deserve to suffer (even if, as Bayle's objection indicates, a loving God would have prevented them from doing wrong): "Men are themselves to blame, I suppose; they were given paradise, they wanted freedom, and stole fire from heaven, though they knew they would become unhappy, so there is no need to pity them" (211). But he scorns the idea of original sin, denying that children too, if they have done no wrong, deserve to suffer: "Children have no solidarity in sin, and if the truth really is that they are in solidarity with their fathers in all their fathers' evil doings, then that, of course, is a truth not of this world and is incomprehensible to me" (212). Indeed, as Ivan goes on, it becomes clear that such an idea is for him not merely incomprehensible, but morally repugnant: "I don't want harmony, for

Bayle's arguments and which contain the notorious pronouncement that this is the best of all possible worlds.

4   See, respectively, the articles entitled "Pauliciens" (note E) and "Pyrrhon" (note B) in Bayle's *Dictionnaire*, Bayle, *Historical and Critical Dictionary*, 177ff and 202ff.

the love of humanity I don't want it. ... They have put too high a price on harmony, we can't afford to pay so much for admission. And so I hasten to return my entrance ticket" (ibid.). Is Ivan not right to rebel? Christian theologians such as Augustine may have argued that children are not really innocent since tainted by original sin. But that rejoinder begs the question. For why should children who have themselves done no wrong be punished with inheriting a sinful nature that makes them deserving of suffering?

Ivan therefore refuses to join in the refrain of the pious, "Thou art just, O Lord!," given all the innocent suffering in the world. Even if those who have caused that suffering are punished, either by other men or by God, there can be no forgiveness for the perpetrators and no justice in the world when children who themselves had no part in the cycle of evil and suffering should have been allowed by God to be hurled into it: "If the sufferings of children go into the replenishment of that sum of suffering that is needed for the purchasing of truth"—by "truth" Ivan means the final revelation of God's purposes in the world—"then I declare ahead of time that all of truth is not worth such a price" (212). Surely, he taunts Alyosha, thinking no doubt of the utopian or revolutionary programs current at the time, you would not set out to create an ideal society, "building the edifice of human destiny with the goal of making people happy in the end," if it required "tortur[ing] one tiny little creation," one single innocent child (213). So how can you then accept that a just God administers the world along just such lines?

There can be no God, Ivan has concluded, because the course of the world contradicts the most elementary principles of justice. The world is "absurd" (211) in that it is morally unintelligible, that is, morally unjustifiable, and Ivan is resolved to "stick to that fact" (ibid.) rather than to betray it by believing that the world is nonetheless, somehow, the creation of a just and loving God. Ivan appears, then, as I have said, to have all the arguments on his side. Our moral sense along with our knowledge of how the world goes—of human evil and the suffering it produces, even among the innocent—show that there can be no God. Significantly, Alyosha offers no other rejoinder to Ivan's arguments than the assertion that Jesus gave his own innocent blood "for all and everything" (213). Ivan is unimpressed. And why should he be moved? For how can Jesus's sacrifice justify God's having created such a world in the first place? Ivan's arguments remain intact.

However, Alyosha's reply is also the occasion for Ivan to relate what he thinks about the figure of Jesus himself. This he does in the story about the Grand Inquisitor he goes on to tell. The aim of the story is to drive home the irrelevance of Jesus's teachings to the human condition, and in this regard it draws upon one of the two cardinal elements in Ivan's thinking we have met: his determination to stick to the evidence about the way the world is. However, the overall view of life he bases on the moral of his story brings him, as we shall see, into contradiction with his other cardinal commitment: his passionate sense of justice.

The Grand Inquisitor

Ivan's "poem in prose" (213) describes Christ returning to sixteenth-century Seville at the height of the Spanish Inquisition and encountering the Grand Inquisitor. It is an encounter rather than a conversation. For to the Grand Inquisitor's justification of the obscurantist and authoritarian religion that Christianity has become, to his "correction," as he puts it (223, 226), of Christ's gospel of spiritual freedom, Christ himself says nothing, just as Alyosha had no counterargument to offer against the reasons that Ivan gave in the preceding chapter for rejecting God's existence. The Grand Inquisitor also appears to have all the arguments on his side. Indeed, he is a persona through which Ivan voices his own opinions about Christ's teachings, based once again on the facts about the way world goes. Thus he too, as Ivan acknowledges, must be understood as having come to believe that there is no God (227).

Let us look more closely at the story Ivan tells. Christ has arrived in Seville, not as part of the Second Coming but for a brief visit to be with the faithful when so many are being burned as heretics *ad majorem gloriam Dei*. When he first appears in the city, all the people immediately recognize him for who he is and flock around him because of his "gentle smile of infinite compassion" (216). Yet when the Grand Inquisitor comes upon the crowd and, arresting Christ, has him taken away, no one protests—an echo of the scene in the garden of Gethsemane in which Jesus's disciples failed to speak up or defend him against arrest by the Roman authorities. Instead, everyone bows and submits to the Grand Inquisitor. Later, once Christ is in prison, the Grand Inquisitor tells him why he has been removed from the people who were welcoming him: "Thou hast no right to add anything to what Thou hadst said of old" (217). For the Church, he explains, has in fact had to correct Christ's work, which was fundamentally defective.

What was the defect? Christ, he objects, had preached a gospel of freedom that is ill-suited to man's nature. He had called for a faith in God that is freely given, unconstrained by bodily needs, awe of the supernatural, or desire for power over others. That was shown by his refusal to give in to the three temptations offered him by the devil in the desert: to make bread out of stones to relieve hunger, to leap from a pinnacle in the expectation that angels would break his fall, and to worship the devil in return for rule of the world. In the same vein he had taught an ethic of universal love, a reflection of his own infinite compassion, which exhorted people to care about others without regard for their own interests. Christ's central message was therefore that men should follow the example of his freedom of spirit in transcending the confines of their usual concerns. But this sort of freedom, the Grand Inquisitor complains, is not at all what people want or can even achieve: "Thou didst choose what was utterly beyond the strength of men" (221).

What human beings most crave are instead "miracle, mystery, and authority" (222, 223), and of these three, authority most of all, a source of direction from the outside showing them how they should think and act and forming therefore an object of awe that they can then revere together in the comfort of a "community of worship" (221). "That is what we have given them," he boasts. "That is how we have corrected Thy work" (223). Authority provides security, security from physical need, but also security from the anxiety of not knowing what to do: "Man is tormented by no greater anxiety than to find someone quickly to whom he can hand over that gift of freedom with which this ill-fated being is born" (221). In saying this, the Grand Inquisitor shows that he does not dispute that human beings have the ability to imagine suspending their immersion in the ways of the world in order to love others for their own sake and to think for themselves. His conviction, however, is that such freedom is a possibility they flee since they lack the strength of mind to exercise it. They want to be free from this freedom, and so much so that they rush to conceive of freedom itself in terms that presuppose a framework of authority. They want to believe that freedom consists in knowing one's way around in the world, according to the conventional definitions of things, and in thus being able to get what one wants. Corrected Christianity has simply sought to meet this need. Its aim, the Grand Inquisitor explains, has been to persuade people "that they will only become free when they renounce their freedom and submit to us" (224). And indeed, he boasts to Christ, the work of redefinition has been successful. "Today people are more persuaded than ever that they have perfect freedom," inasmuch as "they have brought to us their freedom"—that is, the radical freedom that Christ extolled—"and laid it humbly at our feet" (218).

The one-sided debate that Ivan has orchestrated between the Grand Inquisitor and Christ revolves, then, around two opposing ideas of human freedom. The freedom that Christ extolled is the freedom to rise above our own sphere of concerns, and that means first and foremost our deep-rooted need to feel secure in the world, which involves adapting to its ways and reigning assumptions. We have instead the capacity to take up an impartial standpoint toward the world, to judge for ourselves what is right and wrong, and thus to look beyond our own good—whether it is our individual self-interest or the interests of those to whom we happen to feel close—in order to make the good of others generally the object of our attention, in the pure, disinterested "love of humanity" that Christ is portrayed as exemplifying.[5] This *freedom of conscience*, as the Grand Inquisitor calls it (221), is not in his view a freedom that human beings really desire. It is too strenuous and too disorienting. The freedom they seek and that he aims to ensure them is instead precisely the ability to satisfy their own concerns, which are what they most care about, and that means above all a liberation from the insecurity they most dread. This idea of freedom thus sticks to the facts, as Ivan likes to say. It is a freedom, the *instrumental freedom* of being able to get what one wants, that fits in with the evidence about why as a rule we act as we do.

In insisting that such freedom alone is what human beings prize, the Grand Inquisitor is basing himself on the way the world goes. That is why Ivan, whose own thinking he embodies, portrays him as having all the arguments on his side. Thus, Christ does not dispute anything the Grand Inquisitor says. He offers no counterargument, and indeed he says nothing at all during the whole encounter. What is striking is what Christ *does*:

---

5   For more on this conception of the moral point of view, see my essay: Larmore, "Reflection and Morality," *Social Philosophy and Policy* 27, no. 2 (2010): 1–28; also found in *Moral Obligation*, ed. E. F. Paul et al. (Cambridge: Cambridge University Press, 2010), 1–28.

> The old man longed for Him to say something, however bitter and terrible. But He suddenly approached the old man in silence and softly kissed him on his bloodless ageless lips. That was all his answer. (228)

This kiss springs from the pure, other-directed love that Christ professed. It is not, however, merely an expression of that love. It is also, as Ivan says, an answer to the Grand Inquisitor. For though he has no argument to refute the contention that the radical freedom he proclaimed is not what men most desire, all the evidence seeming to favor the Grand Inquisitor, Christ aims to demonstrate by kissing his adversary that transcending the usual course of the world is nonetheless possible. Moreover, the ease with which he steps forward to kiss him suggests that the sort of freedom this act expresses is not so difficult or disorienting as the Inquisitor and many others suppose. Christ's purpose is not to *show by argument* that the Inquisitor's point of view is wrong. It is to *show by deed* the limitations of basing one's view of mankind's possibilities on the evidence of what human beings usually think and do.

It may seem puzzling why Ivan should include in his story so apparently powerful a reply to the arguments of the Grand Inquisitor. How can doing so accord with his belief that one should stick to the facts and fit one's conception of the human condition to what experience tells us is the way things generally go? Yet it is to be remembered whose reply it is. Ivan does not deny, nor does the Grand Inquisitor who speaks for him, that Christ exhibited the freedom of looking beyond one's own concerns and following the impartial dictates of conscience. The point is rather that the rest of humanity has no desire for such freedom, regarding it instead as a source of anxiety. Ivan accordingly intends Christ's kiss to appear as an act that, however magnificent, is so alien to the normal patterns of human motivation that it only confirms the moral of his story. That is why he has the Grand Inquisitor, though initially taken aback, see in it no reason to change his position: "The kiss glows in his heart, but the old man adheres to his idea" (228).

What Ivan does not anticipate is Alyosha replying in the same fashion to the overall outlook his poem in prose is meant to illustrate. When he has finished his story, Alyosha asks him where, "with such a hell in your heart and head" (228), he can draw the strength to live, particularly if he believes, as appeared in a conversation the day before, that since God does not exist there is no moral law and "everything is permitted" (229). Must not such an outlook lead to utter dissolution? Ivan replies that perhaps it must, but that he will not disown the idea that everything is permitted, even if this means his brother will no longer love him. Another question one could well raise is how he can hold such an idea, given his passion for justice, and I shall return to that problem in the next section. Here the important thing to observe is Alyosha's response to Ivan's bleak and negative profession of faith. He presents no counterargument. Rather, "Alyosha got up, went to him and softly kissed him on the lips" (ibid.).

Ivan jokingly dismisses the gesture. "That's plagiarism," he teases. "You stole that from my poem" (229). But Alyosha is not joking. As the novel reveals, he is in earnest about the *imitatio Christi*, earnest in his resolve to practice the self-transcending love of humanity that Christ embodied and taught. Nor, I believe, did Dostoevsky intend Alyosha's kiss to be regarded as a humorous incident. On the contrary, it is meant to impress upon the reader that it is a mistake to base one's estimate of humanity, as Ivan does, on the way the world usually goes. At the same time, Dostoevsky also wanted to convey that the best way to demonstrate that not just Christ but other human beings too can value the freedom of looking beyond their own concerns and caring about others for their own sake is not to invoke various facts and cases to substantiate this conviction. Alyosha produces no arguments against Ivan's contention (any more than Christ does against the Grand Inquisitor's). Given the preponderance of evidence at his disposal, Ivan could easily cast doubt on the reliability of the supposed counterevidence. The best proof of our capacity for radical freedom is instead to exercise it ourselves. It is to *show by our own deeds*, as Alyosha does, that we can choose to set aside our usual preoccupation with our own good.

Everything is Permitted

Ivan is determined to base his view of life on the evidence about how human beings generally think and act. That is why he cannot see the point that Alyosha is making in demonstrating the limitations of this stance. Yet it is also why he fails to see the contradiction that has emerged between his two cardinal commitments—that is, between his devotion to justice and his determination to stick to the evidence. On the one hand, he holds that there is no God, given the manifest injustice in the way the world goes. On the other hand, he has concluded, given the facts about human motivation, that if God does not exist, then there can be no moral law and everything is permitted. He has fallen into this inconsistency because his appeal to our sense of justice rejects the rules of right thinking his hard-headed realism enjoins. It rejects them, moreover, in much the same way as does the kiss that Alyosha gives him—not by way of counterargument, but by the very act it is, though Ivan does not recognize its import.

To see more exactly how the contradiction arises, let us look at how Ivan has arrived at the conclusion that if God does not exist, everything is permitted. That this is what he has come to believe is certain, even if that very sentence—probably the most famous one Dostoevsky is thought to have written—occurs nowhere verbatim in the novel. For Ivan does say things quite close to that sentence a number of times, as when he confirms Alyosha's impression of a conversation that occurred at Father Zosima's monastery the day before. In that conversation, which occurs earlier in the novel (bk. 2, ch. 6), Ivan confirms the report of a still earlier conversation in which he explained why, if there is no God or immortality, "nothing then would be immoral and everything would be permitted, even cannibalism" (65). Here is Ivan's reasoning. If human beings have ever acted morally, it has not been because they happen on their own to "love their neighbors," but only because they believed in God and immortality, that is, believed that God would otherwise punish them in the afterlife. "For every individual like ourselves," he added,

> who does not believe in God or immortality, the moral law of nature must immediately be changed into the exact contrary of the former religious law, and ... egoism, even unto crime, must become not only lawful but even recognized as the inevitable, the most rational, even honorable outcome of his position.

The key premise of this argument is the same analysis of human motives to which the Grand Inquisitor appeals: human beings inveterately pursue their own good alone and feel no impetus to take up an impartial standpoint and concern themselves with the good of others for its own sake. Ivan's justification for this assertion is also the same as the Grand Inquisitor's: it is abundantly confirmed by experience. The only way therefore in which human beings can be moved to treat others morally is that God makes it in their interest to do so. If, however, there is no God, then only "egoism" remains. It becomes a law unto itself, the "inevitable" and indeed the sole "rational" form of conduct. Ivan goes so far as to claim that in the absence of God moral principles themselves, and not just our reason to comply with them, must disappear.[6] He may mean that moral rules only exist if instituted by God. This sort of view, though sometimes voiced, undermines itself, for if one holds God to be the author of moral right and wrong, then one loses any basis for praising God for his goodness. More plausibly, however, Ivan may have in mind some version of the notion that "ought" implies "can": he may mean that it makes no sense to suppose we are bound by certain principles of conduct if we lack any motive that would impel us to comply with them. Such is, after all, precisely what he asserts to be true about the principles of morality if God does not exist.

Yet the difficulty is that Ivan himself relies upon moral principles in explaining to Alyosha why he believes that there is in fact no God. No just God, he argues, could have created a world in which innocent children suffer at the hands of evil-doers. Whence does Ivan draw his conception of what justice requires? And why does he care about the suffering children? These convictions entail looking beyond his own good in order to see in the good of others an object of intrinsic concern, and they do so, moreover, without any regard for the authority of a God. They therefore show Ivan to be moved by the sorts of considerations that, on the basis of sticking to the facts about human motivation, he denies to be within our capacity. They show him to be exercising that radical freedom in which he (like the Grand Inquisitor) denies that we have any interest. As is often true when people end up contradicting themselves, Ivan is not simply confused. Rather, his better self is giving the lie to the narrow-minded doctrine he has reasoned himself into professing.

This is what I meant by saying that one of Ivan's two principal commitments, his zeal for justice, *shows by what it is* the error in his other, that is, in his determination to base his view of humanity on the way the world generally goes. Unfortunately, Ivan fails to discern what that first commitment shows, just as he fails to grasp what Alyosha's kiss expresses. He never comes to see clearly the conflict in which he is caught. That is his tragedy. Perhaps the conflict in his character lies too deep for him to get hold of it. Eventually it leads him into madness, when he learns from his half-brother, Smerdyakov, that he has

---

6 Ivan calls them "the moral law of nature," alluding to the way that one philosophical tradition has conceived of the basic principles of morality as "natural law."

killed their father, Fyodor, in part because Ivan had convinced him that "everything is permitted" (bk. 11, chs. 8–9).

The crucial moral truth all these passages of *The Brothers Karamazov* illustrate is that in our concern for the good of others we demonstrate the freedom we have to transcend what the evidence would otherwise prove to be the character of human motivation. They also suggest that the same freedom shows itself in a faith in God that is freely given, not based in our various needs, a faith of the sort that Christ taught and that Alyosha emulates. Dostoevsky was not fundamentally a philosopher, of course. I am not sure how explicitly he articulated to himself this insight into the self-authenticating power of our freedom to rise above our usual selves. But one can grasp a truth without being able, or without feeling the need, to formulate it with conceptual precision. Indeed, important truths about human life often exert a hold on our attention only when they come embodied in a powerful story.

"If there's no immortality of the soul, … everything is lawful": On the Philosophical Basis of Ivan Karamazov's Idea

Sergei A. Kibalnik

In its various versions, the popular formula "If there is no God, … everything is lawful" is presented in many of Dostoevsky's works. It plays an especially significant role in his novel *The Brothers Karamazov*. It is commonly known that Dostoevsky determined "the main question which is asked" to be "the question of God's existence" (*PSS*, 29[1]:117).[1] As he confessed, that was the question that tormented him all his life.

In the second book of *Brothers Karamazov*, Piotr Miusov recites the words of Ivan Karamazov, who claimed,

> If there is and ever has been any love on earth, this is not from any natural law but simply because people believed in immortality … precisely in this consists the whole natural law, so that if you destroy humanity's faith in immortality, there will immediately dry up in it—not only love but also every living force necessary to perpetuate life on earth. Even more: there will

---

1 Dostoevsky, *Polnoe sobranie sochinenii v tridtsati tomakh* [*PSS*], ed. V. G. Bazanov et al. (Leningrad: Nauka, 1972–90); hereafter cited as *PSS* by volume and page.

no longer be anything immoral, everything will be permissible, even cannibalism. (*PSS*, 14:64–65)

Robert Louis Jackson shows the dialectics of this motive further developed in *Brothers Karamazov*. Let me quote here a long passage from his *Dialogues with Dostoevsky*, which will serve as a good introduction to my analysis:

> The torment of Ivan Karamazov as God-struggler is that he allows for the existence of a religious moral law but does not believe in the immortality of his soul or the goodness of man. He is a victim, finally, of the fatal logic of his position: believing absolutely in the concrete, as it were, day-to-day interdependence of virtue and faith but lacking personal belief in immortality, he arrives at the intellectual position that "all is permissible." His moral nature will not permit him openly to sanction the death of his father, but his ideas are picked up by his disciple Smerdyakov, who implements them with a ruthless logic.

The practical implications of Ivan's proposition—"There is no virtue if there is no immortality"—for an unbeliever are grasped immediately by Dmitry Karamazov: "Excuse me … have I heard things right? 'Villainy must not only be permitted but even recognized as the inevitable and even rational outcome of his position for every atheist'! Is that so or not?" "Precisely," says Father Paissy. "I'll remember that," says Dmitry. Dmitry draws these conclusions; in the end, however, he does not act upon them. "If there is no eternal God, then there is no virtue," he reminds Ivan in his last meeting with him, adding, "And, indeed, there's really no necessity for it."

It is this final conclusion, this simplistic deduction, this intoxicated leap into crime and chaos—"And, indeed, there's really no necessity for it"—that lies hidden in Ivan's speculations and deeply troubles Dostoevsky. How is one to surmount the fatal logic of this either–or: either faith or cannibalism, either beatitude or nihilistic despair? Such are the extreme choices that inhere in Ivan's notion that "there is no virtue if there is no immortality." "You are blessed in believing that, or else most unhappy," Zosima remarks perceptively addressing to Ivan. "Why unhappy?" Ivan asks, smiling. "Because in all probability you don't believe yourself in the immortality of your soul." Ivan has left himself, and mankind, little room for maneuver or morality.

Ivan finds nothing in man, no action of the eternal law in man's conscious-ness, to counteract his criminal tendencies to guide him toward salvation. Hence his reliance on an authoritarian church-state. The position of Father Zosima is quite different. Like Ivan, he believes in a universal church "at the end of the ages." In the meanwhile, however, he does not despair. While Ivan places his hope in social-religious compulsion and excommunication, Zosima believes in the divine law acting in man and in "the law of Christ expressing itself in the recognition of one's own conscience." Zosima essentially affirms a faith in man's conscience, in the possibility of man freely arriving at a sense of truth and good-ness through his own consciousness.[2]

Having placed this motive in the framework of Augustinian and Pelagian theological controversy, Jackson quite reasonably concludes that "Ivan's posi-tion would seem to gravitate toward radical Augustinian doctrine, or Jansenism, according to which post-Fall man lacks the power to abstain from sin and can be saved only by virtue of God's grace," while Zosima's thought "would seem to gravitate in the direction of Pelagian doctrine, which places less emphasis on the original sin and affirms man's perfect freedom to do right and wrong and, in the end, to discover his path of salvation."[3] According to Jackson, Ivan's view-point also evokes quite reasonable parallels with Thomas Hobbes's ideas.[4] For her part, Valentina Vetlovskaya, in her commentaries published in the Academy edition of Dostoevsky's *Complete Works*, refers in this regard to Blaise Pascal (*PSS*, 15:536). Yet, the question concerning the philosophical basis of this motive in the framework of nineteenth-century European philosophy that was contemporaneous for Dostoevsky is still open.

In a way, Ivan Karamazov's formula ("If there is no God . . .") already prom-ises the next step, taken by Nietzsche, who in his *The Gay Science*, published after Dostoevsky's death, declared that "God is dead." However, there was another philosopher who, when Dostoevsky was young, claimed that God—at least in his conventional concept—did not exist, pronouncing religion as the "objectification" of human consciousness. This was Ludwig Feuerbach. The above phrase is to be found in his book *The Essence of Christianity* (1841), of

---

2   Robert Louis Jackson, *Dialogues with Dostoevsky: The Overwhelming Questions* (Stanford, CA: Stanford University Press, 1993), 295–98.

3   Ibid., 298.

4   Ibid., 297.

which, as noted by Sergei Bulgakov and then commented on by Vadim Belopolsky and Igor Smirnov, Dostoevsky was aware. It had an impact on his works, starting at least from *Notes from the Dead House* and *Notes from Underground*.[5]

But in Ivan Karamazov's formula, "If there's no immortality of the soul ... everything is lawful" (*PSS*, 14:93), one can trace not only the impact of Feuerbach's famous book but also of its critique made by another German philosopher of the 1840s—Max Stirner, whose book *The Ego and His Own*, which was published in the end of 1844, produced a shock in philosophical circles of Europe.[6] The influence of this philosopher on Dostoevsky was already discussed by Nikolay Otverzhennyi and Sergei Kibalnik,[7] and by Takayoshi Shimizu and Marcos Galounis.[8] Nevertheless, up to now there has been little attention among Dostoevsky scholars to the fact that the first part of Stirner's book contains a sharp interpretation of Feuerbach's *Essence of Christianity* as an "abolition of faith" and that Stirner's declaration of individualism and immoralism was a direct conclusion from Feuerbach's anthropotheism. All moral relations, affirms Stirner, "are ethical, are cultivated with a moral mind, only where they rank as religious of themselves."[9] Since "higher powers exist only through my exalting them and abasing myself," my "relation to the world,"

---

5   S. N. Bulgakov, "Religiia chelovekobozhiia u L. Feierbakha," in *Sochineniia v dvukh tomakh* (Moscow: Nauka, 1993), 2:181. V. N. Belopolskii, *Dostoevsky i filosofskaia mysl' ego epokhi* (Rostov: Rostov University Press, 1987), 165–85. I. P. Smirnov, "Otchuzhdenie-v-otchuzhdenii: 'Zapiski iz Mertvogo doma' v kontekste evropeiskoi filosofii 1840 gg. (Feuerbach and Co.)," in *Kak literatura otzyvaetsia na filosofiiu* (St. Petersburg: Petropolis, 2010), 59–72.

6   Max Stirner, *Der Einzigee und sein Eigentum* (Leipzig, 1845).

7   N. Otverzhennyi, *Shtirner i Dostoevskii* (Moscow: Golos truda, 1925); S. A. Kibalnik, "Dostoevskii i Maks Shtirner," in *Dostoevskii i sovremennost': Material XXVI Mezhdunarodnykh Starorusskikh chtenii* (Velikii Novgorod: Novgorod Museum Press, 2012), 172–79; S. A. Kibalnik, "On Dostoevsky's Anti-Rationalism, Its European Parallels and Its Followers," in *Russian Thought in Europe: Reception, Polemics, Development*, ed. T. Obolevich, Thomasz Homa, and Josef Bremer (Kraków: Wydawnictwo WAM, 2013), 73–92.

8   See abstracts of their papers: Takayoshi Shimizu, "Dostoevsky and Max Stirner," accessed March 25, 2016, http://catalog.lib.kyushu-u.ac.jp/handle/2324/24632/p%28vi%29.pdf; Marcos Galounis, "Political Nihilism in Dostoevsky's *Crime and Punishment*," paper given at the 15th Simpozium Mezhdunarodnogo obshchestva Dostoevskogo "Dostoevskii i zhurnalism," 34–35 (Moscow: Mezhdunarodnoe obshchestvo Dostoevskogo, 2013).

9   Max Stirner, *The Ego and His Own*, trans. Steven T. Byington, with an introduction by J. L. Walker (New York: Benj. R. Tucker, 1907), 43; http://www.df.lth.se/~triad/stirner/theego/theego.pdf. Hereafter I will use in-text citations by page number.

claims Stirner, is that "I no longer do anything for it, 'for God's sake,' I do nothing 'for man's sake,' but what I do I do 'for my sake'" (158). An introduction to Stirner's book concludes with the declaration: "The divine is God's concern; the human, man's. My concern is neither the divine nor the human, not the true, good, just, free, etc., but solely what is *mine*, and it is not a general one, but is—unique, as I am unique. Nothing is more to me than myself!" (18).

The denial of not only God but of Feuerbach's "God-man," and the declaration of "my self-enjoyment," is the main idea of Stirner's book. So, Ivan Karamazov simply reproduces Stirner's objection to Feuerbach when he declares,

> that for every individual, like ourselves, who does not believe in God or immortality, the moral law of nature must immediately be changed into the exact contrary of the former religious law, and that egoism, even to crime, must become not only lawful but even recognised as the inevitable, the most rational, even honourable outcome of his position. (*PSS*, 14:64–65)

Dostoevsky must have faced the above-mentioned ideas of Feuerbach and Stirner as early as in the 1840s at the parties at Petrashevsky's house. The writer once made a speech there "about personality and individualism" in which he "wanted to prove that there is more ambition than real human dignity between us, and that we all fall into self-abasement, self-annihilation due to petty ambition, egoism, and aimlessness of occupations" (*PSS*, 18:129). This speech is supposedly permeated with Stirner's ideas. But if so, then it is actually directed against them. Dostoevsky could have borrowed a copy of Stirner's book from Petrashevsky.

Apparently, Stirner's ideas were shared by some other members of Petrashevsky's circle, and first of all by Nikolay Speshnev, who is an obvious prototype of several of Dostoevsky's characters (e.g., Nikolay Stavrogin). As it was noted in the commentaries for the Academy edition of the *Complete Works* of Dostoevsky, Speshnev, in his *Letters to Khoetsky* (1847), "criticizes Ludwig Feuerbach's anthropotheism": "Anthropotheism is also a religion but a different one. There is another object of deification—newly made, but the fact of deification itself is not new. Instead of God-man now we have Man-god. Only the word order has changed. Is there a big difference between God-man and Man-god?" (*PSS*,

12:222). The commentators argue that Speshnev "delicately criticizes anthro-potheism" (ibid.).

However, here Speshnev does not offer his own criticism of the anthro-potheism of Feuerbach but rather retells Stirner's. And it is not accidental that this letter was written in German. In *Ego and His Own*, we read: "Man has killed God in order to become now—'sole God on high.'" *The other world outside us* is indeed brushed away, and the great undertaking of the Illuminators completed; but *the other world* in us has become a new heaven and calls us forth to renewed heaven-storming: "God has had to give place, yet not to us, but to—Man. How can you believe that the God-man is dead before the Man in him, besides the God, is dead?" (85). Speshnev also recalls Stirner's thoughts in other passages of his *Letters to Khoetsky* where he emphasizes the difference between "me" and "man" in very similar words. For the sake of brevity, I omit here some textual parallels.

It is obvious then that in the mid-1840s Speshnev was in a way Stirner's follower. (This was overlooked by Speshnev's biographers, including Ludmila Saraskina, the author of the most recent biography of Speshnev.)[10] In 1845, possibly after his reading Stirner, Speshnev called himself a man who "lost shame."[11] At the time, he was living abroad with a Polish woman, who had left her husband for him. That is why he must have enjoyed the dedication in Stirner's book: "TO MY SWEETHEART MARIE DÄHNHARDT" (even though Marie was already Stirner's wife when his book came out).

When Dostoevsky met Speshnev a few years later, he saw him as a strong personality, and afterwards he recognized his extreme influence on his own ideas. At one of Petrashevsky's parties Speshnev gave a speech on religion in which he denied the existence of God.[12] Speshnev's life and behavior in general were marked by "willfulness" and, as is well known, brought to life the character of Stavrogin. As we will see, he also played an essential part in Dostoevsky's shaping of Ivan Karamazov.

In his *Letters to Khoetsky*, Speshnev also predicted that "humanity won't stop at anthropotheism" and that "anthropotheism is not an eventual result, but

---

10 L. I. Saraskina, *Nikolai Speshnev: Nesbyvshaiasia sud'ba* (Moscow: Nash dom—L'Age D'Homme, 2000).

11 Ibid., 125.

12 Ibid., 375.

only a transitional theory. ... To my mind, it is just a track, keeping [to] which Germany and science will come to the complete and unconditional denial of religion."[13] Here Speshnev also openly develops Stirner's idea, which stated that "the fear of God in the proper sense was shaken long ago, and a more or less conscious 'atheism,' externally recognizable by a wide-spread 'unchurchliness,' has involuntarily become the mode. But what was taken from God has been superadded to Man" (100).

Claiming that anthropotheism is just a route on which Germany and science will come to a complete and absolute negation of religion, Speshnev, along with Stirner, sounds similar to Dostoevsky, who regarded Feuerbach's philosophy as a serious step towards atheism. For Speshnev, atheism is an inevitable and justified stage: "And at last, is it really necessary to reduce all the data of a certain period to one and the only idea?"[14] But for Dostoevsky in the 1870s it is, on the contrary, an alarming symptom.

Russian religious philosophers clearly saw Max Stirner's philosophy as a reaction to *Essence of Christianity* by Feuerbach. For example, Semion Frank, in his *Ethics of Nihilism*, wrote: "Strictly logically, from nihilism in the moral field one can conclude only nihilism, that is immoralism, and Stirner did not have many difficulties while explaining this to Feuerbach and his followers."[15] Boris Vysheslavtsev, in his *Ethics of Transfigured Eros*, came close to acknowledging that Dostoevsky's works were a philosophical reaction to the attempts to replace God with man or with the self.[16]

But the specific form of this reaction is a very controversial issue that is still under debate. It is not quite clear whether Dostoevsky, while denying Stirner's position, takes Feuerbach's side. There are some things in *Brothers Karamazov* that make us think so. For example, Rakitin, who finds Ivan Karamazov's way of thinking outrageous, believes in a mankind. "Humanity will find in itself the power to live for virtue even without believing in immortality. It will find it in love for freedom, for equality, for fraternity" (*PSS*, 14:76). This recalls Feuerbach's philosophy. Feuerbach, as he argued himself, "transformed ethics into

---

13 N. A. Speshnev, "Pis'ma k K.E. Khoetskomu," in *Filosofskie i obshchestvenno-politicheskie proizvedeniia petrashevtsev* (Moscow: Gospolitizdat, 1953), 496.

14 Ibid.

15 S. L. Frank, *Sochineniia* (Moscow: Pravda, 1990), 84–85.

16 B. P. Vysheslavtsev, *Etika preobrazhennogo Erosa* (Moscow: Respublika, 1994), 115–16.

religion."[17] Still, it is certainly meaningful that this approach is demonstrated by the character whom the narrator calls "a young man bent on a career" (14:71). Another character who "so loves humanity" that she "often dreams of forsaking" her ill daughter and "becoming a sister of mercy" is Madame Khokhlakov, clearly caricatured by Dostoevsky.

Obviously, Dostoevsky's position is essentially different from those of Rakitin and Madame Khokhlakov. And it is directly formulated in a section of *Diary of a Writer* for 1876 called "Unsubstantiated Statements": "I declare (again, without substantiation, at least *for the moment*) that love for humanity is even entirely unthinkable, uncomprehensible, and *utterly impossible without faith in the immortality of the human soul to go along with it*" (italics in the original).[18] Jackson finds it significant that Dostoevsky's remarks are made in this particular section (also called "Arbitrary Assertions" in another translation) and that Dostoevsky "prefaces his remarks by saying that he intends 'to amuse' those 'gentlemen of ironclad ideas' who believe that love for humanity and its happiness is all set, comes about cheaply and without a thought. Dostoevsky's above-cited remark is provocative and ironical, and directed against interlocutors who have never really confronted or deeply responded to real suffering."[19] But what is provocative in the following Dostoevsky statement, which was more than once rephrased by him in other works?—"My article 'The Sentence' concerns the fundamental and the loftiest idea of human existence: the necessity and the conviction that the human soul is immortal"[20] (*PSS*, 24:46). Isn't Jackson trying to find in Dostoevsky's journalism the ambivalence that is fully present only in his novels? But I do completely share his point of view "that in *The Brothers Karamazov* Dostoevsky finds Ivan's statement acceptable as a theological truism, as an affirmation of the divine unity of all aspects of God's world, but

---

17 Ludwig Feuerbach (anonymous), "*The Essence of Christianity* in Relation to *The Ego and Its Own*," trans. Frederick M. Gordon, http://www.lsr-projekt.de/poly/enfeuerbach.html.
18 Fyodor Dostoevsky, *A Writer's Diary*, ed. with an introduction by Gary Saul Morson, trans. and annotated by Kenneth Lantz (Evanston, IL: Northwestern University Press, 2009), 1:735–36.
19 Jackson, *Dialogues with Dostoevsky*, 294.
20 Dostoevsky, *Writer's Diary*, 1:736.

as a guide to action, he finds Ivan's proposition limited, dogmatic, and dangerous."[21]

Indeed, Dostoevsky approaches the issue of interdependence of virtue and faith in a radically different way than Ivan Karamazov:

> Ivan insists that love and virtue can come to one only through faith. Zosima, however, believes that belief in God and faith are inseparable from love. "Try to love your neighbors actively and ceaselessly," Zosima counsels Mrs. Khokla-kova. "To the extent that you succeed in love, you will become convinced in the existence of God and in the immortality of your soul. But if you reach the point of total self-renunciation in love for your neighbor, then without ques-tion you will believe, and no doubt will be able to enter your soul."[22]

Zosima's idea of active love seems to be close to Dostoevsky's own view of Orthodox Christianity.

Ivan's starting point is the same as Dostoevsky's. Ivan is also convinced of a firm interdependence of faith in God, the immortality of the soul, and morality. Yet, unlike Dostoevsky, Ivan ends up proclaiming immoralism. Dostoevsky appears to see clearly that Stirner's idea of "ego" and "self-enjoyment," which make everything permitted, is just a logical consequence of Feuerbach's philosophy. And Ivan's problem is perhaps an excessive logic, that is, rationalism; a lack of any emotional attitude; and, most of all, a lack of love for other people.

Jackson's statement that Dostoevsky's response to Ivan is to remind him that it is "not virtue through faith but faith through love"[23] seems to me abso-lutely well founded. "Faith which comes through love"—that is certainly true. And, according to Dostoevsky, virtue is achieved through one's love for other people. The "active love" advocated by Zosima turns out to be a recipe both for faith in immortality (not in immortality in general, but in the immortality of one's soul) and at the same time for moral action. Alyosha's kiss, and Christ's kiss in Ivan's poem, presents a symbolic image of such forgiving love.

It may seem, however, that Dostoevsky suggests coming back from Stirner to Feuerbach, who also regarded love as a significant factor. But, according to Feuerbach, "love is practical atheism, the negation of God by the heart, by the

---

21 Jackson, *Dialogues with Dostoevsky*, 294.
22 Ibid., 300.
23 Ibid., 294.

feelings, in fact."[24] Proclaiming himself a "communist," Feuerbach meant "love" as "love for humanity." In the meantime, this principle of "love for mankind" was the target of keen criticism by Dostoevsky, both in his novels and in his journalism.

In "Unsubstantiated Statements," Dostoevsky declares,

> Love for humanity is even entirely unthinkable, uncomprehensible and *utterly impossible without faith in the immortality of the human soul to go along with it.* Those people who deprived humanity of its faith in its own immortality want to replace that faith, in the sense of the meaning of the highest purpose of existence, by "love for humanity." Those people, I say, are raising their hands against themselves; for in place of love for humanity they plant in the heart of a one who lost his faith the seed of hatred for humanity. Let all those wise men of cast-iron convictions shrug their shoulders at this statement of mine. But this thought is wiser than their wisdom, and I believe without a doubt that it will someday become an axiom for humanity.[25]

By "those people" Dostoevsky here apparently means Feuerbach and his followers.

In *Brothers Karamazov*, the confession of a doctor, retold by Zosima, has a similar meaning, compromising Feuerbach's ideal of love for mankind:

> "I love humanity," he said, "but I wonder at myself. The more I love humanity in general, the less I love man in particular. In my dreams," he said, "I have often come to making enthusiastic schemes for the service of humanity, and perhaps I might actually have faced crucifixion if it had been suddenly necessary; and yet I am incapable of living in the same room with anyone for two days together, as I know by experience." (*PSS*, 14:53)

Ivan Karamazov says that his Grand Inquisitor has been "loving ... mankind" "all [his] life" (*PSS*, 14:238).

At the end of the novel, Kolya Krasotkin asks Alyosha Karamazov: "It's possible for one who doesn't believe in God to love mankind, don't you think so? Voltaire didn't believe in God and loved mankind?' ('I am at it again,' he thought to himself.)" Alyosha answers: "Voltaire believed in God, though not very much, I think, and I don't think he loved mankind very much either." The narrator's comment on how Alyosha said this is quite remarkable—"quietly,

---

24 Feuerbach (anonymous), "*The Essence of Christianity* in Relation to *The Ego and Its Own*."

25 Dostoevsky, *A Writer's Diary*, 1:736.

gently, and quite naturally, as though he were talking to someone of his own age, or even older. Kolya was particularly struck by Alyosha's apparent diffidence about his opinion of Voltaire. He seemed to be leaving the question for him, little Kolya, to settle" (*PSS*, 14:500). This comment is in a way analogous to the title of Dostoevsky's article "Unsubstantiated Statements," fairly commented on by Jackson. Alyosha's "diffidence" reminds us of Dostoevsky's proclaiming his own assertions as "arbitrary." Both words are aimed at eliminating any pattern of dogma, which was always alien to the writer. Dostoevsky's manifestations of faith were always styled in such a way, both in his literary works and in the *Diary of a Writer*. Without sharing Stirner's anarchical individualism, Dostoevsky advocates coming back to the "immortality of the soul," which was rejected by Feuerbach.

Ivan's discourse on "if there is no God . . ." clearly fits this pattern. "I don't know whether or not it has been sufficiently pointed out that [Ivan's formula] is not an outburst of relief or of joy, but rather a bitter acknowledgment of a fact," asked Albert Camus, who continued, "The certainty of a God giving a meaning to life far surpasses in attractiveness the ability to behave badly with impunity. The choice would not be hard to make. But there is no choice, and that is where the bitterness comes in."[26] No wonder Jean-Paul Sartre turned Ivan's statement upside down. And the essence of existentialism was formulated by Sartre in the following way: "Nothing will be changed if God does not exist ... even if God existed that would make no difference from its point of view. Not that we believe God does exist, but we think that the real problem is not that of His existence; what man needs is to find himself again and to understand that nothing can save him from himself, not even a valid proof of the existence of God."[27] Ivan Karamazov's idea, which according to Camus is partly Dostoevsky's one, was regarded by Sartre as the starting point of existentialism.

In this respect, both European and Russian existentialism seem to follow Feuerbach and many other partisans of the Pelagian tradition in European philosophy rather than Dostoevsky. But as Jackson has shown, according to

---

26 Albert Camus, *The Myth of Sisyphus and Other Essays*, trans. Justin O'Brien (1955), 44, http://www.dhspriory.org/kenny/PhilTexts/Camus/Myth%20of%20Sisyphus-.pdf.

27 Jean-Paul Sartre, "Existentialism Is a Humanism," in *Existentialism from Dostoyevsky to Sartre*, ed. Walter Kaufman, trans. Philip Mairet (Meridian, 1989), https://www.marxists.org/reference/archive/sartre/works/exist/sartre.htm.

Dostoevsky the primary force is love—"not virtue through faith but faith through love—this is Dostoevsky's reply to Ivan."[28] So one can say that Sartre followed Zosima rather than Ivan Karamazov. And thus he still followed Dostoevsky.

As we can see, the "voices" of Dostoevsky's characters are to a certain extent associated with the ideas of European philosophers of the mid-nineteenth century. And the twentieth- century European and Russian philosophers—Nietzsche and Camus, Semion Frank and Sergei Bulgakov—clearly found their philosophical frameworks in Dostoevsky's novels.

The complicated dialectics of faith and morality, disbelief and Man-godhood, love for one's neighbor and love for mankind in *Brothers Karamazov* cannot be understood without taking into account their interdependence with contemporaneous philosophical discourses.

---

28 Jackson, *Dialogues with Dostoevsky*, 302.

PART

3

Questions of Aesthetics

Once Again about Dostoevsky's Response to Hans Holbein the Younger's *Dead Body of Christ in the Tomb*

Robert Louis Jackson

*Ma qui la morta poesì resurga,
o sante Muse, poi che vostro sono.*

—Dante, Purgatorio 1:7–8

1

I begin my discussion of Dostoevsky's response to Holbein's *Dead Body of Christ in the Tomb*[1] with some commentary by St. Augustine in his *Confessions*[2] on the problem of *formed formlessness*.

Augustine's discussion turns on the first two lines of *Genesis*: "In the beginning God created the heaven and the earth. But the earth was invisible and without form, and darkness was upon the deep."[3] He accepts the notion that "before the Lord formed this unformed matter and fashioned it into kinds,

---

1 Henceforth in the text I refer to Holbein's painting as (*The*) *Dead Christ*.
My earliest discussion of Dostoevsky and Hans Holbein the Younger's painting *The Dead Christ in the Tomb* (*Der Leichnam Christi im Grabe*, 1521/1522) may be found in my study, *Dostoevsky's Quest for Form: A Study of His Philosophy of Art* (New Haven, CT: Yale University Press: 1966), 66–69 et passim. I returned to my discussion of Holbein and Dostoevsky in a paper at the symposium of the International Dostoevsky Society in Naples, Italy, in 2010.
2 Dostoevsky mentions Augustine's *Confessions* in his notebook for 1875–76. See *Polnoe sobranie sochinenii v tridtsati tomakh* [*PSS*], ed. V. G. Bazanov et al. (Leningrad: Nauka, 1972–90), 27:113n; hereafter cited as *PSS* by volume and page.
3 The Russian Slavonic Bible translates the first line of *Genesis* as *Zemlia že bě nevidim i ne ustroen* ("But the earth was invisible and unformed").

there was no separate being, no color, no shape, no body, no spirit," that is, there was only the earth "unformed." He insists, however, that "there was not absolutely nothing"; rather "there was a certain formlessness devoid of any specific character."[4]

"Formlessness" for Augustine, then, is not *nothing*, but *something*. Yet he is bothered: "Why," he asks the Lord, "may I not perceive that the formlessness of matter which you made *without beauty*, but from which you made this beauteous world, is effectively indicated when called "'earth invisible and without form'?"[5]

Augustine's dilemma is plain: the moment he tries to perceive or conceive *formless* matter, he comes up with *forms*, that is, with embodiments of formlessness that are unsatisfactory precisely because they are *forms or images*. The issue for him is not only aesthetic but also ethical and spiritual:

> I formerly conceived [the formlessness of matter] as having countless different forms, and therefore I did not conceive it at all. My mind turned over forms, foul and horrid in confused array, but still forms. I called it formless not because it lacked all form, but because it had such form that, if it ever showed itself, my senses would have turned away from it as from something strange and improper, and man's frail powers would be disturbed by it. But what I was thus thinking about was formless not from lack of all form, but by comparison with better formed things.[6]

Augustine's discussion does not end here. I would like to rest, however, with his posing of the problem of *formless form* and his distinction between lesser and better formed things, a notion essentially of two kinds of beauty.[7]

2

The question of two kinds of beauty, essentially that of formless form, turns up in an exchange between Anna Grigorievna Dostoevsky and Fyodor Mikhailovich Dostoevsky on the occasion of their viewing of Holbein's

---

4 See *The Confessions of St. Augustine*, trans. with an introduction and notes by John K. Ryan (Garden City, NY: Doubleday, 1960), 12.3, p. 306.

5 Ibid., 12.4, p. 306.

6 Ibid., 12.6, p. 307.

7 Augustine earlier in *Confessions* formulates his concept of two kinds of beauty when, in connection with his youthful interest in the pleasures of the flesh, he distinguishes between "lower beauties" and "lower goods," on the one hand, and "lower beautiful creatures" and creatures of "grace and beauty," on the other: "Do we love anything except that which is beautiful? What then is a beautiful thing? What is beauty?" (ibid., 4.13, p. 106).

painting *The Dead Christ* in the Historisches Kunstmuseum in Basel, Switzerland, on August 12, 1867.

In her stenographic *Diary* for this date, Anna Grigorievna contrasts her own view of Holbein's *Dead Christ* with Dostoevsky's response to that work. "This astonishing work simply filled me with horror," she writes, "but Fedya was so struck by Holbein's *Dead Christ* that he proclaimed Holbein a remarkable artist and poet." (*a Fediu tak do togo porazilo, chto on provozglasil Gol'beina zamechatel'nym khudozhnikom i poetom*). Like Ippolit Terentiev in Dostoevsky's *The Idiot* (1868–69), though without his spiritual turmoil, Anna Grigorievna contrasts the usual classical representation of Christ's body —one without marked wounds or lacerations—with what she regards as Holbein's repulsive, albeit well-executed, depiction of Christ's crucified body. She goes on to describe in detail the horrible mutilations inflicted on Christ's body, concluding that Holbein's dead body of Christ so strikingly "resembled an actual corpse that, really, I would not have wanted to be in the same room with it."

"Granted that all this has striking verisimilitude," she writes, "but really it is not at all esthetic[8] [*no, pravo, eto vovse ne estetichno*] and aroused in me nothing but revulsion and a kind of horror." And for the second and final time in her *Diary* account, Anna Grigorievna underscores Dostoevsky's strong dissent: "Fedya, however, was ecstatic over this painting" (*Fedia zhe voskhishchalsia etoi kartinoi*). "Wanting to examine it more closely," she concludes, "[Dostoevsky] stood on a chair to examine it, and I very much feared that he would be fined for it."[9]

Dostoevsky's words, "a remarkable artist and poet," constitute the highest praise he could offer any painter or writer. The word "poet" is sacred in his vocabulary. It embodies not only the notion of inspiration, but of imagination and insight, vision and prophecy, elements central to his concept of fantastic realism. Implicit, then, in his initial response in Basel to the *Dead Christ* is a conception of realism and reality as multidimensional and of an aesthetics of form and beauty as more inclusive than classical beauty, even as the highest Beauty, the beauty of Christ remains for him transcendent and an ever unattainable ideal.

8　The phrase *ne estetichno* suggests also "tasteless."
9　A. G. Dostoevskaya, *Dnevnik* (1867), ed. S. V. Zhitomirskaya (Moscow: Nauka, 1993), Basel, Thursday, August 12 [new style: August 24], 1867.

As his dramatization in *The Idiot* of Holbein's *Dead Christ* attests, Dostoevsky posits in Holbein's painting a powerful and complex spiritual pro and contra. His response to Holbein's *Dead Christ* in Basel, however, is of signal importance in that it underscores the aesthetic and spiritual *point of view* that underlies his employment of Holbein's *Dead Christ* in the apocalyptic universe of *The Idiot*.

Forty years after viewing Holbein's *Dead Christ* in Basel, Anna Grigorievna Dostoevsky returns to the topic of her husband's response in Basel to Holbein's *Dead Christ*. In her posthumous *Reminiscences* (1925), Anna Grigorievna, ignoring entirely her earlier *Diary* account in 1867 of Dostoevsky's affirmative response to Holbein's *Dead Christ*, now speaks of the "devastating impression" (*podavliaiushchee vpechatlenie*) that Holbein's painting made upon Dostoevsky: he stood before it "as though stunned"; she recalls her concern that Dostoevsky might have had one of his epileptic fits.[10] In one of her notes to the 1906 edition of *The Idiot*, referring to the page where Prince Myshkin remarks that "a person looking at this [Holbein's] painting could lose his faith," Anna Grigorievna recalls that Dostoevsky was "terribly shaken up" by Holbein's painting, adding that "at that time" he "told me that 'a person looking at this painting could lose one's faith.'" "Later in life," she writes, "Dostoevsky would often recall the terrible impression this painting made upon him."[11]

There can be no doubt that Holbein's *Dead Christ* made a tremendous impression on Dostoevsky, but why did Anna Grigorievna completely ignore her *Diary* account in 1867? Did she conflate Dostoevsky's response to the *Dead Christ* with Ippolit Terentiev's critique of Holbein's painting? Her unwillingness or inability to reconcile her later account of Dostoevsky's reaction to Holbein's *Dead Christ* with her earlier one suggests not only her own personal bias, but a misunderstanding of art and of an author's relation to his characters. In any case, her later recollections combine with her earlier ones to underscore

---

10 See A. G. Dostoevskaya, *Vospominaniia* (Moscow: Izdatel'stvo "Pravda," 1987), 185–86. See also the English version of these recollections, *Dostoevsky: Reminiscences*, trans. and ed. Beatrice Stillman, with an introduction by Helen Muchnic (New York: Liveright: 1975), 133–34.

11 Cited in L. P. Grossman, *Seminarii po Dostoevskomu: Materialy. Bibliografiia i kommentarii* (Moscow-Petrograd: Gosizdat, 1922), 59.

Dostoevsky's deep and intense involvement with the great pro and contra Holbein's *Dead Christ* in his novel, *The Idiot*.[12]

3

Dostoevsky's writings and criticism in the period following his return from Siberia foreground important concepts of realism and reality that he brought to his interpretation and understanding of Holbein's *Dead Christ*. Central here is the distinction he repeatedly draws between natural or actual truth and artistic truth in the fine arts and in writing. In a harsh review of the Russian painter Valery I. Jacobi's *Prisoners at a Stopping Place* (*Prival arestantov*, 1861), exhibited at a St. Petersburg Academy of the Arts exhibition in 1861, Dostoevsky agrees that the painting's representation of the scene is "exact as it is in nature ... if you look at nature, so to speak, only from the outside, as though you were looking in a mirror or photograph." Yet this simply "attests to the absence of art." There is absolutely no "truthfulness" in Jacobi's painting, Dostoevsky declares. This is not "reality," but a "lie." Of course, he concedes, the artist must know the ABC's of reality, but he "first of all must overcome the difficulties of transmitting actual truth in order to rise to the heights of artistic truth."[13]

This principle of realism was not new to Dostoevsky, but it was one that acquired a deep spiritual and populist meaning for him during his years of trial and prison and exile in Siberia. He embodied this principle in his semi-autobiographical *Notes from the House of the Dead* (1861–62). In this work he depicts the brutal existence of prison convicts, but at the same time sees through what he calls the "repulsive crust" of their condition to their intrinsic humanity. The accomplishment of *Notes from the House of the Dead*, a triumph of artistic and spiritual truth over natural truth (though without concealing the horrendous reality of prison

12 Take, for example, these lines from one of Dostoevsky's early plans for his novel when the Idiot, in a conversation about Christ's moment of despair on the cross ("The passion on the cross shatters the mind"), calls attention to Christ's "terrible cry." "What cry?" his interlocutor asks. "Eloi! Eloi!" "So there was an eclipse." "I don't know—but it was a terrible cry," the Idiot answers. Dostoevsky directly follows this exchange with the line: "The story of Holbein's 'Christ' in Basel" (*PSS*, 9:184).

13 *PSS*, 19:154.

life) was the restoration of the image of the wounded and disfigured image of the Russian people.

Dostoevsky found in the writing of Victor Hugo an aesthetic-spiritual outlook congenial to his own. In a preface to the publication in 1862 of a translation of Hugo's *Hunchback of Notre Dame* (*Notre Dame de Paris*, 1831)[14] Dostoevsky defends the French writer against the charge that his aesthetic method could be summed up in the phrase *Le laid, c'est le beau*—"ugliness is beautiful." Hugo's basic idea, a "Christian and supremely moral one," was the "restoration of fallen man"; Hugo's so-called monster, the deformed but kindly Quasimodo, is for Dostoevsky the embodiment of the "oppressed and despised, dumb and disfigured" (*glukhogo i obezobrazhennogo*) French people of medieval times "in whom there is an awakening of love and a thirst for justice."

Hugo's aesthetics of "beauty and ugliness" early entered Dostoevsky's own stream of aesthetic thought. At the age of seventeen he had read Hugo's ground-breaking *Préface de Cromwell* (1827).[15] Hugo wrote there,

> The division of the beautiful and ugly is not symmetrical with that of nature. Nothing is beautiful and ugly in the arts except through execution. An ugly horrible, hideous thing, transported with truth and poetry into the realm of art, becomes beautiful, admirable, without losing anything of its monstrosity.

Hugo's observations broadly anticipate Dostoevsky's response to Holbein's painting in Basel. The Romantic aesthetic of another writer, the English poet John Keats, opens up pathways to an understanding of Dostoevsky's reception of Holbein's *Dead Christ* and his realism. In a letter to his two brothers in 1817, Keats remarks of the Anglo-American painter Benjamin West's painting, *Death on a Pale Horse*: "It is a wonderful picture, but there is nothing to be intense upon. ... The excellence of every Art is its intensity, capable of making all disagreeables evaporate from their being in close relationship with Beauty and Truth. Examine *King Lear* and you will find this exemplified

---

14   *PSS*, 20:28–29.
15   In a letter to his brother Mikhail, August 9, 1838, Dostoevsky mentions Hugo's *Cromwell* as part of his reading; see *PSS*, 28(1):51.

throughout: but in [West's] picture we have unpleasantness without any momentous depth of speculation."[16]

Keats's idea of "burying" "disagreeables" does not at all mean eliminating them from a work of art. What he looks for, and finds in Shakespeare, and what Dostoevsky found in Holbein's *Dead Christ* and dramatized in *The Idiot*, was an intensity and momentous depth of speculation, a pro and contra, that put the work in close relationship to the highest aesthetic and spiritual values.

What Dostoevsky found in *The Dead Christ* he did *not* find in Mikhail P. Klodt's *The Last Spring* (*Posledniaia vesna*, 1861), a Gold-Medal painting in the Academy of Arts exhibition in 1861. In his review of this exhibition, Dostoevsky sharply condemns *The Last Spring*, along with Jacobi's *Prisoners at a Stopping Place*, for its naturalism. Death is at the center of the painter's attention: "*The Last Spring* depicts a dying young woman in a chair, looking sadly towards a window opening onto a bright spring day." The painting is "a remarkable one," Dostoevsky comments, the "whole painting is beautifully painted, but as a whole," he remarks abruptly, "the painting is far from beautiful. Who wants to hang such a pathological painting in his office or living room? It goes without saying, nobody, nobody." Nobody, he exclaims, needs this "poisonous" "perpetual *memento mori*." "Taken by itself death is a repulsive business. But waiting for death is far more repellent. The artist has chosen for himself an extraordinarily difficult task: nobody will ever succeed in representing the repulsive in a beautiful way."

Dostoevsky allows that there are "dramatic works that represent dying on the stage," but he argues that one cannot depict a dying person on the stage "according to all the rules of pathology, systematically conveying natural truth as it happens in nature." Dostoevsky illustrates his point by offering a verbal sketch of a dying person who sits up, gazes about and "rolls his eyes like a bad provincial actor playing Othello." An audience, he argues, "would rush away from such a performance." But Mr. Klodt, he continues, presents us with the

---

16 Letter of John Keats to his brothers George and Thomas, December 28, 1817; see John Keats, *Complete Poems and Letters*, ed. Clarence DeWitt Thorpe (New York: Doubleday, Duran & Co., 1935), 527–28. In the same letter, Keats amplifies on the quality he finds Shakespeare's achievement: "I mean *Negative Capability*, when a man is capable of being in uncertainties, Mysteries, doubts, without any reaching after fact and reason" (ibid.). In a certain sense we can speak also of Dostoevsky's *Negative Capability* with respect to his dramatization of Holbein's *Dead Christ* in *The Idiot*.

agony of a dying person and the agony of a whole family not just for one day or for a month but "eternally, as long as that beautifully executed, but unfortunate painting hangs on the wall." "No," Dostoevsky concludes, "artistic truth is not that at all, it is something quite different from natural truth."[17]

Whatever the shortcomings of Mikhail P. Klodt's painting, it is not "pathological" in character. Rather, Dostoevsky's angry and agitated response to the *Last Spring* touches on the pathological. Contemporaneous with his review, he was publishing his semifictional recollections of *House of the Dead*: a world where a fatalistic *waiting for death*, on the one hand, and rebellion of all sorts against the fatality of prison life, on the other, marked everyday existence. Klodt's "picture on the wall" plunged Dostoevsky back into the pathos and pathology of the prison world. He found no higher spiritual truth in Klodt's painting, no hint of anything beyond the "last spring," only "natural truth," a perpetual reminder of death as doom.

In Dostoevsky's review of *The Last Spring*, finally, one hears the irascible and strained voice of his Underground Man as he will lash out at the so-called wall in *Notes from Underground* (1864): "Twice two is four, gentlemen, is not life, but the beginning of death." We hear too Dostoevsky's irascible voice—the voice of the critic of *The Last Spring*—in the near hysterical response of Ippolit Terentiev to Holbein's *Dead Christ*—a work, in Ippolit's view, that depicts "nature" crushing a "great and precious being." Yet throughout his depiction of Ippolit's rebellion we also hear in the subtext Dostoevsky's critique of a man, Ippolit, who has suffered a crisis of aesthetics and faith and cannot break through to a broader aesthetic and spiritual vision.

4

The phrase "two kinds of beauty," or, more exactly, "two nice kinds of beauty," turns up in Dostoevsky's notebook on *The Idiot* a little more than six months after he saw Holbein's painting in Basel. The use of the diminutive *obrazchika* signals irony in the question Ippolit puts to Prince Myshkin shortly before he, Ippolit, begins to read his "necessary explanation": "Is it true, Prince, that you said 'beauty' will save the world? ... What kind of beauty will save the world?"[18]

---

17   *PSS*, 19:167.
18   *PSS*, 8:317.

Myshkin has in mind higher beauty, the beauty and perfection of Christ. Ippolit has in mind Holbein's representation in his painting of the disfigured body of Christ, a depiction in which he finds "not a trace of beauty." "What kind of beauty will save the world?" That question, and its implicit challenge to faith, is at the core of Ippolit's critique of Holbein's *Dead Christ*. He in general finds "nothing good about it in artistic respects" (*v nei ne bylo nichego khoroshego v artisticheskom otnoshenii*)—a fact of significance.[19] Yet his feeling of "strange unrest" (*strannoe bespokoistvo*) on looking at *The Dead Christ* indicates that Holbein's painting has struck a spiritual chord in his memory. In looking at this painting it seems to Ippolit as if "nature" in the form of some "huge, implacable and dumb beast" or "huge machine" had senselessly seized, torn up, and devoured "a great and precious being," such a one who was "worth the whole of nature, its laws, and the whole earth which perhaps was created solely for the appearance of this being alone!" It is noteworthy that in his telling, Ippolit does not *name* this "precious being," does not utter the word "Christ," as he does elsewhere; nor does he in any way see or visualize the image, or *obraz*, of Christ, that is, he experiences no epiphany, no sense of Christ's presence or perfection. Rather he experiences Christ as something precious that has been *lost*, as something that remains as a "tremendous thought." What he does directly see, however, is the *disfigured* body of Christ in Holbein's painting.

5

It is a fact of Ippolit's character, of Dostoevsky's characterization of him, that in his egoism and intellection he is to a large extent unaware or unconscious of the latent spirituality within him. He is unaware that he carries within the idea of love and self-sacrifice; he does not know that he is imitating Holbein's Christ when he lies down, eyes wide open and focused on the icon at the foot of his bed. He is like Columbus, Dostoevsky suggests, a man who had discovered America, but without knowing it. Ippolit will never pass over the threshold of egoism to belief. Nonetheless, he has a keen and telling, indeed tormented, interest, in the crisis of aesthetics and faith.

---

19 *PSS*, 8:338–39. Here, of course, is the fault line separating Ippolit's view of Holbein's painting from Dostoevsky's. The failure of Ippolit to see Holbein's painting as a work of art and poetry is correlative in Dostoevsky's view with his failure to recognize, on the conscious plane at least, the spiritual action of the painting. The crisis of faith is inseparable for Dostoevsky from the crisis of aesthetics.

Of great interest in this connection are his brief reflections on the terrible impact the disfigured and crucified body of Christ must have had on his disciples and followers. Noteworthy in his discussion is his use of the Russian word *obraz*—"image, form, icon, beauty,"[20] in the highest sense of the word, the *imago Dei* or perfect image of Christ of Orthodox tradition; its counterpart is *bezobrazie*—literally, that which is "without image," i.e., the misshapen, the deformed, the scandalous, the ugly. Christ suffered not figuratively, but in actuality (*Khristos stradal ne obrazno, a deistvitel'no*), Ippolit remarks: "If precisely such a corpse had been seen by his disciples and apostles; if it had been seen by women who had followed after him and stood by the cross, who had believed in him and worshipped him, then how [*kakim obrazom*; literally, "with what kind of image before them"] could these people, on looking at that corpse, have believed that this sufferer would resurrect?" In short, how could they retain faith in the Resurrection in the presence of the totally disillusioning actuality of a brutally disfigured Christ?[21]

---

20 "'*Obraz*' has been called the 'axis of beauty' in the Russian language"—"L'image, dans la langue russe, est l'axe de la Beauté." See Lydie Krestovsky, *La laideur dans l'art a travers les ages* (Paris: Editions du Seuil, 1947), 36.

21 The crisis of aesthetics and faith is tersely dramatized with respect to dead bodies of family kin—though not, at least overtly, with regard to the dead body of Christ in the tomb—in one of the liturgical verses sung on Trinity Parental Saturday (*Troitskaia roditel'skaia subbota*) or All-Souls Day, the Eastern Orthodox church service commemorating the family dead):

> I weep and sob when I picture death and see lying in the tombs, disfigured, inglorious, without any form, our beauty created in the image of God. O, miracle! What is this mystery that was performed over us? How were we given over to corruption? How were we joined with death? Verily, by the will of God, as is written, giving us the rest that was presented to us.
>
> Плачу и рыдаю, / когда себе представлю смерть / иувижу в гробницах лежащую / по образу Божию созданную нашу красоту / безобразной, бесславной, не имеющей вида. / О чудо! / Что это за совершившееся над нами таинство? / Как мы были преданы тлению? / Как сочетались со смертью? / Воистину повелением Бога, как написано, / подающего преставившимся упокоение.

The singer here *pictures* the disintegration and decay of the bodies of kin, "our beauty created in the image of God," lying in the tomb. He does not speak of shaken faith, but his weeping and sobbing, his leap to "miracle," his agitated questions, suggests a subtext of spiritual anxiety, and a sense of the poverty of words before the *sight* of disfigured (*bezobraznye*) bodies of loved ones in the tomb. It is no accident that this verse is followed by one that offers a reassuring verbal *picture* of joyous family reunion in heaven.

I thank Olga Meerson of Georgetown University for drawing my attention to this liturgical verse.

Ippolit has projected his own crisis of aesthetics and faith onto the followers of Christ. He brings the whole matter to a head with his question, "Can one perceive in an image that which has no image?" (*Mozhet li mereshchit'sia v obraze to, chto ne imeet obraza?*). The question alludes in part to his own despairing response to Holbein's painting: his delirious dreams where he has seen monstrous things. Like Augustine, he is troubled by "strange, impossible form"; he sees all sorts of terrible, unimaginable, so to speak, un-image-able things "even in images." On the other hand, the notion of "a great and precious being" arises in his consciousness as he rages against Holbein's painting. In this context Ippolit's question falls into the same category as the one that perplexed Augustine: Why could he, Augustine, not visualize the beauteous world that the Lord had created out of formless matter?

Ippolit's question may thus be rephrased: Can one perceive *obraz* (the "highest beauty," the "perfection" of Christ) in *bezobrazie*, that which is "without image," in short, ugly, monstrous, disfigured? The answer, in Russian, is hidden in plain view. *Obraz* is the central, indestructible component of *bezobrazie*. Ippolit will never internally *visualize* his ideal, aesthetically and spiritually. As Dostoevsky wrote in his review of Jacobi's painting: "In ancient times they would say that the artist must see with physical eyes and, above all, with eyes of the soul, or with a spiritual eye."[22] Ippolit lacks that kind of "eye." Yet in looking at Holbein's painting he experiences a shock: a collision between his residual ideal, (the "great and precious being") and the reality of a world-historic violation of that ideal, a collision between purity and pollution, form and disfiguration, *obraz* and *bezobrazie*.

"*Les extrêmes se touchent*" ("opposites meet"), Ippolit remarks with reference to himself and Rogozhin shortly after viewing a reproduction of Holbein's *Dead Christ* in Rogozhin's house and before Rogozhin describes the impact Holbein's painting had upon him. Ippolit's words evoke the ancient philosophical concept of the unity of opposites; they speak of an unconscious awareness of the paradoxically affirmative action the pro and contra of Holbein's *Dead Christ*.

Can one perceive *obraz* in *bezobrazie*? Can one perceive the highest beauty in the utmost darkness and degradation? "The need for beauty and the creation

---

22 *PSS*, 19:54.

which it embodies," Dostoevsky wrote in "Mr. –bov and the Question of Art" (1861) not too long after his return from prison and exile, "is inseparable from man, and without it man, perhaps, would not want to live in the world. ... The need for beauty develops most at the moment man is in discord with reality, in disharmony, in struggle. ... In beauty there is both harmony and tranquility."[23]

These thoughts, on the personal plane, echo the profound and transforming spiritual crisis of Dostoevsky in his prison years. On his release from prison in Omsk in January 1854, he writes in a letter to Natalia D. Fonvizina of his sufferings there and of how at moments he would "thirst for faith, like withered grass and find it exactly because truth dawns in misfortune [*v neschast'e iasneet istina*]." This "thirst to believe grows all the stronger in my soul the stronger the opposing arguments." In "moments of complete tranquility," Dostoevsky writes, he would "compose his symbol of faith": that "there was nothing more beautiful, profound ... and perfect than Christ."[24]

The concept of a basic need in man for beauty, a longing for something to venerate, on the one hand, and of truth, beauty, faith emerging in misfortune, struggle, disharmony, in discord with reality, on the other, is at the heart of Dostoevsky's understanding of Holbein's *Dead Christ* in *The Idiot*, of its action, of its pro and contra, of the spiritual movement it arouses in the viewer. There is no final outcome of this action, no grand synthesis and new thesis. Dostoevsky predicts nothing, but he promises *movement*, "*Les extrêmes se touchent*." Rogozhin, reflects Myshkin, "says that 'he likes to look at this painting'; he doesn't; rather it seems, he feels a need .... he wants to get back his lost faith by force.[25] He needs it now to the point of torment. Yes! to believe in something! to believe in somebody!" Myshkin utters these last words as though grasping some new thought; indeed, he appears to have broadened his understanding of the impact of the *Dead Christ*. "But still," he reflects, as though another thought had entered his head, "how strange this painting is." Myshkin does not elaborate. Is he thinking about the pro and contra of Holbein's *Dead Christ*? Myshkin, as we know, declares

---

23 *PSS*, 18:94.
24 *PSS*, 28(1):176.
25 For Dostoevsky, of course, "force" is not a path to faith, as it is not a solution in human relations, a fact that is all too evident in the denouement of Rogozhin's relation to Nastasya Filippovna.

that "some people could lose their faith in looking at this painting." "*Some people*"–but not *everybody*. Again, Myshkin does not elaborate on this point.

Ippolit Terentiev experiences a feeling of "strange unrest" on looking at Holbein's *Dead Christ*.

A sense of permanent unrest and unease, bad dreams, and endless imaging of, and striving for, the unattainable ideal—here is where Dostoevsky leaves us.

6

Early on in the *The Idiot*, Prince Myshkin remarks: "I dare say I am indeed a philosopher, and who knows, perhaps, and in real fact, I have the thought of teaching." In one of his studies, Leonid Grossman suggested that Dostoevsky planned to include in *The Idiot* an interpretation by Prince Myshkin of Holbein's *Dead Christ*: "Questions of atheism and faith, realism and naturalism would have occupied a big space."[26] Dostoevsky plainly concluded that such a broad discussion *from above*, accompanied by aesthetic and spiritual self-awareness from below, would be inconsistent with his development of the character and fate of Myshkin in his apocalyptic novel. Whatever the reasons, Dostoevsky canceled Myshkin's lecture, leaving it to us to ponder again, and again, the great questions surrounding his response to Holbein's *Dead Christ* in Basel in 1867 and his dramatic employment of the painting in *The Idiot*.

---

26 Leonid Grossman, *Dostoevskii* (Moscow: Molodaia gvardiia: 1962), 405–6.

Prelude to a Collaboration: Dostoevsky's Aesthetic Polemic with Mikhail Katkov

Susanne Fusso*

As the editor of the *Russian Herald*, Mikhail Nikiforovich Katkov was one of the most important figures in the development of the nineteenth-century Russian novel. *Fathers and Sons*, the first parts of *War and Peace*, *Anna Karenina*, and the major novels of Dostoevsky all appeared in the pages of his journal. But it seems impossible for us to evaluate his role without emotional distortion. Our understanding of Katkov's literary activity and contribution has been greatly complicated by his vigorous political activity. In parallel with his literary efforts, as the editor of the newspaper the *Moscow News* he was a towering political figure who advocated Russian nationalism and autocracy and agitated vigorously against radical and revolutionary movements. Because of this, seventy years of Soviet-era Russian literary history had to treat him as *persona non grata*. His literary role was consistently minimized or presented in its most unfavorable light. The situation in the West has been somewhat similar. Throughout the twentieth century, Western literary scholars tried to take a critical, objective approach to the ideologically constrained productions of Soviet scholars while

---

* Forthcoming in *Editing Turgenev, Dostoevsky, and Tolstoy: Mikhail Katkov and the Great Russian Novel* by Susanne Fusso; reprinted with permission from Northern Illinois University Press. Copyright © 2017 Northern Illinois University Press.

still relying on their formidable archival, historical, and philological resources. No matter how critical one's approach, it was very hard not to be influenced by the incessant negativity surrounding the image of a figure like Katkov (a negativity that he in many ways deserved). I am working on a study of Katkov's literary activity, in particular his relations with Belinsky, Evgeniya Tur, Turgenev, Dostoevsky, and Tolstoy. My plan is to offer a view of Katkov's literary activity that avoids the two extremes of pariah and paragon, giving him his due as the important figure he was, without vilification or canonization.

Of all Katkov's relationships with Russian writers, his association with Dostoevsky was perhaps the most important and lasting relationship of his literary career. Dostoevsky published all his most celebrated novels in Katkov's *Russian Herald* (founded in 1856): *Crime and Punishment* (1866), *The Idiot* (1868), *The Devils* (1871–72), and *The Brothers Karamazov* (1879–80); his seminal Pushkin speech was published in Katkov's newspaper the *Moscow News* in June 1880, six months before Dostoevsky's death.[1] Dostoevsky's letters from 1865 on make it clear that he relied on Katkov for virtually continuous financial support through payment of advances on his work in progress. Yet their relationship began inauspiciously in 1858–59, with Katkov's rejection of Dostoevsky's novella *The Village of Stepanchikovo and Its Inhabitants*, and continued in the form of a fairly rancorous polemic between the two men, carried on in the pages of their respective journals in 1861–63.

Dostoevsky and Katkov had very little face-to-face contact, even during the years of their most intense collaboration. We have quite a few letters from Dostoevsky to Katkov, but not many from Katkov to Dostoevsky have survived. So the journalistic polemic offers us a chance to study a kind of dialogue between the two men, a dialogue that preceded a long and productive working relationship. In their skirmishes over aesthetics, in general, and Pushkin, in particular, one can see not only their vehement clashes but also the points of inner, fundamental agreement that can help us understand what made possible

---

1   The only lengthy novel that Dostoevsky published elsewhere was *A Raw Youth* (*Podrostok,* 1875), which he published in *Notes of the Fatherland.* Whether coincidentally or not, this novel is considered the least successful of Dostoevsky's major works. The pioneering study in English of Katkov's literary career is by Catharine Theimer Nepomnyashchy, "Katkov and the Emergence of the *Russian Messenger,*" *Ulbandus Review,* no. 1 (1977): 59–89. See also E. V. Perevalova, *Zhurnal M. N. Katkova "Russkii vestnik" v pervye gody izdaniia (1856–1862): Literaturnaia pozitsiia* (Moscow: Moskovskii gosudarstvennyi universitet pechati, 2010).

their fruitful, if sometimes contentious, partnership. In this chapter I will touch on a few of the highlights of this complex interaction.

Toward the end of Dostoevsky's nine years of imprisonment and exile in Siberia that began in 1849, as he was trying to reenter Russian literary life from a seemingly unbridgeable distance, he turned to the *Russian Herald*, which he referred to in a letter of 1857 as "indisputably the primary Russian journal at the present time."[2] In 1858 Dostoevsky requested and obtained an advance from Katkov for his work in progress, one of the first two works he wrote after prison, *The Village of Stepanchikovo*. But after he had submitted the manuscript and asked for a higher honorarium than he and Katkov had agreed to, the *Russian Herald* rejected the work in 1859. One can hardly be surprised by this: both *Village of Stepanchikovo* and "Uncle's Dream," the other work written in Siberia, can be seen today as eccentric masterpieces, but in genre and tone they are farcical and unrealistic, more suited to the 1840s than to the atmosphere of social and political ferment represented by the *Russian Herald*.

Dostoevsky was personally stung by the difficulty of his reentry into Russian literary life. In a letter to his brother Mikhail of October 1859, he despairs about the negotiations with another editor, Nikolai Nekrasov of the *Contemporary*, the man who had been Dostoevsky's first editor in 1846.[3] Dostoevsky suspects that Nekrasov had made inquiries at the *Russian Herald* on the sly, that they had told him "the grapes were sour," and that Nekrasov was consequently offering insultingly low terms for publishing his novella (*PSS*,

---

2 F. M. Dostoevsky, *Polnoe sobranie sochinenii v tridtsati tomakh* [*PSS*], ed. V. G. Bazanov et al. (Leningrad: Nauka, 1972–90), 28(1):288 (letter of November 3, 1857, to M. M. Dostoevsky); hereafter cited as *PSS* by volume and page. William Mills Todd III is completing a study of the poetics and pragmatics of serialization in the nineteenth-century novel, and he has discussed Dostoevsky's working relationship with Katkov in several articles: "The *Brothers Karamazov* and the Poetics of Serial Publication," *Dostoevsky Studies* 7 (1986): 87–97; "Dostoevsky's Russian Monk in Extra-Literary Dialogue: Implicit Polemics in *Russkii vestnik*, 1879–1881," in *Christianity and the Eastern Slavs*, vol. 2 of *Russian Culture in Modern Times*, ed. Robert P. Hughes and Irina Paperno (Berkeley: University of California Press, 1994), 124–33; "Dostoevsky as a Professional Writer," in *The Cambridge Companion to Dostoevsky*, ed. W. J. Leatherbarrow (Cambridge: Cambridge University Press, 2002), 66–92; and "Tolstoy and Dostoevsky: The Professionalization of Literature and Serialized Fiction," *Dostoevsky Studies* 15 (2011): 29–36.

3 *Poor Folk* (*Bednye lyudi*) first appeared in Nekrasov's *Peterburgskii sbornik* (St. Petersburg, 1846).

28[1]:346). Dostoevsky goes on to speak of himself as a "proletarian," dependent on the good will of editors: "But besides all these intrigues with the *Russian
Herald*, Nekrasov is a sensitive animal. After finding out the story with the
Russian Herald and knowing that I, after returning from Siberia, have spent all
my money and am in need, how can he not propose to such a proletarian a
reduction in price? 'He'll agree without fail!' they think" (ibid.). Indeed,
according to an associate of Nekrasov, he disliked the novella and said, "Dostoevsky is all used up. He won't write anything more" (28(1):507). For the man
who was among the first to recognize Dostoevsky's genius to say such a thing
was a devastating indicator of how far Dostoevsky had to go to regain his literary
position. In the end, the novella was published in A. A. Kraevsky's journal *Notes
of the Fatherland* in 1859.

The rejection of *Village of Stepanchikovo* seemed to tell Dostoevsky something important about how to connect with a Russian audience in the reformist
age that followed the death of Nicholas I in 1855. In 1859, in the same letter to
his brother in which he lamented the rejection of *Village of Stepanchikovo* by the
Russian Herald and spoke of the "powerful moral abasement" caused by Nekrasov's
haggling (*PSS*, 23[1]:346), he announced a new project: *Notes from the Dead
House*, based on his life in the Siberian prison: "My personality will disappear.
It is the notes of an unknown man; but I guarantee its interest. The interest will
be of the most capital sort" (28[1]:349). This work, published in the journal
Time that Dostoevsky started with his brother in 1861 upon his return to
St. Petersburg, connected powerfully with a reading audience eager for information about previously hidden sides of Russian life. It reestablished Dostoevsky
as a major writer.[4] Katkov's rejection has to be seen as one of the factors that
ignited Dostoevsky's desire to write a new kind of novel, one that engaged intimately with current Russian events.

Editing his own journal seemed to offer Dostoevsky the best way out of
being a "proletarian," constantly dependent on the whim of editors.[5] In June 1862,

---

4 The first chapters of *Notes from the Dead House* (*Zapiski iz mertvogo doma*, often translated as
   House of the Dead) were published in the journal *Russkii mir* in 1860. After Dostoevsky and
   his brother received permission to start their journal *Vremya*, publication continued there in
   1861. A separate edition appeared in 1862. See *PSS*, 4:276–77.
5 On the history of *Time* and its successor journal *Epoch* (*Epokha*), see V. S. Nechaeva, *Zhurnal
   M. M. i F. M. Dostoevskikh "Vremya," 1861–1863* (Moscow: Nauka, 1972); and Nechaeva,
   Zhurnal M. M. i F. M. Dostoevskikh "Epokha," 1864–65 (Moscow: Nauka, 1975).

when the journal *Time* was well established, Dostoevsky wrote to one of its main contributors, Nikolai Strakhov, "A journal is a great thing [*delo*, also "business," "profession"]; it's the kind of activity that is no risk at all, because, whatever happens, journals as the expression of all the shades of contemporary opinions must remain. And the activity, that is, what precisely is to be done, what one must speak and write about—will always be found" (*PSS*, 28[2]:26). In announcing the journal in the fall of 1860, Dostoevsky tried to stake out a distinctive position, neither Slavophile nor Westernizer, but rather based on the idea of *pochva*, the native "soil" of Russia:

> We know now that we cannot be Europeans, that we are not capable of squeezing ourselves into one of the Western forms of life, lived through and elaborated by Europe out of its own national [*natsional'nykh*] principles, which are alien and opposite to us—just as we cannot wear someone else's clothing, sewn not to our measurements. We have finally become convinced that we too are a separate nationality [*natsional'nost'*], original [*samobytnaya*] in the highest degree, and that our task is to create a new form for ourselves, our own, native one, taken out of our soil, taken out of the people's [*narodnyi*] spirit and out of the people's principles. (*PSS*, 18:36)

This idea of the need for the educated classes of Russia to merge with the common people became the consistent program of the journal and was given the label *pochvennichestvo* (for which no concise and adequate English translation has been coined).[6]

Another part of Dostoevsky's program, directed at least in part at Katkov, is his promise not to be dependent on or submissive to "literary authorities": "Golden mediocrity sometimes, even without regard to personal interest, trembles before opinions established by the pillars of literature, especially if these opinions are boldly, daringly, brazenly expressed. Sometimes only this brazenness and daring is what furnishes the designation of pillar and authority to a clever writer who knows how to make use of circumstances, and at the same time furnishes the pillar with an extreme, although temporary, influence over

---

6 On the idea of *pochvennichestvo* elaborated by the editors of and contributors to *Time*, see Ellen Chances, "Literary Criticism and the Ideology of Pochvennichestvo in Dostoevsky's Thick Journals *Vremya* and *Epokha*," *Russian Review* 34, no. 2 (1975): 151–64; and Wayne Dowler, *Dostoevsky, Grigor'ev, and Native Soil Conservatism* (Toronto: University of Toronto Press, 1982).

the masses" (*PSS*, 18:38). This announcement appeared almost simultaneously with Evgeniya Tur's announcement of her new journal *Russian Speech* in the fall of 1860. That announcement came at the end of a very public polemic between her and Katkov, a polemic to which Dostoevsky made repeated reference in his writings for *Time*. In that polemic Katkov's image was shaped as a man proud of his power in the literary world, arrogant and domineering. Dostoevsky's reference to the pillar of authority who brazenly and arrogantly asserts his influence resonates with the way Katkov was portrayed by Tur and her allies. And Dostoevsky's pledge to keep his journal free of "literary slavery" (ibid.) recalls Tur's pledge to avoid ideological rigidity and to honor the right to independent thought. In her announcement, Tur wrote, "Without allowing any harsh extremes, any doctrinaire attitudes, penetrated by the conviction of the necessity of all-round, independent development of social interests, of the excesses of inordinate centralization, our publication will never betray one great principle: it will not forget that respect for someone else's opinion, respect for the right to independent thought of each of the people who are striving together with us to a single goal, is the main basis for freedom of opinion."[7] Katkov clearly perceived Tur's announcement as an attack on the *Russian Herald*, and he reacted to it accordingly.

Dostoevsky's awareness of Katkov's public image as a domineering editor full of selfish pride (*samolyubie*) comes through clearly in the way he reacts to Katkov in print in the early 1860s. There is a strong personal element to Dostoevsky's writings in *Time* that address Katkov. It is clear that Dostoevsky respects Katkov for the stature his journal has attained, but he also responds almost viscerally to Katkov's perceived arrogance and condescension. Katkov also at times makes personal attacks on Dostoevsky in the course of the polemic, no doubt conditioned by his desire to put a new upstart competitor in his place.

---

7 The version of Tur's announcement I had access to is "Ob izdanii G-zheiu Evgenieyu Tur v 1861 godu gazety Russkaia Rech'. Obozrenie literatury, istorii, iskusstva i obshchestvennoi zhizni na zapade i v Rossii" ["About the Publication by Mrs. Evgeniia Tur in 1861 of the Newspaper *Russian Speech*: A Review of Literature, History, Art, and Public Life in the West and in Russia"], *Moskovskie vedomosti*, no. 258 (1860): 2052. See the discussion of *Russkaia rech'* by Jehanne Gheith, "In Her Own Voice: Evgeniya Tur, Author, Critic, Journalist" (Ph.D. diss., Stanford University, 1992), 141–65; and Gheith, *Finding the Middle Ground: Krestovskii, Tur, and the Power of Ambivalence in Nineteenth-Century Russian Women's Prose* (Evanston, IL: Northwestern University Press, 2004), 36–37, 42, 43, 101.

Dostoevsky refers to Katkov with epithets such as "incontinent and quick-tempered," "limited conceit, unlimited self-satisfaction, a thirst for incense burning and worship," "petty self-worship, Jupiter-like grandeur, childish irritability." Katkov compares Dostoevsky to Gogol's empty-headed braggart Khlestakov, and at one point calls him "a fop perfumed with patchouli."[8] This personal aspect of the polemic has obscured the degree to which Dostoevsky and Katkov actually agree on fundamental issues.

Dostoevsky's 1861 essay "Mr. –bov and the Problem of Art" is often seen as his aesthetic manifesto. In this essay Dostoevsky attempts to define a position independent of adherents of "pure art," on the one hand, and those now demanding that art serve a "useful" social role, on the other.[9] As the editors of Dostoevsky's complete works note, Dostoevsky's position was adumbrated in his testimony in the Petrashevsky case in 1849, when he said about his literary disputes with other members of the Petrashevsky circle, "I was challenged to this literary argument, the theme of which on my side was that art does not need a [social] tendency, that art is its own aim, that the author must worry

---

8   Publications in which Dostoevsky addressed or alluded to Katkov that will be discussed here are "Gospodin –bov i vopros ob iskusstve," *Vremya*, no. 2 (1861), (will be referred to in text as "Mr. –bov"); "Obraztsy chistoserdechiia," *Vremya*, no. 3 (1861) ("Models of Sincerity"); "'Svistok' i 'Russkii vestnik,'" *Vremya*, no. 3 (1861) (*The Whistle* and the *Russian Herald*); "Otvet 'Russkomu vestniku,'" *Vremya*, no. 5 (1861) ("An Answer to the *Russian Herald*"); "Knizhnost' i gramotnost'," *Vremya*, no. 7 (1861) ("Bookishness and Literacy"); and "Shchekotlivyi vopros," *Vremya*, no. 10 (1862) ("A Ticklish Question"). Publications in which Katkov addressed or alluded to Dostoevsky, or that Dostoevsky referred to, include "Neskol'ko slov vmesto sovremennoi letopisi," *Russkii vestnik* 31 (January 1861): 478–84 ("A Few Words"); "Nash iazyk i chto takoe svistuny," *Russkii vestnik* 32 (March 1861): 1–38 ("Our Language"); and "Odnogo polia iagody," *Russkii vestnik* 33 (May 1861): 1–26 ("Birds of a Feather"). References to Katkov's articles will also be cited from M. N. Katkov, *Sobranie sochinenii v shesti tomakh*, ed. A. N. Nikoliukin (St. Petersburg: Rostok, 2010–12); hereafter cited as *SS*. Dostoevsky's epithets for Katkov quoted above are from "An Answer to the *Russian Herald*" (*PSS*, 19:121, 123). Katkov called Dostoevsky "a fop perfumed with patchouli" in "Our Language," 35 (*SS*, 1:364). He compared Dostoevsky to Khlestakov in "Birds of a Feather," 20 (*SS*, 1:389, 390). Dostoevsky caricatured Katkov most pointedly in "A Ticklish Question."

9   See the notes in *PSS*, 18:269–92; Robert Louis Jackson, *Dostoevsky's Quest for Form: A Study of His Philosophy of Art* (New Haven, CT: Yale University Press, 1966); Joseph Frank, *Dostoevsky: The Stir of Liberation, 1860–1865* (Princeton, NJ: Princeton University Press, 1986), 76–85; Nechaeva, *Zhurnal "Vremya,"* 242–44; Perevalova, *Zhurnal M. N. Katkova*, 126–29; and V. A. Viktorovich, "G-n –bov i vopros ob iskusstve,'" in *Dostoevsky: Materialy i issledovaniya*, no. 13 (St. Petersburg: Nauka, 1996), 227–29. See also Susanne Fusso, "Maidens in Childbirth: The *Sistine Madonna* in Dostoevsky's *The Devils*," *Slavic Review* 54, no. 2 (1995): 261–75.

only about artistic quality [*khudozhestvennost'*], and the idea will come of itself; for the idea is the necessary condition for artistic quality" (*PSS*, 18:128–29). In "Mr. –bov," Dostoevsky chastises the advocates of "pure art" for rejecting art that has a social tendency, since that in itself constitutes a restriction on art and thus inhibits its freedom in a way that actually goes counter to their stated aims. The greater part of his article, however, is directed at Nikolai Dobrolyubov ("Mr. –bov") and other utilitarians, who neglect the key issue of artistic quality. In Dostoevsky's view, only art that is free can be of high quality, and only art that is of high quality can be of use to society. In his reading, the artistically feeble stories of Marko Vovchok that Dobrolyubov exalts because they represent the correct political position can only bring harm to that very position because of their lack of truthfulness and compelling realism.

The key passage in Dostoevsky's essay is his admonition that art will only be useful if it is freed of the demand that it be useful. No kind of preconditions can be set on art if it is to be truly artistic and therefore truly of use to humanity: "The more freely it develops, the more normally it will develop, the more quickly it will find its true and useful path. And since its interest and aim are one with the aims of humanity, whom it serves and with which it is inseparably united, then the freer its development, the more usefulness it will bring to humanity" (*PSS*, 18:102). As Robert Louis Jackson has pointed out, this idea is virtually identical to the view of art that Katkov formulated in his 1856 essay on Pushkin, in the very first issues of the *Russian Herald*: "The lines of Raphael did not solve any practical question from the everyday life contemporary to him; but they brought great good and great usefulness for life with the course of time; they powerfully contributed to the humanization of life. The action of great works of art remains not only in the sphere closest to them but spreads far and turns out to be there where there is not so much as a mention of the ideals of the artist."[10]

As Dostoevsky says, supposedly paraphrasing the position of the "pure art" adherents but also apparently representing his own views, "The normal historical progress of the usefulness of art in humanity is as yet unknown. It is

---

10 Katkov, "Pushkin," *Russkii vestnik* 1 (February 1856): 312 (*SS*, 1:266). See Jackson, *Quest for Form*, 38–39; and *PSS*, 20:288. Joseph Frank considers Dostoevsky's source to have been the writings of Valerian Maikov, but the passage he cites from Maikov concerns realism rather than usefulness, and is thus not as close to Dostoevsky's formulation as Katkov's position; see Joseph Frank, *Dostoevsky: The Seeds of Revolt, 1821–1849* (Princeton, NJ: Princeton University Press, 1976), 208; see also Frank, *Dostoevsky: Stir of Liberation*, 84.

hard to measure the whole mass of usefulness yielded to all humanity by, for example, the *Iliad* or the Apollo Belvedere, things that are apparently completely unnecessary in our time" (*PSS*, 18:77–78). Like Dostoevsky, Katkov in the 1856 essay on Pushkin rejects both socially didactic art and an art that is focused only on elegance of form, since both are equally far from the goal of "true art," whose value cannot be assessed either by purely social or by purely aesthetic criteria. Instead, as Katkov writes, the goal of true art is "bring[ing] life into human consciousness and consciousness into the most secret convolutions of life."[11]

Katkov responded to "Mr. –bov" in his essay "Our Language and What Are Whistlers." Given the fact that Dostoevsky's basic aesthetic position in that essay is virtually the same as the one Katkov himself expounded in 1856, one might expect him to welcome Dostoevsky's entry into the discussion. He does, but only up to a point. He acknowledges that Dostoevsky's article includes "some views on art that are very sympathetic to us," but his treatment of the new journal *Time* as a whole is drenched in irony, and he goes on to ridicule the analysis Dostoevsky offered of Afanasii Fet's 1847 poem "Diana" in his article, "Mr. –bov."[12]

Dostoevsky quoted two poems by Fet in his article without giving Fet's name. The first, "Whispers, timid breathing . . .," is presented as the kind of pure aestheticism that, if offered as an appropriate response to a disaster like the Lisbon earthquake, would lead to the enraged citizens' execution of the poet on the spot (*PSS*, 18:76). (Dostoevsky goes on to note that they might fifty years later erect a monument to him for the same poem.) The second Fet poem, "Diana," is introduced as an example of something quite different, a kind of relation to the past and the art of the past that represents not a stale imitation but a "Byronic" enthusiasm. This "Byronic" attitude arises not from "powerlessness before our own life but on the contrary from a fiery thirst for life and longing for an ideal which we are trying to attain in

---

11 Katkov, "Pushkin," *Russkii vestnik* 1 (February 1856): 315 (*SS*, 1:269). Much closer to the time of Dostoevsky's writing, in January 1861, Katkov referred to "art for art's sake" as a sickly art that turns into a course on aesthetics ("A Few Words" 480; *SS*, 1:310). Viktorovich notes the way that Dostoevsky adopts what he finds valuable from both sides of the debate ("G-n –bov," 227).

12 Katkov, "Our Language," 15 (*SS*, 1:343–44).

torments" (*PSS*, 18:96). The poem, which Dostoevsky quotes in full, describes a brilliantly white statue of Diana that the lyric speaker almost expects to come to life and begin to walk through the trees, to look upon Rome and its colonnades and squares. The poem concludes, "But the immobile marble / Shone white before me in incomprehensible beauty." Dostoevsky's following words are quoted by Katkov:

> The last two lines of this poem are full of such passionate vitality, such longing, such significance, that we do not know anything more powerful, more vital in all of Russian poetry. This is the obsolete past, being resurrected after two thousand years in the soul of the poet, being resurrected with such power that he waits and believes, in prayer and enthusiasm, for the goddess to come down now from her pedestal and begin to walk before him, "flashing among the trees with her milky whiteness." But the goddess is not resurrected and she does not have to be resurrected, she does not have to live; she has already attained the highest moment of life; she is already in eternity, for her time has stopped; this is the highest moment of life, after which it ceases—and Olympian calm sets in. Only the future is endless, eternally calling, eternally new, and there is also its own highest moment, which one must seek and eternally seek, and that eternal seeking is called life, and how much tormenting sadness is hidden in the enthusiasm of the poet! What an endless call, what melancholy about the present in that enthusiasm for the past![13] (*PSS*, 18:97)

Again, one might expect Katkov to welcome Dostoevsky's passionate and moving appreciation of Fet's poem. At this time, two camps were clearly emerging in Russian journalism, one of which, led by Chernyshevsky and Dobrolyubov, flaunted its lack of respect for the literary traditions of the past, symbolized mainly by Pushkin. Katkov had recently begun sparring furiously with the "whistlers," a name he coined based on the name of the *Whistler*, the satirical supplement to the *Contemporary*. The "whistlers," in Katkov's parlance, as a kind of precursor term to "nihilist," were those who "move from one negation to another" and "have thrown mud on all literary authorities, have taken away Pushkin's right to the title of national [*natsional'nogo*] poet."[14] In "Mr. –bov" Dostoevsky was also directing his main fire against Dobrolyubov

---

13 Quoted by Katkov, "Our Language," 16 (*SS*, 1:344–45).
14 The quotation about "negation" is from Katkov, "Our Language," 11 (*SS*, 1:341). The quotation about Pushkin is from "A Few Words" 480 (*SS*, 1:310).

and others who showed insufficient appreciation for the values of art and its historical legacy. Yet instead of embracing Dostoevsky's stance in "Mr. –bov," in particular his tribute to art and its enduring power, and the respect for the past that it inspires, Katkov characterizes Dostoevsky's interpretation of Fet's poem as far-fetched and untrue to the text. Katkov describes Dostoevsky's interpretation as "that gurgling stream of half-conceptions, half-images, and half-tones, that puts our little Russian thought to sleep so soundly, so stupefies our innocent intellectual movements, and so irresistibly inundates our humble literature."[15] Katkov is being a strict formalist here; in a narrow sense he is correct that the last two lines of Fet's poem do not obviously contain on their surface all the meaning that Dostoevsky has extracted from them. But Katkov is surely being disingenuous when he pretends not to realize that Dostoevsky is creating his own prose poem inspired by Fet's verse, one that, in fact, is true to the sense of Fet's poem as a whole, even if the last two lines do not literally correspond to Dostoevsky's description. As often happens in their polemic, personal antipathy has obscured essential agreement.

The aesthetic dialogue between Katkov and Dostoevsky can be seen most vividly in their discussions of the significance of Pushkin. In his 1861 essay "A Few Words," Katkov asked, "What is Russian nationality [*narodnost'*]? What is Russian literature, Russian art, Russian thought? Will it be advantageous for Russia that the Russian nationality and the Russian word remain behind every other nationality and every other word in Europe? Will it be good for Russia for us to remain eternal bad boy whistlers, capable only of petty deeds, of small slanders and scandals?"[16] The thrust of Katkov's argument when he asks, "What is Russian literature?," seems to be directed against Russian journalism. Yet the fact that in the parlance of the journals of the day the word "literature" was used to refer both to *belles lettres* and to journalistic writings makes his attack ambiguous. Dostoevsky chooses to read it as a dismissal of the achievements of Russian writers, with Pushkin at their head: "Does the *Russian Herald* really not see in Pushkin's talent a powerful personification of the Russian spirit and Russian meaning?" (*PSS*, 19:112).

---

15 Katkov, "Our Language," 16 (*SS*, 1:345).
16 Katkov, "A Few Words," 482 (*SS*, 1:312).

According to the Soviet-era editors of Dostoevsky's complete works, the question of Pushkin and his significance was one of the major points of disagreement between Katkov and Dostoevsky in their polemic. The editors paint Dostoevsky as defending Pushkin against Katkov's slights. In a typical formulation, they write, "Dostoevsky's surmise about Katkov's far from enraptured personal view of Pushkin was confirmed in the further course of the polemic" (*PSS*, 19:297). They claim that Katkov rejected the idea of Pushkin's status as a national [*narodnyi*] poet. Dostoevsky says something similar about Katkov, if obliquely (19:232).[17]

All of this seems strange if we recall not only Katkov's lengthy essay on Pushkin published in the very first issues of the *Russian Herald* in 1856, but also his 1839 introduction to his translation of Varnhagen von Ense's review of Pushkin's works. Here Katkov had claimed that Varnhagen's recognition of Pushkin gave Russians the right to say "that Pushkin is a universal poet who ranks with those few on whom all of humanity looks with reverence." In that same introduction he wrote, "We are firmly convinced and clearly recognize that Pushkin is the poet not of a single epoch, but the poet of all humanity, not of a single country, but of the whole world."[18] Such characterizations of Pushkin as "a universal poet [*vsemirnyi poet*]" and "the poet of all humanity [*poet tselogo chelovechestva*]" are fully in harmony with Dostoevsky's characterizations of Pushkin in his articles in *Time* as a poet of "universal human striving [*obshchechelovecheskoe stremlenie*]" (*PSS*, 18:99), a poet with "the capability of universality, universal humanness, universal responsiveness [*sposobnost' vsemirnosti, vsechelovechnosti, vseotklika*]" (19:114).[19] So why is

---

17 See also the highly tendentious analysis of V. Ia. Kirpotin, *Dostoevsky v shestidesiatye gody* (Moscow: Khudozhestvennaya literatura, 1966), 96–97.

18 Katkov, "Otzyv inostrantsa o Pushkine," *Otechestvennye zapiski* 3, no. 5 (1839): 1–36 (*SS*, 1:53–84; Katkov, translation of Varnhagen von Ense's review of *Sochineniia A. Pushkina* [*Werke von Alexander Puschkin*], *Jahrbücher für wissenschaftliche Kritik*, no. 61, October 1838. The passage quoted is from *SS*, 1:55.

19 From "Mr. –bov" and "*The Whistle* and the *Russian Herald*." This characterization also lies at the basis of Dostoevsky's 1880 Pushkin speech. Marina Kanevskaya has identified a link between the Hegelian view of art expressed in Varnhagen's essay and Dostoevsky's Pushkin speech: Marina Kanevskaya, "Pushkin as 'Universal' Poet: Varnhagen von Ense and Dostoevsky," in *Cold Fusion: Aspects of the German Cultural Presence in Russia*, ed. Gennady Barabtarlo (New York: Berghahn, 2000), 113–25. Varnhagen's essay first appeared in Russian in Nikolai Polevoi's *Son of the Fatherland* (*Syn otechestva*) in 1839. But Katkov was unhappy with the translation,

there the feeling throughout the polemic between Katkov and Dostoevsky that Dostoevsky has to defend Pushkin against Katkov, that Katkov does not sufficiently value Pushkin?

The answer could be that Katkov's position had changed since 1839, or even since 1856, when he had published his long essay on Pushkin's significance in the inaugural issues of the *Russian Herald*. But I would argue that Katkov did in fact continue to value Pushkin's contribution to Russian literature very highly, especially given that he continued to express his esteem for Pushkin to the end of his life, in the 1880s. The problem lies in the way that Katkov and Dostoevsky respectively view Pushkin's accomplishment. Dostoevsky sees it as something integral, completed, whole. Katkov sees it as an impressive but as yet unfulfilled promise of the greatness of Russian culture. When Dostoevsky read Katkov's essay on Pushkin in 1856, he wrote to a friend that Katkov's ideas were "completely opposite to mine" (*PSS*, 28[1]:229). Dostoevsky did not elaborate on what it was about Katkov's ideas that made them opposite to his, but it seems likely that he was not happy with Katkov's emphasis in that essay on Pushkin's contribution in shaping the Russian literary language. In 1861, in "*The Whistle and the Russian Herald*," Dostoevsky asks Katkov, "Did the phenomenon of Pushkin do nothing more for us than perfect [*vyrabotat'*] the language?" (19:112). The question implies that creating a literary language is somehow an inferior accomplishment, but that was not at all Katkov's view. In two essays of 1861, Katkov looks with envy on the High German language, which has "acquired immortal significance" and "become the palladium of a great nation [*narodnost'*]" because of the great works of culture and thought that have been produced in it.[20] Pushkin greatly advanced the cause

and, in his first act of correcting someone else's work in public, he published his own translation with an extensive introduction in *Notes of the Fatherland* later in 1839.

    Kanevskaya cites the original translation, relegating Katkov's version to a footnote. She surmises that Dostoevsky may have learned of Varnhagen's article from N. N. Strakhov, who quoted it in an article in *Notes of the Fatherland* in 1867. But Strakhov's article quotes *Katkov's* translation of Varnhagen (and his 1856 article on Pushkin); see Strakhov, "Glavnoe sokrovishche nashei literatury," *Otechestvennye zapiski*, December 1867, republished in his *Zametki o Pushkine i drugikh poetakh*, 2nd ed. (Kiev: I. I. Chokolov, 1897), 17–34.

20 Katkov, "Our Language," 11 (*SS*, 1:339), and "A Few Words," 482 (*SS*, 1:312).

of exalting Russian nationality through Russian language and literature. But for Katkov, one writer does not constitute a literary culture of world significance. Katkov wants to spur Russian literature to go further than Pushkin, to add to his accomplishment, not just sit in awed contemplation of it. It was that mission that he had espoused when he founded the *Russian Herald*; it was that mission that he was to further in his subsequent support of Dostoevsky's own work from 1865 to the latter's death.

In contrast to the claims of worldwide recognition of Pushkin that Katkov had expressed in 1839, in his 1861 essay "Our Language" he stresses that Pushkin has not attained universal significance on the world stage. Part of this is because of what Katkov sees as an unfinished, fragmentary legacy: "Pushkin is a great poet, and we feel that he is second to none in terms of power of creation; but tell us whether everything he achieved corresponds to those powers that one feels in him, and tell us also what Pushkin means for the rest of the world, while everywhere, and here as well, we see the powerful influence of the Byrons and Schillers?"[21] In Katkov's view, Pushkin has not been recognized on the world stage partly because Russian society has not matured to the point that such recognition is deserved:

> The point is not the personal powers of one or another writer, but the life of which he serves as the organ, the idea that he carries, the significance that his word has for humanity. ... The strange fate of our talents has long been noted: they disappeared from the stage at the very moment when it was just possible to expect a mature word from them; they appeared in flashes and disappeared at the very moment when they began to become a true force. As if fate wavered about whether to set going those developments that could imprint the Russian word with an immortal significance; as if it had not yet been decided whether the time had come to declare in our life the true principles that are hidden in our calling. Truly, that time has not yet come, and the life of the best minds in our milieu was and remains a life of hopes and aspirations alone.[22]

In his 1861 essay "Bookishness and Literacy," Dostoevsky responded angrily to Katkov's claim that Pushkin was not recognized outside Russia, and he disputed the idea that writers like Shakespeare, Schiller, and Goethe were well known to

---

21   Katkov, "Our Language," 17 (*SS*, 1:346).
22   Katkov, "Our Language," 17, 18 (*SS*, 1:346, 347).

nationalities other than their own. In Dostoevsky's view, Katkov is thinking of Russians themselves, who are deeply aware of the literature of other European nations; the actual knowledge of Schiller or Shakespeare in France, for example, is in fact not that deep or broad (for some reason Dostoevsky substitutes Shakespeare for Katkov's Byron) (*PSS*, 19:17). But in the end he makes a statement that is not so far from Katkov's own orientation toward the possible future of Russian literature and culture rather than toward its past:

> And most importantly, how is Pushkin to blame if he is not yet known in Europe? The point is that Europe doesn't yet know Russia either: it has known it up to now only out of grave necessity. It will be another matter when the Russian element will enter as a fruitful stream into universal human development: then Europe will come to know even Pushkin, and will probably find in him incomparably more than the *Russian Herald* has been able to find up to this time. And then [the *Russian Herald*] will be ashamed in front of the Europeans! Russia is still young and is just now getting ready to live; but that is by no means a cause for blame. (*PSS*, 19:18)

The significance of Pushkin also lay at the heart of the major controversy in which Dostoevsky and Katkov were involved, concerning the public reading by Evgeniya Eduardovna Tolmachova, a civil servant's wife in the provincial city of Perm, of Pushkin's unfinished poem *Egyptian Nights*. In the section recited by Tolmachova, Cleopatra, at a public feast, offers her sexual favors to any man who is willing to sacrifice his life for one night with her. That controversy culminated in Dostoevsky's defense of *Egyptian Nights* from Katkov's charge that as a fragment it was unsuitable for public reading, since without being clothed in artistic detail, its potentially salacious aspects stood out more strikingly. Dostoevsky responds that *Egyptian Nights* is not a fragment, but "the most finished work of Russian poetry" (*PSS*, 19:132).[23]

---

23   In "An Answer to the *Russian Herald*." See Leslie O'Bell, *Pushkin's "Egyptian Nights": The Biography of a Work* (Ann Arbor, MI: Ardis, 1984); V. Kirpotin, "Dostoevsky o 'Egipetskikh nochakh' Pushkina," *Voprosy literatury*, no. 11 (1962): 112–21; Frank, *Dostoevsky: Stir of Liberation*, 86–87; Lewis Tracy, "Decoding Puškin: Resurrecting Some Readers' Responses to *Egyptian Nights*," *Slavic and East European Journal* 37, no. 4 (1993): 456–71; and S. V. Berezkina, "F. M. Dostoevsky i M. N. Katkov (iz istorii romana 'Prestuplenie i nakazanie')," *Izvestiia RAN, Seriia literatury i iazyka* 72, no. 5 (2013): 16–25. During the discussion at the conference Dostoevsky beyond Dostoevsky at Brown University in March 2014, Olga Meerson pointed out that the introductory part of *Egyptian Nights* is centrally concerned

There is no question that the poem declaimed by Mrs. Tolmachova was left unfinished at Pushkin's death. But as in the disagreement between Dostoevsky and Katkov over how to interpret Fet's poem "Diana," here Katkov takes a narrow, formalistic view, while Dostoevsky reacts as a creator, not strictly an interpreter. Rather than seeing the poem's unfinishedness as a defect, Dostoevsky valorizes the very fragmentariness of Pushkin's work:

> Pushkin set himself the task (if it is at all possible that he set a task in advance for his inspiration) to present a moment of Roman life, and only one moment, but in such a way as to produce by it the fullest spiritual impression, in order to convey in a few lines and images the whole spirit and meaning of that moment of the life of that time, so that by this moment, by this little corner, one could guess in advance and understand the whole picture. And Pushkin achieved this and achieved it in such artistic fullness that it appears to us as a miracle of poetic art. (*PSS*, 19:133)

We can see here on the micro level the same disagreement the two men had about Pushkin's legacy on the macro level: for Katkov, Pushkin's accomplishment is unfinished, an unfulfilled promise, a fragment in a sense, while for Dostoevsky, it is an integral and complete achievement.

Dostoevsky's second point is that any sexual material in the work has been transformed by a mysterious artistic process: "Here reality has been transformed, *having passed through art*, having passed through the fire of pure, chaste inspiration and through the poet's artistic thought. This is a secret [*taina*] of art, and every artist knows about it" (*PSS*, 19:134; emphasis in original). Third, Dostoevsky argues that if any salacious impression is received, it is the fault of the audience, not the artist: "The *chastity* of an image does not save it from a coarse and even perhaps a dirty thought" (ibid.; emphasis in original). Finally, he offers his own interpretation of *Egyptian*

---

with the question of usefulness in art that Dostoevsky had discussed in "Mr. –bov." But strangely neither he nor Katkov ever refers to this aspect of *Egyptian Nights* in the course of their polemic. On the fragmentary nature of *Egyptian Nights*, see the excerpt from Strakhov's unpublished article that Dostoevsky appends as a "letter" to the end of "An Answer to the *Russian Herald*": "*Egyptian Nights* is not a fragment at all. Where have you found in it signs of unfinishedness, fragmentariness? On the contrary—what a full picture! What marvelous correlation of the parts, definiteness and finishedness! ... *Egyptian Nights* is an improvisation, but it is a complete, finished improvisation" (*PSS*, 19:137–38).

Nights as a work that produces not a "Marquis de Sade" effect but a powerful moral effect: "This *ultimate expression* [of passion], about which you so often talk, in our opinion can indeed be a temptation, but in our opinion it represents only the perversion of human nature, which has reached such horrible dimensions and is presented *from such a point of view* by the poet (and the point of view is the main thing) that it produces not an obscene but a shattering impression" (19:135; emphasis in original). Pushkin's depiction of the spiritual bankruptcy of decadent Alexandria "makes it clear to what kind of people our divine Redeemer came" (19:137). Dostoevsky is rightly celebrated for the artistically visionary interpretation of *Egyptian Nights* he gives in this essay.

The Tolmachova controversy provoked the most direct and personal public interaction between Dostoevsky and Katkov. It reveals some of the dynamics that would make possible the later working relationship between the two men. Most important here is that we see Dostoevsky rising to a challenge posed by Katkov. Katkov's questioning of the artistic form of *Egyptian Nights* inspired Dostoevsky to one of his best pieces of literary criticism. This is a kind of foreshadowing of the way in which Dostoevsky was moved to write cogently about his own artistic aims when "pitching" new ideas for novels in his letters to Katkov during the later years they worked together. We also see some of Dostoevsky's uneasiness with the radicals, whom he seems to have decided to court during his editorship of *Time*. Unlike M. L. Mikhailov, Dostoevsky could not defend Mrs. Tolmachova with unalloyed righteous indignation, because he felt too strongly the viewpoint of the "old mommies" whose daughters were subjected to her provocative performance.[24] In this uneasiness we can see that he did not so vehemently disagree with Katkov as it would seem on the surface. But the bare-knuckled nature of nineteenth-century Russian journalism led the two men into making fairly sharp personal attacks on each other. Dostoevsky had the advantage of the clear public image of Katkov that had been developed

---

24 [M. L.] Mikhailov, "Bezobraznyi postupok 'Veka,'" *Sanktpeterburgskie vedomosti*, no. 51, March 3, 1861. In "Models of Sincerity," Dostoevsky had written that the opinions of the "old mommies [*starykh mamenek*]" in Mrs. Tolmachova's audience should be respected because of their concern for their daughters: "Indeed, for those of *adolescent* age such a reading *might* even be dangerous. In an adolescent age a person is not formed either physically or morally, and on him even the Medici Venus might not produce a fully artistic impression" (*PSS*, 19:103; emphasis in original).

in the Tur polemic: the selfishly proud, overbearing, intelligent but arrogant editor throwing his weight around. Dostoevsky's public image was not as well defined at this time, but no one who knew him would have described him as a "perfumed fop"; Katkov's barb was much less apt than Dostoevsky's (but it did seem to cause Dostoevsky some pain).

Time was closed down in 1863 because of an article by Strakhov on the Polish question that was interpreted by the authorities as being seditious. By the fall of 1863, with *Time* closed down and a new journal not yet officially approved, Dostoevsky had fallen back into the role of a journeyman writer, or what he called a "proletarian." He wrote to Strakhov asking him to approach the editor of the *Library for Reading* about publishing a new work. He instructed Strakhov to make it clear that he needed to be paid in advance: "I am a proletarian writer, and if someone wants my work, he has to secure my services in advance" (*PSS*, 28[2]:50). Later in the same letter, Dostoevsky says that if Strakhov is unable to make a deal with the *Library for Reading*, then he should approach the newspapers but avoid the *Notes of the Fatherland*, and "of course not the *Russian Herald*" (*PSS*, 28[2]:52). After writing so many highly personal attacks on Katkov, Dostoevsky at this point could not contemplate turning to Katkov with his work. But the next two years would be some of the hardest in Dostoevsky's life and would bring him back, despite everything, to the man he first approached in 1858.

Dostoevsky spent much of 1863 in a difficult love affair with Apollinarya Suslova; his wife, Mar'ya Dmitrievna, died in April 1864 and his brother Mikhail died in July, leaving Dostoevsky to try to carry on the journal *Epoch*, which never really took off and closed in March 1865. Financially crushed by family needs and gambling debts, in September 1865 Dostoevsky wrote his famous letter to Katkov describing his conception of *Crime and Punishment*. At virtually the same time, he expressed his fears about this step in a letter to A. E. Vrangel': "While *Time* was being published, our two journals had some brawls. And Katkov is such a selfishly proud, vain, and vengeful person that I am very afraid now that, remembering the past, he might haughtily refuse the story I am offering and make a fool of me" (*PSS*, 28[2]:140). Dostoevsky saw before him in his mind's eye the caricatured, vain, and vengeful Katkov of his public polemics, which is part of the story of Katkov, but not the whole story.

Katkov was never so selfishly proud as to lose sight of the best interests of his journal, or of the larger mission of making Russia a world-historical nation through the medium of a great literature. Contrary to Dostoevsky's fears, Katkov agreed to work with him and sent him an advance of 300 rubles for the first of the four major novels that were to secure Dostoevsky's place on the world literary stage.

Dostoevsky's Postmodernists and the Poetics of Incarnation

Svetlana Evdokimova

The Struggle over Aesthetic Ideals

"Alyosha, do you believe than I am not merely a buffoon?—I do believe that you are not merely a buffoon."[1] With these words Dostoevsky undoubtedly anticipated the reader's temptation to view Fyodor Pavlovich Karamazov as nothing more than a buffoon, for the characters in the novel, including Karamazov the father himself, and the narrator of *The Brothers Karamazov* frequently refer to Fyodor's scandalous behaviour as buffoonery. I propose, however, to consider Fyodor not only as a traditional carnivalesque fool but as a character who poses questions of modern aesthetics. I interpret his behavior as artifice in the context of Dostoevsky's critique of the modern crisis of artistic representation.

As it has been frequently pointed out, the philosophical thought of Dostoevsky owes a great deal to the Platonic tradition. I suggest that the contradictory aesthetic ideas expressed in *The Brothers Karamazov* reflect the crisis of Platonic aesthetics and of Romantic representation. The "Pro et Contra" of *The Brothers*

---

1 F. M. Dostoevskii, *Polnoe sobranie sochinenii v tridtsati tomakh* [*PSS*], ed. V. G. Bazanov et al. (Leningrad: Nauka, 1972–1990), 14:123; hereafter cited as *PSS* by volume and page. All translations are mine unless otherwise specified. In cases when translation may not render some important aspects of the text, the original text will be provided in a footnote. I would like to express my gratitude to Alexandar Mihailovic for his careful reading of this chapter and his invaluable comments and suggestions.

Karamazov is not only the pro et contra of the Grand Inquisitor and Zosima but also the pro et contra of Plato and anti-Plato.

Gilles Deleuze's critique of Platonism could provide a useful tool for considering the aesthetic problematic of *The Brothers Karamazov*, for it addresses the anti-Platonic turn in modern philosophy. Discussing the "overthrowing" of Platonism in modern philosophy in his essay "Plato and the Simulacrum," Deleuze insists that modernity "is defined by the power of the simulacrum": "The problem no longer concerns the distinction Essence/ Appearance or Model/Copy. The whole distinction operates in the world of representation. The goal is the subversion of this world."[2] Jean Baudrillard also succinctly addresses the simulacra's annihilating power to efface the Platonic idea of God:

> But what becomes of the divinity when it reveals itself in icons, when it is multiplied in simulacra? Does it remain the supreme power that is simply incarnated in images as a visible theology? Or does it volatilize itself in the simulacra that, alone, deploy their power and pomp of fascination—the visible machinery of icons substituted for the pure and intelligible Idea of God? This is precisely what was feared by Iconoclasts, whose millennial quarrel is still with us today. This is precisely because they predicted this omnipotence of simulacra, the faculty simulacra have of effacing God from the conscience of man, and the destructive, annihilating truth that they allow to appear—that deep down God never existed, even God himself was never anything but his own simulacra—from this came their urge to destroy the images. If they could have believed that these images only obfuscated or masked the Platonic Idea of God, there would have been no reason to destroy them. One can live with the idea of distorted truth. But their metaphysical despair came from the idea that the image didn't conceal anything at all.[3]

For both Deleuze and Baudrillard, the simulacrum is either a floating signifier that has been divested of its signified or a referent to an object that does not in fact exist. As we shall see, the postmodern understanding of aesthetics as the study of ossified simulacra—a practice expressing what Baudrillard calls a

---

2 Gilles Deleuze, "Plato and the Simulacrum" (trans. Rosalind Krauss), *October* 27 (Winter 1983): 55, 52–53.

3 Jean Baudrillard, *Simulacra and Simulation* (Ann Arbor: University of Michigan Press, 1994), 4–5.

"fascination for desert-like and indifferent forms"[4]—is fully embodied by Fyodor Karamazov's poetics of destabilization and aleatory verbal defilement.

I read Fyodor's behavior as an artifice that reverses the Platonic system of ideas, which may be central to the religious aesthetics of Dostoevsky. Fyodor Karamazov, along with other "adulterers of thought," such as Rakitin and Fetyukovich, and Foma Fomich Opiskin (from *The Village of Stepanchikovo*), are precisely representatives of this new aesthetic trend.

Dostoevsky is acutely aware of the two competing kinds of aesthetics, an aesthetic based on likeness, or similitude, to an Idea (that is, a Platonic tradition that finds its expression in iconicity) and the aesthetics that has no referent but itself. These two kinds of aesthetics are represented by images, such as icons, on the one hand, and by creations-phantasms, on the other. Insisting on Plato's distinguishing between the "*iconic copies* (likeness)" and the "*phantasmatic simulacra* (semblances)" (emphasis in the original), Deleuze explains: "The copy is an image endowed with resemblance, the simulacrum is an image without resemblance. The catechism, so fully inspired by Platonism, has familiarized us with this notion. God made man in His own image and to resemble Him, but through sin, man lost the resemblance while retaining the image. Having lost a moral existence in order to enter into an aesthetic one, we have become simulacra. The remark of the catechism has the advantage of stressing the daemonic character of the simulacrum."[5] Fyodor pertains to this particular aesthetic existence and exemplifies a type of aesthetics that is also represented by Ivan Karamazov's devil and referred to by Dmitri in his famous opposition of the two types of beauty: the beauty of the Madonna and beauty of Sodom.[6]

Dmitri's words about the ideal of Sodom and the ideal of the Madonna are often interpreted as indication of Dostoevsky's awareness of beauty's ambiguity and his ambiguous attitude toward beauty, but it is also important to consider this opposition as an opposition of two kinds of representational aesthetics. By referring to "the ideal of the Madonna," Dostoevsky uses the term "Madonna" to link

---

4 Ibid., 160.

5 Deleuze, "Plato and the Simulacrum," 48–49.

6 On the subject of "two kinds of beauty" in Dostoevsky, see Robert Louis Jackson, *Dostoevsky's Quest for Form: A Study of his Philosophy of Art* (Bloomington, IN: Physsardt, 1978), 40–70.

it to the European representational canon.[7] The "aesthetics of the Madonna" implies that the notions of beauty, goodness, and truth merge; whether this is a Byzantine icon or a Renaissance Madonna, this aesthetics is based on Platonic (or Neoplatonic) representation, that is, on the assumption that a painting represents a visual image of the unrepresentable Truth. Although Plato himself criticized artistic representation as unable to grasp the true reality, later Christian Neoplatonists validated representation based on the idea that there is continuity between God and the world.[8] For Plato, the object of representation in painting is a copy in respect to the idea of the object, *eidos,* but there is an original behind this copy. The notion that there is an invisible image prototype that can be glimpsed in the icon is central to the theology of the icon and Platonic mimesis. Plato distinguishes between the two types of the art of mimesis: the first one he calls the *art of creating images,* the second one the *art of creating phantasms.* These phantasms, according to Plato, *seem* beautiful but do not stem (emanate) from the beautiful. I suggest that Dmitri's notion of the idea of Sodom represents this particular kind of aesthetics of phantasm, implying negation of the higher inaccessible truth, which may be found behind the representation. This ideal of Sodom, or phantasm, only seems beautiful, but it does not emanate from the beautiful. As opposed to the beauty of the Madonna that presupposes the existence of an

---

7   On the subject of Dostoevsky's choice of "Madonna" rather than "Virgin Mary" (or "the Mother of God") in this opposition, see Grigorii Pomerants, *Otkrytost' bezdne: vstrechi s Dostoevskim* (Moscow: Sovetskii pisatel', 1990), 178. As has been thoroughly discussed in scholarly literature, the ideal of the Madonna was connected in Russian literary tradition with the Romantic cult of Renaissance paintings of the Madonna, especially Raphael's *Sistine Madonna.* See Andreas Schönle's discussion of the role of Raphael's Madonna in Russian romantic imagination in Schönle, "O tom, kak Sikstinskaya Madonna pokrovitel'stvovala russkomu romantizmu," in *Sed'mye tynianovskie chteniia: Materialy dlia obsuzhdeniia* (Riga-Moscow, 1995–96), 135–50. See also Ksana Blank's detailed overview of "the Madonna cult in Russian literature," in Blank, *Dostoevsky's Dialectics and the Problem of Sin* (Evanston, IL: Northwestern University Press, 2010), 85–93.

8   As Tom Rockmore argues, Plato criticized artists for their inability to know what they depict and, therefore, to depict it correctly. Aristotle and later medieval Christian thinkers, however, were anti-Platonic in the sense that they committed to the view of an unbroken continuity between God and the visible created universe; see Rockmore, *Art and Truth after Plato* (Chicago: University of Chicago Press, 2013). He writes: "The basic claim is the assertion of an unbroken ontological continuity between God and the world, God and nature, a continuity which sustains the characteristic triple cognitive link between human beings who in imitating nature imitate and know God" (104). Rockmore interprets this medieval Christian position as "the anti-Platonic belief that in imitating the world due to God we can reliably claim to know God," that is, as anti-Platonic only in the sense of art's cognitive function (ibid.).

original referent, the ideal image of the Virgin Mary, "the ideal of Sodom" does not have this referent, because Sodom is merely a metaphor of sin, of something that does not exist as an entity. The beauty of Sodom then, like simulacrum, is built upon dissimilarity, dissimilitude, perversion, and deviation from true beauty. The beauty of the Madonna may imply a certain similitude; the beauty of Sodom may not. Significantly, in contrast to the very extensive European pictorial tradition of the representation of the Madonna, the iconography of Sodom is very scarce and, for the most part, either does not depict the city of Sodom at all (using representational displacement by focusing on the theme of Lot, his daughters, and his wife) or portrays images of burning and destruction. As opposed to the Madonna, Sodom does not have an ideal form, but represents formlessness.[9] The aesthetic of Sodom, rooted as it is in fragmentation, results in the disintegration of representation and its possibility. Sodom does not have a claim of the copy and as such resists representation. The ideal of Sodom is therefore the beauty of phantasm or, in Dostoevsky's terms, the state in which man finds out that "the aesthetic idea got blurred." Whereas Dmitri Karamazov seems to be torn between the two types of beauty, Fyodor is firmly on the side of Sodom, understood not in the narrow sense as a particular kind of debauchery, but as an aesthetic impulse thriving on phantasms and creating simulacra rather than icons.[10]

Fyodor Karamazov's "Postmodernism"

Fyodor's blasphemy could be seen as a direct reflection of his rejection of Platonic representation and an embracing, instead, of the "aesthetic existence" of simulacrum. Angered by his wife's piety, he spits at the icon of the Virgin Mary: "I'll

---

9 For an illuminating discussion of the paradox of the form of formlessness in Augustine and in Dostoevsky, see Robert Louis Jackson's presentation in chapter 9 in this volume.

10 Lev Karsavin argues that Fyodor Karamazov is susceptible to pure beauty and, therefore, is capable of love; see Karsavin, "Fyodor Pavlovich Karamazov kak ideolog liubvi," in *Russkii eros ili filosofiia liubvi v Rossii* (Moscow: Progress, 1991), 350–63. Indeed, Fyodor is sensitive to various kinds of beauty, including the "innocent beauty" of Alyosha's mother, but Fyodor's response to beauty, and probably pure beauty, especially, is destructive. Pure beauty only ignites in him the desire to profane and to destroy it. Although Karsavin is right in pointing out that "the very desire to defile is understandable only on the basis of a very acute sensitivity to that which is being defiled," it is obvious that Fyodor derives aesthetic pleasure primarily in the acts of pollution and distortion. His aesthetic impulse is based on perversion and the pleasure of defilement. By the turn of the century, Fyodor Sologub would pick up on this new type of aesthetics in his portrayal of Peredonov in his novel *Petty Demon*.

knock that mysticism out of her, thought I. 'Here,' I said, 'here you see your holy image. Here it is. Here I will take it down. Look then, you believe it's miraculous, but here, I'll spit on it in front of you and nothing will happen to me for it!'" (*PSS*, 14:126). Iconic representation is based on the assumption that an icon is a visual image of the unrepresentable Truth. By rejecting the image as likeness, as a referent to an idea, or an original, Fyodor also implicitly rejects iconic aesthetics. Since Fyodor does not believe in God, he views icons, church, and the institution of religion as simulacra of sorts. For an atheist, icons (viewed as icons rather than merely works of art) are offensive not only because icons claim to represent Christ's divine nature, which cannot be circumscribed (a heresy that, according to the iconoclasts, represents idolatry), but also because they pretend to refer to something that does not exist. By spitting at the icon, he does not simply commit an act of profanation, but he also questions Christian aesthetics (which are central to iconic representation), that is, questions the existence of proto-image behind the image, of the original behind the copy, that is, image as likeness.

The world for Fyodor appears as a vertigo of images without any foundation behind them. His discussion of the "hooks" in hell is indicative of this view:

> And so I wonder: hooks? Where would they get them? What of? Iron hooks? Where do they forge them? Have they a foundry there of some sort? In the monastery, the monks probably believe that there's a ceiling in hell, for instance. Now I'm ready to believe in hell, but only without a ceiling ... And then if there's no ceiling there, there are no hooks either. If there are no hooks it all breaks down, which is again improbable: who would then drag me down to hell with hooks, for if they don't drag me down, what will happen then, what justice is there in the world? *Il faudrait les inventer*, those hooks, on purpose for me alone. (*PSS*, 14:23–24)

By paraphrasing Voltaire's words, "If there were no God, one would have to invent Him," Fyodor seems to insist that God, devil, and hell do not exist but are merely simulacra. An image for him does not have any proto-image or original: "Yes, yes, only the shadows of hooks. I know, I know. That's how a Frenchman described hell: 'J'ai vu l'ombre d'un cocher, qui avec l'ombre d'une brosse frottait l'ombre d'une carrosse'" (*PSS*, 14:24).

The world for Karamazov the father is a shadow of the shadow of the shadow, or a copy of the copy *ad infinitum*, so that it is impossible to find the original in an infinite recession of seemingly isomorphic units. Even when he speaks about the shadow of the shadow, he turns to literary texts that he consciously distorts, as if in demonstration of defilement as the last refuge of true agency. The referenced text is the parody of the sixth song of *Aeneide* written by Charles Perrault and his brothers, which was frequently assigned to Paul Scarron, the author of *Le Virgile travesti*.[11] Thus, Fyodor's speech represents infinite production of copies of copies completely obscuring the original.

Fyodor Karamazov is a performer, and the main strategy of his performance is defilement and the destabilization of meaning. One of the best examples of his creative simulation is his behavior in Father Zosima's cell and his absurd story about von Sohn (from German for "son"). The story of von Sohn referred to a man who existed in reality and who was murdered in St. Petersburg; this story was also used as a parody of one of the hypostases of the Trinity and of the resurrection of Christ. By using the name of von Sohn in reference to Maksimov, Fyodor explains:

> Your reverence, do you know what is von Sohn? There was a famous murder case: he was killed in a house of harlotry––I believe that is what such places are called among you—he was killed and robbed, and in spite of his venerable age, he was nailed up in a box, locked, and sent from Petersburg to Moscow in the luggage compartment with a number attached. And while they were nailing him up, the harlot dancers sang songs and played the harp, that is to say, the piano. So this is that very von Sohn. He has risen from the dead, hasn't he, von Sohn? (*PSS*, 14:81)

However, this story does not merely travesty the resurrection of Christ. Karamazov the father creates a simulacrum of sorts, a story that has no basis underneath it and has no original source—this is merely a copy of a nonexistent copy, which he confirms himself. Likeness is merely a simulation:

> —"He is like von Sohn," Fyodor Pavlovich said suddenly.

> —"Is that all you can think of? [...] How is it that he is like von Sohn? Have you ever seen von Sohn yourself?"

> —"I've seen his photograph. It's not the features, but something indefinable. He's a purest second copy of von Sohn."

> (*PSS*, 14:34)[12]

---

11 See editorial comments in Dostoevsky, *PSS*, 15:526.

12 [...] shall indicate suspension points in the original.

Thus, Maksimov as von Sohn is a verbal simulacrum, created by Fyodor, "the purest second copy" having no semblance or likeness and taken not from a real prototype, but from a photograph of someone Fyodor never saw. Fyodor creates untranslatable neologisms but these words have no referents, they are signifiers without the signified: "'There, didn't I say he was von Sohn!' cried Fyodor Pavlovich, enraptured. 'He is a real von Sohn, risen from the dead! Why, how did you tear yourself away from there? What did you *vonsohn* there and how could you get away from dinner?'"[13] (*PSS*, 14:84). Similarly, his neologism, *naafonit'*, a word derived from the name of the holy Mount Athos but turned into a verb form prefixed with *na*, implying intense cumulative action, suggests activity resulting in a negative outcome, such as in the words *nadelat'*, *natvorit'*, *nakhuliganit'*, *nabedakurit'*, thus completely subverting the metaphorical meaning of Mount Athos, which stands for monastic holiness, and turning it in its very opposite: "I've pulled off plenty of pranks [*naafonil*, literally "atho-sized"] in my time"[14] (14:125). His lies and slanders are not merely false and misleading statements intended to damage someone's reputation, not merely untruths (which presuppose the existence of truth), but verbal simulacra ungrounded in reality; they are the actualizations of something in itself incommunicable and nonrepresentable. The destabilizing discourse of Fyodor's garrulous buffoonery is based on a hodgepodge of distorted quotations, which stand on their own without reference to the thing they have originally represented. Karamazov's witticism, "Credo, but I don't know in what" (14:124)—the words that he absurdly and maliciously attributes to Father Zosima and that travesty the Orthodox Symbol of Faith (Nicene Creed) beginning with the words "I believe in one God, the Father Almighty, Maker of heaven and earth"—targets the transcendental Signified by implicitly denying the existence of God. As a "sponger" (*prizhival'shchik*) and similar to Ivan Karamazov's devil (also referred to as a "sponger"), Fyodor is a "sponger" on someone else's word, an aesthetic sponger of sorts.

Speaking about his own buffoonery, Fyodor emphasizes the aesthetic motivation of his behavior: "Yes, exactly, I have been all my life taking offense

---

13 "—Ну не говорил ли я,—восторженно крикнул Федор Павлович,—что это фон Зон! Что это настоящий воскресший из мертвых фон Зон! Да как ты вырвался оттуда? Что ты там нафонзонил такого и как ты-то мог от обеда уйти?"

14 "Наафонил я, говорит, на своем веку немало."

for the pleasure of it, taking offense on the *aesthetic* grounds, for it is not so much pleasant as *beautiful* sometimes to be insulted—that you had forgotten, great elder, it is *beautiful*!"[15] (*PSS*, 14:41). Moreover, this "beauty" and this peculiar aesthetic sense are based not on likeness but on falsehood, and they are explicitly linked to demonism by Fyodor Karamazov himself:

> But I have been lying, lying decidedly my whole life long, every day and hour of it. Truly I am a lie and the father of lies! But probably I am not the father of lies, I am getting the texts mixed up, but then at least the son of lies, and that will be enough. (*PSS*, 14:41)

Lies are understood here not merely as misinformation, false logic, or appearance, but as ontological lies, which question the very relation between the image and the original. The reference to the "father of lies" points to the demonic nature of the phantasms, created by Karamazov the father. Fyodor's buffoonery, his sophistry, his language-making, produce, indeed, a "reverse Platonism" by generating verbal simulacra and by making them affirm their rights among authoritative scriptural word. Fyodor erases the distinction between truth and falsehood, denies the difference between the original and the copy. He discovers the lure of the false, the intoxicating power of lies and the aesthetic pleasure of creation that obliterates any sense of reality. Father Zosima criticizes Fyodor's "drunkenness and incontinence of speech" and explains his behavior by a perverse aesthetic pleasure of lying:

> It is sometimes very pleasant to take offense, isn't it? A man may know that nobody has insulted him, but that he has fancied the insult himself and lied for the beauty of it, that he has exaggerated all to create a picture, has caught a word at a word and made a mountain out of a molehill—he knows that himself. (*PSS*, 14:41)

Thus, Fyodor appreciates a particular kind of aesthetic sense that leads to the creation of images (*kartiny*) based not on reality but on lies, or the beauty of phantasms. Indeed, Fyodor lies for the "beauty of it" and creates a mountain out of a molehill. The "father of lies," he is an artist of simulacra, as his stories

---

15 "Именно, именно, я-то всю жизнь и обижался до приятности, для **эстетики** обижался, ибо не токмо приятно, но и **красиво** иной раз обиженным быть;—вот что вы забыли, великий старец: **красиво**!" (my emphasis).

about von Sohn and about Diderot's visit to the Russian Metropolitan Platon signify. His story about Diderot's "christening" is an improvisation based on phantasmal logic, continuously affirming that there is no logic, no foundation to this verbal creation, which is merely a figment of his imagination:

> Did you ever hear, Your Reverence, how Diderot the philosopher came to the metropolitan Platon during the reign of the Empress Catherine? He entered and said straight out: "There is no God." To which the great prelate lifted up his finger and answered, "The fool has said in his heart there is no God." And he fell down at his feet on the spot. "I believe," he cried, "and accept christening." And so he was baptized on the spot. Princess Dashkov was his godmother, and Potemkin his godfather [...] ... Great elder! Forgive me, the last story about christening of Diderot I invented just now, this very minute, just as I was telling the story, but I never thought of it before. I made it up for the piquancy of it. (*PSS*, 14:39)

Fyodor's aesthetics with its complete obliteration of the real and its disconnect between essence and appearance defies the concept of representation. Distorted quotations, references to the nonexistent originals, deconstruction of the cultural intertext, hypertextuality, signifiers separated from the signified, the substitution of the beautiful with the witty, the vertigo of performance and provocation—all these features link Fyodor's behavior to postmodern aesthetics. Fyodor rejects images/icons and fabricates verbal simulacra, such as his stories about von Sohn or Diderot; he creates signs that merely dissimulate the absence of the signified.

Realism and the Aesthetics of Incarnation

In pondering the problems of aesthetics and striving to create his own "realism in the higher sense of the word" or "fantastic realism," based not on surface semblance, but on spiritual likeness, on the reality of ideas, that is, realism in the medieval scholastic sense of the word, Dostoevsky acutely sensed the pending crisis in the aesthetic and religious consciousness of modernity. For Dostoevsky, this crisis consisted more specifically of a fully articulated rupture with the epistemological foundations of the Platonic tradition, later so poignantly discussed by Deleuze and others. While polemicizing with the naturalistic understanding of realism, Dostoevsky critiques this realism for merely touching the surface and limiting itself to the exterior similarity. Let us recall how Dostoevsky describes the portrait of his narrator in "Bobok":

> I think that artist painted me not for the sake of literature, but for the sake of the two symmetrical warts on my forehead: a phenomenon, he says. They have no ideas, so now they exploit phenomena. Well, but how well he painted my warts—just like life! That's what they call realism. (*PSS*, 21:42)

In other words, Dostoevsky is skeptical of art based merely on the depiction of phenomena and strives for the type of art that would be able to penetrate into the world of ideas (*noumena*) and would be based on images referring to ideas. Plato, as we recall, presupposed three levels of reality: the ideal forms, the visible objects (which are "shadows" of ideal forms), and images that comprise the mimetic arts. Although a direct literary imitation is located two steps below the essential nature of things, Dostoevsky wanted to grasp the more genuine reality of ideal forms, without bypassing, however, the realm of sensible reality. He was equally suspicious of naturalism without "ideas" and of the art of simulacra (of the kind that Fyodor Karamazov practices, playing with phantasms disconnected from the realm of sensible reality).

In *The Brothers Karamazov*, Dostoevsky implicitly juxtaposes two types of realism by making Ivan Karamazov's devil proclaim that he loves "earthly realism" but suffers from the fantastic: "Just like you, I suffer from the fantastic, that is why I love your earthly realism. Here with you, everything is circumscribed, there is a formula, a geometry, while we have nothing but indeterminate equations" (*PSS*, 15:73).[16] The "earthly realism" about which the devil is so nostalgic is the material world, the world of phenomena. Being himself an "ideal form" or, rather, a "fallen ideal form, he "suffers from the fantastic," as he puts it, and, therefore, rebels against this "fantastic realism" of immaterial existence. His greatest envy is precisely embodiment, enfleshment, incarnation: "My dream is to incarnate—but only irrevocably and decidedly—in some kind of fat two-hundred-fifty-pound merchant's wife" (15:73–74).[17] An "impure form,"

---

16 "Ведь я и сам, как и ты же, страдаю от фантастического, а потому и люблю ваш земной реализм. Тут у вас все очерчено, тут формула, тут геометрия, а у нас все какие-то неопределенные уравнения!"

17 "Моя мечта—воплотиться, но чтоб уж окончательно, безвозвратно, в какую-нибудь толстую семипудовую купчиху."

so to speak, he feels doomed to be merely a "sponger" (*prizhival'shchik*), an imposter, an impersonator deprived of its own independent phenomenal existence. Ivan continuously reminds the devil that he lacks material existence, that he is merely his fancy, a phantom: "'Never for a single minute have I taken you for reality [*real'nuiu pravdu*],' Ivan cried with a sort of fury. 'You are a lie, you are my illness, you are a phantom [*prizrak*]. … You are the incarnation of myself, but only of one side of me [...] of my thoughts and feelings, but only the nastiest and the stupidest of them'" (15:72). As an "idea," he could inhabit, take possession of someone, but only temporarily, always in fear of being exorcised.

This kind of "fantastic realism" is his curse, for he is yearning to be also part of the "earthly realism" similar to Christ with his two natures, human and divine. The devil, however, can only pretend to have two natures without ever achieving their unity, as follows from his peculiar theological non sequitur: "Satan *sum et nihil humanum a me alienum puto*" (*PSS*, 15:74).[18] His failure to achieve the unity of the dual nature of Christ is exposed in his incompatible combination of Russian and Latin in one sentence, with "satanic" and "human" natures being rendered by two distinct languages. He flaunts his logical blunder, distorting Terence's famous quotation and insinuating the identity of the demonic and human natures. The devil, as he admits, "suffers," but does not "exist": "I am suffering, but nevertheless I do not exist. I am an X in an indeterminate equation" (15:77).[19] His suffering consists precisely in the fact that he lacks sensible material existence and has only the "reality" of an idea. He is a concept (a universal) without material embodiment in the particular. It is not surprising, then, that he considers realism in opposition to materialism: "I want to join the society of the idealists, create an opposition among them: that is, I am a realist, not the materialist, ha-ha" (15:72).

Dostoevsky himself, as we remember, juxtaposes his own realism (and idealism) to materialism. Contrasting himself to conventional realists (or "earthly realists," in the devil's terms), Dostoevsky writes in his letter to A. N. Maikov (December 11, 1868):

> I have an entirely different notion of reality and realism from those of our realists and critics. My idealism is more real than theirs. My God! If you only render sensibly that which we, Russians, have lived through in our spiritual

---

18 "Сатана sum et nihil humanum a me alienum puto."
19 "Я страдаю, а все же не живу. Я икс в неопределенном уравнении."

development, would not the realists scream that this is a fantasy? Meanwhile, this is an original, true realism. This is precisely realism, only a more profound one, while their kind is merely on the surface. ... With their kind of realism you cannot explain so much as a hundredth part of the real facts, which have actually occurred. But with our idealism we have even prophesied facts. (*PSS*, 28(2):329)

Dostoevsky's realism, therefore, strives not merely at representation of the phenomenal material world but also at revealing the very essence of reality. It is for this reason that Dostoevsky views Christ as both an aesthetic and moral principle, for Christ's human nature coincides with his ideal form, and his "reality" is not bound by "earthly realism" of material facts and "truths," but at the same time he is fully palpable, visible, embodied, and, therefore, representable. The rivalry of the devil with Christ is the rivalry for incarnation, and, therefore, for the legitimacy of representation. Characteristically, in *The Brothers Karamazov*, both Christ and the devil are creations of Ivan's mind. However, though Christ is granted the status of real personality and has an embodied existence in Ivan's narrative, the devil remains merely his hallucination, or a phantasm.

Dostoevsky formulates his religious and aesthetic Christological creed in his oft-quoted letter to Natalia D. Fonvizina (January 1854):

This creed is very simple. Here it is: to believe that there is nothing more beautiful, deeper and more sympathetic, more rational, more manly and more perfect than Christ. And I say to myself with jealous love that not only is there no one else like him, but that there could be no one. Moreover, if anyone could prove to me that Christ is outside the truth, and if the truth *in actuality* were outside Christ, I should prefer to stay with Christ, rather than with truth. (emphasis in original) (*PSS*, 28(1):176)

The view of God (in the Christian tradition, of Christ) as the supreme beauty is hardly new, and the roots of it go back at least as far as Plato. What is important, however, about Dostoevsky's "creed" is his insistence on the particular aesthetic value of Christ's earthly, material existence, for such words as "sympathetic" (*simpatichnyi*) and "manly" (*muzhestvennyi*) could refer only to Christ's human hypostasis, that is, God incarnate. Significantly, in the Christian iconographic tradition, pictorial representation of Christ was justified by his incarnation. As Jeremy Begbie explains, "It is especially instructive to notice that those who

were reluctant to accept that Christ was God incarnate were also often opponents of icons."[20] Iconophiles insisted that it was possible to "circumscribe"
Jesus because of the Incarnation. Jaroslav Pelican summarizes the Byzantine
argument in favor of the iconic representations of Christ as follows:

> The dogma of the person of Jesus Christ, as this had been codified by the
> ecumenical councils and the creeds, was to supply the fundamental justifica-
> tion for the Christian icons in the church. ... Thus the incarnation of Christ
> as divinity made human did make it possible for Byzantine theology to
> affirm the validity of aesthetics and of representational religious art, but in
> the process it also transformed both art and aesthetics into something that
> had never quite been before. [21]

It is not a coincidence that Dostoevsky refers to his proclaimed ideas about the
beauty and perfection of Christ as his creed. Christ's divinity made human is
precisely what provides an aesthetic justification for his realism. We recall that
Ivan's devil, on the other hand, is jealous of Christ's incarnation and, therefore,
jealous of his "earthly realism." Since the devil cannot incarnate, there is no
possibility for his consistent representation either, for he inhabits or "possesses"
various human and animal forms, depending on "aesthetic preferences" of his
audience. Not surprisingly, as opposed to the Madonna or Christ, there is no
consistent iconographic representational tradition of the devil (just as there is
no consistent representational tradition of Sodom). The devil is an aesthetic
"sponger" and as such he could appear with horns and claws to please "the spir-
itualists" (as Ivan's devil mockingly refers to those seeking "material proof" of
his existence) or in the guise of Mephistopheles, in the Romantic rebellious
splendor or, finally, according to the aesthetic preferences of nineteenth-century
naturalism or realism, as a gentleman in a worn-out jacket and soiled under-
wear. Ivan's devil explains his own sponger nature: "C'est charmant, a sponger.
Yes, I am in my natural shape. For what I am on earth if not a sponger?" (*PSS*,
15:72). The Incarnation gives Christ the legitimacy of representation. The
devil, by contrast, is doomed to the representational uncertainty because of his
lack of embodiment. It is through Christian theology and aesthetics that

---

20 Jeremy Begbie, ed., *Beholding the Glory: Incarnation through the Arts* (Grand Rapids, MI:
    Baker, 2001), 87.
21 Jaroslav Pelikan, *Imago Dei: The Byzantine Apologia for Icons* (Princeton, NJ: Princeton
    University Press, 1990), 77.

Platonic dualism is overcome, that the intrinsic goodness of the created world (held in question by Plato) is reaffirmed, for incarnation creates a possibility of continuity between the absolute ideal form and the sensible world. Although rooted in the Platonic tradition, Christian aesthetics validates representation on the basis of continuity between the unrepresentable divinity and the world of phenomena, justified by incarnation.[22] The incarnation of God is what constitutes for Dostoevsky the highest beauty (letter to S. A. Ivanova, January 1, 1868): "In the world there is only one positively beautiful person—Christ, so that the appearance of this immeasurably, infinitely beautiful person is already an infinite miracle" (28, 2: 251).

If we consider the importance of the concept of incarnation for Christian aesthetics, then Dostoevsky's complex and much discussed response to Hans Holbein the Younger's *The Body of the Dead Christ in the Tomb* might elucidate his concept of realism in art. Arguably, Holbein's painting does not portray Christ's dual nature, or the Word made flesh. It is realist only in the "earthly" sense. Some would claim that it destroys continuity between the realm of "universals" and "particulars" ensured by incarnation. Thus, Anna Grigorievna Dostoevsky's reaction to the painting is similar to the one of Prince Myshkin, who in Dostoevsky's novel *The Idiot* asserts that one could lose one's faith from looking at this painting. According to this interpretation, Holbein's Christ pertains only to sensible reality, abjuring the ideal of absolute beauty. He is not God incarnated. This view is implicitly echoed in Julia Kristeva's analysis of this painting. She claims that the image transmits the new vision of mankind and that Holbein's representation is anti-iconic in the sense that it is void of transcendence and contains no promise of resurrection: "The unadorned representation of human death, the well-nigh anatomical stripping of the corpse conveys to viewers an unbearable anguish

---

22 The aesthetics of Russian icon art have been widely discussed by scholars and theologians who insisted that the "reverse perspective" of the icon gives the illusion of our standing inside the scene portrayed before us. The icon is not so much an artifact that is mimetic of reality as it is a portrayal of our participation in it; it creates, therefore, the opportunity of achieving direct contact with the Platonic *eidos*. See Pavel A. Florenskii, "Obratnaia perspektiva (1919–1922)," in *Filosofiia russkogo religioznogo iskusstva XVI-XX vv* (Moscow: Progress: 1993), 247–64. Florenskii points out that the iconic representation only "signifies, points to, hints at, leads to the idea of the original, but by no means reproduces this *image* in some *copy* or *model*" (259). See also Boris A. Uspenskii, "Semiotika ikony," *Semiotika iskusstva* (Moscow: Shkola "Iazyki russkoi kul'tury," 1995), 221–303.

before the death of God, which here is mingled with our own death because there isn't the slightest suggestion of transcendency."[23]

However, Dostoevsky's own approach to Holbein's painting is much more complex and is not dismissive of the painting's power of transcendence. Obviously, Dostoevsky would not have called Holbein a "remarkable artist and poet" if he did not see in the artist artistic qualities that were congenial to his own view of "realism in a higher sense." Robert Louis Jackson is undoubtedly right when he insists that Dostoevsky's references to Holbein as "a remarkable artist and poet"

> are foundational for any understanding of his response to Holbein's *Dead Christ*. They constitute the highest praise he could offer any painter or writer. The word "poet" is sacred in his vocabulary. It embodies not only the notion of inspiration, but imagination and insight, vision and prophecy, elements central to his concept of fantastic realism.[24]

Even though one of the characters of *The Idiot*, Ippolit Terentiev, seemingly critiques Holbein's painting and does not see it as a work of art, he points out to some crucial aspects of Christ's artistic representation:

> There is not a trace of beauty in Rogozhin's picture [that is, a copy of Holbein's painting]; this is a full representation of the corpse of man who has endured endless torments even before crucifixion—wounds, torture, beatings from the guards, beatings from the people when he was carrying the cross and fell beneath it, and finally, the passion of the cross lasting six hours (according at least to my calculations). True, this is a face of man, *just* taken down form the cross, that is, a face that preserves a great deal of its liveliness and warmth; nothing has had time to stiffen, so that the face of the dead man still expresses suffering, as though it were still being experienced (this is very well captured by the artist); but still this face has not been spared in the

---

23 Julia Kristeva, "Holbein's Dead Christ," in *Fragments for a History of the Human Body: Part One*, ed. Michael Feher, Ramona Naddaf, and Nadia Tazi (New York: Zone, 1989), 241. In her account of Kristeva's interpretation of Holbein, Sara Beardsworth elaborated upon this perception: "The image of flesh caught between a wounded body and decomposition transmits a feeling of permanent death. The effect is compounded by other features of the painting, for Holbein has voided it of any representation of transcendence. No vista stretches out behind the dead Christ to link him to the beyond, and no mourners tie him to the human realm"; Beardsworth, *Julia Kristeva: Psychoanalysis and Modernity* (Albany: SUNY Press, 2004), 146.

24 See Robert Louis Jackson's brilliant study in the present volume, chapter 9.

slightest; this is bare nature, and indeed this is how the corpse of man must look, whoever it may be, after such tortures. I know that the Christian church decreed in the very first centuries that Christ's passion was not figurative, but actual, and that his body on the cross must have been, therefore, wholly and entirely subject to the laws of nature. In the painting, this face is terribly mangled by blows, swollen, with terrible swollen, bloody bruises, the eyes are open, the pupils are askance; the whites wide open, gleaming with a kind of deadly, glass-like lustre. (*PSS*, 8:338–39)

Of particular importance here are Ippolit's words about theological interpretation of Christ's passion as an actual, rather than a figurative or symbolic, event. The triumph of Christian representation is precisely in the humanness of the divine.

The prescience of Dostoevsky's characterization of the crucifixion as an apotheosis of the ontological notion of divine materiality—in which the phenomenal and noumenal are brought into their necessary correlation—can be seen in the work of any number of contemporary theologians. Hans Urs von Balthasar elucidates the significance of Jesus's passion and death on the cross for Christian aesthetics:

This law extends to the inclusion in Christian beauty of even the Cross and everything else which a worldly aesthetics (even of a realistic kind) discards as no longer bearable. This inclusiveness is not only of the type proposed by a Platonic theory of beauty, which knows how to employ the shadows and the contradictions as stylistic elements of art; it embraces the most abysmal ugliness of sin and hell by virtue of the condescension of divine love, which has brought even sin and hell into that divine art for which there is no human analogue.[25]

Dostoevsky saw in Holbein this type of "inclusive" Christian aesthetics that was beyond the "worldly aesthetics" of conventional "realists," an aesthetic that was justified by the divine incarnation and could, therefore, embrace even the ugliness of the corrupted flesh. Holbein's Christ might very well evoke not divine but mundane and material prototype. However, this proto-image does not need to be that of God, who is uncircumscribable, but could be simply that of a dead man whose divinity is always a matter of faith and cannot, therefore, be

---

25 Hans Urs von Balthasar, *The Glory of the Lord: A Theological Aesthetics*, vol. 1, *Seeing the Form* (San Francisco: Ignatius, 1982), 124.

shaken by any "material proofs."[26] Admiring Holbein as an "artist and poet," Dostoevsky viewed this painting not as simulacrum (in modern parlance), but as an iconic representation, evoking a prototype through its glaring absence within this particular representation. It is iconic in a sense that the representation of the dead Christ is, in fact, an image referring to a proto-image. However, even though the human nature of Christ is representable, the divine nature is unrepresentable and unportrayable. In this sense Holbein's painting exemplifies the main challenge of Christian representation based on the dialectic of the Incarnation. Pelikan explains the Iconoclasts' argument with the Iconodules as stemming from their emphasizing "one polarity of this dialectic of the Incarnation at the expense of the other: 'Christ,' they said, 'is uncircumscribed and incomprehensible and impassible and immeasurable.'"[27] Iconoclasts, in a sense, dismissed the "earthly" Christ, for they believed that his human nature was also uncircumscribable and unportrayable. By contrast, the Iconodules believed that "the flesh was circumscribed, as it was seen upon earth during the years of Christ's life on earth, and therefore it was legitimate to iconize it now."[28] Seen from the point of view of the Iconodules' logic, then, Christ's flesh, even if it is a flesh of a dead Christ taken down from the cross, can be legitimately represented. Not only could it be represented, but even the corruption of the flesh cannot deny Jesus's divine nature because Jesus's human nature can never exist alone but must be the total divine-human person of Christ. As Kristeva reminds us, Holbein's painting does not have the "slightest suggestion of transcendency."[29] While there is certainly *mimesis* here—the scrupulous copying of an object—the real subject of the painting may very well be of the transformation to come, which is in no direct way suggested by the tableau that we see before us. The miraculous nature of the imminent resurrection is vividly communicated to the viewer by means of this appalling spectacle, of the body of Christ in its inert, scarified, and grotesquely cadaverous state. That is precisely why, so it seems,

26 We recall how Dostoevsky mocks the search for material proofs in the matter of faith through the ironic words of Ivan's devil and through his "theological" interpretation of St. Thomas the Apostle's faith: "Besides, no proof is of any help to faith, especially material proofs. Thomas believed not because he saw the resurrected Christ, but because he wished to believe, even before he saw" (*PSS*, 15:71).

27 Pelikan, *Imago Dei*, 78.

28 Ibid., 79.

29 Kristeva, "Holbein's Dead Christ," 241.

Dostoevsky both admires Holbein's painting and finds it profoundly disturbing: this image does evoke a prototype, but a very uncertain and highly ambiguous one—it could either affirm or destroy faith, depending on the position one takes in respect to the Incarnation. Dostoevsky was fascinated by Holbein's Christ as an image that refers to an event (the Resurrection) without attempting a direct representation of it. Like Russian icon art that Fyodor Karamazov scorns in *The Brothers Karamazov*, the painting is not so much a copy of the real—or, for that matter, a simulacrum untethered from any actual object—as it is a specular access point for encountering it.

In his own art, Dostoevsky strove to convey the inner likeness of humans to an idea, but he felt that contemporary art chose a different path by completely separating image from the proto-image and paying tribute only to the outer semblance. For him, Holbein's humanist painting was, as it were, on a threshold of modernity. The next logical step would be a complete disappearance of the original or proto-image. In the postmodern world this kind of aesthetic is linked to the triumph of simulacrum, which destroys hierarchy and denies any privileged point of view. Fyodor Karamazov, with his ontological disorder, his buffoonery, and destructive behavior, which eliminates the distinctions between the originals and copies, with his speech generating infinite phantasms, is a harbinger of this seductive new world of simulacra. And so is Ivan's devil, longing nostalgically for incarnation. Dostoevsky's own "realism in a higher sense" is rooted in the aesthetics of incarnation, an aesthetic that dissolves the Platonic severance between the world of forms and the world of appearance, and affirms the unbroken continuity between God and the world. Dostoevsky's aesthetics is close to Balthazar's "theological aesthetics" in its inclusiveness of worldly ugliness in the Christian beauty. This was Dostoevsky's powerful, although desperate, attempt to defend Neoplatonic representation in the wake of the new wave of iconoclasm, to which Jean Baudrillard refers in his *Simulacra and Simulation*.

PART

4

The Self and
the Other

XII

....

What Is It Like to Be Bats?
Paradoxes of *The Double*

Gary Saul Morson

After all, what would be left of what it was like to be
a bat if one removed the view point of the bat?
—Thomas Nagel, "What Is It Like to Be a Bat?"[1]

"The eternal silence of these infinite spaces terrifies me," wrote Pascal.[2] Somehow, the "I" that is my universe is located at an infinitesimal point. How can infinity be so compact?

In *War and Peace*, Pierre finds this mystery comic. Captured by the French, and seated by a campfire, he bursts into laughter: "They took me and shut me up ... Who is 'me'? ... Me—is my immortal soul!" Pierre looks around at the fields, forest, "the bright shimmering horizon luring one on to infinity," and thinks, "And all that is within me, and is *me*! ... And they caught all that and put it in a shed and barricaded it with planks!"[3] The moment provokes Pierre's laughter because the fact it reports—consciousness located in a body—is absurd. It is unbelievable but true, which is a contradiction. And it is also both outlandish and the most common thing in the world. The fact that Pierre laughs, as if for the first time, at something we all know is what provokes the reader's

---

1   Thomas Nagel, *Mortal Questions* (Cambridge: Cambridge University Press, 1979), 173.
2   As cited in Fred R. Shapiro, ed., *The Yale Book of Quotations* (New Haven, CT: Yale University Press, 2006), 584.
3   Leo Tolstoy, *War and Peace*, trans. Ann Dunnigan (New York: Signet, 1968), 1217.

laughter (or smile). Even to know about this fact is to experience it. "I am here"—we say it all the time—turns out to be an amazing thing to say.

How can something that has no physical presence and can contain the universe be somewhere in particular? It's like the mystery of the burning bush—something material but defying the laws of matter—except that each of us is the one on fire. Seen tragically, it is the mystery of death. When my body dies, my consciousness dies with it. "We all die alone," as Pascal also says, and that would be true even if some nuclear Armageddon made us all die simultaneously.[4] Consciousness cannot be shared. Pierre here expresses one of the ultimate mysteries. And for both Tolstoy and Dostoevsky, the important thing is to recognize that it *is* a mystery.

For the materialists of the Russian intelligentsia, it was not. For them, as for today's "new atheists," selfhood and consciousness do not constitute anything radically different from all those other things explained by physical science. Jacob Moleschott is supposed to have said that the brain secretes thought the way the liver secretes bile. Today some reduce thought to the firing of nerve endings, others to a sort of computer program. Daniel Dennett called his best-known work *Consciousness Explained*. For Dennett and Richard Dawkins, as for Chernyshevsky and Sechenov, there is no mystery.

Nagel wrote his classic essay on what it is like to be a bat to show that there is indeed a mystery. What makes consciousness mysterious is the existence of experiences that by their nature involve a point of view, a subjectivity, and so cannot be reduced to anything without a point of view:

> For if the facts of experience—facts about what it is like *for* the experiencing organism—are accessible only from one point of view, then it is a mystery how the true character of experiences could be revealed in the physical operation of that organism. The latter is a domain of objective facts *par excellence*, the kind that can be observed and understood from many points of view. (emphasis in original) (Nagel, *Mortal Questions*, 172)

In part 1, chapter 7 of *Anna Karenina*, Levin overhears a debate on this question, which has remained substantially the same from that time to this.

For one group of thinkers, it is an article of faith—I use the term advisedly—that there can be no mystery, because the whole point of science, as they conceive it, is to show that the world conforms to the categories of the mind and is scientifically

---

4   Shapiro, *Yale Book of Quotations*, 584.

knowable. Theirs is the position of Sophocles's Oedipus, who believes that human intellect can solve all riddles, but the play itself, and Greek tragedy generally, proclaims the opposite: the world defies human understanding.

Euripides ends five plays with lines affirming the ultimate unknowability of things. In *Medea* the chorus concludes:

> Many things the gods
> Achieve beyond our judgment. What we thought
> Is not confirmed and what we thought not god
> Contrives.[5]

And at the end of *Alcestis*, the chorus advises:

> Many are the forms of what is unknown.
> Much that the gods achieve is surprise.
> What we look for does not come to pass;
> God finds a way for what none foresaw.[6]

If we step back to consider, is not the presumption that the universe must conform to the capabilities of our minds the rankest anthropomorphism? Isn't it even more anthropomorphic than the personification of natural forces, since it involves the whole universe? And does not evolution strengthen Euripides's point by prompting us to ask why the evolution of minds to suit the conditions of earth should just happen to suit everything else? Isn't that a concealed argument by design?

Dostoevsky found this presumption—that the world, including the people in it, is readily intelligible—ridiculous. And so where others saw things as easily graspable, he kept creating for the reader the sense of the mysterious. He and his characters keep telling us that human behavior does not fit existing or conceivable scientific categories. Moral questions do not reduce to physical ones. Above all, there is the mystery of consciousness.

In *The Brothers Karamazov*, Dmitri paraphrases Rakitin's version of Dennetry: "Imagine: inside, in the nerves, in the head—that is, these nerves are there in the brain ... (damn them!) there are these sort of tails ... and when they

---

5 Translation by Rex Warner in *The Complete Greek Tragedies*, vol. 5, *Euripides I*, ed. David Greene and Richmond Lattimore (New York: Modern Library, 1956), lines 1416–19.
6 Translation by Richmond Lattimore in ibid., lines 1159–62.

quiver an image appears … that is an object, or an action, damn it. That's why I see and then think, because of those tails, not at all because I've got a soul."[7] "An image appears"—to whom? The explanation stops short just at the most important point, which is not how images can be created, but how they can appear as images to me, to a subjectivity. In a physical universe that in and of itself lacks point of view, each of us has one.

It should be obvious that any account of the world that does not include this point-of-viewness is leaving something out, is "incomplete," as Nagel likes to say. But science as today's materialists and those of the Russian intelligentsia understood it deals with explanations that allow for no point of view. Indeed, part of the thrill of materialist taboo-breaking comes from reducing the personal to the impersonal. Today, that is what provides the frisson to the manifestly absurd claim that authors are nothing more than the vehicle through which social forces operate. Such thrills worked its magic in Dostoevsky's time, and so he developed a series of counterthrills designed to make the opposite point. The tails of nerves don't know anything, and so they are unaware of their own existence. There is no point-of-viewness about them.

One thing we all share is that we each have something we do not share. That is why we all die alone. My consciousness is precisely mine. Typically, philosophical thought experiments about selfhood work by supposing the opposite and generating absurdity. This sort of reduction to the absurd was one of Dostoevsky's favorite kinds of humor.

Consider: If I am nothing but how I appear to the outside, why could I not be copied? If I could be, would there be two of me? (This is sometime called "the amoeba problem.") Would these two of me directly sense each other? If so, would they really be one of me in two bodies? As Siamese twins are two selves sharing part of a body, could there be Siamese selves sharing part of a me? Or would me and copy-me each be a separate me, albeit absolutely identical to its counterpart, and each sensing only its own subjectivity?

Is your double you? Our deep fascination with identical twins, still more with Siamese twins, derives from our sense that subjectivity must be unique. Golyadkin considers twinning as something resembling his experience when his precise double appears, but doubling goes a step further. *Ex hypothesi*, a person and his double are absolutely identical from the external standpoint.

---

7   Fyodor Dostoevsky, *The Brothers Karamazov*, trans. Constance Garnett (New York: Modern Library, 1950), 716–17.

Identical twins do not have the same name, but the two Golyadkins do, and that is one reason our hero is especially horrified to learn that the other Golyadkin is also Yakov Petrovich! The story would not be nearly so funny if the double were, let us say, Akaky Akakievich.[8]

"Both together is impossible"

If there were someone exactly like me, would it be me? For a materialist, that would have to be the case, since identical causes must produce identical results. If one imagines a sort of biological 3-D printer that could make a molecularly correct exact replica of me, would there therefore be the same me in two heads? Or what? If someone exactly like me were to replace me, and no one could notice any change, would I still be there? (Does that perhaps happen when they "beam up" someone in *Star Trek*?)

The identity of the Golyadkins' names is, if anything, weirder than mere identity of appearance. As we would say today, it cannot be the result of DNA. It suggests an identity of *persons* even where we see two *men*, and so creates a metaphysical comedy. If the two Golyadkins are objectively absolutely the same, perhaps they are also subjectively the same, but without knowing it? Do they each have the same point-of-viewness? What would that be like?

Dostoevsky constantly plays on the identity of names suggesting an identity of identity. He milks the absurdity for all it is worth when Yakov Petrovich addresses a letter to Yakov Petrovich. Actually, and appropriately, he addresses two such letters:

Dear Sir, Yakov Petrovich!

... Your obstinate desire to persist in your course of action, sir, and forcibly to enter the circle of my existence, ... transgresses every limit imposed by the merest politeness ... I imagine there is no need, sir, for me to refer to ... your taking away my good name. ... I will not allude here to your strange, one may even say, incomprehensible behavior to me in the coffee house ...

Your most humble servant,
Ya. Golyadkin
(*PSS*, 1:175; 218–19)[9]

---

8 Of course, the story alludes to Akaky Akakievich, who is a copyist and has a double name.

9 Cited passages from *The Double* are from Dostoevsky's 1866 revision of the novella as it appears in F. M. Dostoevsky, *Polnoe sobranie sochinenii v tridtsati tomakh* [*PSS*], ed. V. G. Bazanov et al. (Leningrad: Nauka, 1972–1990); hereafter cited as *PSS* by volume and page. The

Dear Sir, Yakov Petrovich!
Either you or I, but both together is impossible! ... However, I remain
ready to oblige or to meet you with pistols.
Ya. Golyadkin
(*PSS*, 1:188; 234)

The endlessly varying metaphysical joke is that the two who somehow think
they are different people are indeed the same person. But how can one person
think he is not himself? He might somehow forget or be brainwashed about his
name and even his past, but how could he be wrong about his subjectivity? To
cite a famous example from John Locke, if a prince's consciousness should
change places with a cobbler's, the prince would still feel his own *me* even if he
must repair shoes.[10] Others could be mistaken because they must judge from
the outside, but I *am* me, am I not?

Locke explains: "I know that in the ordinary way of speaking, the same
person, and the same man, stand for one and the same thing," but if we are
really to understand "what makes the same spirit, man, or person," we must
carefully distinguish these terms.[11] Locke concludes that personhood is
precisely consciousness. And consciousness can be in only one place at a
time. If we imagine a person whose finger is cut off, and further suppose
that consciousness went with the finger—so that, in a sense, it was not the
finger but the rest of the body that was cut off—we would see that personhood goes with consciousness. (That is part of the joke in Gogol's "The
Nose," from which Dostoevsky borrowed liberally.) Wherever consciousness
may be, Locke concludes, it must still be either here or there at any given
moment.

Or as Golyadkin says: "Either you or I, but both together is impossible!"
Of course, he has not read any philosophy and means something like "This
town isn't big enough for the two of us!" But the reader also detects the literal
sense of the words: either you are me or I am me, but not both. More than one

---

translations are from Fyodor Dostoevsky, *The Double*, in *The Eternal Husband and Other
Stories*, trans. Constance Garnett (New York: Macmillan, 1956), cited second by page
number, but I have often adjusted the translation, sometimes extensively.

10   See Locke's fascinating exploration of the problem in the chapter "Of Ideas of Identity and
Diversity," in John Locke, *An Essay Concerning Human Understanding*, ed. Alexander Camp-
bell Fraser (New York: Dover, 1959), 1:439–70.

11   Ibid., 1:457.

me is "impossible"—not just in the sense of "unacceptable" but also "logically incoherent." It is not taboo but senseless to say, except figuratively, that another can "enter the circle of my existence." My existence as me cannot be in two persons, and two persons cannot be one me.

And yet: the very fact that Golyadkin has to prove his point by threatening a duel suggests that he himself believes the opposite. (After all, if the two people were really one, and one Golyadkin shot the other, would he not be killing himself too? In the world of doubles, murder can be suicide, and vice versa.) Golyadkin insists, without expecting to be believed, "He's another person, your Excellency, but I'm another person too; he's apart and I am also myself by myself [*sam po sebe*]; I am really myself by myself," he explains, as if he needs convincing (*PSS*, 1:213; 264).

The story's deep humor derives, in short, from Golyadkin's recognition, and simultaneous refusal to recognize, that the double is not just like him but *is* him, and that he is his own impersonator. Jean Cocteau is supposed to have said that "Victor Hugo was a madman who thought he was Victor Hugo," but Golyadkin is a madman who worries that he *isn't* Golyadkin. We might sum up the point of Gogol's *Dead Souls* and *The Inspector General* as "everything is a counterfeit and there is no original," and by the same token we might paraphrase *The Double* as "everything is an impersonation but there is no person."

One could almost say that the master joke in all of Gogol is first to offer a fake, a copy, a forgery, a counterfeit, an impersonation, an imitation, a replica, or a representation, all of which by their very logic demand something else that is being faked or copied or impersonated or replicated, and then to deny the existence of that something else. What if (as Nozdrev suggests) there are only lies? Oh, do not trust that Nevsky Prospekt!

Dostoevsky adapts this joke, which relies on sheer nonsense, to the problem of identity. It makes no sense to deny one's own existence, but that denial expresses a fundamental human anxiety. The Underground Man needs proof that he exists, so he tries to get himself thrown out of the window, since one does not humiliate a mere object, but the officer instead moves him aside like a piece of furniture. In the same Dostoevskian spirit, Ralph Ellison's Invisible Man, remarks that not being seen, "you often doubt if you really exist."[12]

---

12 Ralph Ellison, *Invisible Man* (New York: Vintage, 1972), 3.

Horror stories (or films like Roman Polanski's *The Tenant*) often work by suggesting an existential threat to the hero's identity, and overtones of horror pervade *The Double.* If anything, Golyadkin's double is more truly him (if comparatives have any meaning here) than he is.

When Golyadkin encounters the double, we get an absurd variation on a device that goes back to Greek tragedy, Shakespeare, Gogol, and countless other dramatists—the recognition scene: "He perfectly recognized his nocturnal visitor. The nocturnal visitor was no other than himself [*ne kto inoi, kak on sam*]—Mr. Golyadkin himself, another Mr. Golyadkin, but perfectly the very same as he himself [*sovershenno takoi zhe, kak on sam*]," a double in every respect (*PSS*, 1:143; 179).

The real horror, which the hero constantly tries to ward off, is that although subjectivity is indeed unique and only one of a *me* can exist, the real me is not mine but his, and I am the one who does not have a *me*! I am the pretender! This possibility is hard even to state precisely because we all believe that a me is directly present to itself. I might, for instance, discover that a man people took to be a certain person is his twin, and, in fact, numerous murder mysteries have turned on this possibility of misidentification from the outside. No one knows the suspect has a twin, and so he can easily create an airtight alibi while his twin commits the crime. This plot has become so familiar that it has generated a variant in which people know there are twins, and suspect the twin ruse, but both twins have airtight alibis—only they are not twins, but two of triplets.

But these "mysteries" are not at all mysterious in any fundamental way, as they would be if there were a misidentification of a subjectivity *from the inside.* The absurdity of such an idea suggests that we simply know, in the sense that we cannot sensibly doubt, that we have a subjectivity.

Someone might say, "Prove that it is you!," meaning that you are the person you say you are, but that would mean *prove it to someone else.* Proving it to yourself—proving that your *me*, experienced from within, is really your *me*—would constitute a rather different sort of challenge. In fact, proof, if one means making something that has overcome doubt, completely misses the point, because one's own existence can't be doubted to begin with. Something literally indubitable not only does not need proof, but would be compromised by it, because where there is proof there is the possibility of doubt. Usually proof is the strongest way to establish a point, but in this case it is inferior to the direct experience.

This stronger-than-proof indubitability arises precisely because there *is* a point-of-view aspect of the world. We arrive again at Dostoevsky's intense sense that we cannot truly believe that a purely objective, point-of-view-less description of the world could ever be complete. The materialists must be wrong precisely because for them that description is complete.

To believe that, you might as well—Descartes notwithstanding—doubt your own existence. Strangely enough, Golyadkin does: he "even began to doubt his own existence" (*PSS*, 1:147; 183). For that matter, so does the devil in *Brothers Karamazov*, but there the devil himself knowingly plays the role of a metaphysical nihilist. Despite his status as a supernatural being, he is not sure whether he believes in the supernatural. What's more, he may be a merely possible being, living a merely hypothetical existence, which is why he professes to wish he could be incarnated into a fat old lady of simple faith. He even knows he is Ivan's double, perhaps just a figment of Ivan's fevered imagination, and so might very well not exist at all. Dostoevsky never tired of this joke.

The Thinking Rag

The best known passage in Pascal joins the mystery of selfhood to the nobility of thought:

> Man is but a reed, the most feeble thing in nature, but he is a thinking reed. The entire universe need not arm itself to crush him. ... But if the universe were to crush him, man would still be more noble than that which killed him, because he knows that he dies and the advantage the universe has over him; the universe knows nothing of this.[13]

The Double seems to transform these lines. Golyadkin, who is the opposite of noble, tells himself he will not "allow himself to be insulted" since he is a man, not a thing. He insists he will not "be treated like a rag ... I am not a rag. I am not a rag, sir!" As if paraphrasing Golyadkin's own uncertainties from within, the narrator mocks this statement:

> Possibly if someone wanted, if someone, for instance, actually insisted on turning Mr. Golyadkin into a rag, he might have done so, might have done so

---

13 I borrow the translation used as the epigraph for Rebecca West's novel, *The Thinking Reed* (New York: Viking, 1936), facing title page.

without opposition or punishment (Mr. Golyadkin himself felt this at times)—and there would have emerged a rag and not Golyadkin—yes, a nasty, filthy rag; but this rag would not have been a simple rag, this would have been a rag with self-esteem, this rag would have had animation and feelings, even though it would have been a timid pride and timid feelings, hidden far away and deep within the folds of this rag, but all the same they would have been feelings. (*PSS*, 1:168; 210)

I was forced to retranslate this passage to preserve the constant repetition of the word "rag," which seems to provoke a wince of pain in Golyadkin every time it is uttered, with every wince inspiring the narrator to say it again and again.

Since only a non-thing could say it either is or is not a thing, one would think that there would be no reason to insist on one's non-thing-ness. And yet, Golyadkin does insist that he is not a thing, that he has self-esteem and feelings. For Pascal, man is a reed, but a thinking reed; for this narrator, the hero is a rag, but a feeling rag. Not just thinking, but feeling—because, for Dostoevsky, it is not consciousness, or even self-consciousness, but the particular sort of agonizing self-consciousness we call humiliation that makes us human.

We have moved from man as *un roseau pensant* ("a thinking reed") to man as *un chiffon tremblant* ("a trembling rag"). Pascal's thinking reed is overwhelmed only by the universe's physical force, but Dostoevsky's rag is also overwhelmed by society's moral force. Physical force at least leaves the self with nobility, but social force strips away that, too. When Dmitri Karamazov must strip, he feels his very self exposed. All stripping, physical or moral, is unspeakably painful— Dostoevsky's Underground Man compares it to being flayed alive—and it seems to explain the etymology of the hero's name, Golyadkin (from *golyi*, "naked"). The narrator seems to revel in inflicting such pain.

Descartes pointed to thought, but other philosophers have argued that pain proves consciousness still more clearly. When in pain, even a materialist who regards thought as analogous to bile cannot doubt, can barely pretend to doubt, that he is in pain. That is why the Underground Man speaks of an educated man of the nineteenth century who is suffering from toothache. Just try to be a materialist with aching teeth! As there are no atheists in foxholes, so there are no materialists in dental chairs.

But Dostoevsky knows that pain is not enough to make us human. Animals, after all, also suffer pain. What they are missing is humiliation. Pain proves we have a subjectivity, but humiliation proves we have a *social* subjectivity, and human subjectivity is essentially social. I am humiliated, therefore I am human. It has been said that all of Dostoevsky's novels could be called *Crime and Punishment*, and we may add that they could also be called *The Insulted and the Humiliated*.

Golyadkin's inner discourse constantly reflects his awareness of being spied on, judged, regarded as strange. And so he constantly assures himself that he is all right, just like everyone else, and why should he not be? When he leaves the doctor's office, he looks up and sees the doctor watching him from the window. It is a sort of early study in Stavrogin's resentment of Tikhon as a spy into his soul.

The "feeling rag" passage captures this sense of humiliation at its most vertiginous. Constantly, as Bakhtin notes, Golyadkin simulates "independence and indifference … directed not outward, not toward another, but toward Golyadkin's own self: he persuades himself, reassures and comforts himself, plays the role of another person vis-à-vis himself. Golyadkin's comforting dialogues with himself are the most prominent trait of the whole story."[14] And these dialogues are themselves the result of "the total nonrecognition of his personality on the part of others," including the narrator—and even, we may add, of himself.[15] Because of the narrator's taunting tone, readers simultaneously occupy the role of humiliator and humiliated, as they both identify with Golyadkin and laugh at him.

The Bad Samaritan

At the beginning of the "Rebellion" chapter, Ivan Karamazov maintains that one cannot truly love one's neighbor, simply because he is he and I am I and that difference is unbridgeable. There can be no real empathy, any more than my *me* can be experienced as if it were someone else's *me*. Ivan breaks out of this circle of self when he returns to help the drunken peasant freezing in the snow. The incident alludes to Jesus's story of the man who had "fallen among thieves" and been left naked and half-dead. A priest sees him and passes by "on the other

---

14 Mikhail Bakhtin, *Problems of Dostoevsky's Poetics*, trans. Caryl Emerson (Minneapolis: University of Minnesota Press, 1984), 212.

15 Ibid., 215.

side," as does a Levite. But a good Samaritan "had compassion on him" (Luke 10:33). Jesus tells the story to explain what it means to "love thy neighbor," which, after caring for the peasant, Ivan now recognizes is indeed possible. For Ivan, the discovery comes too late, but for Golyadkin it does not come at all. That is why we sense there is hope for Ivan's, but not Golyadkin's, recovery from insanity.

I think the key incident in *The Double* has been overlooked. Let us call it "the bad Samaritan." When the double follows Golyadkin home, Golyadkin takes him in and, apparently, pities him. The new Golyadkin is a picture of humiliation as only Dostoevsky can describe it:

> There was a downtrodden, crushed, scared look about all his gestures, so that—if the comparison might be allowed—he was at that moment rather like the man who, having lost his clothes, is dressed up in someone else's: the sleeves work up to the elbows, the waist is almost up to his neck, and he keeps every minute pulling down the short waistcoat; he wriggles sideways and turns away, tries to hide himself, or peeps into every face, and listens whether people are talking of his position, laughing at him or putting him to shame—and he is crimson with shame and overwhelmed with confusion and wounded vanity. (*PSS*, 1:153; 191)

He is more naked clothed than nude. This poor soul is fallen among Petersburgers, stripped not physically but morally. For a moment, Golyadkin is "genuinely touched" (*PSS*, 1:156; 194). But almost immediately his mood takes on—if the phrase may be allowed—a Dostoevskian quality: "In short, Mr. Golyadkin was quite happy ... because, so far from being afraid of his enemies, he was quite prepared now to challenge them all to mortal combat ... [and] because he was now in the role of a patron" (*PSS*, 1:157; 195).

Golyadkin has the chance to show compassion and care for the other person for the sake of the other person. But he treats the other as—well, as an extension of himself. He sees in his pitiful companion someone who will toady up to him as Golyadkin has toadied up to others; and, still worse, he values him as someone who will be his ally in intrigues against those others.

For Golyadkin, others exist either to intrigue against him or to be intrigued against, much as the Underground Man can only imagine love as dominating or being dominated. The only empathy Golyadkin knows comes from recognizing another person as an inflictor of pain or an object of patronage. When the double starts to torment Golyadkin, he is only enacting Golyadkin's own intentions. It is, of course, because the double knows Golyadkin so intimately that he can touch his sore spots with such uncanny accuracy.

Empathy is necessary for morality, but not sufficient, as every good con man knows. The reason that, as Dostoevsky repeatedly suggests, former victims make the most skilled torturers is that they know just what hurts the most. For the same reason empathy can be used not to comfort but to exacerbate. The double makes full, sadistic use of this privilege. For who knows better how to torment oneself than one's own replica, and who loves being in the dominating position more than Golyadkin himself? This is one case where the punishment fits the crime precisely. In this sense, *The Double* is an early version of *Crime and Punishment*. Golyadkin gets exactly what he deserves, and his suffering (and ours along with him) is all the more acute because of it.

From this point on, the story logically unfolds with a mounting humiliation leading to the madhouse. The story ends: "Our hero shrieked and clutched his head in his hands. Alas! For a long while he had been haunted by a presentiment of this!" (*PSS*, 1:229; 284). A presentiment, or fore-feeling, is a sort of temporal double. The sense of inevitability derives from the fact that the fore-felt event is a repetition of what was already long there. And yet: for one moment, the moment when he felt genuine sympathy, he could have escaped the logic of doubling, leaving his own shadow behind.

One can see each of Dostoevsky's works as intensifying one or another sense of the mysterious. When Svidrigailov and Stavrogin come to disbelieve absolutely in the mysterious, and see the world as completely banal, they kill themselves, but they are not the characters furthest from Dostoevsky's own viewpoint. At least they look for mystery. That is why Svidrigailov sees, and is glad he sees, ghosts, even if they are themselves banal spirits. Fyodor Pavlovich at least feels mystical terror. No, the characters most distant from the author are those who do not even look for mystery and who are smugly sure that only the stupid, the superstitious, and the religious believe in it. The real villains of *Brothers Karamazov* are Smerdyakov and his petty double, Rakitin.

It is sometimes said that with the passing of communism, Dostoevsky's relevance has faded a bit, but I think that the prevalence of both sociological and neurologic challenges to the ultimate mysteries makes him more pertinent than ever. The intellectual West has grown hostile to religion because, as Dostoevsky foresaw, it has come to disbelieve not just in God but in the very subject who could experience belief. Killing subjectivity has proven harder than killing God because subjectivity is directly experienced. But it can still be treated as a mirage, a double of something that does not exist.[16]

---

16 I have developed these ideas on *The Double* in a longer essay, "Me and My Double: Selfhood, Consciousness, and Empathy in *The Double*," in *Before They Were Titans: Essays on the Early Works of Dostoevsky and Tolstoy*, ed. Elizabeth Cheresh Allen (Boston: Academic Studies Press, 2015), 43–60.

Interiority and Intersubjectivity in Dostoevsky: The Vasya Shumkov Paradigm

Yuri Corrigan

Indwelling Self/Relational Self

Among studies of Dostoevsky's conception of personality, two largely incompatible and equally influential schools of thought can be discerned. On the one hand, Dostoevsky has been read as a neo-Romantic "expressivist" who situated the roots of the personality, and of the world itself, in the inexhaustible depths of the "human soul."[1] The elder Zosima's teaching in *The Brothers Karamazov* on the organic nature of the personality whose roots "touch other worlds" provides a vivid illustration of this view: Zosima describes our "secret innermost sensation" of a "connection with ... a celestial and higher world," and our sense that "the roots of our thoughts and feelings are not here, but in those other worlds" (*PSS*, 14:291).[2] It was in this mystical Romantic vein that Vladimir Solovyov

---

1 By "expressivist," I mean the view that the human personality is an expression of the sources of nature that lie in its depths. For Charles Taylor's espousal of the term "expressivism," see "The Expressivist Turn," in *Sources of the Self: The Making of Modern Identity* (Cambridge, MA: Harvard University Press, 1989), 368–92. On Dostoevsky and expressivism, see Malcolm V. Jones, *Dostoyevsky after Bakhtin* (Cambridge: Cambridge University Press, 1990), 3.

2 F. M. Dostoevskii, *Polnoe sobranie sochinenii v tridtsati tomakh* [*PSS*], ed. V. G. Bazanov et al. (Leningrad: Nauka, 1972–90); hereafter cited as *PSS* by volume and page. All translations are mine.

spoke of Dostoevsky's belief in "the divine power in the soul" and in its "divine origin."[3] The personality, understood thus, becomes not only a repository for divinity but also an "all-encompassing," "microcosmic" universe within itself.[4] Various traditions of selfhood stand behind this notion of personality, among them the Neoplatonic Augustinian self that turns inward to discover the presence of the divine in its depths, or the German Romantic self that reaches, in its dark inscrutable basis, into the very sources of nature and of the universe.[5]

In observing the radically social, relational nature of Dostoevsky's characters, however, readers have questioned whether this apparent belief in the infinite inward capaciousness of the self extends to his active psychological portraits.[6] Thus, a second school of thought finds its center in what can be described as Bakhtin's Dostoevsky: a remarkably contemporary, potentially postmodern writer who reconceived traditional notions of self in intersubjective dialogical space. This is the Dostoevsky who, according to Tzvetan Todorov, "rejects an essentialist conception of man," and locates the "psychic structure" of the personality entirely in human relationships, and for whom "the human being has no existence prior to the other or independent of him."[7] Bakhtin called attention to the absence of a psychologized

---

3 Vladimir Solovyov, *Sobranie sochinenii Vladimira Sergeevicha Solov'eva* (St. Petersburg: Knigoizdatel'skoe Tovarishchestvo "Prosveshchenie," 1914), 3:185.

4 Dmitrii Chizhevskii, "Dostoevskij—psikholog," in *O Dostoevskom: Sbornik statej* (Prague, 1929), 1:55.

5 "If everything in nature is living, and if we ourselves are simply its most self-conscious representatives, the function of the artist is to delve within himself, and above all to delve within the dark and unconscious forces which move within him, and to bring these to consciousness by the most agonizing and violent internal struggle. This is Schelling's doctrine"; Isaiah Berlin, *The Roots of Romanticism* (Princeton, NJ: Princeton University Press, 1999), 98.

6 Edith Clowes articulates some of this ambivalence when, after having compared Dostoevsky to Nietzsche as a proponent of the Romantic emphasis on integrating the subliminal natural forces that undergird consciousness, she nevertheless point out that "Dostoevsky's moral consciousness is much more socially oriented than Nietzsche's" and that Dostoevsky is less interested in "penetrating the complex interactions of subliminal forces in the *intra*personal sphere" and more focused on "resolution of conflicts … in the *inter*personal sphere"; Clowes, "Self-Laceration and Resentment: The Terms of Moral Psychology in Dostoevsky and Nietzsche," in *Freedom and Responsibility in Russian Literature: Essays in Honor of Robert Louis Jackson* (Evanston, IL: Northwestern University Press, 1995), 133.

7 Tzvetan Todorov, "Notes from the Underground," in *Genres in Discourse* (Cambridge: Cambridge University Press, 1990), 89. Todorov, echoing Bakhtin, asserts that

and naturalized sense of self in Dostoevsky's characters, who lack the detailed interiority or personal biography of realist literature, and whose radical inner formlessness abates only in the activity of interpersonal dialogue.[8] These characters, Bakhtin observed, are always on the "threshold," looking outward, existing fully in the "living *present*," never determined or limited by unconscious lives or biographical pasts.[9] Bakhtin's perspective helps illuminate the relational nature of personhood in Dostoevsky, whose characters apprehend their depths *outside* of themselves, "in the souls of *others*."[10] From this perspective, if the self is rooted in other worlds, as Zosima espouses, then those other worlds are not transcendent essences but rather the worlds of other personalities.

Thus, the self in Dostoevsky is thought of, on the one hand, as an *essence*, a bottomless depth, encompassing and expressing the entire universe, and, on the other hand, as an *activity*, *event*, or *point of view* that constitutes itself outwardly through relationships. My present treatment here engages this

---

Dostoevsky locates "the essence of being in the other" (87). For a similar view, see also Julia Kristeva, "The Ruin of a Poetics," in *Russian Formalism: A Collection of Articles and Texts in Translation*, ed. Stephen Bann and John E. Bowlt (Harper and Row, 1973), 102–21.

8 Malcolm Jones accepts "expressivism" as an important aspect of Dostoevsky's philosophical outlook and argues, interestingly, that the "fantastic realism" of a Bakhtinian Dostoevsky is "not to be located in the process of spiritual evolution described by Dostoyevsky … but in the 'deviations,' … the destabilizing effects of what Bakhtin calls heteroglossia in urban life where man is torn from his roots" (*Dostoevsky after Bakhtin*, 6–7).

9 Bakhtin, *Problems of Dostoevsky's Poetics*, ed. and trans. Caryl Emerson (Minneapolis: University of Minnesota Press, 1984), 108. See Irina Sandomirskaia's forceful critique of Bakhtin's concept of the self: "A body without a name, without a personality and without borders—such is the subject in the inhuman political economy that goes by the name of dialogue"; Sandomirskaia, "Golaia zhizn', zloi Bakhtin i vezhlivyi Vaginov: Tragediia bez khora i avtora," in *Telling Forms: 30 Essays in Honour of Peter Alberg Jensen*, ed. Karin Grelz and Susanna Witt (Stockholm: Almqvist & Wiksell, 2004), 338.

10 Bakhtin, *Problems of Dostoevsky's Poetics*, 61; emphasis in original. See Holquist's discussion of Bakhtin's move against "untrammeled subjectivity," the "old conviction that the individual subject is the seat of certainty, whether the subject so conceived was God, the soul, the author, or my self" (19); see Michael Holquist, *Dialogism: Bakhtin and His World*, 2nd ed. (New York: Routledge, 2002), esp. 14–27. For an example of Bakhtin's resonance in the fields of psychology and cultural theory as a thinker who "challenges the idea of a core, essential self," see Hubert J. M. Hermans, "The Dialogical Self: Toward a Theory of Personal and Cultural Positioning," *Culture and Psychology* 7, no. 3 (2001): 243–81.

duality in commentary by examining the tension between interiority and inter-subjectivity already distinctly evident in one of Dostoevsky's much-neglected early stories, "A Weak Heart" ("Slaboe serdtse"), published in 1848. Both the indwelling and relational models of selfhood are evoked in this portrait of how two personalities of significant interior complexity unravel themselves in external, intersubjective space. I shall focus on the paradigm of the collapse of the collective, intersubjective personality in "A Weak Heart" as a window into Dostoevsky's career-long meditation on the problem of personal essence (or soul). In using the early story as point of entry into Dostoevsky's expansive meditation of the self, I shall also explore "A Weak Heart" as a blueprint for the portrait of collapsed interiority in *Crime and Punishment*.

Intimate Friendship and the Collective Self

"A Weak Heart" depicts the anxious travails and gradual descent into madness of one Vasya Shumkov, a humble, ardent, slightly disfigured clerk who has been entrusted with a large amount of copying work by his superior and benefactor, Yulian Mastakovich. Because of a newly formed engagement with his beloved Liza, whom he has fervently pursued for weeks, Vasya has egregiously neglected his work. His roommate and best friend, Arkady Nefedevich, tries to help him finish the copying, attempting at all costs to shore up his friend's sanity, but Vasya, overwhelmed by the emotions of his newfound happiness, and tormented by his "ingratitude" before his benefactor, whom he feels he has betrayed, is ultimately beyond saving. Vasya undergoes a pitiful public collapse, is removed to an asylum, and Arkady is left alone without his friend in the cold and ghostlike city of St. Petersburg.

The work has been consistently read, for good reason, as "a story of social protest" in its illustration of how a lowly civil servant is crushed by the hierarchical rank-and-file nature of imperial Russia.[11] According to this traditional reading,

---

11 Victor Terras, *The Young Dostoevsky* (1846–49) (The Hague: Mouton, 1969), 39. See also W. J. Leatherbarrow, "Idealism and Utopian Socialism in Dostoyevsky's Gospodin Prokharchin and Slaboye serdtse," *Slavonic and East European Review* 58, no. 4 (1980): 524–40; and Joseph Frank, *Dostoevsky: The Seeds of Revolt, 1821–1849* (Princeton, NJ: Princeton University Press, 1979), 318–22. Donald Fanger avoids the political context, characterizing Vasya as prototype for "the generous dreamer" who "cannot stand the anomalous burden of happiness in an imperfect world"; see Fanger, *Dostoevsky and Romantic Realism: A Study of Dostoevsky in Relation to Balzac, Dickens, and Gogol* (Evanston, IL: Northwestern University Press, 1998), 168.

the meek Vasya Shumkov, in his wrenching psychological collapse, is a representative of Dostoevsky's "downtrodden" (the focus of his early, socially oriented writing), his breakdown the result of his having utterly internalized his subordinate status.[12]

When read in the context of Dostoevsky's extended inquiry into the notion of relational personhood, however, the passionate, intimate attachment between Vasya and his roommate, Arkady, seems less a facet of Dostoevsky's social commentary and more the kernel of a larger philosophical and psychological project. The loving friendship vividly expresses the dangers of intimacy in Dostoevsky's world, as the friends' closeness leads directly to the replacement of aspects of the self with the activities of the other. In this sense, the relationship provides a concept of intersubjective selfhood notably different from, and considerably more pathological than, the dialogical model espoused by Bakhtin: in Vasya and Arkady we see an overwhelming need for the other as a completion of one's own unfinished personality, a personality that degenerates as it becomes gradually subsumed and supplanted by its loving but overpowering counterpart. As we shall see, Vasya's escape from assimilation by Arkady's personality prefigures numerous scenes and paradigms from the later works in which characters struggle to be released from their imprisonment within intersubjective personalities, while encountering within themselves a lack of architecture, an atrophied self, propped up and supplemented by the tireless activity of another person.

The friendship between Arkady and Vasya enacts a complementary distribution of faculties between adjacent personalities, of a vigilant administrative mind (Arkady) that binds itself to a subordinate, largely irrational, intensely feeling, obedient nature, or "weak heart" (Vasya). Arkady plays the role of the friends' collective superego, having "loved [Vasya] so, watched over him, instructed him at every step with saving advices" (*PSS*, 2:28). As Vasya's external conscience, he takes on full responsibility for his friend's work deadline, beseeching Vasya to look to him for guidance, to "hold to me," as he puts it, so that "I will stand over you with a stick today and tomorrow, and all night, and I will torment you in your work: finish up! Finish up faster, brother!" (2:29). Arkady's zealous solicitude often resembles an invasion, or annexation, of his friend's agency. He consistently bemoans the fact that he cannot take over for Vasya entirely, that he cannot save

---

12   See N. A. Dobroliubov, "Zabitye liudi," in *Literaturno-kriticheskie stat'i* (Moscow, 1937), 480–81.

his friend by simply occupying his place: "How annoying that I cannot help you," he exclaims to Vasya, "or else I would have taken it and would have written it all for you ... Why don't you and I have the same handwriting?" (2:29). Arkady constantly expresses the desire to substitute himself for Vasya, stressing, for example, his ability to sign Vasya's name: "I sign your name terribly similarly and make the same curl ... Who would notice!" (2:31). Vasya, in turn, apparently conceives of his own existence as directly dependent on Arkady's, and he continually declares, rather mysteriously, that he "would not be living in this world" were it not for his love for Arkady (2:18, 26). The weaker of the two men, Vasya is generally inclined to accept Arkady's administration, looking at his friend "ever so timidly ... as if his decision ... depended on him" (2:22), his pathetic "feeble" (2:17) physicality repeatedly overwhelmed by Arkady's "leonine," (2:22) "powerful greedy ... embraces" (2:33) and "strong arms" (2:17).

As co-joined personalities, Arkady and Vasya exhibit an extreme degree of intimacy. They constantly throw themselves into each other's ardent, loving embraces (*PSS*, 2:17, 18, 36, 42, 44, 47). Early in the story, Arkady lifts Vasya up and carries him around the room like a child, "pretending that he was lulling him to sleep" (2:17).[13] Later on, "Arkady thr[ows] himself upon him, like a mother whose kindred child is being taken away" (2:44). At times, the friends are so intimately connected that they appear to share a nervous system: "Vasya held him by the shoulders, looked into his eyes and moved his lips as if he wanted himself to say the words for him" (2:22). Their intimacy, moreover, extends beyond the physical. Arkady claims to have special insight into Vasya's inner processes—"I understand you; I know what is happening within you" (2:37)—and Vasya wonders at his friend's uncanny powers of perception: "For a long time now I've wanted to ask you: how is it that you know me so well?" (2:39).

Like Ivan and Smerdyakov in *Brothers Karamazov*, Arkady sees Vasya's actions as realizations of his own private intentions. At first surprised by Vasya's decision to get married, he then recalls the impulse in himself: "I myself, brother, thought about getting married; and now suddenly you're getting married, so it's all the same" (*PSS*, 2:19). He then quite suddenly discovers in himself the same passionate love for the same woman (he "was in love, fatally in

---

13   Katherine Strelsky has suggested "feminine identification resulting in homosexual panic" as the real reason for Vasya's demise; Strelsky, "Dostoevsky's Early Tale, 'A Faint Heart,'" *Russian Review* 30, no. 2 (1971): 148.

love with Liza"): "Just as she looks after you, let her look after me too. Yes, friendship for you and friendship for her; you are indivisible now; only I will have two beings like you instead of one" (2:29); to which Vasya, "terribly pleased" with Arkady's plan to invade his marriage, "pointed out that this was just how it should be and that now they will be even greater friends" (2:28–29). For her part, Vasya's fiancée intuitively understands the bizarre fluidity between the friends' identities when she cries out, "in the most naïve rapture," her hope for the future: "We will be the three of us like one person!" (2:28).

In this portrait of intimate friendship, we encounter another curious detail: the two heroes, utterly preoccupied with their shared concerns over Vasya's predicament, have no tangible pasts, except for some intentionally obscured details—for example, that they are both orphans, and that Vasya, unlike Arkady, is initially presented without patronymic, a detail the author promises to explain but then never does. Concerning Arkady's past, the narrator promises to recount an episode—"once it even happened that ... But this can wait until later" (*PSS*, 2:26)—and again conspicuously fails to deliver on his promise. These references to the past, appearing as obvious ellipses in the text, emphasize a lack within these characters, a blank space where memory or personal biography fails to reside. Indeed, their personalities appear to be unfolded entirely in their intense mutual interactions.

The intimate relationship of extension into the other evidently recalls elements of the doppelgänger tradition, and in fact replays many of the scenes from Dostoevsky's *The Double*, which was published two years earlier: we think of Golyadkin Senior when Arkady rushes through the streets of St. Petersburg, trying to anticipate and preemptively reverse the self-destructive behavior of his counterpart; or when he suddenly runs into the guilty Vasya, "nose to nose," like Golyadkin with his double on the street, and Vasya stops "like one caught in a crime" (*PSS*, 2:35); or especially in the public scandal at the end, when Vasya appears before his superiors in a deluded, incoherent, and trembling state and, like Golyadkin, is removed to an asylum. The story represents a departure from *The Double*, however, in that, unlike Golyadkin, who encounters a perfect replica of himself, Arkady and Vasya are unmistakably two separate individuals. Here Dostoevsky emphasizes his growing interest not in one personality that projects itself onto the outside world, externally dramatizing its own self-consciousness, but in the psychology of two discrete, sovereign individuals who come to enact the behavior of a single self.

Pretending to Sleep: Escape from the Other

As mentioned above, the story dramatizes a crisis in the friendship, in which Vasya, because of some nascent and concealed inner anguish, begins to refuse Arkady's administrative instructions. We discover that Vasya, by the time the story begins, has recently begun nurturing a sense of interior privacy. Just as he keeps the shameful secret of his neglected, unfinished work—"five of the thickest notebooks" (*PSS*, 2:37)—hidden from Arkady in a box, he has told Arkady nothing of his engagement to Liza, and when Arkady teasingly holds his friend down, trying to force the confession out of him, Vasya insists on the dignity of his personal interior space, exclaiming that "'if you had gone on to ask me 'what's her name?' I swear I'd have killed myself before answering you" (2:18). Vasya's secrecy is symptomatic of a larger transformation in his character, a change that he himself does not understand. He tries to explain his newfound inner complexity to Arkady, vaguely describing a growing consciousness of himself as separate from others, with an attendant longing for dignity and responsibility:

> "It seems to me that I didn't know myself before … and I only discovered others yesterday too. I … didn't feel, didn't value fully. The heart … in me was callous. … Listen, how did it happen that I hadn't done any good to anyone on the earth, because I was incapable, … And so many have done good to me! Take you first: do you think I don't see. I was … only keeping quiet!" (*PSS*, 2:39)

The experience of being loved and recognized by his fiancée has evidently shaken Vasya, forcing him to evaluate himself as a discrete personality. "I am undeserving of this happiness!" he protests to Arkady, "what have I done that was special, tell me! … And I! Such a woman loves me, me … as I am" (2:25). Thus, a distinct moral ambiguity accompanies the emergence of interior secrecy, since it is connected, on the one hand, with the discovery of self-worth at being loved and, on the other hand, with the subliminal criminal secrets of the neglected work and the hidden notebooks.

Arkady perceives danger in his friend's emergent complexity. He beseeches Vasya to "reveal [his concealed] torments" so that he can take responsibility upon himself. He repeatedly offers to act as intermediary between Vasya and his "benefactor," Vasya's section head, Yulian Mastakovich, who is, to Vasya, a divine, omnipotent being. "I'll save you!" he offers to Vasya, "I'll go to Yulian Mastakovich … don't shake your head, no, listen! … I'll explain … how you're destroyed, how

you're tormenting yourself.... I'll sacrifice myself for you ... don't contradict me!"
(*PSS*, 2:38). Vasya, however, is determined to free himself from Arkady's government. Faced with Arkady's intention to take his place, he "cries out, turns white as
a wall," and protests vehemently: "Do you know that you're killing me right now?"
(2:37). He is especially anxious about Arkady's helpful plan to sign Yulian Mastakovich's visitors' books for him (in other words, to subsume his identity), afraid
that his benefactor will notice "that it's a different hand" (2:31). In Arkady's presence, he accepts his orders docilely and agrees to stay home to copy the neglected
work. When Arkady leaves, however, Vasya's agency awakens. As Arkady rushes
to the benefactor's residence to sign, he notices that Vasya has secretly escaped to
sign his own name—"imagine his surprise when before him appeared Vasya
Shumkov's very own signature!" (2:35)—Vasya's gesture, as it were, of insistence
upon his own unannexable personality. Thus, the awakening of the self is portrayed
through these irrepressible desires in Vasya: to sign one's own name, to atone for
one's crimes, to feel the full weight of one's "guilt" before "God," to repent and to
pray for divine mercy, to "tell him myself," to "go myself": "I'll explain everything
myself ... he'll see my tears, he'll be moved by them" (2:38–40).

The story provides us with a clear vantage point onto one of Dostoevsky's
most ubiquitous leitmotifs of the emergence and concealment of interiority (and
thus of the instability of the intersubjective self): the action of pretending to sleep.
In Arkady's dream, he sits over a sleeping Vasya, symbolically enacting the structure
of their relationship, with Arkady as a vigilant consciousness to Vasya's supine,
malleable, unconscious body. The dream—an important moment in Dostoevsky's
early conception of the collective personality—dramatizes Vasya's transformation:

> It seemed that he [Arkady] was not sleeping and that Vasya, as before, was
> lying on the bed. But the strangest thing! It seems Vasya is pretending, that
> he is even deceiving Arkady and is now getting up ever so quietly, observing
> him out of the corner of his eye and stealing to the desk. A burning pain
> seizes Arkady's heart; it was vexing, sad and difficult to see that Vasya doesn't
> trust him, that he's hiding and concealing from him. He wanted to grab him,
> to cry out and carry him to the bed ... Then Vasya screamed out in his arms,
> and Arkady was carrying a lifeless corpse to the bed. (*PSS*, 2:43)

The events of the dream vividly portray Vasya's attempt to emancipate himself
from Arkady's will, to overcome his role as the passive, sleeping body to
Arkady's administrative mind. Still pretending to be subdued, he has secretly

awakened to his own agency, and Arkady attempts to seize control of his friend, to force him into unconsciousness, even by destroying him—reducing him to a "lifeless corpse"—in the process. This image of pretend sleep, as a motif of the unstable intersubjective self, extends throughout Dostoevsky's writing—for example in *The Demons*, in Stepan Trofimovich's attempt to escape Varvara Petrovna's vigilant administration (*PSS*, 10:502) or in Maria Timofeevna's flight from Stavrogin (10:219), and later, in Smerdiakov's murderous pretend sleep in *Brothers Karamazov*, which dramatizes all too literally Ivan's submerged, suppressed intention.

Self without Soul

The story's final passage—in which Arkady, lamenting his friend's demise, experiences a vision of an unearthly St. Petersburg, as though "a new city were taking shape in the air"—presents a fascinating description of the severed collective self. The episode has received a great deal more commentary than the rest of the story, as an autobiographically derived epiphany that Dostoevsky extracted from the story thirteen years later and inserted into a journalistic feuilleton.[14] Because Dostoevsky himself tore the passage from its original context, criticism has followed and has weighed it on its own merits. Readers have argued that Arkady's glimpse into "the fantastical, magical reverie" of the city "that will disappear in its turn and waft into steam to the dark blue sky" (*PSS*, 2:47–48) is an early presentiment of Dostoevsky's program of "fantastic realism," of his separation from quotidian, earthly reality and his discovery of another, spiritual realm.[15] In treating Arkady's experience as a form of mystical initiation into an otherworldly realm, however, readers overlook the implicit emphasis upon Arkady's *bereaved* status, since he encounters this vision of a second, disembodied, ethereal city in the air after an element of his personality has collapsed and vanished.

---

14 Arkady's vision is repeated almost verbatim, now from the first person, in Dostoevsky's 1861 "Peterburgskoe snovidenie v stikhakh i proze" (*PSS*, 19:67–85).

15 See, for example, Fyodor Stepun, *Vstrechi* (Munich: Tovarishchestvo zarubezhnykh pisatelei, 1962), 15; and Fanger, *Dostoevsky and Romantic Realism*, 168. Bakhtin reads the vision as a "carnivalized sense of Petersburg" (180n), a way of placing the city itself "on the threshold" so that it too, like Dostoevsky's personalities, is "devoid of any internal grounds for justifiable stabilization." Bakhtin, *Problems of Dostoevsky's Poetics*, 167.

Perhaps as a result of reading the scene outside of its narrative context, critics consistently gloss over the strangest part of the passage—the peculiar physiological reaction that Arkady suffers as he looks out over the Neva. We are told that he experiences a sudden insight into Vasya's experience and shudders, feeling "the surge of some powerful and hitherto unknown sensation" as a "spring of blood" fills his "heart":

> Some kind of strange thought visited the orphaned comrade of poor Vasya. He gave a start, and his heart was as if filled in this moment with a hot spring of blood, which suddenly boiled up from the surging of some powerful sensation, hitherto unknown to him. It was as if he only now … discovered why his poor Vasya, who had not been able to bear his happiness, had lost his mind. His lips quivered, his eyes blazed, he grew pale, and it was as if his eyes were opened to something new in this moment. (*PSS*, 2:48)

The bizarre description suggests that, in the absence of Vasya as cathexis, as externalized bearer of his suppressed emotional life, Arkady painfully feels the upsurge of the atrophied faculties within himself that had formerly been replaced externally by his friend's activity. Vasya too, when he attempted to escape Arkady's protection, felt stricken and overwhelmed by the new burden of thought that the absence of Arkady awakened in him, a sensation he experienced physically: "He ran his hand over his forehead as if wanting to remove from himself some kind of heavy, oppressive weight that had lain on his entire being" (*PSS*, 2:43). Arkady's vision on the Neva in this context can be seen as a depiction of the anguish of the disembodied personality, which has used the other as a substitution for its own interior life, and is now forced, quite suddenly, to encounter these dimensions within.

One is tempted to venture a Bakhtinian reading of Arkady's predicament on the Neva—his lonely disembodied existence in the wake of Vasya's demise—as a natural consequence of the dialogical nature of selfhood. In Bakhtinian terms, Arkady's bereft status as I-for-myself, his sensation of ghostly semiexistence or soul-lessness could be read as a result of the "dialogical need for the other." Since the fullness of being exists only within human relationships, Vasya, as a beloved other, acted as "bestower" of "soul" upon Arkady.[16] In Vasya's

---

16 Bakhtin, "Author and Hero in Aesthetic Activity," in *Art and Answerability: Early Philosophical Essays by M. M. Bakhtin*, ed. Michael Holquist and Vadim Liapunov, trans. Vadim Liapunov (Austin: University of Texas Press, 1990): 101. In Gerald Pirog's words, "It is in this sense that we can speak of our absolute aesthetic need for the other, who alone can

absence, the lonely consciousness is reduced to a "spurious and disjected subjectivity" that can have no soul on its own.[17] Such an argument, however, would dramatically contradict the tenets of Bakhtin's thought, since Bakhtin, who tended not to see the darker aspects of dialogue in Dostoevsky,[18] insisted that dialogical interaction takes place between "unmerged" and "sovereign" consciousnesses.[19] These sudden interior sensations (the surges of blood from an unknown source) that emerge in the absence of the external soul indicate that there is another level of complexity underlying Arkady's radical solitude—that his need to enact his personality intersubjectively is the result of pathologically suppressed or erased interior life. Dostoevsky's return to this relationship in *Crime and Punishment*, as we shall see, points to the collapse of the intersubjective self as a moment of central and sustained importance in his thought.

Fear of the Interior

For good reasons, Raskolnikov's lineage is most often traced to the radical idealists of Dostoevsky's earlier prose, the "dreamers" who long to "transform the world and bring it into conformity with [their] visionary longings," and the intellectual rebels, from Golyadkin to the Underground Man, who attempt to

---

create my completed personality. This personality would not exist if the other did not create it. ... We are ... in a constant state of complementarity with others, who must also seek in us their own completed selves"; Pirog, "Bakhtin and Freud on the Ego," in *Russian Literature and Psychoanalysis*, ed. Daniel Rancour-Laferriere (Amsterdam: John Benjamins, 1988), 407–8.

17 Bakhtin, "Author and Hero in Aesthetic Activity," 101.

18 "Remarkably," observes Caryl Emerson, "Bakhtin assumes that the other's finalizing efforts are always benign—or at least a given self is presumed resilient enough to incorporate, or counter, any definition the other might thrust upon it"; Emerson, "Russian Orthodoxy and the Early Bakhtin," *Religion & Literature* 22, nos. 2–3 (1990): 116. Sasha Spektor argues that dialogue in Dostoevsky is "the site of an intense struggle for authorial power," a struggle fueled by characters' "metaphysical anxiety" concerning the absence of a divine author; Spektor, "From Violence to Silence: Vicissitudes of Reading (in) *The Idiot*," *Slavic Review* 72, no. 3 (Fall 2013): 557. For an extensive examination of the difference between the ideal of harmonious intersubjectivity and the "abyss ... where polyphony threatens to become cacophony," see Jones, *Dostoevsky after Bakhtin*, xiv. For an authoritative look at some of the most persuasive challenges mounted against Bakhtin's theory of polyphony and dialogue with regard to Dostoevsky, see Caryl Emerson, *The First Hundred Years of Mikhail Bakhtin* (Princeton, NJ: Princeton University Press, 1997), esp. 130–49.

19 Bakhtin, *Problems of Dostoevsky's Poetics*, 26. On this aspect of Bakhtin's thought, see especially Alina Wyman, "Bakhtin and Scheler: Toward a Theory of Active Understanding," *Slavic and East European Review* 86, no. 1 (2008): 58–89.

stage a "revolt against the established social-moral order."[20] Innumerable analyses of Raskolnikov's internal divisions have refined for us his image as an exacerbated intellect, testing out the postulates of ideological theories while hindered by his inescapable status as a "trembling creature" subject to natural laws and impulses.[21] Raskolnikov's connection with Vasya Shumkov, however, opens up a markedly different aspect of his character: through this lens we see Raskolnikov as a weak, damaged, and incomplete personality who attempts hysterically to escape domination by external administrative minds. A brief examination of some of the resonances between *Crime and Punishment* and the early, little-studied story helps us further grasp the tension between interiority and intersubjectivity that underlies both texts and that helps define the problem of selfhood in Dostoevsky.

The first, most apparent repetition from the earlier template lies in the description of Raskolnikov and Razumikhin's friendship. When in Raskolnikov's presence, Razumikhin reminds us distinctly of Arkady in his struggle to annex and take over his friend's functioning; his "powerful arms" (*PSS*, 6:150), like Arkady's (2:33), grasp hold of Raskolnikov and forcefully direct him toward health, prudence, and recuperation. Razumikhin's surname (formed from *razum*, "reason") takes on a much more literal meaning in this context since, like Arkady, he enacts the faculty of the executive mind externally for the incomplete self.[22] We see him "taking charge at once," deftly "grasping" Raskolnikov's "head with his left hand, regardless of the fact that [Raskolnikov] would have been able to get up himself," and bringing soup and tea to the latter's lips (6:95). He immediately takes over Raskolnikov's finances and personal appearance, buying clothes for his helpless counterpart, and he even overcomes indignant opposition ("Leave me be! I don't want it!") in changing Raskolnikov's

---

20 Joseph Frank, *Dostoevsky: The Miraculous Years, 1865–1871* (Princeton, NJ: Princeton University Press, 1995), 98–99.

21 See, for example, Richard Peace's foundational reading of Raskolnikov as "above all else, a man whose actions are based on cool and calculating reason"; Peace, *Dostoevsky: An Examination of the Major Novels* (Cambridge: Cambridge University Press, 1971), 19.

22 Marina Kostalevsky describes Razumikhin as "the positive personification of rational good"; Kostalevsky, *Dostoevsky and Soloviev* (New Haven, CT: Yale University Press, 1997), 154. Frank, who notes the similarity between Arkady and Razumikhin, suggests that his surname "indicates Dostoevsky's desire to link the employment of this faculty not only with the cold calculations of utilitarianism but also with spontaneous human warmth and generosity" (*Dostoevsky*, 99).

undergarments, while the latter, defeated and humiliated, eventually complies (6:101–2). The struggle of wills concerning the problem of signature (the desire to annex the identity of the other) is repeated from the earlier story. When Raskolnikov refuses to sign for his mother's gift of money, Razumikhin attests to his ability to "direct" the invalid ("we will direct him, that is, simply guide his hand"), and, we are told, "was seriously getting ready to guide Raskolnikov's hand," before Raskolnikov, like Vasya, insists on signing himself (6:94).

In "A Weak Heart," we follow Arkady's agony closely as he gradually loses all control over his counterpart; in the later novel, the entire emphasis is upon the fugitive self, Raskolnikov, protecting an interior personal realm in which is concealed, among other, more deeply buried memories, a recent crime. As Raskolnikov attempts to escape Razumikhin's vigilant surveillance, he, like Vasya, has no defined intention of his own—only a suppressed sense of agency that fuels disorganized, frenzied activity. In the absence of external surveillance, he is unable to stay in his room and sleep, unable to fulfill the sensible command of his external superego, but he "leaps up, half crazed from the bed" as soon as he is left alone "with burning convulsive impatience" to do something (PSS, 6:99). The descriptions of Raskolnikov released from Razumikhin's supervision emphasize simultaneously a desperate desire to exert agency and an utter incapacity for thought or self-administration: "He didn't know and didn't think about where to go; he knew one thing: 'that it was necessary to end all *this* today, in one go, at once . . .' How to end it? With what? About this he didn't have any idea, and he didn't want to think" (6:21). Raskolnikov's subsequent hysterical bustling about the city directly repeats Vasya's. When Arkady leaves, Vasya simply cannot stay at home, for all the good it would do him. Instead, he feels a frantic compulsion to go directly to the authorities, to confess his "crime," though he can give no rational explanation for his impulse. Arkady's desperate, agonized search for Vasya, who has run away from his incarceration in their room, is replayed in the novel, as the friends collide suddenly, like Arkady and Vasya, on the street—"Neither had caught sight of the other up to the last step, so that they almost collided heads" (6:129)—and Razumikhin scolds his disobedient friend—"I'm going to take you up under my arm, … and carry you home, then lock you in!" (6:129)—implying a real sense of ownership over him.

In *Crime and Punishment*, the pathology of the shared personality is still more pronounced than in "A Weak Heart." For all of Raskolnikov's attempts to evade Razumikhin, we see that he exhibits a desperate need for his friend as a result of his own incapacity for self-administration. From the beginning, despite himself, he is deeply, actively embroiled in the shared self that his friendship with Razumikhin enacts. Upon receiving the devastating news of his sister's intended marriage, he seeks out Razumikhin compulsively, in a state of despair, as if hypnotized, crying out for his friend's surveillance, though unaware of it himself:

> "And where am I going?" he thought suddenly. ... The question, why had he now set off to see Razumikhin bothered him more than it even seemed to him; ... "Could I really have wanted to fix the whole business through Razumikhin alone and find the solution to everything in Razumikhin," he asked himself in surprise. (*PSS*, 6:43–45)

The murder is committed in that moment when Raskolnikov, panicked and distraught, overcomes his mysterious compulsion to visit Razumikhin, and attempts to assume responsibility himself for his family dilemma. The crime is committed outside of Razumikhin's purview, as an expression of Raskolnikov's own hysterical attempt at personal agency. We discover later in the novel that Raskolnikov cannot survive for long without an external mind—when he finally shirks Razumikhin's supervision, he immediately binds himself to other kinds of external minds and agencies, most prominently to those of Svidrigailov and Sonya. In this sense, the novel comes to explore not only the collapsed interior life of the incomplete personality but also the ways in which this atrophied self succumbs to various external sources of intellection.

The image of pretend sleep as a symbol of concealed interiority (or of the collective self's instability) finds immense resonance in the novel. Vasya's pretend sleep in Arkady's dream, as examined above, dramatized the externalized relationship of the prostrate, malleable body to the executive mind: the subdued being feigns docility while hiding a secret, interior life, planning its escape and bid for independent agency. Pretending to be a compliant limb of Razumikhin's administrative will, Raskolnikov, like Vasya, "conceals his power" from his friend with a "feral cunning" (*PSS*, 6:95–96), "closing his eyes and pretending to be asleep" as he hears Razumikhin entering the room

(6:210). As Raskolnikov transfers to the administration of Svidrigailov, the nature of their relationship is quickly established (as if by shorthand) by use of this image (6:214, 219). Later, we discover that Svidrigailov (who incidentally has the same name and patronymic—Arkady Ivanovich—as Vasya Shumkov's friend and mentor) comes to suicidal despair after his dream in which he is confronted by the image—"horrific" to him—of a child, pretending to sleep, concealing depravity and mockery under closed eyelids: "Her long dark eyelashes seem to shiver and wink, and from under them looks out a sly, sharp, unchildlike-winking little eye, as if the little girl is not sleeping and is pretending." When the child's eyes finally open, we infer from Svidrigailov's acute terror that he sees something from his own much-avoided unconscious realm in the "boundlessly ugly and offensive … filth" that no longer conceals itself under the winking eyelids. In each of these instances, the unconscious interior life—that which is hidden behind closed eyelids—is a region of shame, ugliness, disgust, the unwanted memory of a violent crime or a case full of neglected notebooks. It is the shame over and avoidance of what is hidden beneath the veneer of this pretend sleep that propels the personality beyond the threshold of the self into a world of frantic intersubjective activity. In each case these hateful interior phenomena are placed outside of the self, into another person, until that other person refuses to be subsumed, awakens covertly from an enforced sleep, and launches a rebellion against the colonizing other.

Some Conclusions

The intersecting personalities of Vasya and Arkady testify to the brokenness of dialogic interaction in early Dostoevsky and to the pathologies inherent in his conception of the open-ended, relational self. Whether we prefer a diagnosis of "morbid codependency" or "projective identification,"[23] or whether we suspect subliminal sexual anxieties or repressed desires in Arkady and Vasya, it is clear that Dostoevsky is describing disturbed characters who suffer from some form of collapsed interiority, and that the deficiency of the interior dimension causes them to cling to each other with greater convulsive energy. Even Razumikhin,

---

23 "Morbid codependency" in early Dostoevsky is examined by Thomas G. Marullo, *Heroine Abuse: The Poetics of Codependency in "Netochka Nezvanova"* (DeKalb, IL: Northern Illinois University Press, 2016).

the most refreshingly level-headed of Dostoevsky's characters, nevertheless exhibits all the hungry embraces of a disturbed psyche. Though Pulkheria Alexandrovna and Dunya do not "want to notice these eccentric details," still he grasps onto their hands "as if in a vise," pressing them "to the point of pain," grasping them "even more firmly" if they attempt to "tear their hands away" as they realize that it is "impossible to run away from him" (*PSS*, 6:154). In the context of these ravenous, colonizing personalities, both the early story and the later novel approach the question of introspection—of stepping back from the compulsive threshold through the discovery and acknowledgment of what is concealed within: whether in Vasya's passionate desire to confess his "crime" to Yulian Mastakovich, or in Raskolnikov's to confess his murder and to atone for it. Both crimes, though obviously different in their degree of seriousness, can be understood as metaphors for the recognition of interior, personal space, especially since the crimes themselves, we suspect, point to the presence of earlier, more deeply buried memories in these characters whose personal biographies and "former past," rarely mentioned, are glimpsed, if at all, from afar, in the waters of the Neva, "in some depths, below, somewhere barely visible" (6:90).

Vasya Shumkov's interior awakening sheds some light on the tension between interiority and intersubjectivity in Dostoevsky, since it suggests that if the self is simply the site of consciousness, a point of view, or an activity of addressivity directed toward the other, then the gulf between selves cannot be preserved: the self falls into and becomes subsumed into the other. As Ivan's formulation goes in *Brothers Karamazov*, "If there is no immortality of the soul, then all is permitted, even anthropophagy" (*PSS*, 14:65). The example that occurs to Ivan—*anthropophagy*—is significant, and his idea could be rephrased thus: without the positing of an essential interior principle within the self, human beings will consume each other. In early Dostoevsky, we are left simply with a depiction of the need to recover an interior essential space in the self as a psychological quandary, but one which takes us back with renewed attention to Dostoevsky's novelistic examinations of the reconstitution of the interior realm from its dispersal into adjacent, convulsively embracing selves.

XIV

Dostoevsky's Angel—Still an Idiot, Still beyond the Story: The Case of Kalganov

Michal Oklot

> What is a seraph? Maybe a whole constellation. And maybe that whole
> constellation is just some chemical molecule.[1]
> —Dostoevsky, The *Brothers Karamazov*

> Have the angels turned discreet![2]
> —Rainer Maria Rilke, *Vergers*, 22

Jacob's Dream

In his essay "The Multi-visage Icon" ("Mnogolichnaia ikona," 1900), Akim Volynsky (1865–1926) exercises a reading of the first of a number of scandal

---

1 Fyodor Dostoevsky, *Polnoe sobranie sochinenii v tridsati tomakh* [*PSS*], ed. V. G. Bazanov et al. (Leningrad: Nauka, 1972–90), 15:85–86 (*BK*, 651); hereafter *PSS* by volume and page. The page numbers in parentheses refer to the English translations Fyodor Dostoevsky, *The Idiot*, trans. Richard Pevear and Larissa Volokhonsky (New York: Vintage Classics, 2003), and *The Brothers Karamazov*, trans. Richard Pevear and Larissa Volokhonsky (New York: Farrar, Straus, and Giroux, 2002), abbreviated *Idiot* and *BK*, respectively.
2 *The Complete French Poems of Rainer Maria Rilke*, trans. A. Poulin Jr. (Saint Paul, MN: Graywolf, 1986), 151.

scenes in *The Brothers Karamazov* (1881), explicating it as an *ekphrasis* of a peculiar icon devoted to the theme of life as *theophilia*.[3] Fyodor Dostoevsky's "icon," he writes, does not represent so much a divinized figure in a frozen image as it does a figure present in its full vividness. His images are woven into the dynamic fabric of the realist narrative. In the background of this "dramatic icon," as he called the scene at Zosima's cell, Volynsky distinguishes two silent novice figures, Alyosha and Porfiry, whom he calls "angel-like young men,"[4] as if they had entered the narrative having stepped down from the lowest step of Jacob's ladder to make a detour in their eternal journey between the earth and heaven. So, perhaps, demons are not the only intermediary creatures—or rather, half-creatures—that populate Dostoevsky's worlds. Those worlds are also inhabited by angels—accidental guests, confused and lost in their earthly (or narrative) detours. They may, for instance, take the disguise of an idiot, like Prince Myshkin, or a jaded melancholic, like Pyotr Fomich Kalganov, a marginal character in *Brothers Karamazov*, who puzzles the reader with his discreet, hardly noticeable presence. But let us look at this analogy not through the ethical problem of humans' capacity for good and evil, which is usually provoked by the allusion to the demonic and the angelic, but rather through the angelic ontology, so to speak. The analogy can be understood through three concepts: transitoriness, incompleteness, and surplus. Each of these concepts also gestures at certain distinctive qualities of Dostoevsky's text, in both narrative and ideological dimensions. Following this discussion, now equipped with the conceptual framework the second part of this essay will take a closer look at Kalganov and his role in the novel.

Balzacian Trope

First, we must ask if we can find evidence of Dostoevsky's interest in angels in his own readings. One of the possible paths of such an inquiry can lead through Emanuel Swedenborg (1688–1772), for it is impossible not to pass under an angel's wing when reading Swedenborg. Czesław Miłosz (1911–2004) was the first who experimented with a more comprehensive reading of Dostoevsky in

---

3 See Akim Volynsky, *Dostoevsky*, ed. V. A. Kotel'nikov (St. Petersburg: Akademicheskii Proekt, 2007), 281.
4 Ibid., 297.

the context of Swedenborg,[5] following a trace left by Leonid Grossman, who, in his reconstructed library of Dostoevsky, put on the shelf A. N. Aksakov's translations of Swedenborg's works and his two brochures devoted to Swedenborg's exegeses of the Bible.[6] Yet, we do not need to look at the works of Aksakov from the 1860s to establish such a parallel. A more natural lead takes us straight to the Romantic reception of Swedenborg, especially in one of Dostoevsky's "teachers," Honoré de Balzac (1799–1850) and his *Études philosophiques—Seraphita* (1834), *Louis Lambert* (1832), and *Exiles* (1831). Balzac develops his theme of the evolution of the spirit, moving from the natural to the divine world (not unfamiliar to Dostoevsky's readers) in his trilogy precisely through angels—and not figurative ones but actual ones (if this modality applies to angels at all), as in the angelological treatises of Swedenborg. The angels in Balzac (and Balzac's Swedenborg) unveil certain limitations of Enlightenment reason, which is incapable of comprehending the infinity of the divine intellect. This is also a lesson hidden behind Dostoevsky's narratives, and, in particular, *Brothers Karamazov*. So this theme alone, shared with Swedenborg's Romantic disciple, Balzac, can justify our search for angels in Dostoevsky.

Transitoriness: D. H. Lawrence's Problem with Dostoevsky's Angels

In searching for angels in Dostoevsky, we can also experiment with the perspective of modernism, especially with one of the modernists' "angelologists," D. H. Lawrence (1885–1930), who was interested in an ontological dimension of the angelic in literature. In a letter to his friend S. S. Koteliansky—a translator of Russian literature—Lawrence expresses his irritation with the omnipresence of the fallen angel theme in Dostoevsky: "I could do with Dostoevsky," he writes, "if he did not make all men fallen angels. We are not angels. It is a tiresome conceit.... It doesn't matter what Stavrogin does.... It is his affair. It bores me. People are *not important*: I insist on it. Let them die."[7] Here, one can easily

---

5   See Czesław Miłosz, "Dostojewski i Swedenborg," in *Rosja: Wiedzenie transoceaniczne*, vol. 1, *Dostojewski – nasz współczesny*, ed. Barbara Toruńczyk et al. (Warsaw: Fundacja Zeszytów Literackich, 2010), 115–31.

6   N. F. Budanova et al., *Biblioteka F. M. Dostoevskogo: Opyt rekonstruktsii. Nauchnoe opisanie* (Moscow: Nauka, 2005), 132–35.

7   George J. Zytaruk, ed., *The Quest for Rananim: D. H. Lawrence's Letters to S. S. Koteliansky* (Montreal: McGill-Queen's University Press, 1970), 68; emphasis in original.

sympathize with Lawrence's irritation, and his call for a broader, ontological understanding of the angelic; and indeed, it might be good hermeneutical advice to avoid reading Dostoevsky's characters—"silly blighters, fools, and two-penny knaves"[8]—through their capacity to fall. This rings especially true when bearing in mind that Dostoevsky himself was rather skeptical about the "fallen angel," the troublesome Byronic heritage of Russian literature. Further into *Brothers Karamazov*, it is none other than the infernal phantasmagoric guest of Ivan Karamazov's who will be as suspicious of a fallen angel as Lawrence.

Declaring that people (meaning their psychological and ethical motivations) are *not important*, the mystical materialist Lawrence was referring to the general ontological and cosmogonic perspective that he developed extensively in his *Study of Thomas Hardy*. In the chapter titled "Work and the Angel and the Unbegotten Hero," Lawrence sees the angel as a "more perfect being than ourselves with more extended knowledge of that which is not ourselves."[9] For him, an angel is a trace of individuality, sheer distinctiveness of "a complete melody or a pure color" in the "utterly homogenous infinity, a great non-being, at once a positive and negative infinity."[10] Lawrence's discreet angel is also a vector of "some reaction, infinitesimally faint, stirring somehow through the vast homogenous inertia"[11] in the process of liberation of life from matter. However, in his literary iconography, he, like Dostoevsky, sticks to the conventional Christian imagination: "My Angels and Devils," he writes in a letter to E. M. Forster, "are old-fashioned symbols for the flower into which we strive to burst. . . . I am just in love with medieval terms, that is all— Fra Angelico and Cimabue and the Saints."[12] Not accidentally, Lawrence's novel *Rainbow* (1915)—which, next to *Women in Love* (1920), and *Plummet Serpent* (1926) could be read as a part of novelistic triptych concerning the mystic ontology of life not far from that of Vasily Rozanov (1856-1919)—is populated by Fra Angelico's angels, vectors of the "progress of life" and the emergence of nonselfish individuality.

---

8 Ibid.

9 D. H. Lawrence, *Study of Thomas Hardy and Other Essays*, ed. Bruce Stelle (Cambridge: Cambridge University Press, 1985), 42.

10 Ibid., 43.

11 Ibid., 42.

12 George. J. Zytaruk and J. T. Boulton, eds., *The Letters of D. H. Lawrence*, vol. 2, *June 1913– October 1916* (Cambridge: Cambridge University Press, 1981), 275.

Having in mind Balzac's Romantic angel, which unveils the invisible, and Lawrence's modernist angel, let us look at Dostoevsky's own thought on angels (and demons). While experimenting with Stavrogin's unstable, transitory ontology in one of the manuscript sketches of conversations between Stavrogin and Shatov titled "The Fantastic Hour," Dostoevsky has Stavrogin utter the famous "fantastic" thought about potentiality as the fundamental modality of human existence, unveiled to the broader reading public by Rozanov. "Certainly, we are transitory creatures [*shushchestva perekhodnye*]," Stavrogin says:

> and our existence on earth is, certainly, the uninterrupted existence of a chrysalis, transforming into a butterfly. Remember the saying: "the angel never falls, the demon has fallen earlier before, so it has been always lying fallen, the man always falls and rises." I think, people become demons or angels. ... But the earthly life is a process of transformation. ... Also do not forget that "there will be time no more," as the angel [of the Apocalypse] swore. ... It is impossible to die. Being is, while nonbeing is not.[13]

This passage does not necessarily concern our condition of a fall. Reading Dostoevsky through Stavrogin's thought we may say that Dostoevsky's novelistic characters are somewhat suspended between two antipodal types: the angelic Myshkin and the demonic Stavrogin (a particular kind of an angel). Both emerge and disappear among the mountain ranges of the Swiss Alps: Myshkin in the bright, blue infinite of the sublime; Stavrogin in the negative infinity of the dull place, a ravine cramped by the mountains. Let us note that the finale of their earthly trajectory is almost the same. They both lose themselves—Myshkin "in his own light,"[14] and Stavrogin in his own darkness—in two infinities, as Lawrence would say in his aforementioned angelic digression. And it is precisely these two characters, dissolved in two infinities, who determine the two directions of man's "incomplete entelechy." The fantastic lepidopteric thought that Stavrogin utters in this moment of brilliance—an interruption of his manic–depressive trajectory of the demonic, in the angelic key—demonstrates the need of these subtle half-beings to understand our own ontological position of *transitoriness*—our source of hope for nontranscending

---

13 *PSS*, 11:184.
14 Walter Benjamin, *Selected Writings*, vol. 1, *1913–1926*, ed. M. Bullock and M. W. Jennings (Cambridge, MA: Belknap, 1996), 80.

immortality—which could be yet another formulation of one of the main themes in Dostoevsky.

The anthropological dimension of such an understanding of the angelic is not far from Russian Orthodox theological interpretations. To stay in the context of devoted readers of Dostoevsky, in Sergei Bulgakov's (1871–1944) sophiological angelology, angelic love is a form of metaphysical abjuration—not only of one's own wealth but also of anything that is one's own. This character of angelic love is manifested negatively in the image of the fall of the fallen demons, who desired precisely their *own*: demanding to establish their kingdom with the prince of this world. The "good" angels abjured this wish, "and they loved not their lives unto the death" (Rev. 12:11).[15] The life of the Holy Trinity, Bulgakov writes, is characterized by the mutual self-exhaustion of the divine hypostases, which have their lives not in themselves but in *the Others*: the Father in the Son and the Spirit, the Son in the Father and the Spirit, and the Spirit in the Father and the Son.[16] The angel's life, then, is, in a sense, a potential life. An angel, Bulgakov writes, is the other (*drugoi*) and a friend (*drug*). Thus, as Andrei Pleşu noted in the spirit of Bulgakov's writings, angels are our "identical otherness," "our latent openness," "the surplus negating a possibility of finding our own identity."[17] An angel stands for everything that is different in us and, yet, is not different, at the same time, since, to put it oxymoronically, its identity is in its impossibility; as Pleşu argues, it teaches us a radically different anthropology from that of the concept of identity that is hysterically reinforced in contemporary art and the humanities.

Incompleteness: Life in "unfinished half-tails . . ."

If we project Dostoevsky's angels onto Pseudo-Dionysius's celestial hierarchy, and while considering their roles in the narratives, they would belong to the lowest rank of ordinary angels: those closer to the world and in charge of revelation; those that take care of our own hierarchy so that the uplifting return toward the Principle of principle, God, might occur.[18] An example of such an

---

15 Quoted in Sergius Bulgakov, *Jacob's Ladder: On Angels*, trans. Thomas A. Smith (Grand Rapids, MI: William B. Eerdmans, 2010), 162.

16 See ibid., 162–63.

17 I am referring to the Polish translation from Romanian: Andrei Pleşu, *O aniołach* [*On Angels*], trans. Tomasz Klimkowski (Krakow: Universitas, 2003), 17.

18 See Pseudo-Dionysius, *The Complete Works*, trans. Colm Luibheid (New York: Paulist, 1987), 170–71.

angel, a messenger lost in his otherness, is Prince Myshkin. By taking a closer look at him, we can see how his angelic role is related to Dostoevsky's angelic ontology and narrative topography.

In a memorably insignificant scene at the beginning of *The Idiot*, Myshkin takes a thick leaf of white, blank, richly textured paper and begins to write separate phrases, playing with various types of handwriting from both old and new times, as if, to use Volynsky's observations once again, "merging with everything that has lived and still lives on the earth."[19] As a result, some sort of "parallel world begins to emerge,"[20] Volynsky writes. This world, enclosed in the trajectories of characters and spaces between them, is so much richer than the one that surrounds Myshkin, flattened by his idiocy. This act of copying handwriting styles creates an impression of Myshkin trying on various costumes or masks, as if he were experimenting with the possibilities of living in various forms of human life (which brings to mind the dark experiments with masks and life scenarios of another tenant of intermediary space, the demon Stavrogin). Volynsky, summing up his analysis of the calligraphy passage, writes that Myshkin "is playing with various individual characters with the discrete smile, as if he was some bodiless angel."[21]

The confusion starts when the idiot, Myshkin, tries to enter the story. Not having a life of his own, he tries on several roles that he does not understand. Here, he loses himself in grandiose gestures, which do not communicate anything in particular, and experiments with various lives, trying them on like his all-too-fashionable clothing. In so doing, he always looks awkward (he is not as experienced with borrowed lives and ideas as is his evil twin brother, Stavrogin). So he becomes a radical Slavophile, a suitor from Nikolai Gogol's (1809–52) *Marriage* (1842), a husband, a prophet, a "millionaire-philanthropist," a player in a banal love triangle. Later in the novel, Aglaya will capture Myshkin's lack of qualities by comparing him to Pushkin's "Poor Knight" (1836), which we may also interpret in an angelic key as the poetic portrait of anonymity, a face upon which one can imprint anything. Unlike a true calligrapher, whom Myshkin describes in his calligraphy demonstration, he makes attempts at extra flourishes, "unfinished half-tails," from which "the whole military

---

19 Volynsky, *Dostoevsky*, 120.
20 Ibid.
21 Ibid.

scrivener's soul is peeking out of it."[22] What is Myshkin showing us, then, when he adds such a "half-tail" of his assumed individuality? Behind the chaos of his grandiose gestures, the broken lives and Chinese vase, we see the idiot's (the modern angel's) quality: facelessness. Angelic, faceless individuality can only be perceived beyond a temporal order—once Myshkin is thrown back into the chronology (the story), he returns to his clinical idiocy. We may say that Myshkin experiences an experimental world, the world as possibility, which in actuality leads to disappointment, a melancholy of fulfillment. In the rare moments of assuming his true identity, he plunges back into the infinite beyond the horizon line, losing consciousness. Myshkin aligns with himself only during an epileptic fit.

But what would his angelic message be after all? Peter Sloterdjik gives an ambiguous answer, which could be reconciled with the theological ontology of an angel. For Sloterdjik, Myshkin the idiot is "an angel without a message—an undistanced, intimate augmenter of all coincidently encountered beings."[23] Moreover, Sloterdjik sees Dostoevsky's theological and philosophical brilliance precisely in his recognition of "the chance to shift the focus of Christology from angeletics to idiotics and thought it through to its limits"—"the crises of sender metaphysics."[24] The idiot, a modern angel, does not invoke "transcendental radiance," Sloterdjik argues, but "naiveté and disarming benevolence in the midst of a society of role players and ego strategists,"[25] leading his life as the main character in his own story; exchanging places with his afterbirth, he "make[s] space for its being-in-the-world as itself"[26]—emerging life, in Lawrence's vocabulary. To translate this argument back to Bulgakov's ange-lology, Myshkin lives only outside himself, in others' lives, in metaphysical self-exhaustion, being just an angel, sheer capacity, no less, and no more. Mysh-kin's angelic quality, or rather its lack, is ontological poverty and emptiness: he is a *half-being* (*polu-bytie*), in Bulgakov's terminology, which, through its *incompleteness*, gives us ontological hope for immortality, for that which is not complete cannot die. As Ernst Bloch, another modernist student of Dostoevsky,

---

22 *PSS*, 8:29 (*Idiot*, 34).
23 Peter Sloterdjik, *Spheres, Vol. 1: Bubbles*, trans. Wieland Hoban (Los Angeles: Semiotext(e), 2010), 473.
24 Ibid., 472.
25 Ibid., 473.
26 Ibid., 475.

would say in the spirit of Stavrogin's angelic thought, our kernel of existence, being never actualized, transcends death without resorting to metaphysical transcendence.

Surplus: The Case of Kalganov

So, then, we might ask what happened to Dostoevsky's angel (or demon) after his misadventures in St. Petersburg, Pavlovsk, and Skvoreshniki, and beyond the limit of the Alpine arête. In *Brothers Karamazov*, Dostoevsky's summa and his return to the native flatland of the Mother-Moist Earth (*Mat' syra zemlia*), Myshkin's life in potentiality becomes actualized in Alyosha's body; faceless Myshkin-Stavrogin finds a face (not a mask)—the lively, healthy, full-blooded face of Alyosha. Still, he is not fully actualized in the plot. Alyosha retains the role of messenger, carrying letters and notes in a world devoid of face-to-face communication, one enmeshed in "the crises of the sender metaphysics." He remains at the threshold: between the monastery and "our town," in intermediary space. If Myshkin preserves his marginal status, occupying the center of the novel, Alyosha seems to lose his transparency, gradually materializing in the *fabula*.

Instead, let us take a closer look at a marginal character, Kalganov, who consistently preserves his status of marginality throughout the novel. In many respects, he could be representative of the collection of characters that populate the margins of Dostoevsky's novels, who never try to move to the center like Prince Myshkin. To be more precise, Kalganov belongs to a peculiar cluster of marginal characters that include young, good-looking men who do not have any specific role assigned to them in the plot, whose novelistic existence is episodic, and whose absence would not disrupt the narrative flow. Their origins are unclear: they wander without any specific goal, precisely like Kalganov; they may spread gossip or carry messages, like Rakitin or Perkhotin, also from *Brothers Karamazov*; or even engage in blackmail, like Trishatov from *The Adolescent*. Their status is often morally ambiguous. Trishatov is a perfect example of this moral and narrative suspension. He is a member of the blackmailers' gang and, at the same time, helps save Versilov from committing murder and suicide.[27] These men often wander in pairs, for example, Trishatov with Andreev, and Kalganov with Maximov, Rakitin, or Alyosha.

---

27 In a chapter devoted to Trishatov, Susanne Fusso—pursuing the argument of her book, summarized by its title, *Discovering Sexuality in Dostoevsky*—gives enough evidence for a

Certainly from the perspective of the ostensible themes and motifs in Dostoevsky's novels, Kalganov might be seen as a literary portrait of a typical young man of the 1870s, one with no ideological or spiritual spine, the son of liberals of the 1840s, an incurable melancholic—the "dreamer"—or a dandy, an echo of Onegin; perhaps he is a candidate for suicide, a literary double of Alexander Herzen's daughter, as if he just stepped from the pages of the *Diary of the Writer*. Perhaps Kalganov carries some dark secret, as do Dostoevsky's other ambiguous characters Svidrigailov, Stavrogin, and Verkhovensky. Seen from the latter perspective, he might also be a double of nihilistic Smerdyakov, the dramatized "contemplator," as represented in a famous painting by Ivan Kramskoy.

Who or what else might this fair creature with Prince Myshkin's blue eyes be, "with the strange fixity in [its] gaze"? Victor Terras, a devoted reader of Plotinus—a philosopher who inspired many medieval and modern era angelologies—classifies Kalganov as typical for Dostoevsky—"unnecessary," "extra," "a trademark" of Dostoevsky's art.[28] He is unrelated to anything in the book, like some sort of a narrative surplus. Following this hint, but stretching our imagination a bit further by putting into movement a chain of literary associations, we may consider Kalganov to be a close relative of a certain young dandy in white pantaloons who passes like a ghost through the opening pages of Gogol's *Dead Souls*. If this is the case, he can be a figure of a narrative detour, first giving us flickering hope for the possibility of the story and then bringing us back into an entangled assembly of empty sets, leaving behind only a narrative surplus, the logic of which is described so well by Nabokov in his playful study of Gogol. This choice could be explained by the realist narrative itself, which demands an excess of random details and a procession of so-called flat characters. Nonetheless, for our purposes here, we can focus more closely on the anagogic dimension of this character.

Robert Belknap finds for Kalganov a well-defined role within the structure of the novel, suggesting that his presence could be explained on the level of the inherent structural relationships in the text, as an "installed" "reminder," whose

---

desexualized reading of this puzzling character, especially in the section devoted to Trishatov's imaginary project of the operatic transposition of Goethe's *Faust*. See Fusso, *Discovering Sexuality in Dostoevsky* (Evanston, IL: Northwestern University Press, 2006), 42–68.

28   Victor Terras, *A Karamazov Companion* (Madison: University of Wisconsin Press, 2002), 142.

role is to recall Alyosha and his states.[29] As in the case of Terras's observation, we might also develop Belknap's thought, stretching it beyond the structural. Indeed, it is hard to resist the impression that Kalganov is a substitute for Alyosha in two of the most important scenes of the novel, both of which are structurally and ideologically significant. Kalganov, as Terras also notes, "keeps turning up on the fringes of the novel."[30] These are the places that frame the story beyond the ostensive *fabula* with their two gestures: Zosima's prophetic bow to Dmitri, and weeping Kalganov's farewell to the arrested Dmitri.

Kalganov's indifference to carnal passions and our inability to catch him *in flagrante delicto* with a woman might prompt some eager scholars to build a case for his having a homosexual orientation. Perhaps yes, perhaps no. The problem with this approach, putting aside its interpretative value, is that he is not caught *in flagrante* with a man either. Should the enigma of Kalganov be hidden in his sexuality? As a twentieth-century admirer of Dostoevsky, one of the melancholic ghosts of European twentieth-century literature, Emil Cioran (1911–95), once said, "Sexuality is a great leveler; better, it strips us of our mystery."[31] So let us not consider urgent the question of the sexual preferences of Dostoevsky's characters in order to leave the question open for yet another interpretation.

Still, if we insist on looking at Kalganov through his sexuality, there is another option—impotency, which also constitutes a great enigma. Cioran noted in regard to Gogol's "secrets" that "no flow isolates more." "Impotent, a man possesses the inner strength that makes him singular, inaccessible," Cioran writes.[32] And this is what we may also say about Kalganov, a temporary protector of another marginal character, Maximov—an orphaned, old-fashioned landowner, who himself, in the potent space of Mokroe, conjured up another layer of surplus, phantom characters from *Dead Souls*, as if resurrecting them. The impotence (or sexual indifference) of Kalganov as a key to the enigma of his appearance in the novel could be a promising interpretative hypothesis, if understood precisely beyond the leveling sexuality, perhaps in the sphere of— and this is the point—the angelic.

---

29   See Robert Belknap, *The Structure of "The Brothers Karamazov"* (Evanston, IL: Northwestern University Press, 1989), 55–56.

30   Terras, *Karamazov Companion*, 363.

31   Emil Cioran, *The Temptation to Exist*, trans. Richard Howard (London: Quartet Encounters, 1987), 184.

32   Ibid.

Dostoevsky inserts the portrait of Kalganov in the novel twice. In both, he appears as a financially independent, melancholic, beautiful man. He is a relative of Miusov and "friendly with Alyosha." Yet, the reason why he enters the plot is unclear. The narrator describes him in short, precise sentences, as if painting a portrait. For example, at the very beginning of the novel, we meet Kalganov in the first of the scandalous conclaves, which puts into motion the tragedy of transfiguration. We see him for the first time at the beginning of the scene, on his way to the elder Zosima's cell—he is giving a handout to the beggars, but he is not doing so spontaneously, rather, it is as if he were fulfilling some script, seeming embarrassed, and not without some unexplained irritation.[33] In the cell of the elder Zosima, he stands out from the rest of the characters by forgetting to join the theater of bows: "Kalganov was so confused," the narrator writes, "that he did not bow at all."[34] Later, Kalganov witnesses the elder Zosima's prophetic bow—one of the most important gestures of the entire novel. He also prompts the rhetorical question that Dmitri automatically utters, which later will become one of the "proofs" of his guilt, as if directing Dmitri toward the trajectory of sin and redemption.

Yet, before he disappears from the story, Kalganov makes one more gesture. He takes with him the landowner Maximov, who is wronged and humiliated not only by his two wives and Ivan Karamazov but also, as we learn from him later, by the character of the Gogolian surplus, Nozdrev, the demon of chaos from Gogol's novel. So we may say that this originary scandal ends with a departure of those two enigmatic Gogolian characters, Kalganov and Maximov, whose actions proper may take place only in the surplus.

Being absent for more than three hundred pages of the novel, Kalganov reappears in book 8: we find him in Mokroe, on the sofa next to Grushenka, who is clutching his hand. Kalganov remains "somehow insensible" to her caresses, as the narrator reports. From the previous pages, we know of Grushenka's inclination toward angels, and toward men. (Later, Dmitri will also hold Kalganov's hand in his joyful greeting; in Mokroe, as in the earlier, infernal part of book 8, each grotesque gesture, each instance of verbal excess, each act of buffoonery has emblematic significance.) We learn that Kalganov and Maximov

---

33 See *PSS*, 14:33 (*BK*, 35).
34 *PSS*, 14:36 (*BK*, 39).

turned up in Mokroe by sheer chance. While Trifon Borisich is reporting to Dmitri on the situation at the inn and the available possibilities of entertainment, he cannot even recall Kalganov's name. The narrator—perhaps assuming that the reader, too, has also forgotten about this taciturn and giggly melancholic—inserts the same portrait of Kalganov, as if by mistake. Yet, if we agree that the proper space for Kalganov is in the narrative surplus, this repetition, which creates some sort of a rhyme, is perfectly justified.

There are, however, some changes in the second portrait, but it would be an exaggeration to say that these changes indicate a "development" of the character; it is rather a matter of accents and angles from which we look at him. Is it Kalganov's double, the second identical-looking angel? This reinsertion of Kalganov's portrait makes an impression, as if Dostoevsky were trying to lead our gaze twice toward the same place of this peculiar icon. When we meet Kalganov for the second time in Mokroe, he is perhaps more capricious, even inexplicably irritated, filled with disgust for the world, as if it had deeply disappointed him; he is bored and tired with it. His melancholic gaze makes an impression, "as if he soiled himself with something."[35] He also loses interest in Maximov, or, perhaps, this time he is just focused on Dmitri and his coming "transformation." Perhaps it is just a coincidence, but the fact that in the absence of Gypsies, Borisich sends for Jews to play at "Rozhdestvenskaia" (Christmas might have a symbolic meaning similar to that of the Jewish constable who meets Svidrigailov before the latter's last journey in *Crime and Punishment*, to which another angelologist of Russian literature, Rozanov, once turned our attention.

Initially in this scene, Kalganov still accompanies his Gogolian protégé, Maximov, hysterically laughing at his braggadocio. But, perhaps, his laughter is supposed to turn Dmitri's attention away from the crime he was about to commit—the most terrible, irredeemable crime in the spiritual jurisdiction of Christendom. Let us note that the angelic character from *The Adolescent*, Trishatov, explicitly prevented a suicide. The world of Dostoevsky's last novel is assembled much more subtly, so Kalganov, a peculiar guardian angel—"a benefactor," as Maximov calls him—also assists Dmitri, the central actor of the pagan-Christian drama, but in more trivial tasks, as, for instance, in helping

---

35 *PSS*, 14:392 (*BK*, 434).

him open a bottle of wine. It is as if Dostoevsky, in parody, wanted to present the drama of a modern guardian angel, but one who is unable to actively protect us. He then tries to prevent Mr. Musialowicz and Mr. Wroblewski from cheating at cards. Kalganov is a much subtler and more discreet angel than the unleashed Prince of Lightness, Myshkin, whose marginality takes over the center. So, finally feeling somehow estranged from the entire scene, Kalganov falls asleep: "But he was not merely drowsy from drink," the narrator comments, "he felt suddenly dejected, or, as he said, 'bored.'" "What a dear, charming boy he is!" Grushenka will say looking at him. We then hear the distorted verses from Pushkin's "The Prophet" from Dmitri, the words anticipating his transformation, which could only be made with the help of the Six-Winged Seraphim, grotesquely distanced from its parody—the impotent Kalganov. Once Dmitri has chosen new, vivid life in the embraces of Grushenka, Kalganov exits the scene: "'Well, now I really shall leave,' thought Kalganov, and going out of the blue room, he closed both halves of the door behind him,"[36] as if disappearing behind the panels of the iconostas.

In the following sequence of Dmitri's three ordeals, titled, nonaccidentally, "The Soul's Journey through Torments," Kalganov returns to testify in Dmitri's favor, but not without indignation. Kalganov then gives him his clothes. This Christian gesture is also distorted: the clothes are too tight, exposing Dmitri's excessive, grotesque carnality. The sequence ends with Kalganov running out of the inn and, following Dmitri to the carriage, exclaims ardently, "Farewell, you dear man, I won't forget this magnanimity!" "The bell jingled—Mitya was taken away." Here we stay with Kalganov, sitting down in a corner of the front hall, "ben[ding] his head, cover[ing] his face with his hands, and [beginning] to cry."[37] After Dmitri has been taken away, we may assume that the crying and disoriented Kalganov has been prefigured in the fable of Grushenka, which ends with the exit of the weeping angel: "And the woman fell back into the lake and is burning there to this day. And the angel wept and went away."[38] Kalganov also brings to mind the Archangel Michael, who assisted the Virgin Mary in her descent to hell, from the formal and ideological prototype of Ivan's poem,

---

36 *PSS*, 14:398 (*BK*, 441).
37 *PSS*, 14:461 (*BK*, 511–12).
38 *PSS*, 14:319 (*BK*, 352).

especially if we take into account the titles of the chapters that narrate the interrogation—the torments of the soul.

In the remaining sections of the book, Kalganov will reappear twice more: first in a fantasy of Lise, "the little devil" (*besenok*), as one of her imaginary suitors, and a man who lives as if in a dream. Here, allegedly, he says, "Why live in reality, it's better to dream. One can dream up the gayest things, but to live is boring."[39] Yet, he is making a Gogolian marriage proposal, like his twin brother, the idiot. Next, we see him for the last time at the trial of Dmitri, during which he testifies in favor of Dmitri, confirming the dishonesty of the "infernal" Poles. (In Dostoevsky, Catholic Poles always signify "fake" Christians, who need some rationale for their faith, be it historical or messianic.) So, even if he is a creature of the margin, Kalganov is still the only character in *Brothers Karamazov* who is present in both scenes: during the prophetic bow—a prefiguration of Dmitri's transformation—and at the pagan-Christian passion in Mokroe.

Therefore, perhaps, the decision of the directors of the various cinematic adaptations of *Brothers Karamazov*—from Fyodor Otsep, to Richard Brooks, to a recent Russian television soap-opera-style adaptation—to remove Kalganov to focus on the commercial success of their films tells us something important about Kalganov. Although Kalganov interacts with the main characters of the novel, and is even related by blood to one of them (Miusov), he remains mysterious, as if living on the *parergon* ("subordinate activity or work") not able to become actualized in *the story*, understood as a chronological sequence of narrative events. The promise he brings into the narrative is never fulfilled on the novel's narrative plane. Certainly, he reemerges from the narrative fog in Mokroe, but only by chance, as he readily admits. Moreover, this scene belongs to a different order than that of the ostensive narrative—it belongs to the visionary. It is hard to resist the impression that by introducing Kalganov, Dostoevsky was carrying the Gogolian surplus into his last novel, as he did with his first major works. Kalganov's case, however, might help us better understand the meaning of this Gogolian (or angelic) surplus, leading us through the anagogic detour.

---

39 *PSS*, 15:22 (*BK*, 581).

Resorting to the terminology of medieval exegetes, we may say that Kalganov belongs to *parergon*, "which gives meaning to the very way that the pictorial signs shift in work, become *translata*."[40] So, perhaps the marginal presence of Kalganov can be interpreted on the anagogic level. As Massimo Cacciari noted, "In guiding from visible things to invisible ones, the Angel is the figure of the *anagogy*, of the sensus anagogicus, that pertains to future life and heavenly things ... can lead *hic et nunc* to a sort of vision of the eschaton, ad *contemplanda caelestia*,"[41] unlike the demons that bind us to fate. Anagogia, one of the extensions of the spiritual meaning of history (the story)—in scholastic exegetic practices, as Georges Didi-Huberman reminds us—designates the ultimate of tropological conversions, the meaning of Scripture viewed from the eschatological perspective, constituting the theological, and the theological atmosphere, of meaning par excellence.[42] Thus the narrative surplus on the anagogic level can be interpreted as the modality of the angel. As Michel de Certeau wrote in his remarkable essay "Angelic Speech," the angel is "the signature of an excess (even when it is the index of a different "order" of things), and by a 'more' or a 'too much,' he opens a horizon of "sublime" that overflows, and must overflow, the common rules of veridiction."[43]

The *Sistine Madonna*: "Das Unbeschreibliche/ Hier ist's getan . . ."

The theme of angels in Dostoevsky was introduced in this chapter through Volynsky's analogy of the arrangement of Orthodox icons to the literary conclaves of *Brothers Karamazov*. Let us close with a brief visit to the Old Masters Gallery in Dresden, taking a closer look at Raphael's *Sistine Madonna*, one the most important paintings not only for Dostoevsky but for modern aesthetic reflection, in general. It was discussed most notably by Johann Winckelmann, and from then on by almost every major European writer and philosopher.

---

40   Georges Didi-Huberman, *Fra Angelico: Dissemblance and Figuration*, trans. Jane Marie Todd (Chicago: University of Chicago Press, 1995), 31.

41   Massimo Cacciari, *The Necessary Angel*, trans. Miguel E. Vatter (Albany: SUNY Press, 1994), 4.

42   Didi-Huberman, *Fra Angelico*, 40–41.

43   Michel de Certeau, *The Mystic Fable*, vol. 2, *The Sixteenth and Seventeenth Centuries* (Chicago: University of Chicago Press, 2015), 170.

In addition to Dostoevsky, the list of admirers of the *Sistine Madonna* includes Goethe, Balzac, Wagner, Nietzsche,[44] and Heidegger, to mention just a few.[45]

We should not be surprised, then, at seeing its copy, which Dostoevsky received from Vladimir Solovyov, hanging over the sofa in Dostoevsky's reconstructed study room in the Dostoevsky Museum Apartment in St. Petersburg. Dostoevsky's copy, however, is just the cropped, central fragment of the entire composition, featuring St. Mary with the child. Further, we may have the impression that in his novels that refer to the *Sistine Madonna*—*The Idiot, Demons,* and *The Adolescent*—Dostoevsky seems to be focused just on the central Madonna, not noticing the drama of representation (a significant portion of the composition) or the cherubs, who rest on the represented frame of the painting, long fascinating so many art historians and writers. Obviously, Dostoevsky saw the original painting in Dresden, so we are fully justified to look for allusions to this painting in *Brothers Karamazov*. Moreover, the absence of direct references to Raphael in this novel may imply a subtler and more discreet presence, one not reduced to a discussion of the eternal beauty embodied in the Madonna, as in the previous novels.

The Romantic viewers of the painting shifted their critical attention from the central Madonna to the background and margins of the work, provoking questions concerning the tension between reality and artificiality, and the limits of representation. As Hans Belting argues, since the beginning of the nineteenth century, Raphael's vision has been imagined in the topos of the dream—as mirage-playing tricks in the imagination of a modern artist. It became the paradigmatic work for the Romantic point of view, in which artistic contemplation replaced religious practice. Heidegger, as Belting reminds us, compared the Dresden picture to the sacrament, in which the bread is transubstantiated into the body of art.[46] In a way, Belting argues, this painting shows "the ambivalence between work and idea," which liberates "every painted image from its externality and transform[s] it into an internal image."[47]

---

44 Like Dostoevsky, Nietzsche also received an engraving of the *Sistine Madonna* to be hung "above the sofa." See Hans Belting, *The Invisible Masterpiece*, trans. Helen Atkins (Chicago: University of Chicago Press, 2001), 66.

45 For a discussion of the critical and philosophical reception of this painting, see ibid., 50–70.

46 Ibid., 50, 67.

47 Ibid., 63.

Taking into account the Romantic interpretations of the *Sistine Madonna*, we may risk the hypothesis that its themes are also present in *Brothers Karamazov*, and not only those concerning the question of beauty but in the structure of the entire novel, or, at least, in its spiritual and aesthetic center—the scene in Mokroe, anticipated earlier in the novel in "The Confessions of the Passionate Heart." The questions formulated from the Romantic point of view could also be related to one of the central problems for Dostoevsky—who belonged [to] the Romantic generation, after all—and to *Brothers Karamazov*: the possibility of the narrative to capture the moment of the embodiment, the ineffable moment of suspension between the possibility and the actuality of the Incarnation. If *The Idiot* is an apocalyptic experiment with the image of the world after the crucifixion of Christ and the impending Second Coming, *Brothers Karamazov* might pose questions on the Incarnation and on the possibility of its representation related to the question of realism in art.

In Raphael's painting, the Madonna is not represented as an actualized vision. As Christian Kleinbub writes, Raphael "dramatizes, as if in an *istoria*, the transient moments when the vision is coming into being, when the invisible is becoming visible, grasping the cloak of materiality and clothing itself in phenomenal form."[48] Kleinbub goes on to write that Raphael's composition indicates "that if we might only see a little further or make out the emergent form of a cloud putto, we might glimpse what it means to 'see' beyond seeing itself."[49] Thus stated, the painting, unable to present a natural phenomenon, instead offers "a virtual apparition staged according to the rules of Aquinas's theory of the physical visionary. In this sense it is truly a simulacrum."[50] Viewed in this way, it is about the materialization of the vision and its rendering in art. The theatricality of the painting stresses its focus on the accommodation of the invisible in a visible medium, which is done, as Kleinbub argues, by "maintaining in precarious balance the irreconcilable dialectic of bodily and spiritual seeing, a balance that could slip dangerously

---

48 Christian Kleinbub, *Vision and the Visionary in Raphael* (University Park: Pennsylvania State University Press, 2011), 44.

49 Ibid.

50 Ibid.

close to the total materialization, and thus banalization, of the invisible divine."[51]

In "The Confessions of the Passionate Heart," Dmitri—as if paraphrasing Stavrogin's fantastic thought quoted above—also situates us between two winged creatures: insects and angels, the "storm" of sensuality and corruption.[52] This "fantastic" anthropology leads Dmitri to the question of spiritual transformation, and to eternal beauty and its visibility: "Beauty is a fearful and terrible thing! Fearful because it's indefinable, and it cannot be defined, because here God gave us only riddles. Here the shores converge, here all contradictions live together."[53] Rainer Maria Rilke's poetic rhyme to this thought in *Duino Elegies* seems to be most appropriate in the context of Dmitri's thought, for he relates the question of the terror in beauty (*das Schöne ist nichts als des Schrecklichen Anfang*) directly to the question of the angel (*Ein jeder Engel ist schrecklich*). Rilke's angel, like that of Dmitri's, makes us aware of our spiritual task, that is, our transformation of the phenomenal world (of Sodom and "Bernardy," of lust and modern science) through spiritual value, through pure inwardness, as unveiled by the angel. At the same time, the angel also unveils the terrifying truth that hope within the visible is unattainable. Following the angelic vector, we must do some work of the heart (*Hertzwerk*) that aims at the most radical renunciation—a more active renunciation than any monk has ever imposed upon himself—however, as we learn from Rilke's angels, this is not about transcendence: nowhere can the world exist but within. The knowledge of the internal, Rilke would say, is beyond the visible. Thus, this is the angel's horrifying truth. Commenting on the opening verses of Rilke's "First Elegy," Robert Vilain writes, "Beauty may be seen as the visible world that has been (trans)formed and shaped . . .,

---

51 Ibid., 45.
52 In Fyodor Tiutchev's translation of "Ode to Joy," quoted by Dmitri, this metaphysical suspension of man between angels and insects is strengthened by the symmetry of the translated verses: "To insects—sensuality / Angel—stands before god" (*Nasekomym—sladostrastie / Angel—bogu predstoit*) (*PSS*, 14:90). What is more, in Tiutchev's version, "der Cherub" is translated as "an angel," prompting the reader to go back to this passage when encountering other angelic motifs. Both nuances are lost in Pevear and Volokhonsky's translation, which relies on a standard English translation rather than rendering into English the Russian version of Schiller's poem.
53 *PSS*, 14:100 (*BK*, 108).

whilst dread is the invisible that has yet to be transformed."[54] And in a letter to Witold von Hulewicz, Rilke writes that the "Angel of the Elegies is that being which guarantees the recognition of a higher degree of reality in the realm of the invisible.—It is therefore 'terrible' to us because we, who love and transform it, still cling to the visible."[55] In Dostoevsky, this realization of the ambiguity of beauty, formulated explicitly for the first time by Dmitri during his "fantastic hour" in his mono-mystery-drama, performed in front of his "angelic" brother, Alyosha, takes us to the pagan rites in Mokroe, where he begins his *Hertzwerk*, the legacy of Doctor Hertzenstube, another angelic visitor, a foreigner as lost in the Russian language as Kalganov is in the reality of everyday Russia. However, as we learned from the Romantic reception of the *Sistine Madonna*, it is not only the internal affairs of the figures represented in the work of art but also those of the observer—in this case, the reader; the image must come to life "within the observer himself."[56] This is also a lesson of *Duino Elegies*.[57]

Encouraged by Rilke's sense and intuition of the angels' presence in Dostoevsky, we may wish to glimpse Raphael's painting once more, and, in particular, its lower section, occupied by the famous twin angels. What is their role in the entire composition? They are not simply ornamental surplus, and even if this were the case this angelic ornament would not escape from the regime of the anagogic content of the painting. The physicality of putti and their status—God's creations, but still not men—gesture not so much toward the transubstantiation of the divine, which is still suspended between the visible and the invisible at the center of the painting, as toward our bodily creature's own transformation, directed inward, still invisible; Madonna and the *babe* are still floating in the clouds as a dream or an idea, while the putti, embodied as the vision, rest on the solid frame. Kalganov's status is similar. We barely notice him and his role in the narrative, and yet we cannot forget his two elaborate physical descriptions. He feels uncomfortable in his body, almost embarrassed by his own physical presence; his melancholic gaze

---

54 Rainer Maria Rilke, *Selected Poems*, trans. S. Ranson and Marielle Sutherland (Oxford: Oxford University Press, 2011), 304.
55 Quoted in Rilke, *Selected Poems*, 304.
56 Belting, *Invisible Masterpiece*, 63.
57 Ibid.

arrests the world in half-comprehension and half-actualization—the world seen through his gaze does not constitute a coherent structure. Yet, his physical image, and at the same time, narrative discreetness, situates the frenzied rioters on the threshold between the visible and the invisible. Kalganov (or the two identical Kalganovs—one from the scandal scene and one from Mokroe), resting on the lintel of the novel's narrative frame, like Raphael's two angels, might be a vector pointing at the space between the representation of the frame and the material frame. Similarly, Maximov, coinciding with neither the diagetic nor the extradiagetic world, nor even with his own phantasms, brings forward the issue of the materiality of truth and vision, or its parody, by "resurrecting" Gogol's characters (as if responding to Smerdyakov, who was famously concerned with the untruth in Gogol, as during the dispute at Fyodor Pavlovich's home over cognac).

Thus, if we read the book through the analogy of Raphael's painting, in the Mokroe sequence, the novelistic translation of the center of Raphael's work— which Dostoevsky began in "The Confessions of the Passionate Heart"—becomes complete: the telluric, almost pagan Madonna, as Winckelmann noted, is holding the *babe*, the embodied God. But she is still on the threshold, of the visible and the invisible; the babe in Mokroe is still a vision. In Dostoevsky's eclectic fresco, the *babe* belongs to a dream, so we can say that the entire composition is suspended between vision and artistic realization, just as we find in Raphael's painting. The movement of the scene in the book, and, indeed, in the entire novel, seems to lead from the material of the narrative toward its spiritualization. Dmitri is standing naked, as if ashamed of his body with all its details; and our gaze, directed by the narrator and the investigators, is fixed on those material details. Dmitri is also distracted by the material excess of the scene. This excess of materiality, or "realism," as Dmitri would say, is narrative surplus that counterbalances Dmitri's spiritual visions, or, perhaps, the realization of his singularity, his nonselfish self, to use Lawrence's terminology. As he exclaims at one point during the interrogation, "This time it's not a dream! Realism, gentlemen, the realism of actual life!,"[58] as if he is saying that there are two orders of reality. Not only does Dmitri dream in this novel, but so do Ivan and Alyosha. Kalganov, as we know from Lise and the narrator, actually lives in the

---

58 *PSS*, 14:425 (*BK*, 471).

dream, disgusted with actual life. And by the end of the Mokroe sequence, the whole composition is completed in the ambiguous miracle of transubstantiation, the vision is fulfilled in Dmitri's dream, just as with the Romantic interpretations of Raphael's painting.

It is not an accident that in *Brothers Karamazov*, the word "angel"—the expectation of some angelic role to be fulfilled, the need of an angel— emerges from the chatter of the characters throughout the entire novel. Here, we may risk a fantastic hypothesis in order to have our own "fantastic hour": that is, that no one notices the "true" angel, Kalganov, who, disoriented in his mission, and with no clear message, turns our attention to the event of the self-transformation of Dmitri, like angels in Goethe's *Faust, Part Two*, which "lift up the immortal part of Faust to a celestial apotheosis that reunites him with Gretchen."[59] As at the end of *Faust, Part Two*—a poetic response to Raphael's painting[60]—at the end of the Mokroe sequence, which arguably should end the anagogical dimension of the novel, the idea of redemption also brings the apprehension of the absolute in art. We find that Dmitri's ecstasy in the apprehension of Madonna from the beginning of the novel precisely anticipated the coming transformation in Mokroe. This incredible sequence of iconic arrangements in Mokroe could easily have ended with the verses of the closing stanza of Goethe's *Faust*, chanted by the "mystical chorus":[61] "What is ineffable / Here is accomplished." Thus, what is also at stake in Mokroe, and in the entire novel, is the embodiment of religious vision.

As Pleşu notes when referring to the writings of the Church Fathers, after the Incarnation, humans know more about the divine than the angels do; people better know the depth of the divine, which becomes obvious and, in a way, visible after the Resurrection.[62] Quoting Dumitru Stăniloae, Pleşu writes that man preserves the image of God better than the angels, which are messengers, servants, assistants, or, sometimes, just spectators. So, the true angel of the world, in waiting for the fulfillment of the promise of the Second Coming, would be more like Myshkin's relative, a pale

---

59 Belting, *Invisible Masterpiece*, 66.
60 For the discussion of the *Sistine Madonna* and *Faust, Part Two*, see ibid., 63–66.
61 Quoted in ibid., 64.
62 Pleşu, *O aniołach*, 29.

Kalganov, and not Alyosha, to whom most of the characters explicitly prescribe the angelic role. As we see in Dostoevsky's synthetic vision, which combines the Gospel with the realist narrative, and where all the events are in the midst of the interaction of three biblical planes—heaven, earth, and hell—the angelic allusions, as in the Bible and Patristic literature, hint at the possibility of mediation among all of these planes. Thus, the characters of *Brothers Karamazov*, who are looking so desperately for their guardian angels, need them not so much for protection as for mediation. Kalganov, in his marginal presence in the crucial scenes of the novel, could be the bearer of such a mission, showing just such a direction, or, rather, its trace, having in mind that he is a modern messenger, capricious and indecisive in his melancholy. To again use Pleşu's symbolic vector graphics and his distinction between angels and humans, we find that the angel, Kalganov, is a trace of the vector, while the man, Dmitri, is the cross.

XV

The Detective as Midwife in Dostoevsky's *Crime and Punishment*

Vladimir Golstein

It is easier to write about Socrates than about a young lady or a cook.

—Chekhov, in his Jan 2, 1894, letter to Suvorin

Truth is the daughter of Time, and I feel no shame in being her midwife.

—Johannes Kepler

When, in the final chapter of *Crime and Punishment*, Raskolnikov climbs the stairs and arrives at the police station to confess, he encounters a tipsy police lieutenant, Ilya Petrovich, who launches—quite unexpectedly—into an attack on nihilists and ... midwives:

> "There are such a lot of nihilists now, all over the place, and indeed it is easy to understand why, what times these are, I ask you. You and I, however ... of course, you aren't a nihilist, are you? ... You can be open with me, you needn't hesitate ... There are an extraordinary number of midwives cropping up all over the place."—Raskolnikov raised his eyebrows questioningly ...— "I am talking of those short-haired females,"—went on the garrulous Ilya Petrovich. "It is my own idea to call them midwives and I think the name is very satisfactory ... They push themselves into the Academy and study anatomy; well, tell me, if I fall ill am I going to call in a girl to cure me? He,

he!" Ilya Petrovich laughed, delighted with his own wit ... "Then again, look what a lot of these suicides there are: you can't imagine ... Why, only this morning we had the case reported to us of a gentleman newly arrived in St. Petersburg. Nil Pavlovich, what was his name?" ... "Svidrigailov!" answered a hoarse voice. ... Raskolnikov started. (447–48)[1]

This somewhat humorous passage is clearly pregnant with meanings that only a good midwife can deliver. Ilya Petrovich's references to the new fashion of female education and the new trends of emancipation should not obscure the fundamental fact that the profession chosen by female radicals, besides its medico-scientific dimension, is deeply steeped in myths, history, and cultural tradition. Various cultures, Russia's included, imagined a midwife as a particular type of woman, capable of functioning at the cross-section of biological and spiritual, medical and religious. In the spirit of this cross-section, a midwife was expected to be some sort of a mediator (as the English word "midwife" clearly implies). Likewise, midwives were expected to be postmenopausal women, preferably widows not engaged in erotic activity, as if their sexuality and ability to conceive would hinder their ability to deliver somebody else's children. Consequently, we can understand the tension that Russian society experienced at the time of *Crime and Punishment*, the tension that the Russian language clearly captures: traditional midwives were called *poval'niye babki*, while younger girls who preferred the medical and scientific approach to the issue wanted to be known by the French variant of the term, *akusherka* [акушерка]" ("obstetrician"). The very term *babka*, of course, suggests a grandma, hardly a proper name for a young educated girl. Dostoevsky's own novel *The Demons* features Shatov's pregnant wife requesting the help of a cheaper, older peasant midwife, but she is persuaded to employ the young radical *akusherka*, Virginskaya.

Besides elaborating the tension of old and new, Ilya Petrovich's diatribe inadvertently describes emerging cultural trends that Dostoevsky had always been ready to observe and discuss, such as nihilism, scientism, and suicide.

---

1 All references to Dostoevsky are to the *Polnoe sobranie sochinenii v tridsati tomakh* [*PSS*], ed. V. G. Bazanov et al. (Leningrad: Nauka, 1972–90); hereafter cited as *PSS* by volume and page. I have relied on the English translation of the novel in *Crime and Punishment*, 3rd ed., Norton Critical Edition, ed. George Gibian, trans. Jessie Coulson (New York: Norton, 1989). The page number is given in parenthesis following the quotation itself. All other translations are my own.

Thus, his *Diary of a Writer* pays special attention to the suicide of a young radical woman, named Pisareva, who got her medical education as a midwife. The fictional variant of this interlink of deaths, suicides, and midwives is elaborated on the pages of *The Demons*, where Dostoevsky demonstrates how well aware he was of the cultural expectations connected with midwifery; the radicalism of the young nihilistic women (Virginskaya, or Shatov's sister, Darya) is underscored by the fact that they combine erotic affairs and midwifery.[2]

But leaving Dostoevsky's own preoccupation with radical youth aside, what is interesting about Ilya Petrovich's diatribe is that it captures the new reality that the novel depicts. The times are different, and they produce new cultural types: nihilists and feminists. The traditional old woman in a village is replaced by a short-haired, educated, gentry girl; the traditional violent murderer (a character in the novel's epilogue insists that "it is not a nobleman's job to kill with an ax") is replaced with an intellectual student; the traditional pleasure seeker and seducer, Svidrigailov, is replaced with a Nietzschean superman bound on suicide.

Ilya Petrovich's comical claim about the "overabundance of midwives" and other nihilists—implying a new reality that the novel captures—highlights another important dimension of Dostoevsky's text: practically all the novel's characters (ranging from Marmeladov and Sonya to Svidrigailov and Luzhin) function as midwives, as people who help Raskolnikov to deliver his confession, to undergo his spiritual rebirth.

Images of birth and delivery accompany Raskolnikov from the beginning to the end of the novel. Thus, the very first sentence announces the process of emerging—mostly metaphorically, but with the sufficient stress on the physical activity: "Toward the end of a sultry afternoon in July a young man came out of his little room" (1). The physical movement of Raskolnikov prefigures not only the miraculous image of Lazarus coming out of his grave but also a rather mundane thing, such as the birth of a child. A few chapters later, we hear Nastya's comment on Raskolnikov's nightmare, in which Ilya Petrovich appears to be beating Raskolnikov's landlady: "It is your blood that makes a noise. It's when it hasn't got an outlet, and it begins to get all clotted, and then you begin to get visions" (99). In connection with this search for outlet, it is worth

---

2   Cf. Muireann Maguire, "Dostoevsky and the Politics of Parturition: Childbirth as Political Motif in Demons," *Modern Language Open* 1 (2014): 1–9.

remembering Porfiry Petrovich's own incessant reminder to Raskolnikov that the latter needs "air," an open space, an outlet. Likewise, in the epilogue to the novel, we encounter the reference to the nine-month gestation period, when we read of Raskolnikov's mother yearning for her son: "One morning she roundly declared that by her reckoning Rodya ought soon to be with them, and that she remembered his telling her ... that they must expect him in nine months" (именно через девять месяцев) (456).

The key role in this process of Raskolnikov's delivery, however, is played by Porfiry Petrovich, a character embodying a new type of a detective. A traditional policeman, a dogged pursuer of the criminal would not do in this novel of new types. It is my claim that Porfiry Petrovich is this strange combination of old and new, of pursuer and pursued, of nihilist and midwife, of a person who upholds the law, yet operates outside it. In other words, the reversals and paradoxes of various gender and cultural roles, to which Ilya Petrovich alludes so boldly, have also touched upon Porfiry.

For attentive readers, Porfiry Petrovich does appear as an uncanny figure, as someone who is less of a character and more of a device. Thus R. P. Blackmur claimed that Porfiry is an unreal character, serving as an agency of the plot, something "to make the wheels go round."[3] Joseph Frank elaborates the point in the following manner: "Unlike Poe's Dupin, he is far from being a monster of rationality; nor is he, like Hugo's Javert, a relentless incarnation of the Law. ... Porfiry's role-playing is very much like that of a novelist, who embodies his own personality in a whole range of characters."[4] In terms of "embodying a whole range of characters," Porfiry should remind us of a well-known (real-life) nineteenth-century detective, Eugène-François Vidocq—one of the founders of modern criminology and a precursor of the comic Inspector Clouseau—who was notorious for his ability to assume different personalities when in pursuit of his suspects. Yet, what is important about Porfiry's shifty character is not so much his ability to camouflage himself into different masks, but rather his own protean nature, which connects him to another intellectual investigator known since the time of antiquity.

---

3 Edward Wasiolek, ed. and trans., *Notebooks for "Crime and Punishment"* (Chicago: University of Chicago Press, 1967), 132.

4 Joseph Frank, *Dostoevsky: The Miraculous Years 1865–1871* (Princeton, NJ: Princeton University Press, 1995), 125.

I refer to Socrates, of course, a brilliant and versatile thinker, who compared his own intellectual pursuit of truth to the art of midwifery while claiming that his purpose was to bring forth what's latent in his students.[5] Indeed, besides its obvious medical side, the art of midwifery—at least since the time of Socrates—implied psychological, philosophical, and aesthetic dimensions: to bring forth, to facilitate and trigger inner transformation and rebirth. That aspect of Socrates has been the subject of scrutiny of various scholars, including the recent studies by Myles Burnyeat and Radcliffe Edmonds.

Besides the similarities in appearance (short, stout, paunchy, snub-nosed, large round head) or dress (both were frequently seen in what looks like robes, or the Russian *khalat*), Porfiry Petrovich and Socrates share goals (to bring forth the beautiful inner person) and methods. They both are forever ironic, meta-literary, and ready to deconstruct, expose, and scrutinize their own methods, while skillfully using verbal traps and other rhetorical tricks of the trade. Their complex verbal strategy stems from the fact that even though they are clearly more skillful than sophists in one case, or detectives in another, their purpose is not to win an argument or capture a criminal, but rather to produce change in their interlocutors, to bring forth justice, temperance, truth, and other qualities that were hidden before their interference.

Similar to Socrates's role vis-à-vis his interlocutors, Porfiry doesn't simply want to catch Raskolnikov, he wants to bring forth a transformation and change in consciousness. Dostoevsky—writing at the time of the novel—formulated his ideas on change in the following manner: "Man is not born for happiness … because the knowledge of life and consciousness … is acquired by experience pro and contra, which one must take upon oneself. (By suffering, such is the law of our planet, but this immediate awareness, experienced through the life process,

---

5 The fact that a number of *Crime and Punishment*'s characters function as Socratic midwives has been observed by M. W. Russell, "Beyond the Will: Humiliation as Christian Necessity in *Crime and Punishment*," in *Bloom's Modern Critical Interpretations: Fyodor Dostoevsky's Crime And Punishment*, ed. with an introduction by Harold Bloom (New York: Chelsey Publishing House, 2004). Russell states, "Of course Dostoevsky is … recalling that Socrates described himself as a midwife in Plato's *Symposium*. As the wise woman from Mantinea, Diotima, helped Socrates bring forth his soul in beauty and reach Sophia or wisdom, so Sonya serves as a midwife for the soul of Raskolnikov, even as a spiritual physician who helps cure him of his madness" (240).

is such a great joy that one gladly pays with years of suffering for it.)"[6] In other words, Dostoevsky views suffering as "labor," as the process required for the birth of new awareness. By referring to "the law of our planet," Dostoevsky clearly invokes the verdict of the Almighty, who associated earthly gains with the pain of labor: "In sorrow thou shalt bring forth children ... in the sweat of thy face shalt thou eat bread" (Gen. 3:16–18).

Porfiry Petrovich, a police investigator in search of the pawnbroker's murderer, is entrusted with helping Raskolnikov with all kinds of deliveries. Raskolnikov's first labor is clearly connected with his guilt and confession. As many criminals before or after him, Raskolnikov is suffering from the "compulsion to confess," an affliction known in literature at least since Chaucer, "Murder will out—*that* see we day by day," and Shakespeare, "Foul deeds will rise / Though all the earth o'erwhelm them, to men's eyes,"[7] and studied in detail by German psychiatrist and great admirer of Dostoevsky, Theodor Riek.[8] Raskolnikov's guilt surely wants out, and it forces him to act stupidly in front of Zametov, as he does when he revisits the scene of the crime. By the way, this scene of revisiting the pawnbroker's apartment is the longest chapter of the novel (eighteen pages; pt. 2, ch. 6), only approximated by the scene describing one of Raskolnikov confrontations with Porfiry (seventeen pages; pt. 3, ch. 5). The length and the tortuous content of these chapters clearly invoke the images of labor.

It is hardly surprising, therefore, that during this scene of revisiting the pawnbroker's apartment, Raskolnikov encounters another strange "midwife" figure—a mysterious man who eventually accuses him of crime. This stranger is described as a classic Russian "midwife" (*povival'naya babka*): "A little man who looked like a superior workman or small tradesman, but since he was wearing a sort of long robe (*khalat*) and a waistcoat, from a distance he resembled a peasant woman ... His whole figure seemed to stoop. From his flabby wrinkled face he seemed to be over fifty; his sunken little eyes looked hard, morose, and discontent" (230). This female-like tradesman will appear again, during another labor scene with Porfiry when Porfiry hides the man in a closet with the purpose

---

6 PSS, 7:154-5.
7 Geoffrey Chaucer, "The Nun's Priest's Tale," in *The Canterbury Tales*, line 15,058; and Shakespeare, *Hamlet*, 1.2.256–57 (act, scene, lines).
8 See Theodore Riek, *The Compulsion to Confess: On the Psychoanalysis of Crime and Punishment* (New York: Farrar, Straus and Cudahy, 1959).

of surprising and eliciting Raskolnikov's confession. This time the connection between Porfiry and his double, the tradesman, is made blatantly clear:

> Porfiry Petrovich was informally dressed, in a dressing gown (khalat) and slippers trodden down at the heel … He was a man of about thirty-five, rather short and stout, and somewhat paunchy. He was clean-shaven, and the hair was cropped close on his large round head, which bulged out at the back … His fat, round rather snub-nosed, dark skinned face had an unhealthy yellowish pallor, and a cheerful slightly mocking expression. It would have seemed good-natured were it not for the expression of his eyes … The glance of those eyes was strangely out of keeping with his squat figure, almost like a peasant woman's. (211)

Socrates's remarkable appearance is well known from Plato and other contemporary works, such as Xenophon's *Symposium* and Aristophanes's *Clouds*.[9] He is described as rather ugly with a snub, broad nose, piercing eyes, and a wide mouth. He wore a simple, unadorned robe-like garment (*himation*) wrapped about his pot-bellied body.

It is worth stressing that Socrates's appearance—besides leaving its mark on both Porfiry and the tradesman—invokes that of Dostoevsky himself. According to the memoirs of Dr. Yanovsky, a close friend of Dostoevsky, "His wide forehead and round head, and wide put eyes made his head look like that of Socrates. He was very proud of this similarity."[10] Likewise, A. N. Maikov, describing the early, Petrashevsky period of Dostoevsky, wrote that he remembers Dostoevsky, in the manner of dying Socrates, in a nightgown, delivering speeches to his friends about the sacred task of saving the motherland.[11]

Judging by drafts of the novel, Porfiry was initially presented as a rather realistic figure with various concrete details relating to his life and his professional activity. Yet, even this realistic figure had a rather metaphorical and suggestive last name—Semenov,[12] referring to the seed (*semia*): a potent

---

9 Plato, *Symposium* 215a–c, 216c–d, 221d–e (566–67, 572), and *Theaetetus* 143e (848). Translations, and page numbers in parentheses, are taken from Plato, *The Collected Dialogues*, ed. Edith Hamilton and Huntington Cairns (Princeton, NJ: Princeton University Press, 1961).

10 O. V. Marchenko, "Sokraticheskaya tema u Dostoevskogo," in *Istoriko-filosofskii ezhegodnik: 2001* (Moscow: Nauka, 2003), 155.

11 *PSS*, 18:192.

12 *PSS*, 7:68. At another moment Porfiry is called Porfiry Semenovich (*PSS*, 7:166).

image of birth and transformation in the universe of Dostoevsky, as the very epigraph to *The Brothers Karamazov* suggests. Despite the symbolism suggested by Porfiry's last name, he is presented in the drafts as a rather realistic detective, who hesitantly gropes for the truth, as he circles around Raskolnikov and interrogates Raskolnikov's friends. In the final version of the novel, however, we encounter a rather different Porfiry: a person who is not so much an investigator as he is a spiritual guide. In this respect, it is highly relevant to recall Father Tikhon from Dostoevsky's later novel *The Demons*—whose probing psychological questions provoke the following response from Stavrogin: "The monk would have made the greatest police investigator."[13] Stavrogin's comment clearly foreshadows G. K. Chesterton's famous detective, Father Brown.

This ease with which a monk in Dostoevsky's world can become a police investigator explains why Porfiry—as Dostoevsky's work on *Crime and Punishment* continues—became more symbolic, more Socrates-like, anticipating future characters such as Father Tikhon or even Father Zosima, whose role as a spiritual midwife has been revealed in his encounter with another murderer— the so-called mysterious visitor in *Brothers Karamazov*.

It is clear that to accomplish his roles of spiritual guide, midwife, and police investigator, Porfiry has to be a rather oxymoronic figure, the figure that embraces all possible contradictions. Despite his "official status," Porfiry appears to be strangely uprooted. There is nothing that will tie him to something particularly human or concrete. He lives in a "state-owned apartment," even though in the drafts he was supposed to rent from Lebezyatnikov;[14] he does not have a family name—a rare instance in the world of Dostoevsky; he has a peculiar sexuality: we learn that now he wants to join the monastery, now prepares to get married. In that respect, Porfiry Petrovich cuts a figure similar to Prince Myshkin or Kalganov.

According to Socrates's *modus operandi*, it is precisely his "wide nature"—to borrow Dostoevsky's term—that enables him to succeed in bringing new truths into the world. His feigned ignorance, his strength and endurance hidden behind clumsiness, his rhetorical prowess hidden behind deliberately crass language are well-known features. On that level, Socrates has a long list of heirs in various cultural traditions, including holy fools (*yurodivye*) of Russian tradition.

---

13 *PSS*, 12:110.
14 *PSS*, 7:186.

This protean or Socratic nature of Porfiry makes the discussion of his character difficult. Unless we create some sort of equivalent Socratic discourse, we are bound to reduce and impoverish him. The part of this discourse should stress the radical difference between Porfiry and the rest of the characters, the same difference that characterizes Socrates and his follows or opponents. In articulating his superman idea, Raskolnikov frequently refers not just to Napoleon but also to the ancient Greek figures of Lycurgus and Solon, who—in a radical difference from the historical Socrates—relied on coercive state power to accomplish their goals. Socrates, on the other hand, insisted that radical reform can and should be secured through persuasion alone. And that's the path that Porfiry also strives to follow.

It is also worth stressing that the ability to dwell in all possible domains is what gives great fictional detectives their insights into crime. They all tend to act like Socrates. As in the case of traditional midwives who succeeded at their trade only after they moved beyond a well- defined sexual role, there exists a conviction that the lack of concrete identity, be it social, sexual, or any other is what enables these characters to solve their mysteries. From Sherlock Holmes to the heroes of Agatha Christie, to Chesterton's Father Brown, to TV's Columbo with his ever-absent wife, we see the strange correlation between their insights into criminals and diffused identity and sexuality.[15]

In fact, Socrates's failure to pay attention to erotic advances is a feature frequently commented on in Plato's dialogues. Socrates is much more interested in his role as a tutor or mentor than as a lover—for all his charm and tricks, Alcibiades, for example, fails to get Socrates to bed.[16] In *Theaetetus*, Socrates is quite articulate about his function as an intellectual and moral midwife: "I am childless in such things, and I am only trying to assist in the birthing, and to that end uttering charms over you and serving up things from each of the wise for you to task, until I bring out with you into the light your own belief." He also reminds us that Greek tradition also expected midwives to abstain from procreation themselves: "You know … that women never practice as midwives while they are still conceiving and bearing children themselves. It is only those who are past child bearing who take this up."[17]

---

15 Christopher Wallace, "The Case of the Celibate Detective," Salon.com, accessed January 21, 2016, http://www.salon.com/2013/02/03/the_case_of_the_celibate_detectives/.
16 *Symposium* 219b–d (570).
17 *Symposium* 149b (854).

This line of reasoning is worth elaborating, since it suggests a rather complex process behind various transformations of Dostoevsky's characters. In the *Symposium*, Plato depicts his teacher not as the progenitor or begetter of ideas, but as Socrates the Beautiful, who assists as a midwife at the labor of the fertile young men, helping them bring their spiritual progeny to light. It is a young man (a lover) who is already pregnant by virtue of his stage in life who now gives birth assisted by the object of his admiration (the beloved one). Radcliffe Edmonds explains the process in the following way:

> The entire process of procreation takes place within the lover: arousal, begetting, pregnancy and parturition ... Diotima describes the lover as a young man in search of beauty to relieve his pregnant soul. This lover is in search of the beloved who is possessed of beauty, at least in his soul ... and the presence of this beloved allows the lover to bring to birth the spiritual progeny with which he is in travail. Or in the words of the "Symposium": "whenever something pregnant draws near to beauty, it becomes glad and rejoicing, it lets and begets and gives birth. ... Hence, for the one who is pregnant and already swelling, there is much excitement about the beautiful because of the possibility of relieving the enormous labor pains.[18]

The object of veneration, the beloved, for Plato, acts as a midwife, as someone who brings forth the progeny that the lover has been carrying for a long term ... It is through the contact with the beauty of his beloved that the admirer (the lover) is delivered of his pregnancy. Beauty thus works as a midwife; it is this instrument that—in the words of Socrates—"utters charms" upon the soul and brings forth the progeny.[19]

---

18 Radcliff G. Edmonds III, "Socrates the Beautiful: Role Reversal and Midwifery in Plato's *Symposium*," *Transactions of the American Philological Association* 130 (2000): 266–67.

19 Dostoevsky's musings on the beauty that should save the world acquire new urgency and new understanding once we consider the role of beauty in the process of delivery. "The world would become Christ's beauty" (Мир станет красота Христова), Dostoevsky observed in his drafts for *The Demons* (PSS, 11:188). The beauty of Christ, of his image and actions, brings forth the best in us and in the world. Consequently, Porfiry can be connected to *porfira* ("purple"), the beautiful color associated with regal power and glory. Dostoevsky, who viewed beauty as something truly redeeming, had to share this Socratic sensitivity. In other words, it is not just Socratic dialogue or Socratic intellectual provocations that produced the necessary changes in the subject, but rather something more mysterious, akin to the skills of traditional midwives who—while working at the cross-section of medicine and religion—would charm the soul into delivery. Seen from this perspective, Porfiry's vague, submerged sexual interests imply a

Porfiry's purpose is not just to catch Raskolnikov, and not just to debunk him by challenging his intellectual, emotional, and moral defenses, but rather to facilitate the rebirth of a new man, a new Raskolnikov. It is hardly a coincidence that from the very first interview, Porfiry makes Raskolnikov focus on such images of transformation as Lazarus's resurrection or the New Jerusalem.

Unexpected as the roles of a spiritual guide and midwife are for a police investigator, it is this trajectory that Porfiry travels. In the process of investigation, Porfiry understands what kind of a criminal he is dealing with. He keeps on praising Raskolnikov's heart, soul, and nobility. Consequently, he understands that Raskolnikov's crime is not just of a legal but also of an ideological and moral nature. So it is Raskolnikov's ideology that has to be defeated, and it is Raskolnikov himself who has to acknowledge his defeat. Only then can the transformation begin. Spiritual progress can be achieved only after genuine remorse and attrition. Porfiry thus facilitates the birth of the new self, the "rebirth" of Raskolnikov, or rather of these aspects of Raskolnikov that the latter has tried to suppress and cut out.

On Raskolnikov's moral and spiritual "pregnancy," Dostoevsky observed, "His moral development begins with the crime itself. The very possibility of such questions did not exist before. In the last chapter, in prison, he said that without this crime, he would not have confronted such questions, desires, feelings, needs, strivings, and development."[20]

Porfiry plays the central part in the process of Raskolnikov's transformation, as he tries to disarm Raskolnikov ideologically and encourage him to reverse the trajectory of his thoughts. Porfiry as a police detective has to disappear, giving place to a spiritual midwife. Let us trace this trajectory as it is revealed in their three interviews.

The first interview starts on a Gogolian note, as Porfiry appears on the stage quoting a well-known line from Gogol's *Inspector General*. This early reference to Gogol's play sets the tone for what's to follow: it introduces theatrical terms and the very concept of play-acting so relevant to both Porfiry, who wants to trick Raskolnikov, and to Raskolnikov, who pretends to be innocent. Furthermore, Gogol intended his play as a vehicle "to catch the conscience of Russia,"

---

person whose sexuality has been transcended and transformed into inner beauty that serves as a magnet for the spiritual beauty of Raskolnikov.

20   Wasiolek, *Notebooks for "Crime and Punishment,"* 11.

to make it undergo self-scrutiny and consequent transformation. This ability of the theater to induce moral transformation by making the criminal confess has been known at least since the time of Shakespeare:

> I have heard that guilty creatures sitting at a play
> Have, by the very cunning of the scene,
> Been struck so to the soul that presently
> They have proclaimed their malefactions.
> For murder, though it have no tongue, will speak
> With most miraculous organ. . . .
>
> . . . The play's the thing
> Wherein I'll catch the conscience of the king.
> (*Hamlet*, 2.2.575–580; 591–92)

Dostoevsky, who knew Gogol practically by heart, was clearly aware of both literal and metaphorical meanings of Gogol's famous comedy. So it is hardly surprising that Porfiry is presented as a Gogolian figure who intends to disarm, catch, and transform Raskolnikov.

Besides its theatrical underpinnings, the first dialogue between Porfiry and Raskolnikov also has features of a Platonic dialogue. Besides Porfiry and Raskolnikov, several other people are present in Porfiry's apartment (Razumikhin and Zametov), and the gathering has the elements of some kind of a soiree or symposium. The participants discuss the nature of the crime, socialism's view of it, the role and impact of the environment. The discussion eventually focuses on the exchange between Porfiry and Raskolnikov as the former begins to question Raskolnikov's theory. He subjects it to ironic taunting, takes extreme extrapolations from his theory, and personalizes the debate by forcing Raskolnikov to personalize his abstract theory. Porfiry concludes their conversation with an intellectual trap for Raskolnikov (asking him about the details of the crime scene), which Raskolnikov skillfully avoids. In other words, following the illustrious examples of Plato, Shakespeare, and Gogol, Porfiry wants to capture Raskolnikov through some sort of verbal trap. Or to be more precise: the elements of Gogol's play skillfully hide Porfiry's own art, his Socratic attack on Raskolnikov's reason, and his intellectual defenses.

The second dialogue between the Porfiry and Raskolnikov presents their confrontation in a different key, as it becomes more focused on the technical aspects of crime and investigation. The action moves into Porfiry's office, and the conversation becomes less intellectual and abstract as it focuses on human nature and its failures to act according to logic. Instead of Raskolnikov's theories, the two discuss the behavior of a criminal and the detective strategies of capturing him. Rather than setting up an intellectual trap, Porfiry tries to provoke Raskolnikov into confession. He works on Raskolnikov's emotional defenses and uses everything in his repertoire to mock and tease him. Porfiry skillfully mixes criminal themes with his banter on gymnastics, hemorrhoids, and other health issues (258): "He was dropping empty phrases, frequently falling into nonsense" (260). At one moment, the detective is described as a ball bouncing from one wall into another (256); at another, Porfiry's laughing body is compared to a rubber eraser, suggesting the lack of a definitive shape (257).

In a complex irony fitting of Socrates, Porfiry attacks the formalism of various police methods. "The form is nonsense," he pronounces, while asserting that "one cannot restrict the investigator with the form, he is a free artist" (260). A protean, free artist, a figure capable of being simultaneously everywhere and nowhere, not only implies a policeman whose net is spread wide, but more importantly, it takes us back to the very essence of Socrates, who in his paradoxical exchanges has also proven to be nowhere and everywhere, knowing all and nothing. Even in his manner of conversation, Porfiry is similar to Socrates, as both are very good at switching the tone, using all possible verbal registers, ranging from banter to philosophical moralizing. In fact, Porfiry's language is by far more rich and diverse than that of any other character in the novel. Not just physically, but verbally, Porfiry manages to be nothing and everything, creating thus a net to catch Raskolnikov.

This discussion, as it focuses on the psychological state of the criminal, raises issues pertinent to Porfiry's midwife function. As Porfiry talks about "catching the criminal," he discusses the revolt of the criminal's human nature, the revolt that "ripens" the criminal, prepares him for confession. "Why should I bother him before his due time [*do sroka*]," he admits (260). This concept of ripening toward the allotted date suggests, of course, the time of pregnancy. The combination of guilt, uncertainty, and suspense forces the criminal into confession, but only after a period of time needed for gestation, without which no midwife is able to deliver. Furthermore, Porfiry discusses aesthetic issues during this dialogue, implying the role of beauty needed in this process of gestation.

In this interview, Porfiry reminds us that he has other fish to catch besides the criminal. He keeps returning to the concept of "higher mission" for which Raskolnikov is destined—in contrast to Porfiry himself: "I am a bachelor, I am a finished man, I went to seed" (*v semia poshel*) (257). While pointing to the contrast between the "finished" Porfiry and the younger Raskolnikov, Porfiry's comment is deliberately contradictory and paradoxical. How can a bachelor "go to seed"—an expression usually applied to the family man with children—unless it is the loner who is in the business of delivering other people's seed. Porfiry clearly uses the term metaphorically: he refers to the "children" that he has delivered, that is, to the criminals whose spirit he helped to resurrect by bringing them back to God.

Porfiry's rhetoric finds its perfect equivalent in Socrates's claims that he is nothing but a midwife, a person incapable of giving birth to wisdom, but capable of helping others to deliver "the admirable truths" that have been hidden within them. Socrates is rather articulate about the nuances of his skill:

> My art of midwifery is in general like theirs [real midwives]; the only difference is that my patients are men, not women, and my concern is not with the body but with the soul that is in travail of birth. And the highest point of my art is the power to prove by every test whether the offspring of a young man's thought is a false phantom or instinct with life and truth. I am so far like the midwife that I cannot myself give birth to wisdom, and the common reproach is true, that, though I question others, I can myself bring nothing to light because there is no wisdom in me. The reason is this. Heaven constrains me to serve as a midwife, but has debarred me from giving birth. So of myself I have no sort of wisdom, nor has any discovery ever been born to me as the child of my soul. Those who frequent my company at first appear, some of them, quite unintelligent, but, as we go further with our discussions, all who are favored by heaven make progress at a rate that seems surprising to others as well as to themselves, although it is clear that they have never learned anything from me. The many admirable truths they bring to birth have been discovered by themselves from within. But the delivery is heaven's work and mine.[21]

Porfiry's reference to "seed" (*semia*), the word with which he is frequently associated, brings to mind another instance of "seed": *Brothers Karamazov*'s "seeds from other worlds," the divine seeds waiting for growth and delivery. By invoking this concept of "seed," Porfiry foregrounds his role as a spiritual

---

21   *Theaetetus* 150 b–c (855).

midwife. Zosima in *Brothers Karamazov* explains the concept in the following manner: "God took seeds from different worlds and sowed them on this earth, and His garden grew up and everything came up that could come up but what grows lives and is alive only through the feeling of its contact with other mysterious worlds. If that feeling grows weak or is destroyed in you, the heavenly growth will die away in you."[22]

This concept of "spiritual seeds," to which Porfiry alludes during the second interview, gets further articulation in the final interview. Here we witness an altogether different Porfiry: he is now a somber and wise person, appealing to Raskolnikov's spiritual and religious values. The interview takes place in Raskolnikov's room, his home turf, so to speak. Here Porfiry does his best to level with Raskolnikov: he is serious, thoughtful, and sincere—as much as he can be. He no longer mocks or taunts Raskolnikov; he almost insists on being his peer. He claims to understand and appreciate Raskolnikov's soul and heart, his ambitions, his impatience, his nobility and idealism. It is exactly to these qualities that he appeals, and he insists that Raskolnikov is not the type who escapes and persists in his criminality while losing the ideology that can back him up. Consequently, Porfiry offers a different type of resolution: a voluntary confession rather that arrest and trial.

Porfiry argues that Raskolnikov would eventually ripen for the confession: "If I lock you up, you'll wait for a month or two, and then come with confession, unexpectedly to yourself" (352). In describing Raskolnikov's turmoil, and his "readiness" for the delivery, Porfiry resorts to the metaphors of pregnancy and birth: "I understand what it means to carry it all on yourself" (344). "To carry" (*peretashchit'*) is a term that implies carrying a burden, as if during the pregnancy.

It is also important to stress that Raskolnikov enters the final interview with the very strong feeling of being closed in, of "needing fresh air." Having witnessed Mikolka's confession, and realizing that he has temporarily beaten Porfiry's suspicions, he feels trapped: "Until this, everything had been too oppressive and confining, had crushed him with its overwhelming weight, and a sort of stupefaction had descended on him. From the moment of the scene

---

22   Fyodor Dostoevsky, *The Brothers Karamazov*, trans. Richard Pevear and Larissa Volokhonsky (London: Vintage, 2004), 276.

with Mikolka at Porfiry's, he had begun to feel suffocated and hemmed in, without escape" (376). On a metaphorical level, the gestation period is over: Raskolnikov has reached the moment when he wants to be caught and delivered from his old criminal self into a new one, and his readiness becomes obvious even to him (345).

Altogether, Porfiry mentions God and saints, invokes religious concepts, and refers to the Bible no less than fifteen times in this dialogue. At one moment, he asserts,

> How much do you know? Seek and ye shall find. Perhaps it is through this that God seeks to bring you to himself... Perhaps you ought to thank God: how do you know that He is not sparing you just for that? Keep your heart high and don't be so fearful! Do you flinch from the great fulfillment that confronts you? No, that would be shameful ... I know you do not believe me, but it is the sacred truth that life will sustain you ... Now you need only air, air, air ... Who am I? I am a man who has developed as far as he is capable, that is all. A man, perhaps, of feeling and sympathy, of some knowledge, perhaps, but no longer capable of further development. But you—that's another matter: the life God destined you for lies before you ... Become a sun, and everybody will see you. The first duty of the sun is to be the sun. (389)

In a complex argument, Porfiry suggests that Raskolnikov has to return to himself first in order to return to God through becoming what God destined him to become. This transformation clearly implies not so much birth as rebirth. That's exactly what Socrates was striving to achieve through his communication with his various interlocutors. Describing Socrates's complex interaction with the youth, Edmonds writes,

> On the one hand Socrates is ... the needy barefooted philosopher who is eternally seeking ... He seeks out beautiful youth, and engages them in conversations about the good life and virtue ... But Socrates is also Socrates the beautiful, ... whose outward ugliness hides supreme beauty ... This beauty serves as midwife to the thoughts of all the young men with whom Socrates consorts ... relieving them of the pains of their spiritual pregnancy and helping them actively pursue philosophy. Socrates plays the role of both lover and beloved in these relationships.[23]

---

23   Edmonds, "Socrates the Beautiful," 262.

Indeed, the aesthetic dimension of Socrates's midwife activity is made explicit by Alcibiades. Alcibiades is very specific about Socrates's goal to educate, to induce the transformation, to bring out the best in men by acting as an aesthetic catalyst or magnet. By appealing to their ethical and aesthetic sense, by revealing his own inner beauty, Socrates makes them act in accordance with what is the best in them:

> He loves to appear utterly uninformed and ignorant.—isn't that like Silenus ... Don't you see that it's just his outer casting, like those little figures I was telling you about. But believe me, friends and fellow drunks, you've only got to open him up and you'll find him so full of temperance and sobriety that you'll hardly believe your eyes ... He does not really care about a row of pins about good looks ... or money, or any of the honors that most people care about. He doesn't care a curse for anything of that kind, or for any of us either ... and he spends his whole life playing his little game of irony and laughing up his sleeve at all the world. I don't know whether anybody else has ever opened him up when he's been serious, and seen the little images inside, but I saw them once, and they looked so godlike, so golden, so beautiful and so utterly amazing that there was nothing for it but do exactly what he told me.[24]

One of the most important features of Socrates—according to Alcibiades—was his ability to provide his audience with moral education when they least expected it. By mocking and undermining their presuppositions, Socrates didn't just reveal the inadequacy of his interlocutors' reasoning, he clearly had a bigger fish to catch: encouraging moral growth and eventual delivery of a new self. Alcibiades's rhetoric and imagery describes the process in the following way:

> Anyone listening to Socrates for the first time would find his arguments simply laughable: he wraps them up in just the kind of expressions you'd expect of such an insufferable satyr. He talks about pack asses and black-smiths and shoemakers and tanners, and he always seems to be saying the same old thing in just the same old way, so that anyone who wasn't used to his style and wasn't very quick on the uptake would naturally take it for the most utter nonsense. But if you open up his arguments, and really get into the skin of them, you'll find that they're the only arguments in the world that have any sense at all, and that nobody else's are so godlike, so rich in images of virtue, or so peculiarly, so entirely pertinent to those inquiries that help the seeker on his way to the goal of true nobility.[25]

---

24 *Symposium* 216d–e, 217 (568).
25 *Symposium* 221e–222a (572).

Alcibiades continues, stressing Socrates's art of inducing his audience to recognize their erring ways, while provoking them to experience shame, to acknowledge their lost status, and to embark on restoration or improvement:

> And then again, he reminds me of Marsyas the Satyr.
>
> ... And aren't you a piper as well? I should think you were—and a far more wonderful piper than Marsyas, who had only to put his flute to his lips to bewitch mankind. It can still be done, too, by anyone who can play the tunes he used to play. Why, there wasn't a note of Olympus' melodies that he hadn't learned from Marsyas. And whoever plays them ... the tunes will still have a magic power, and by virtue of their own divinity they will show which of us are fit subjects for divine initiation.
>
> Now the only difference, Socrates, between you and Marsyas is that you can get just the same effect without any instrument at all—with nothing but a few simple words, not even poetry. Besides, when we listen to anyone else talking, however eloquent he is, we don't really care a damn what he says. But when we listen to you, or to someone else repeating what you've said, even if he puts it ever so badly ... we're absolutely staggered and bewitched. ...
>
> But this latter-day Marsyas, here, has often left me in such a state of mind that I've felt I simply couldn't go on living the way I did. ... He makes me admit that while I'm spending my time on politics I am neglecting all the things that are crying for attention in myself.[26]

That is the trajectory that Raskolnikov himself seems to undertake, encouraged and helped by Porfiry, who, similar to Socrates, assumes the role of a midwife in Dostoevsky's text, of someone who brings forth what has already been inside of his patient. Furthermore, in true midwife fashion, Porfiry disappears by the end of the novel. (According to Russian folklore tradition, on the day of the birth, the midwives were supposed to arrive to and leave the house without being noticed.[27]) He made sure, however, that there is no "evidence" against Raskolnikov among the police documents, so that Raskolnikov's "unexpected" confession mitigated his sentence. Porfiry deliberately dismisses his own professional activity and accomplishment, only to

---

26 *Symposium* 215b–216a (566–67).

27 G. I. Kabakova, "Otets i povitukha v rodil'noi obriadnosti Poles'ia," in *Rodiny, deti, povitukhi v traditsiakh narodnoi kul'tury*, ed. S. Neklyudov (Moscow, 2001), 109.

help Raskolnikov on his path toward rebirth. The police investigator gives way to the spiritual midwife, thus fully assuming the role played by Socrates in his society. In a rather revealing gesture, Dostoevsky last refers to Porfiry when he mentions that Porfiry, along with Raskolnikov's doctor, Zosimov, attends Dunya and Razumikhin's wedding, an event more closely related to childbearing and rebirth than to criminal investigation.

Conclusion

It is interesting to observe that another literary masterpiece written at the time of *Crime and Punishment*—Tolstoy's *War and Peace*—also features a character who functions like a midwife, bringing forth everything that was gestated in Pierre Bezukhov's soul. I refer to Platon Karataev, another figure whose manners and appearance are compared to those of a peasant woman (*baba*), and whose gestures—as he brings Pierre back to life—clearly invoke the gestures of a midwife.

In Tolstoy's rendering, we witness the collapse and then restructuring of Pierre, who has just witnessed the senseless execution of Russian prisoners during the French retreat from Moscow:

> From the moment Pierre witnessed those horrifying murders committed by men who had no wish to commit them, it was as if the mainspring of his soul, on which everything depended and which made everything seem alive, had collapsed into a heap of meaningless rubbish. Though he was not even aware of it, his faith in the right ordering of the universe, in humanity, in his own soul and in God, had been destroyed ... Now he felt that through no fault of his own the world had crumbled before his eyes, and only meaningless ruins remained. He felt that it was not in his power to regain his faith in life.[28]

And yet, after experiencing this collapse, Pierre undergoes both physical and intellectual rebirth, assisted in this process by Platon Karataev, clearly a midwife figure:

> Beside him, sitting in a stooped position was a little man whose presence made itself known to him by the strong smell of sweat that emanated from him every time he moved ... Having *unwound a cord* that was wrapped

---

28 Leo Tolstoy, *War and Peace*, trans. Ann Dunnigan (New York: Signet, 1968), 1156.

around one leg, he *carefully coiled it up*, and, glancing at Pierre, immediately set to work on the other leg… In his way, with swift deft circular motions, one following the other without pause, he took off whatever things he was wearing on his feet and hung them on pegs in the wall overhead. *Then he took out his knife and cut off something … Pierre was conscious of something pleasant, soothing, and complete in those deft, circular movements*, in the man's well-ordered arrangements in his corner … "Eh, don't fret, dear man," he said in the gentle, caressing, *singsong voice in which old Russian peasant women talk.* "Don't fret, friend; suffer an hour, live an age … Here, have a bit of this, sir," he said, and … untying the rag he handed Pierre several baked potatoes … He took a potato, drew out his clasp knife, cut the potato into two equal parts on the palm of his hand, sprinkled some salt on them from the rag, and handed them to Pierre … "You try 'em like that!" Pierre thought he had never tasted anything so delicious. "Oh, I am all right," he said, "but why did they shoot those poor fellows? The last one wasn't even twenty." … "Tsk, tsk, what a sin, what a sin!" … Sounds of screaming and shouting were heard somewhere in the distance, and the glare of the fire was visible through the cracks of the shed; but inside it was dark and quiet. Pierre didn't sleep for a long time, but lay with wide-open eyes listening to the rhythmic snoring of Platon, who lay beside him in the darkness, and he *felt that the world that had been shattered was beginning to rise again in his soul, but with a new beauty, and on new, unshakable foundations.*[29] (all emphasis is mine)

It is a fascinating fact that both authors invoked a similar image of a midwife in two of their greatest novels written in the 1860s. The period of Great Reforms must have filled the authors and their public with heightened expectations when Russian society, long pregnant with reforms and modernization, was waiting for the delivery. In other words, the image of midwives was clearly in the air as the country was on the eve of transformation, waiting for a new society to emerge from the old one based on serfdom.

Both Raskolnikov's and Pierre's examples reveal a certain optimism, the hope that a positive transformation was possible, that a new protagonist can be delivered. The optimism was slightly dampened by the fact that in Tolstoy's novel, Prince Andrei's wife dies in childbirth. Yet, as a certain disillusionment with reforms had set in in the 1870s, we witness a different image of a midwife or even of child delivery. Anna Karenina, for example, is tormented by nightmares,

---

29 Ibid., 1156–60.

in which she dies in childbirth. Furthermore, no new Anna emerges by the conclusion of the novel.

This issue becomes even more pronounced in Dostoevsky. In fact, the image of midwives, or failed child-deliveries, continues to haunt him, acquiring more and more negative and satirical connotations, as great expectations were giving way to lost illusions.

The Demons is rife with imagery of childbirth and midwifery, all of which go awry. It is therefore hardly surprising that in *The Demons* physical or spiritual beauty is mostly absent, and rationalism and violence defeat aesthetics. As Shatov's wife is getting ready to give birth she requests a traditional midwife. Instead, she is introduced to the modern-day radical *akusherka*, Virginskaya, who, despite her professionalism, delivers death, disharmony, and disintegration. The very fact that modern radicals— including young educated midwives—are disconnected from spirituality and beauty is highlighted by Kirillov: an ugly, clumsy, and self-destructive individual who can't even speak coherent Russian. Kirillov's emblematic failings are made obvious in this dialogue with Shatov, in which Shatov's grotesque masculine imbecility is matched by Kirillov's clumsiness and utter lack of coherence:

> —"Kirillov, my wife's giving birth!"
> —"How's that?"
> —"Giving birth, to a baby!"
>
> —"You're not … mistaken? … It's a great pity that I'm not able to give birth," Kirillov answered pensively, "that is, not that I'm not able to give birth, but that I'm not able to make it so that there is birth … or … No, I'm not able to say it."[30]

Although he is not able to say what is involved in "giving birth," Kirillov persists in belaboring, and eventually carrying out, his highly paradoxical and equally ugly theory of suicide.

Despite his ugly surroundings, Shatov is given a chance to glimpse the beauty and mystery of childbirth. In his rapture he declares to the radical midwife, Virginskaya, "The mystery of the appearance of a new being, a great mystery and an inexplicable one, Arina Prokhorovna, and what a pity you don't

---

30   Fyodor Dostoevsky, *The Demons*, trans. Richard Pevear and Larissa Volokhonsky (New York: Vintage, 1994), 581.

understand it! ... There were two, and suddenly there's a third human being, a new spirit, whole, finished, such as doesn't come from human hands; a new thought and a new love, it's even frightening ... And there's nothing higher in the world!"[31]

Virginskaya feels the instant need to drag this exaltation through the mud. She resorts to a cynically utilitarian retort by insisting that childbirth is only "the further development of the organism, there's nothing to it, no mystery ... That way every fly is a mystery. But I tell you what: unnecessary people shouldn't be born. First reforge everything so that they're not unnecessary and then give birth to them. Otherwise, you see, I've got to drag him to the orphanage tomorrow."[32]

This refraction of the image of a midwife throughout Dostoevsky's oeuvre reveals that this topic was hardly accidental in *Crime and Punishment*. Dostoevsky's explorations of the mysteries of Russian cultural development, of its complex and contradictory search for rebirth, clearly unite his earlier and later novels. Numerous midwives, to whom *Crime and Punishment* alludes, appear in realized form in *The Demons*; yet, they no longer function in the mythical and ancient role of a spiritual midwife that goes back to Socrates. Instead, the stage is set for the modern, medically educated, yet spiritually nihilistic midwives and their stillborn children to preside over the scenes of murder and suicide.

---

31 Ibid., 593.
32 Ibid.

Metaphors for Solitary Confinement in *Notes from Underground* and *Notes from the House of the Dead*

Carol Apollonio

1. "They were almost obliterated socially. They became permanently withdrawn, and they lived as outcasts—regularly set upon, as if inviting abuse."[1]
2. They "lose the ability to initiate behavior of any kind—to organize their own lives around activity and purpose. Chronic apathy, lethargy, depression, and despair often result. ... They have difficulties with 'irrational anger.' Many ... become consumed with revenge fantasies."[2]
3. "He observed himself becoming neurotically possessive about his little space, at times putting his life in jeopardy by flying into a rage if a guard happened to step on his bed. He brooded incessantly, thinking back on all the mistakes he'd made in life, his regrets, his offenses against God and family" (about Terry Anderson's experience of solitary confinement as a hostage of Hezbollah in Lebanon).[3]
4. "Paranoia, aggressive fantasies, and impulse control problems . . ."[4]

---

1 Atul Gawande, "Hellhole," *The New Yorker*, March 30, 2009, 36.
2 Ibid., 40.
3 Ibid., 38.
4 Rick Raemisch, "My Night in Solitary," *New York Times*, February 21, 2014, A23.

The reader of Dostoevsky's *Notes from Underground* (1864) would be forgiven for assuming that these observations concern the work's misanthropic hero. He too is withdrawn, depressed, neurotic, emotional, vengeful, irrational, angry, regretful, and brooding. The story he tells about his encounter with the prostitute Liza is precisely a tale of, as quote number 3 puts it, "mistakes he'd made in life, regrets, and offenses." Yet the referents here are not fictional characters but real-life subjects of experiments—inside and outside the lab. The socially inept, withdrawn creatures described in the first quote are rhesus monkeys raised without their mothers in psychology professor Harry Harlow's Wisconsin lab in the 1950s. Though the monkeys' basic physical needs were met, the absence of a living caregiver led to profound psychological and emotional disturbances. They were the first scientifically studied sufferers of what is now known as reactive attachment disorder, a syndrome diagnosed in children, whose symptoms include the following:

> persistent failure to initiate or respond in a developmentally appropriate fashion to most social interactions, as manifest by excessively inhibited, hypervigilant, or highly ambivalent and contradictory responses (e.g., the child may respond to caregivers with a mixture of approach, avoidance, and resistance to comforting, or may exhibit frozen watchfulness)."[5]

A similar experiment (though inadvertent) was conducted on the so-called Romanian orphans who emerged profoundly disturbed from behind the Iron Curtain in the early 1990s. These children had also been raised in institutional settings without loving caregivers.[6]

The subjects described in the other quotes are convicts or hostages held in solitary confinement. As physician and writer Atul Gawande shows, in all these cases—monkeys, orphans, prisoners—the psychological effects are similar and suggest manifestations of the same underlying problem. Psychologists and specialists in penology offer a precise and, in fact, obvious explanation for this

---

5 "Diagnostic Criteria for 313.89 Reactive Attachment Disorder of Infancy or Early Childhood," *BehaveNet*, accessed February 22, 2016, http://behavenet.com/node/21499.

6 For one overview, see Felicia Iftene and Nasreen Roberts, "Romanian Adolescents: Literature Review and Psychiatric Presentation of Romanian Adolescents Adopted in Romania and in Canada," *Journal of the Canadian Academy of Child and Adolescent Psychiatry* 13, no. 4 (2004): 110–13, accessed February 22, 2016, http://www.ncbi.nlm.nih.gov/pmc/articles/PMC2538707/.

cluster of behavior patterns: an absence of loving contact with members of their own species. In the case of the monkeys, the results were so egregious that they led to a new ethical code, forbidding researchers to treat lab animals this way. When human beings (children, prisoners) are subjected to similar conditions, the issue gets very complicated. In the present day, social workers are overwhelmed as they try to care for unloved children, and tens of thousands of convicts are held in isolation units.[7]

There is a great gulf in time and space between these subjects and Dostoevsky's disturbed hero, not to mention the ontological differences: they are "real," nonfictional creatures subjected to analysis via "-ologies"—psychology, sociology, criminology, penology, statistics. He, or "it," is a purely fictional creation and as such requires specialized analytical approaches that move beyond those of the social sciences. The Underground Man clearly manifests symptoms of reactive attachment disorder, but the real question is, in the words of Oblomov, "Why am I the way I am?"[8] Exploring this question will lead into the hero's back story, into the historical context within which he was created, and into a deeper question about the human condition: *Why is the I the way it is?* Our exploration leads to the paradox of what any of this has to do with prison and with solitary confinement, in particular. Even the most casual reader will note that the Underground Man is not in prison. And there are lots of people around, so he's not solitary either. To get to the bottom of this we need to read the book as literature, subjecting these obvious facts to a metaphorical reading in which Dostoevsky presents an abstract problem (that of the ego and the nature of its freedom) using tropes of spatial confinement. We will start with some easy truths. I offer three sequential lines of analysis, on an increasing scale of complexity:

1. Debates on punishment and solitary confinement in Dostoevsky's time
2. Dostoevsky's experience of imprisonment
3. Intertextual paradox of setting: *Notes from the House of the Dead* and *Notes from Underground*

---

7 Gawande, "Hellhole," 42.

8 "Отчего же это я такой?—почти со слезами спросил себя Обломов и спрятал опять голову под одеяло,—право?" Ivan Goncharov, *Oblomov*, accessed February 22, 2016, http://www.klassika.ru/read.html?proza/goncharov/oblomov.txt&page=18.

Debates on Punishment in the Mid-Nineteenth Century

As Anna Schur shows in her excellent 2012 book on the subject, in the middle of the nineteenth century, Russian thinkers and government administrators were paying close attention to emerging Western theories and practices of punishment. These developments are highly relevant to a reading of Dostoevsky's works relating to problems of justice, crime, and punishment, not to mention his own experience of prison and exile. By deemphasizing corporal punishment in favor of incarceration regimes, the Russian Criminal Code of 1845 aimed to reduce arbitrariness in punishment.[9] Here lies what will be one important theme for Dostoevsky: the contrast between direct human physical contact (whether violent or tender), on the one hand, and abstract social systems, on the other. In *Notes from the House of the Dead*, Dostoevsky offers literal depictions of both corporal punishment and the physical structures of incarceration. In *Notes from Underground*, I will argue, he addresses the issues of punishment in enigmatic, figurative ways that relate to the work's central problem of solipsism, using the master spatial metaphor of solitary confinement.

As Schur shows, correctional impulses were at work in the establishment of punitive solitary confinement by Western reformers, reflecting the influence of the evangelical tradition. According to the strict isolation of the "separate" or "silent" regime, prisoners were locked in a solitary cell with a Bible and other edifying texts. The point was to nurture reflection on their misdeeds, to spark moral reform from within and bring about, in the words of David Copperfield in 1850, "the reduction of prisoners to a wholesome state of mind, leading to sincere contrition and repentance."[10] Schur notes that Dostoevsky would undoubtedly have been aware of a detailed article on the subject of Western penal practices by N. G. Frolov, published in *Sovremennik* in 1847.[11] As can be the case, optimistic and ambitious social reform led to unexpected consequences. Dickens directs his satire at the system's ineffectualness—prisoners are not reformed. The model prisoner Uriah Heep, ensconced in his comfortable solitary cell, learns only a new vocabulary of piety to mask his unchanging

---

9   Anna Schur, *Wages of Evil: Dostoevsky and Punishment* (Evanston, IL: Northwestern University Press, 2012), 83.

10 Charles Dickens, *David Copperfield* (London: Bradbury & Evans, 1850), ch. 61, accessed February 22, 2016, http://etc.usf.edu/lit2go/166/david-copperfield/3188/chapter-61-i-am-shown-two-interesting-penitents/.

11 Schur, *Wages of Evil*, 85.

hypocritical and villainous character. Responding to a visitor's question as to whether he was comfortable in his cell: "Yes, I thank you, sir!" said Uriah Heep, "I see my follies, now, sir. That's what makes me comfortable."[12] But the system was not merely ineffectual as a means of rehabilitation. It in fact proved disastrous for inmates' physical and mental heath. Among the most frequently discussed evils of strict isolation, Schur reports, were "physical deterioration, psychological disorders, and mental disturbances"; prisoners experienced "loss of hearing, weakening of the limbs, severe depression, delusions, madness, and suicidal behavior."[13] They were affected similarly regardless of their nationality, but, as Schur points out, the practice of solitary incarceration met with opposition in Russia; its reliance on the individual's moral responsibility clashed with what were assumed to be distinctly Russian values of community.[14] These issues, of course, will be central to Dostoevsky's mature works, not limited to those directly addressing problems of crime and punishment.

Dostoevsky's Experience of Solitary and Communal Punishment

After his arrest in 1849 in connection with the Petrashevsky affair, Dostoevsky and the other prisoners were held in what (to any reader of Gulag memoirs, at least) seem to have been relatively benign conditions of solitary confinement in the Peter and Paul Fortress. The prisoners were visited five times a day; even General Nabokov, who headed the Commission of Inquiry, stopped by.[15] Nabokov personally showed concern for the prisoners' welfare and requested that they be provided with fresh clothing and linens.[16] In the summer of 1849, M. V. Petrashevsky wrote to the Commission, asking permission for his comrades to read books and walk in the garden, "for prolonged solitary confinement … in people with a strongly developed imagination and nervous system

---

12 Dickens, David Copperfield, chap. 61.

13 Schur, *Wages of Evil*, 86.

14 Ibid., 88.

15 Andrei M. Dostoevskii, *Vospominaniia*, "Kvartira piataia" (Leningrad: Izdatel'stvo pisatelei, 1930), accessed February 22, 2016, http://az.lib.ru/d/dostoewskij_a_m/text_1896_vospominania.shtml.

16 Liudmila Saraskina, *Dostoevskii: Zhizn' zamechatel'nykh liudei* (Moscow: Molodaia Gvardiia, 2011), 222.

may bring about mental collapse."[17] Petrashevsky names Dostoevsky among those prisoners who could suffer deleterious effects, noting that he was on the point of hallucinating.[18] Whether for this reason or some other, after two months in prison Dostoevsky was provided with books to read and given permission to take walks in the garden and, most importantly, to write.[19]

The effects of imprisonment on Dostoevsky and on his writing have been hotly debated. The same facts from the Peter and Paul Fortress experience are interpreted differently depending on the critic's point of view. So Schur focuses attention on a "marked decline of physical and mental health" that she finds in the letters Dostoevsky wrote from the fortress. His symptoms—"nightmares, heightened impressionability, and nervous deterioration"[20]—accord with those documented among prisoners in solitary confinement. For her part, Liudmila Saraskina writes,

> Unexpectedly for himself, Dostoevsky did not lose his mind or suffer spiritu-
> ally. ... Eight months of incarceration, during which he had to draw
> exclusively on his own means, that is, on his own head ... did not come
> easily. ... But it turned out that during the most arduous minutes of life, he,
> an inveterate hypochondriac with shattered nerves and a ruined digestive
> system, with an eternally sore throat, was able to manifest a psychological
> calm and a rare spiritual fortitude. ... He no longer suffered his fear of
> "lethargic sleep" ..., and ceased discovering in himself countless illnesses. ...
> He dreamed "quiet, good, pleasant dreams."[21]

To some extent, then, it has been argued that the conditions of Dostoevsky's solitary imprisonment in the Peter and Paul Fortress served to nurture the writer's strength of character and resilience, not to mention his resources as a writer— over and beyond the actual literary production of the story "A Little Hero," which he wrote in the fortress. I note again that according to the original Western model for strict correctional solitary confinement, prisoners were

---

17 Ibid., 229.

18 Ibid., citing *Delo Petrashevtsev*, ed. V. R. Leikina, E. A. Korolchuk, and V. A. Desnitskii (Moscow-Leningrad, 1937–51), 1:148–49.

19 Dostoevsky's future adversary Nikolai Chernyshevsky similarly used his time in the fortress to powerful literary effect; it was there that he wrote *What Is to Be Done?*, the book that Dostoevsky's narrator was to attack so pointedly in *Notes from Underground*.

20 Schur, *Wages of Evil*, 93.

21 Saraskina, *Dostoevskii*, 228–29.

given paper and pen with which they were expected to record their thoughts and presumably document the salutary effects of this compulsory introspection. To readers in search of irony, therefore, Dostoevsky's experience in solitary confinement could serve as a validation of the "silent system" advocated by Western evangelical reformers. Reading, reflection, and isolation from dangerous comrades brought about positive moral effects, which were documented, to say the least, in writing.

The torments of the Siberian prison for Dostoevsky were precisely the opposite. Both in *Notes from the House of the Dead* and in letters he wrote upon his release, Dostoevsky repeatedly claims that his greatest suffering came from having to live constantly in a crowd of people, what his *House of the Dead* narrator Goryanchikov calls "compulsory communal cohabitation." (*vynuzhdennoe obshchee sozhitel'stvo*).[22] Dostoevsky craved silence and solitude, complaining of

> constant hostility and brawls on all sides . . . always under guard, never alone, and this for four years without change. (To his brother Mikhail, January 30–February 22, 1854)[23]

> For almost five years now I have been under guard or in a crowd of people, never alone for a single hour. To be alone is a normal need, like drinking and eating; otherwise in this forced communism you become a misanthrope. The company of human beings becomes a poison and a plague, and it was this unendurable torment that caused me the most suffering for these four years. There were moments when I detested everyone who crossed my path, whether they deserved it or not, and I regarded them as thieves who had stolen my life with impunity. (To Fonvizina, February 20, 1854, from Omsk)[24]

The language, as so often with Dostoevsky, conveys "proof by opposite example" that conditions of solitude are salutary for an individual's spiritual and moral development. This point is not unique to the originators of the solitary incarceration regime, or to Dostoevsky. Chronicling her experience both in horrendous conditions of solitary confinement and in group incarceration, Eugenia Ginzburg writes, "Prison, and especially solitary confinement, ennobled and purified

---

22   F. M. Dostoevskii, *Polnoe sobranie sochinenii v tridtsati tomakh*, ed. V. G. Bazanov et al. (Leningrad: Nauka, 1972–90), 4:22; hereafter cited as *PSS* by volume and page.
23   *PSS*, 28:171.
24   *PSS*, 28:177.

human beings, bringing to the surface their finest qualities, however deeply hidden."[25] And as recently as 2012, Pussy Riot prisoner Ekaterina Samutsevich sought solitary confinement as an escape from the boring, dreary conditions of a group cell: "She had heard that if you went on hunger strike, you were trans-ferred to solitary. She would like that."[26]

Dostoevsky wrote in letters immediately upon his release from prison in 1854,

> I regard those four years as a time in which I was buried alive and enclosed in a coffin. I do not have the power to tell you, my friend, how horrible that time was. It was inexpressible, endless suffering, because every hour, every minute weighed upon my soul like a stone. There was never a moment during the entire 4 years when I was not aware that I was in hard labor prison. (To his brother Andrei, November 6, 1854)[27]

As in his thinly fictionalized memoir about the Siberian prison experience, Dostoevsky here offers the metaphor of death for communal incarceration. The external picture matches the inner one: memoirists from his prison years observe that Dostoevsky kept to himself, appeared constantly gloomy, silent, and depressed, and sought solitude.[28] Interestingly, to judge by all accounts, it was precisely the conditions of solitary confinement that Dostoevsky craved while in Siberian prison—his behavior and demeanor can be interpreted as an attempt to create these conditions on a psychological level.

Any discussion of Dostoevsky's mature writing and worldview must grapple with his experience of prison and exile. The writer later claimed that living among the convict prisoners enabled him to bridge the gap between himself and the common people, contributed to the development of his philosophy of "return to the soil" (*pochvennichestvo*), and supported his spiritual growth. Though still dominant, this judgment has endured many challenges and refinements. Naturally, critics have focused on *Notes from the House of the Dead*, offering a range of interpretations, which differ primarily in the amount of weight they give to the work's fictional or nonfictional elements and the different layers in

25 Eugenia Semyonovna Ginzburg, *Journey into the Whirlwind*, trans. Paul Stevenson and Max Hayward (New York: Harcourt, 1995), 341.

26 Masha Gessen, *Words Will Break Cement: The Passion of Pussy Riot* (New York: Riverhead, 2014), 150.

27 *PSS*, 28:181.

28 For an excellent sampling in English, see *The Dostoevsky Archive*, ed. Peter Sekirin (Jefferson, NC: McFarland, 1997), 107–41.

its narrative frame. Robert Louis Jackson offers a symbolic interpretation of the book as a narrative of resurrection; Robin Feuer Miller argues that Dostoevsky's conversion actually came before his journey to Siberia;[29] Linda Ivanits focuses attention on the workings of the Christian religious imagery in the text, suggesting that Dostoevsky imbues it with ambiguities that would persist through the major writings to follow;[30] Nancy Ruttenburg argues grimly that *Notes from the House of the Dead*, far from offering a story of redemption and reconciliation, reinforces existing class differences;[31] Schur argues that the key experience for the book's narrator was his separation from the other prisoners, rather than any communion with them.[32]

Certainly, Goryanchikov's isolation, misanthropy, and, in fact, his death upon his release from prison seem to support this latter view. Whatever the perspective, it seems justified to note that Dostoevsky's self-segregation from the other prisoners contributed to his growth as a writer—this despite the fact that, at least officially, he was not permitted to write. He was carrying on the writer's internal work of observing the world around him and pondering the significance of what he saw: "I cannot express to you how much I suffered from not being able to write in prison. Though it is true that internally I was working intensely. Something good came of it; I could sense that" (to Maikov, January 18, 1856).[33]

Of course, during the prison years, Dostoevsky did have access to reading material beyond the famous Bible given to him by the Decembrists' wives; during his stays in the prison hospital, a local priest brought him issues of religious journals, prison guards provided him with Dickens, and he had occasional access to newspapers. The prison doctor not only allowed Dostoevsky to write observations in what is now called his "Siberian Notebook" but also kept it safe for him when he returned to the prison barracks.[34]

---

29 Robin Feuer Miller, *Dostoevsky's Unfinished Journey* (New Haven, CT: Yale University Press, 2007), 28.

30 Linda Ivanits, *Dostoevsky and the Russian People* (Cambridge: Cambridge University Press, 2008), 31.

31 Nancy Ruttenburg, *Dostoevsky's Democracy* (Princeton, NJ: Princeton University Press, 2008), 89–90.

32 Schur, *Wages of Evil*, 13.

33 *PSS*, 28:209.

34 Saraskina, *Dostoevskii*, 261.

Judging from all the evidence, in response to the oppressive communal conditions of his imprisonment, the writer drew on his inner resources to develop a psychological and emotional strategy of self-discipline that contributed to his development as a writer. Indeed, this condition of internal exile—let's call it solitary confinement within a crowd—was to bring extraordinary literary results. Upon his release, Dostoevsky set pen to paper and created one of the world's greatest body of works. A long period of silence sparks the urge to communicate. Here, too, the trope holds: hostages released from solitary confinement "initially … [experience] the pure elation of being able to see and talk to people again. They can't get enough of other people, and talk almost nonstop for hours."[35] Ginzburg chronicles a similar, cathartic experience upon her release into communal incarceration after two years in solitary: "At present, purified by our sufferings and full of the joy of meeting other human beings after two years of solitude, we felt like sisters in the highest sense of the word. … We chattered about everything that had happened to us."[36]

The literary works that emerge reflect this craving to communicate, in addition to serving as a writer's testimony to the truths observed and experienced in prison. This close relationship between imprisonment and first verbal, then literary eloquence has been particularly powerful in the Russian and Soviet context, where it has produced a major literary tradition, beginning with *Notes from the House of the Dead*, continuing with the works of such authors as Ginzburg, Alexander Solzhenitsyn, and Varlam Shalamov, and leading to who knows what future writing.

The Underground Man transforms this truth into fictional form, imparting to it the added force of enigma, paradox, and metaphor. A literary creature trapped in the solitary underground dreams of this moment of release: "Although we're capable of sitting silently in the underground for forty years, once we come out into the light of day and let loose, we talk and talk and talk."[37] As with his experience of solitary confinement, we note in passing the parallel irony that, in the case of Dostoevsky, the Siberian prison system seems to have

---

35   Gawande, "Hellhole," 39.
36   Ginzburg, *Journey into the Whirlwind*, 264–65.
37   Fyodor Dostoevsky, *Notes from Underground*, trans. Boris Jakim (Grand Rapids, MI: Eerdmans, 2009), 34; *PSS*, 5:121.

brought about its desired effects: the reform of a political revolutionary into a productive citizen.

Paradox of Setting: *Notes from the House of the Dead* and *Notes from Underground*

Clearly, I have been developing a paradox: a person can live in solitary confinement, even when surrounded by people. Paradox is a dominant principle in Dostoevsky's works. The most obvious example of this in *Notes from Underground* is its narrator's constant self-contradiction—he says one thing, and then says the opposite. But the paradoxes extend to other layers of the text, most particularly here: setting. Sometime the obvious facts—the man lives in a densely populated area (a prison, a city)—can get in the way of a truth: he is alone. Extending the sphere of study beyond a single written work can illuminate the underlying principles of how this works. Let's call it, say, a poetics of *intertextual paradox.*

Notes from the House of the Dead and *Notes from Underground* can be regarded as two integral parts of one writerly project. Introducing Alexander Petrovich Goryanchikov's manuscript, the frame editor of *Notes from the House of the Dead* notes that the ex-con's description of the prison was occasionally interrupted by "some other narrative, … some strange, horrible recollections written down in uneven, convulsive handwriting, as if under some sort of compulsion."[38] The identity of this set of writings has been the object of speculation among readers; might it be Goryanchikov's own confessional tale—something paralleling Shishkov's story of his murder of Akulka? Jackson, for example, parenthetically suggests that this may be "an account of his domestic tragedy."[39] Gorianchikov's entire prison memoir, in that case, would represent an elaborate evasion of the most important moral point: the narrator's guilt for murdering his wife. But while keeping that possibility in mind, I will follow Jackson's other speculation that the text could be the soon-to-be-written *Notes from Underground.*[40] Reading this way allows us to

---

38   Fyodor Dostoevsky, *Notes from the House of the Dead,* trans. Boris Jakim (Grand Rapids, MI: William B. Eerdmans, 2013), 7; *PSS,* 5:8.

39   Robert Louis Jackson, *The Art of Dostoevsky: Deliriums and Nocturnes* (Princeton, NJ: Princeton University Press, 1981), 34.

40   Ibid., 170.

see *Notes from Underground* as a paired work offering the narrator's internal perspective—his introspection and focus on his own guilt and responsibility, which is lacking in *Notes from the House of the Dead*. Its working title—"Confession"—reinforces this point; the purpose of the underground narrator's monologue is in fact to tell the tale of his own misdeeds. Given this focus on language's ethical function, *what* the teller is guilty of is less important than *the fact* of his guilt and his need to confess it. This helps universalize the work's message, rather than deflecting it onto a safer, more tightly delineated set of concerns, such as tropes of Romantic literature, Russian debates of the 1860s, the influence of Rousseau, and so on. The narrator, named "Я," is not somebody else; rather it is "I"—me or, better, my ego alone. The prison is metaphorical—it is our human world, with our inborn guilt at its heart. To become free we must "tell our guilt." The underground is a state of self-punitive, metaphorical solitary confinement that internalizes the physical space of the prison. I am there too.

In *Notes from the House of the Dead*, the prison is a set of realistically described physical structures situated in a mythological landscape. The external frame narrator presents Siberia (not without irony) as a promised land, a bounteous paradise:

> ... one can lead a blissful existence in Siberia not only from the point of view of government service but from many other points of view as well. The climate is superb; there are many remarkably rich and hospitable merchants; there are many extremely prosperous non-indigenous inhabitants. The young ladies blossom like roses, and they're moral to the highest degree. Wild game flies about the streets and practically bumps into the hunter. Champagne is drunk in unnatural quantities. The caviar is amazing. In some places the harvest yields fifteen-fold. ... In general, it's a blessed land.[41]

This is a legendary, imaginary land, a paradise only visible between the palings of the prison wall and identified by Goryanchikov at the beginning of his narration as "God's world": "Sometimes you'd look through the chink in the fence at God's world: surely there must be something to see?—but the only thing you'd see would be a little corner of the sky and the high earthen ramparts, overgrown with coarse weeds, and on the ramparts the sentries would walk back and forth, day and night."[42]

---

41 Dostoevsky, *Notes from the House of the Dead*, 3–4; *PSS*, 4:5–6.
42 Ibid., 8; *PSS*, 4:8.

This doubled image of the world outside prison as a paradise prompts us to view the prison metaphorically as the whole material, empirical, tangible world. From that perspective, its inhabitants are not just convicts serving time for specific crimes under the tsarist regime but, rather, humanity generally, living as we do in our self-made structures of habitat and confinement. The setting, then, offers a paradox: the "house of the dead" is actually a world teeming with life. In this metaphorical vision, the common factor shared by both worlds is the guilt of its inhabitants. From our world no one escapes alive; Goryanchikov's death, once he leaves the prison walls, is inevitable. (By the way, that famous eagle, the novel's central image of freedom, will also die; he is unable to fly.) This does not by any means disable the message of resurrection that Jackson finds in the text; it just reminds us that the message must be discovered through metaphorical readings.[43]

The paradox of setting challenges readers to seek freedom from our universal imprisonment. We must look within. Tolstoy's Pierre Bezukhov discovers this truth when he sits by the road and realizes that the French have no control over his immortal soul:

> "Ha, ha, ha!" laughed Pierre. ... "They caught me, locked me up. They're holding me prisoner. Me who? Me? Me?—my immortal soul! Ha, ha, ha! ... Ha, ha, ha!"[44]

True freedom is presented here as a challenge to all humanity. This does not mean that Dostoevsky (and Tolstoy) believe that political structures of oppression, including prisons, are meaningless; both of them hold passionate views on the subject. But in their great novels they tell a poetic truth, offering visions of freedom that concern all human beings, regardless of the specifics of our habitats and enclosures.

Paired with *Notes from the House of the Dead*, *Notes from Underground* offers numerous metaphorical structures with ambiguous function—shelter or imprisonment: wall, chicken coop, squalid apartment, billiards hall, brothel, Crystal Palace—all of which, not coincidentally, are man-made. The underground itself

---

43 I offer an expanded reading of the metaphorical setting of *Notes from the House of the Dead* in Carol Apollonio, "*Notes from the House of the Dead*: An Exercise in Spatial Reading, or Three Crowd Scenes," *Rossiiskii gumanitarnyi zhurnal* 3, no. 5 (2015): 354–67.

44 L. N. Tolstoi, *Voina i mir, Polnoe sobranie sochinenii*, 90 vols., ed. V. G. Chertkov et al. (Moscow-Leningrad: Gosudarstvennoe izdatel'stvo khudozhestvennoi literatury, 1928–58); series 1, *Proizvedeniia* 12 (1933): 105–6.

is not described as a specific physical space, rather, it serves to convey the meta-phor in its broader sense. Here I take advantage of an ambitious statement that Jackson makes in his introduction to *The Art of Dostoevsky*: "It would appear that [Dostoevsky] insists that *man is his own environment*" (my emphasis).[45] Indeed the reading I am offering for *Notes from Underground* recognizes that the bound-aries between character and setting are smudged in a way that, though mind-bending, can help clarify this problem of freedom and isolation.

Why is the Underground Man the way he is? Our first answer is psycholog-ical and primitive: he was an unloved orphan, a product of the broader family breakdown in mid-century Russian society—hence the attachment disorder. His attachment disorder renders him unable to engage in healthy, loving rela-tionships. His need to avoid human interactions predisposes him to make unhealthy choices: for example, he turns down a lucrative career offer upon graduation from high school in order to escape intimacy (specifically, the company of his schoolfellows). Similarly, he has chosen to live in a separate apartment: "I couldn't live in *chambres garnies*: my apartment was my solitary refuge, my shell, my lair, in which I concealed myself from all humankind."[46] The Underground Man's apartment is in fact the material product of his choice to live alone; Dostoevsky's use of an organic metaphor ("my shell") reinforces the point. He has created his own environment, it is part of him. It is his "dead house," out of which he seeks freedom in "real, living life."[47]

At this point it is easy to treat the Underground Man as an individual case, a troubled individual with a unique past. Such a reading lets readers off the hook too easily. Dostoevsky's character is not an individual but a representation of the ego separated from community, not due to some personal idiosyncrasy, but as the result of factors and forces that concern all humanity. In this sense he reflects his own time (1860s Russia under the reforms) and ours. These factors—social, historical, philosophical, psychological, religious, literary—have been the focus of an extraordinary body of criticism, with *Notes from Underground* at its center. The point of my metaphorical reading has been to show that the work's hero is not a dead, psychopathic Russian from a distant time and place, but that he is I, myself, facing problems of freedom and solipsism that are integral to the

---

45 Jackson, *Art of Dostoevsky*, 9.
46 Dostoevsky, *Notes from Underground*, 103; *PSS*, 5:168.
47 Ibid., 114; *PSS*, 5:176.

human condition. Reading the work jointly with its companion, *Notes from the House of the Dead*, brings these problems into high relief.

Notes from the House of the Dead and *Notes from Underground* represent different ways of conceptualizing the problem of freedom. The former offers the external, material, literal image of the prison; the latter probes within the individual's psyche. Both convey their message through paradox: freedom and life can be found in the "house of the dead"; a free individual can be imprisoned in himself. Dostoevsky's use of "the language of freedom" is crucial; what is "will" in *Notes from Underground* is actually a spatialized image of "freedom" in the previous work. The word is *volia*. From the perspective of the House of the Dead, freedom is outside its walls, where people live "*na vole*":

> There were men who had been totally reckless and overstepped all bounds when they were *free* ... [*na vole*] "We're lost men," they'd say. "We weren't able to live *in freedom* [*na vole*], so now we have to walk the green street."[48] (my emphasis)

It is no coincidence that the Underground Man seeks freedom using the same word, *volia*, but it emerges into English not as "freedom," but as "will," or "free will." On the level of word choice, as with setting, the idea of freedom has moved from its spatially situated context in (outside of) the House of the Dead, inward. Often what we see in an English translation as "*free* will" is, in the original, "*one's own* will" (*svoia volia*) (my emphasis). For example, at the end of part 1, chapter 8:

> You'll scream at me ... that no one's infringing on my *free will*; that they're merely busy arranging things in such a way that my *will* [*volia*] should, of *its* own free *will* [*svoei sobstvennoi volei*], coincide with my normal interests ... Good God, gentlemen, what sort of *free will* [*svoia volia*] can there be when it all comes down to tables and arithmetic ... ? As if that's what *free will* [*svoia volia*] is![49] (my emphasis)

Conclusion

In part 1 of *Notes from Underground*, the Underground Man diagnoses himself as a creature of acute self-consciousness, and a product of modern secular science. Dostoevsky makes him an orphan. When the Underground Man

---

48 Dostoevsky, *Notes from the House of the Dead*, 13; PSS, 4:13.
49 Dostoevsky, *Notes from Underground*, 30; PSS, 5:117.

suggests that he emerged "not out of the womb of nature but out of a test tube,"[50] from here it is not even a leap, but just a little sidle over into Harlow's monkey cage, not to mention the Romanian orphans. The Underground Man is basically a lab mouse: "This test-tube man … , genuinely regards himself not as a man but as a mouse."[51] Switch the mouse for a monkey and you have a textbook specimen, the sufferer of attachment disorder, torn from his mother, and brought up by cold, hard science.

At the end of part 2, Dostoevsky's underground hero writes, "I've been feeling ashamed all the time I've been writing this story: it's not so much literature as corrective punishment."[52] Dostoevsky's works chronicle the miseries caused by the individual's separation from community. This individual, I, is both the victim and the villain in *Notes from Underground*—its suffering, brooding, depressed, neurotic, vengeful antihero. It suffers because it is alone, and because it is not free. This solitude, ironically, is a condition it shares with all modern humanity. By confessing his guilt in an act of writing, the individual atones for it, endures his earned punishment, and offers his text to readers as a way to overcome our shared isolation.

50 Dostoevsky, *Notes from Underground*, 10; *PSS*, 5:104.
51 Ibid.
52 Ibid., 117; *PSS*, 5:178.

XVII

Moral Emotions in Dostoevsky's "The Dream of a Ridiculous Man"

Deborah A. Martinsen

Dostoevsky's "The Dream of a Ridiculous Man" is a philosophical tale that explores the emotional dynamics of its eponymous first-person narrator. "Dream" recounts the story of a "vile Petersburgian" infected by Western Enlightenment thinking who sees a little star in the dark sky, decides to commit suicide, encounters a little girl who begs him for help, feels pity then anger, drives her away, returns home, speculates about his emotions, has a dream vision of an Edenic paradise that floods him with love, and awakens with a thirst for life.[1] His story recounts the conversion of a fallen man whose journey of self-knowledge gives him a life-saving dream vision that includes a version of the Christian myth of paradise, fall, and redemption. His story reflects Dostoevsky's message that beauty can save us: the Ridiculous Man starts with

---

1 Noteworthy studies of "Dream" include Joseph Frank, *Dostoevsky: The Mantle of the Prophet, 1871–1881* (Princeton, NJ: Princeton University Press, 2003), 351–58; Robert Louis Jackson, *The Art of Dostoevsky: Deliriums and Nocturnes* (Princeton, NJ: Princeton University Press, 1981), 272–303; Robin Feuer Miller, *Dostoevsky's Unfinished Journey* (New Haven, CT: Yale University Press, 2007): 105–27, 148–61; Gary Saul Morson, *The Boundaries of Genre: Dostoevsky's "Diary of a Writer" and the Traditions of Literary Utopia* (Austin: University of Texas Press, 1981): 177–82; and V. Tunimanov, "Satira i utopiya ('Bobok,' 'Son smesh-nogo cheloveka' F.M. Dostoevskogo)," *Russkaia literatura* 9, no. 4 (1966): 70–87.

a narrow view of the world, has a dream that expands his vision, and awakens with a living image of truth, beauty, and unity in his heart. The story's emotional dialectic mirrors its mythic vision: the Ridiculous Man starts from a position of flat affect (his chronic shame has given rise to negative emotions and defenses that inure him to the greater emotional pain of feeling unlovable), his encounter with the little girl and his dream vision flood him with positive emotions that break down his emotional defenses, and his love for others persists after he awakens. I will examine the Ridiculous Man's spiritual awakening by focusing on two images—the little star in the sky and the little girl on the earth—and four of the story's salient moral emotions—pity, shame, pride, and *toska*, a particularly Russian anguish that signals metaphysical longing in Dostoevsky's work.

Following the philosophers Gabriele Taylor and Jesse Prinz, I hold that moral emotions are characterized by their evaluative and moral dimensions, that is, they help us recognize whether an action is bad, and they motivate us to be good.[2] On these terms, not all emotions are moral: fear for one's life is not, whereas fear for one's soul is. Since moral emotions entail judgment, they awaken both our cognitive and affective capacities—a dual action Dostoevsky deploys to involve us in the action and affect of his writing. In exploring the moral function of *toska*, I am extending the work of Arpad Kovacs, who shows that *toska* has ontological, aesthetic, and poetic functions in Dostoevsky's work.[3] I will also show that *toska*, like shame, works by paradox: in both emotions, the underlying sense of alienation heightens the sense of lost or desired connection.[4]

In "Dream," Dostoevsky lays bare the dismantling of emotional defenses that the philosopher David Velleman argues is essential to the opening of our hearts.[5] Whereas the story's first-person narrator protects himself from the

---

2 Gabriele Taylor, *Deadly Vices* (Oxford: Clarendon, 2006), 55; Jesse Prinz, "The Moral Emotions," *The Oxford Handbook of Philosophy of Emotion*, ed. Peter Goldie (Oxford University Press, 2010), 520.

3 Arpad Kovacs, "Angustia: *Toska u Dostoevskogo*," in *Russica Hungarica: Issledovaniya po russkoi literature i kul'ture, Rusistika v Budapeshtskom Universitete imeni Etvesha Loranda* (Budapest-Moscow, 2005), 100–25. I cite a manuscript copy whose pages do not correlate to the volume's pages.

4 Unlike shame, *toska* does not primarily stem from feelings of personal inadequacy, although it can express similar feelings of social and metaphysical loss. Moreover, unlike shame, which often paralyzes a person emotionally, *toska* often impels a person not only to express that sense of longing, as Kovacs demonstrates, but also to seek something outside the self.

5 J. David Velleman, "Love as a Moral Emotion," *Ethics* 109, no. 2 (1999): 338–74.

shame and pain of being considered ridiculous with walls of pride, ratiocination, and indifference, his unexpected pity for the little girl exposes the falsity of his self-protective self-image and breaks down those defenses. His pity arouses his anger, his philosophical speculation distances him from unsettling emotions, and his dream reconciles mind and heart. Dostoevsky thus engages the Romantic debate with Enlightenment thinking[6] and devises a synthesis that heals his Ridiculous Man's divided self. Dostoevsky's solution also resembles his doctrine of *pochvennichestvo*—a union of native Russian moral intuition and imported European education that can heal the rift between Russia's noneducated and educated populations.

While the story has many generic sources, I will show how Dostoevsky turns "Dream" as a philosophical tale into a Christmas story.[7] Dostoevsky signals his engagement with Enlightenment thinking by explicitly referring to Voltaire throughout the story. First, he draws attention to the story's genre as a philosophical tale by having the Ridiculous Man note that he is sitting in a Voltairean armchair, first as he speculates, then as he dreams. Next, by having the Ridiculous Man confess his intention to shoot himself in the head yet dream that he shoots himself in the heart, Dostoevsky underscores the story's mind–heart thematics. Finally, by evoking Voltaire's philosophical tale "Micromegas," whose eponymous space-traveling philosopher hails from Sirius, Dostoevsky highlights his narrator's penchant for rational analysis. By contrast, Dostoevsky's implicit references to Dickens's *A Christmas Carol* signal his intention to combat Enlightenment rationality with Romantic sentiment. Pity for a child in pain will open a heart that has defended itself from the vulnerability of connection.[8]

---

6 Frank, *Mantle of the Prophet*, 357. Frank argues that although Dostoevsky's story has similarities to Cabet's *Voyage to Icaria* and Victor Considerant's *La Destinée sociale*, which reflect his utopian socialist roots and moral sympathies, "Dream" is written "*as an answer* to the rational utopias of the Socialists." He agrees with N. I. Prutskov that Dostoevsky's story is not anti-utopian but anti-Enlightenment: "Its foundation is anti-Enlightenment (the primacy of feelings of the heart and their opposition to truths of the head, the precedence of moral actions prompted by conscience in opposition to those actions motivated by convictions)"; Prutskov, "Utopia ili anti-utopia," in *Dostoevsky i ego vremya* (Leningrad, 1971): 352.

7 Miller, *Dostoevsky's Unfinished Journey*, 105–27.

8 Ibid., 121. Miller continues, "The paradoxical notion of a preacher who knows he has lost the knack for words renders his life, rather than his words about that life, a living symbol of faith as opposed to reason" (ibid.).

The little star and the little girl initially represent the Ridiculous Man's mind–heart conflict. In the biblical Christmas tale, a star in the sky signals hope and inspires three wise men to journey to Bethlehem. In "Dream," the little star extinguishes hope and inspires the Ridiculous Man to kill himself. When the Ridiculous Man sees that same little star again during his dream journey, he mistakes it for Sirius. In evoking Voltaire's tale, which explores how one's sense of self affects one's perspective, Dostoevsky suggests that Enlightenment thought has perverted his narrator's thinking.[9] Read as part of Dostoevsky's 1876–77 *Diary of a Writer*'s polemic on suicide, this story illustrates the limits of the Ridiculous Man's moral imagination: instead of marveling at the vastness of the universe and the fact that he is part of it, the Ridiculous Man feels metaphysically insignificant.[10] As the psychiatrist Richard Rosenthal observes, the Ridiculous Man uses suicide as a defense: "He carries it around in his back pocket, so to speak, as the ultimate escape. When he feels inadequate, rejected, and humiliated, he can always kill himself. This gives him a sense of control."[11] Comforted by the thought that he has determined the moment to kill himself, the Ridiculous Man heads to his fifth-floor room, a location that signals both his poverty and his alienation from the life-giving Russian soil.

The little girl shows that the Ridiculous Man's mental construct is false. She needs him. Anticipating Zosima's doctrine that all are responsible for all, Dostoevsky shows readers that the Ridiculous Man *can* help the little girl. But he doesn't, and the Ridiculous Man cannot kill himself without speculating on why his commitment to non-being does not nullify either his "feeling of pity for the little girl" or "his feeling of shame after the base act committed" (*PSS*, 25:108). These two emotions—pity (*zhalost'*) and shame (*styd*)—dramatize the Ridiculous Man's internal conflict. His pity is a positive, other-directed emotion, and his shame is a negative, self-directed emotion.

---

9   Voltaire's tale "Micromegas" also explores how rational inquiry affects belief.

10 Dostoevsky opens his 1876 *Diary of a Writer* with reflections on suicide, and he contrasts contemporary, unthinking suicides with Goethe's Werther, who bids farewell to the Milky Way, thereby signaling his sense of connection to God's creation (*PSS*, 22:6). I cite F. M. Dostoevsky, *Polnoe sobranie sochinenii v tridtsati tomakh* [*PSS*], ed. V. G. Bazanov et al. (Leningrad: Nauka, 1972–1990), as *PSS* by volume and page. All translations are my own.

11 Richard J. Rosenthal, M.D., email correspondence, January 23, 2014. I am grateful to Richard for sharing his thoughts and insights about the story with me as I wrote this article; they were a tremendous help in formulating my own.

The elided emotion—anger—momentarily protects him from the pain of sympathy. Dostoevsky's readers will recognize this underground dynamic: the positive emotion's heart-flooding affect threatens the individual's sense of self, and he or she responds by withdrawal, aggression against self, or another, or both.

The Ridiculous Man identifies with the little girl's fear: "in her voice resonated that sound, which in very frightened children signifies despair. I know that sound" (*PSS*, 25:106). In short, the little girl instantiates the Ridiculous Man's fear of isolation, exclusion, or abandonment. This identification arouses his pity—a positive emotion that entails the capacity to imagine another's pain. The little girl's words—"Mamochka! Mamochka!" (25:106)—activate the Ridiculous Man's moral imagination. He understands "that her mother is dying somewhere, or something had happened there with them, and she ran out to call someone, to find something to help her mama" (25:106). The little girl's pain and fear breach the Ridiculous Man's hardened emotional defenses and open his eyes. He recognizes how much she loves and depends on her mother and how terrified she is of losing her. His spontaneous pity reveals the Ridiculous Man's innate moral sensitivity, but her vulnerability reminds him of his own. His anger exposes his defenses against the pain of vulnerability and the shame of not living up to his ideals.[12]

The little star and the little girl, signs of head and heart, heavens and earth, alienation and connection, are also linked to the Ridiculous Man's *toska*, his anguished longing for wholeness or belonging. As Nabokov explains, "No single word in English renders all the shades of *toska*. At its deepest and most painful, it is a sensation of great spiritual anguish, often without any specific cause. At less morbid levels it is a dull ache of the soul, a longing with nothing to long for, a sick pining, a vague restlessness, mental throes, yearning."[13] Kovacs shows that in Dostoevsky's early work, *toska* expresses an anguished longing for

---

12 People who pride themselves on their self-sufficiency or moral superiority see positive emotions as a sign of weakness. See Deborah A. Martinsen, "Shame and Punishment," *Dostoevsky Studies* 5 (2001): 51–70.

13 Aleksandr Pushkin, *Eugene Onegin: A Novel in Verse*, trans. with commentary by Vladimir Nabokov (Princeton, NJ: Princeton University Press, 1981), 2:141. This statement is found in Nabokov's commentary to chap. 1, stanza 34, line 8. The quote continues, "In particular cases it may be the desire for somebody or something specific, nostalgia, love-sickness. At the lowest level it grades into ennui, boredom, *skuka*."

an absent or nonexistent object, a desire for it, for beauty, for living life.[14] Kovacs also demonstrates how *toska* simultaneously acts as both the signal and subject of narrativity, the symptom of will and its expression, an anguish for an unattained reality that leads to a need for expression and a search for new words.[15] In "Dream," the Ridiculous Man's *toska* expresses an anguished longing for both human community and metaphysical unity. His *toska* also motivates the Ridiculous Man to articulate his vision.

Dostoevsky first introduces *toska* in the story's second paragraph as the Ridiculous Man confesses that "earlier I felt anguish because I seemed ridiculous" (*PSS*, 25:104). Using the verb form *toskovat'*, he identifies his anguish with a sense of social alienation and painful self-awareness. Like his literary predecessor, the Underground Man, the Ridiculous Man acknowledges his painful self-awareness: he claims that he did not merely seem ridiculous, but actually was. The unnamed emotion here is shame: the Ridiculous Man feels insignificant and unlovable. Shortly thereafter, Dostoevsky explicitly ties his narrator's anguish to his indifference: "Perhaps because a terrible anguish was growing in my soul due to a certain circumstance that was already infinitely beyond me: namely the conviction that had come upon me that in the whole world *nothing matters*" (всё равно; emphasis in original) (25:105). The Ridiculous Man's mind has strangled his heart with a philosophy of indifference that protects him from painful self-consciousness and "terrible anguish." He uses the language of revelation—his conviction arises "suddenly" (вдруг) and he *feels* it with his "whole being" (25:105). In fact, from the moment that the narrator accepts his indifference, he "suddenly stopped feeling angry" (25:105). Behind his narrator's back, Dostoevsky informs us that the Ridiculous Man's philosophy of

---

14   Kovacs, "Angustia," 13. I indicate page numbers from my printout. Kovacs argues that the untranslatable *toska* derives from the concept of *angustia* as used variously in the works of St. Augustine, Martin Luther, Pascal, Kierkegaard, Berdyaev, Heidegger, and Tillich. Kovacs asserts that even though *toska* is not synonymous with German *Angst*, it more closely approaches the German and French sense of existential angst (1). Unlike depression in Dostoevsky's work, which is negatively associated with pointless ideation, fantasy, and images of darkness and shadows, *toska* is positively associated with insightfulness (прозрение), the heart, and images of light (10). It entails a suffering that derives from others' suffering and that concentrates our sympathy for them (11). Finally, *toska* simultaneously and paradoxically signals a constriction of the heart and a longing for something beyond it (15).

15   Ibid., 9–12.

indifference is a perverse emotional defense against awareness.[16] Like the Underground Man, he bumps into people on the street, but unlike the Underground
Man, who hones his painful self-consciousness and spends months preparing
for a sidewalk duel to restore his honor, the Ridiculous Man dulls his.

By linking the Ridiculous Man's "terrible anguish" to something "infinitely
higher," Dostoevsky stresses the metaphysical dimension of his narrator's
alienation. He also supplies a solution: the Ridiculous Man's dream reconnects
him to his positive emotions. Unlike Voltaire's Sirian philosopher Micromegas,
who travels the external universe seeking knowledge about other worlds,
Dostoevsky's Ridiculous Man seeks answers to moral questions by dream
travel: "Dreams, it seems, are impelled not by rationality, but desire, not the
head, but the heart" (*PSS*, 25:108).[17] His dream companion saves him from his
self-enclosed hyperrationality by taking him outside of himself—beyond the
earth, past the stars, to a prelapsarian paradise. The Ridiculous Man's dream
vision turns his thoughts toward the divine: "How could I alone conceive it or
dream it with my heart? Is it possible that my petty heart and capricious,
insignificant mind could be elevated to such a revelation of truth?" (25:115).
The Ridiculous Man's inner journey of self-knowledge thus leads him to a
reality outside and higher than himself.

The Ridiculous Man's higher reality is associated with images of light,
which Kovacs connects to *toska* in Dostoevsky's early work.[18] In part 3 of this
1877 story, the Ridiculous Man feels a terrible anguish while traveling through
space: "I expected something in the terrible anguish tormenting my heart"
(*PSS*, 25:111).[19] Yet no sooner does the Ridiculous Man feel *toska*—not in the
past but in the present—than he sees the sun, which resurrects him: "I suddenly

---

16 Here I am adopting Melvin Lansky's model of defense as "defense against awareness";
    Melvin R. Lansky, "Hidden Shame," *Journal of the American Psychoanalytic Association* 53
    (2005): 870.
17 Moreover, dreams do not follow the rules of logic: the Ridiculous Man knows that he is dead,
    but also that he continues to feel and think. In dream logic, feelings come first.
18 Kovacs, "Angustia," 10.
19 Dostoevsky shows readers his first-person narrator's emotional defenses (*PSS*, 25:110–11):
    the Ridiculous Man anticipates humiliation, exposes his fear of contempt to his traveling
    companion, and then experiences humiliation for revealing his fear (a very underground
    dynamic). Voltaire describes a similar experience, one regarding rational prejudices rather
    than emotional defenses: Micromegas and his companion from Saturn initially dismiss the
    possibility that earth's inhabitants could have intelligence because of their relative minuteness,
    which Micromegas then realizes is an intellectual prejudice with no basis in reality.

saw our sun! ... the native power of light, that same light that gave birth to me, resounded in my heart and resurrected it, and I felt life, my former life, for the first time since my grave" (25:111). The clear Christian imagery of this second revelation undoes the Ridiculous Man's earlier revelation that nothing matters. It also emphasizes the Augustinian connection between self-knowledge and knowledge of the divine—to know oneself is to know God in oneself. In the Ridiculous Man's story, as in Augustine's *Confessions*, confession is both acknowledgment of shortcoming and profession of faith.

In part 4, as the Ridiculous Man notes that his hatred for people on earth always included *toska*, Dostoevsky links *toska* and the moral emotions. The Ridiculous Man can only understand the prelapsarian dream people with his heart. He claims that they elicit a "responding anguish" in "the dreams of his heart" (в снах моего сердце) and "the dreams of his mind" (в мечтах ума моего). As in *Crime and Punishment*, Dostoevsky employs the Russian word *son* to signify unconscious dreams, like Raskolnikov's dream of the mare (*PSS*, 6:46–49), and *mechta* to signify conscious dreams, like killing the pawnbroker (6:275–78). In "Dream," these words signal the split between the Ridiculous Man's compassionate heart and his calculating mind. The Ridiculous Man's moral emotions give rise to philosophical questions: "My hatred for people on our earth always included anguish: why can I not hate them, not loving them, why can I not forgive them, and in my love for them there's anguish: why can I not love them, not hating them?" (25:114). The Ridiculous Man longs for authentic connection, but here Dostoevsky reveals that alienation from his own feelings impedes his narrator's connection to others. The Ridiculous Man cannot fully hate, love, or forgive because he suffers from a persistent shame that prevents him from seeing himself as a worthy self-presenting agent. [20] Rather than attempting to repair the social bond, the Ridiculous Man withdraws.

---

20 Lansky, "Hidden Shame," 886. Lansky observes, "The inability to forgive often hides shame that attends one's complicity in betrayals and rejections." He also observes that shamed persons can act in a way that seems to solve the problem of "the shame of felt powerlessness, helplessness, contempt, and worthlessness" (including the act of withdrawal). Such acts then afford the shamed person "an experience of power (and possibly guilt) that also pushes shame into hiding" (ibid.). The philosopher David Velleman sees shame as anxiety about exclusion from the social realm where individuals act as self-presenting agents; see J. David Velleman, "The Genesis of Shame," *Philosophy and Public Affairs* 30, no. 1 (2001): 27–52.

In his dream and in his confession, however, the Ridiculous Man tries to repair the social bond. He takes responsibility for the fall by claiming that he corrupts the dream people. Yet he seems to corrupt them not by anything he does, but by who he is—a fallen, shame-filled man, whose knowledge of good and evil infects others. The Ridiculous Man's dream thus echoes earlier Dostoevskian works: the Underground Man identifies consciousness as a disease, and Raskolnikov dreams of trichinae that infect individuals with a divisive hyper-rationality. Yet these earlier cerebral protagonists consciously harm others, in part to alleviate the pain of their shame,[21] whereas the Ridiculous Man simply acts as a source of consciousness. Unlike the Underground Man, who refuses to accept his guilt, and unlike Raskolnikov, who confesses but does not repent,[22] the Ridiculous Man accepts both his fallen state and responsibility for others' fall. Like Eve and Adam in the garden of Eden, he first hides his shame and guilt but then confesses—he reaches out and accepts responsibility. Moreover, he believes that he can save those who laugh at him by sharing his shame—the universal, human condition.

The Ridiculous Man's *toska* thus shares the paradox of shame: separation entails union, a sense of longing implies a sense of loss. From story's beginning to end, Dostoevsky's first-person narrator is acutely aware of what he has lost, even if it may be a dream ideal of connection to all living things. And Dostoevsky, behind his narrator's back, associates that sense of loss and longing to the little star in the heavens and the little girl on earth. Initially the little star makes him think—"that little star gave me an idea" (*PSS*, 25:106)—and the little girl makes him feel—"I had felt pity not long ago" (25:107). The Ridiculous Man's awakened conscience moves him to speculate about what it means to be human: "It seemed clear that if I am a person, and still not nothing, and while I have not turned into nothing, then I live, and consequently can suffer, get angry, and feel shame for my actions" (25:107). The suffering, anger, and shame mentioned here reflect the action of the story's opening frame: the Ridiculous Man feels

---

21 Deborah A. Martinsen, "On Shame and Human Bondage," in *Dostoevsky on the Threshold of Other Worlds: Essays in Honour of Malcolm V. Jones*, ed. Sarah Young and Lesley Milne (Ilkeston, Derbyshire: Bramcote, 2006), 157–69; Martinsen, "Shame and Punishment," 51.

22 Richard J. Rosenthal, "Raskolnikov's Transgression and the Confusion between Destructiveness and Creativity," in *Do I Dare Disturb the Universe? A Memorial to Wilfred R. Bion*, ed. James Grotstein (Beverly Hills, CA: Caesura, 1981; London: Karnac Books, Maresfield Library, 1984), 197–235.

pity for the young girl, angrily stomps his foot and yells at her, and then feels shame for his action. Dostoevsky thus demonstrates that the Ridiculous Man's moral emotions drive his actions and reflections.

The Ridiculous Man speaks of moral suffering, but early in the story Dostoevsky links moral and physical pain. The Ridiculous Man claims that he feels both: "You see: although it made no difference to me, I did, for example, feel pain. If someone were to strike me, I would feel pain. Exactly the same in the moral sense: if something very pitiful were to happen, I would feel pity, just as when things still made a difference to me in life" (*PSS*, 25:107). Dostoevsky identifies the Ridiculous Man's pity not only as a form of suffering but also as an emotion he felt before his revelation that nothing mattered. In his dream, the opposite holds. He feels moral, then physical pain: "A profound indignation suddenly burned in my heart, and I suddenly felt a physical pain in it" (25:110). Here Dostoevsky identifies the Ridiculous Man's indignation as a form of moral suffering that awakens his sense of bodily pain, thereby signaling his narrator's return to physical awareness. This reversal, emphasized by the repetition of the Dostoevskian "suddenly," prefigures the Ridiculous Man's final conversion.

Dostoevsky's pre-dream, pre-conversion narrator suffers from acute chronic shame—he sees himself as ridiculous in others' eyes. To protect himself, he owns the label "ridiculous" and guards this defensive knowledge with pride: "I was always so proud, that I would never under any circumstances acknowledge it to anyone" (*PSS*, 25:104). His pride leads to increased self-enclosure, which he equates with survival: "That pride grew in me ... and if it happened that I were to confess before anyone whomsoever that I was ridiculous, then it seems to me that I would on the spot, that very evening, shatter my head with a revolver" (25:104). As this confession reveals, the Ridiculous Man's shame is so acute that it has become a matter of life and death. In order to protect himself from the painful self-consciousness and vulnerability of connection, he withdraws emotionally. The Ridiculous Man thus suffers from what Taylor calls "a shriveled self," a condition accompanied by its own negative feedback loop: in depriving himself of interactions with others, he deprives himself of crucial knowledge about the world and himself.[23]

---

23 Taylor, *Deadly Vices*, 79.

By closing down emotionally, the Ridiculous Man, like the Underground Man before him, loses the opportunity to know himself. Dostoevsky conveys the extent of the Ridiculous Man's narcissistic self-enclosure by having him wonder whether the world and its people are "I myself alone" (*PSS*, 25:108). This speculation reveals the paradox of pride: to desire is to want something one lacks, but the proud desire godlike perfection and self-sufficiency, a desire that leads to spiritual death[24] (like Kirillov in *Demons*). The Ridiculous Man's pride leads to a self-enclosure so complete that he no longer feels a need to be in the world. His pride makes him feel that to have feelings is a weakness (like Raskolnikov in *Crime and Punishment*) and that to show them would betray a vulnerability so painful as to require complete extinction. The Ridiculous Man's moral emotions betray him. He thought that his indifference would protect him from the pain of being human, but his pity for the little girl causes him pain. He suffers morally because he identifies with her, and he experiences shame because he failed to live up to his false ideal of indifference. His moral emotions save him by changing his way of perceiving the world and his place in it.

Although Dostoevsky loads hyperrationality with negative connotations, he values philosophical speculation.[25] Significantly, the Ridiculous Man's dream begins with moral speculation: if he were to commit a shameful act on the moon or Mars, would it matter to him? The Ridiculous Man thus asks himself, Am I a moral being or not? Even before providing the dream as answer, the story affirms that he is: his pity and shame mark the Ridiculous Man as a moral being. His philosophical question takes concrete form in the Ridiculous Man's dream travels, where he explicitly links the little girl to his love for the earth he has quitted. As he shakes with "an uncontrollable, ecstatic love for that former, native earth," which he had abandoned, the Ridiculous Man has a vision: "The image of the poor little girl, whom I had offended, flashed before me" (*PSS*, 25:111). The little girl connects him to life and love.

The Ridiculous Man's dream not only answers his speculation but heals the shamed-based alienation that causes him to drive the little girl away. Her plea for help awakens his moral emotions and thus prepares for the dream journey in which he feels connected to and responsible for others. His dream

---

24 Ibid., 80.
25 Frank, *Mantle of the Prophet*, 357–58. Frank speculates that "Dream" is a first version of a "Russian Candide," an idea Dostoevsky jotted down five months after writing the story.

shows him that a meaningful life requires both emotional and intellectual engagement. It demonstrates that reasoning used as a defense harms, whereas reasoning used as a means of self-knowledge heals. In short, his dream heals the Ridiculous Man's divided self and gives meaning and purpose to his life. When he awakens, he seeks and finds that little girl.

By story's end, Dostoevsky has expanded the little girl's functions by creating a web of associations around her. At story's opening, she is the agent of the Ridiculous Man's change of heart and mind; at story's end, the vehicle for his expiation. Psychologically, she represents the narrator's vulnerable, abandoned self. Thematically, she represents connection to the earth, to the Ridiculous Man's native soil. And ideologically, she represents a pure Russia, uncontaminated by Western thought. In finding her, the Ridiculous Man thus enacts Dostoevsky's dream of *pochvennichestvo*—the union of Western-educated upper classes with the unlettered but Christ-following Russian masses.

By story's end, Dostoevsky has also expanded the little star's functions. Initially the agent of the Ridiculous Man's decision to kill himself, in mid-story the little star becomes the vehicle for his *toska*. Psychologically, the little star shifts association from the Ridiculous Man's choice of death to his love of life. Thematically, the little star mistaken for Sirius represents Enlightenment rationality and alienation from emotions, whereas the little star identified as earth represents Romantic longing and love for the fallen earth and its inhabitants. Once linked to the earth, the little star merges emotionally with the little girl, preparing for its ideological rebranding as Isis-Sirius, Mother Russia, the earth that gives him birth. The philosophical tale yields to the Christmas tale, in which the star leads the wise men to the Mother of God, or *Bogoroditsa*, the off-stage figure in this drama of compassion.[26] It's not surprising that the Ridiculous Man calls the earth star *rodnaya* (from *rod* meaning "family or genus") and claims that it has *rodnaya sila*, or "native power" (*PSS*, 25:111). In the philosophical tale, Sirius is the home of Voltaire's space-traveling Enlightenment philosopher Micromegas, but Sirius is also mythically linked to the Christmas tale as the bright star that leads the magi to Bethlehem and as the star that signals the advent of Isis, the life-giving Egyptian maternal figure associ-

---

26 I am grateful to Richard Rosenthal for pointing out the importance of the off-stage mother (correspondence, February 28, 2014).

ated with myths of death and reincarnation. Behind his narrator's back, Dostoevsky thus shows readers how the heart can change our perceptions: a star that leads to death can signal rebirth. Using the poetics of paradox, Dostoevsky activates our cognitive and affective faculties, challenging us to go beyond either/or thinking.

The dream gives Dostoevsky's narrator a new sense of self: he must preach the truth it has revealed to him. Although he has lost the words, he is sustained by the "living image" of the truth in his heart.[27] He knows that it is an ideal, not realizable on earth. He does not articulate Zosima's doctrine of all responsible for all, but he feels it. He now loves those who ridicule him: he identifies with them because they are like his pre-vision self. Full of pride, they are trapped in themselves and limited in their perceptions. They long for an Edenic unity but cannot find it. They project blame outward, mocking him rather than examining themselves.

As many great scholars have observed, the Ridiculous Man experiences conversion. He starts in a world of *nothing matters* (всё равно), a world where positive moral emotions like love, pity, and *toska* have been repressed by indifference. The little star in the Petersburg sky confirms this mental construct. The little girl on the Petersburg streets refutes it. She insists that things matter, her mother matters, *she* matters. Her plea for help proves that the Ridiculous Man's mental construct is a self-protective lie. His dream reveals the truth contained in the little girl's plea—all are responsible for all. Feelings of pity and love are natural parts of being human.

The Ridiculous Man's drama with little star, little girl, and *toska* has two acts. The first starts on earth and ends in his dream: the Ridiculous Man sees the little star, which can signify either religious hope or Enlightenment death; he chooses death, sees the little girl who restores him to life, and dream-travels past that little star, leaving his Enlightenment thinking behind. The second act starts in his dream and ends on earth: he sees another little star, which is the earth, experiences a rebirth, visits the prelapsarian earth, causes the fall, wakes up,

---

27   Jackson notes the difference between the Ridiculous Man's *pravda* (a "lower earthly truth of the flesh," i.e., that he has corrupted the dream people) and his *istina* ("a higher Truth of beauty and spirit"), which reflects "the paradoxical structure in Dostoevsky's philosophical thought: the notion of two kinds of beauty" (*Art of Dostoevsky*, 290–91). In my reading, the higher truth provides the answer to the Ridiculous Man's existential angst.

finds the little girl, and starts preaching the truth of his vision. In act 1, the Ridic-ulous Man's *toska* is associated with his feelings of shame, alienation, and defensive indifference. In act 2, however, his *toska* expresses the natural condi-tion of fallen humanity, an anguished longing for love and connection with other people and the divine.

In evoking the myth of the fall, Dostoevsky reminds us that the moral emotions of shame and guilt are the price of knowledge. "Dream" demonstrates that knowledge in the Dostoevskian world also comes with *toska*, a longing for lost unity with God and all living things. The story proposes that positive moral emotions represent the bridge back. The Ridiculous Man begins and ends his story by expressing love for those who ridicule him: he loves and identifies with them because they are like his pre-dream self, full of pride and blame, humans in a fallen world who erect defenses to protect themselves from knowledge of their incompleteness and of their responsibility for one another. Their longing for Eden expresses knowledge of lack. To lack is human; to strive is human; to love and be vulnerable is to be fully human, not self-sufficient but part of some-thing higher. "The Dream of a Ridiculous Man" thus shows that the moral emotions, including *toska*, are essential to human community. For Dostoevsky, belief in something greater than self, something that links all living beings, is essential to morality. The Ridiculous Man concludes his story by stating his mission—to turn others around, that is, to convert them, so that they can see the beauty within. To do so, he argues, "the main thing is to love others as oneself"; and "'The consciousness of life is higher than life, knowledge of the laws of happiness is higher than happiness'—that's what needs to be fought!" (*PSS*, 25:119). Dostoevsky's Ridiculous Man thus chooses Christian love over Enlightenment thinking. Romantic sentiment trumps Enlightenment reason. The philosophical tale is converted into a Christmas story.

XVIII

Like a Shepherd to His Flock: The Messianic Pedagogy of Fyodor Dostoevsky—Its Sources and Conceptual Echoes

Inessa Medzhibovskaya

In fond memory of Robin Mookerjee—wordsmith, poet, friend, a remarkable mentor to students and colleagues

> A disciple is not above his teacher, but everyone who is perfectly trained will be like his teacher. ... For a good tree does not bear bad fruit, nor does a bad tree bear good fruit
> —Gospel of Luke 6:40, 43, 44

> Plants are shaped by cultivation, and men by education.
> —Jean-Jacques Rousseau (1762).[1]

> We have realized the necessity of uniting with our native soil, our popular foundations. Our aim is to create a new form for ourselves, our own, native form, derived from our own soil.
> —Dostoevsky (1860)[2]

---

1   Jean-Jacques Rousseau, *Émile, or On Education*, trans. and intro. Allan Bloom (New York: Basic, 1979), 38.

2   "Ob'iavlenie o podpiske na zhurnal Vremia na 1861," in F. M. Dostoevsky, *Polnoe sobranie sochinenii v tridtsati tomakh* [*PSS*], ed. V. G. Bazanov et al. (Leningrad: Nauka, 1972–1990),

Oswald Spengler's *The Decline of the West* (1918) is remembered mainly for its doomsday verdict on Western culture. It is less known, however, for a place reserved in it for Dostoevsky's posthumous leadership in the new millennial Reich. Since the "history of higher mankind fulfills itself in the form of great culture," which lasts roughly a millennium, the future belongs to Russia, the Russia of Dostoevsky: "To Dostoevsky's Christianity will the next thousand years belong."[3] It is tempting to explain Spengler's admiration for Dostoevsky by his proven dependence on Hippolyte Taine, the inventor of theories of the rise and decline of historic-cultural types and of racism in culture. Dostoevsky was also influenced by Taine and was well familiar with his *De l'intelligence* and *L'Ancien Régime* (PSS, 27:113, 377; 30[1]:30). But I will take another route.

At the turn of the century in German-speaking lands, every significant artist and thinker nurtured on Nietzsche's affirmation of suprahistorical heroism was simultaneously looking for a way out of the stalemate faced by cultures of liberal democracy.[4] The humanistic ideals of Goethean Weimar did not produce citizens of the world but a society of professionals, public servants, and consumers. Nietzsche likens their state of mind to the happiness of masti-cating cattle, curious about the world beyond the slope only to the extent that richer outlying pastures could be found. With matching scorn, Dostoevsky sati-rizes German *Bildungsbürgertum* alongside the hedonistic frivolity of the French bourgeois in *Winter Notes on Summer Impressions* (1862) (PSS, 5:46–98). According to Georg Lukács, Nietzsche and Dostoevsky were providing the answers to unfulfilled revolutionary yearnings of a bourgeois man born around 1870 (the same year as Lenin)—"the generation whose formative literary influ-ences were Dostoevsky and Nietzsche and who has not moved from the anti-liberal apostasy fashionable at the time."[5]

18:36. Unless otherwise noted, this and all further references to Dostoevsky's work are to this academic edition, cited as *PSS* by volume and page.

3   Oswald Spengler, *The Decline of the West*, trans. Charles Francis Atkinson, rev. Arthur Helps, ed. Helmut Werner (New York: Vintage, 2006), 81, 273–74.

4   I mean primarily the arguments in Nietzsche's "On the Uses and Disadvantages of History for Life" and "Schopenhauer as Educator" in his *Untimely Meditations* (1874); see Friedrich Nietzsche, *Untimely Meditations*, trans. R. J. Hollingdale; ed. Daniel Breazeale (Cambridge: Cambridge University Press, 2000), 57–194.

5   Georg Lukács, "In Search of a Bourgeois Man," in *Essays on Thomas Mann*, trans. Stanley Mitchell (New York: Grosset and Dunlap, 1964), 34.

No wonder, therefore, that instead of returning to the patrician equanimity of Goethe's Weimar in the maiden days of the Weimar Republic, Thomas Mann found his ideal in Dostoevsky's method "relating to the national necessity for a religious ideal transcending individual prosperity."[6] When asked in 1919 to comment on the growing success of his work in the Bildungsroman genre, Mann's friend Hermann Hesse chose to defer to the author of *The Brothers Karamazov* as the true leader of European youth, whose ideal was beginning to devour the spirit of Europe:

> The young people of Europe, and especially the youth of Germany, feel Dostoevsky to be their great writer, not Goethe, not even Nietzsche. . . . This is what I call the decline of Europe. . . . Briefly put, it is a turning away from every fixed morality and ethic in favor of a *universal understanding*, a universal validation, a new, dangerous, terrifying sanctity such as the elder Zosima.[7]

A twenty-five-year-old Walter Benjamin, the very representative of that young generation, had stated the core of the matter even more succinctly in 1917. His novel of choice was *The Idiot*:

> Dostoevsky depicts the destiny of the world in the medium of the destiny of the people. This point of view is typical of the great nationalists, according to whom humanity can unfold only in the medium of a national historical heritage . . . in the aura of the Russian nation.[8]

These tendencies in the German wave of enthusiasm for Dostoevsky at the turn of the century and in the interwar period are more than simply intriguing. They require a serious assessment of Dostoevsky's messianism, which hinges on his conviction that European civilization brings new elements into Russian popular life by widening its horizons rather than luring it away from its predetermined route. In the best traditions of classical liberalism, he believes that the receipt of a

---

6 Mann notes this idea in the diary entry of January 21, 1920; Thomas Mann, *Diaries, 1918–1939*, selection and foreword Hermann Kesten; trans. Richard and Clara Winston (London: Robin Clark, 1984), 84.

7 Hermann Hesse, "*The Brothers Karamazov*, or The Decline of Europe: Thoughts on Reading Dostoevsky," in *My Belief: Essays on Life and Art*, trans. Denver Lindley, ed. and intro. Theodore Ziolkowski (New York: The Noonday Press, 1975), 70–71.

8 Walter Benjamin, "Dostoevsky's *The Idiot*," in *Early Writings, 1910–1917*, trans. Howard Eiland et al. (Cambridge, MA: Belknap, 2011), 275–80. Written in 1917, the Benjamin's note was published in 1921.

diploma does not complete the soul (*PSS*, 21:128). It may appear that Dostoevsky therefore can no longer be reduced to a simple commitment to the ideology of the soil (*pochvennichestvo*) taken strictly in its Russian historical context.[9] But the picture is more complex. For the same reason as he was inspiring the Germans before 1933, Dostoevsky had failed as a leader in the eyes of Russian liberal youth. Consider a previously overlooked formative episode in the career of Paul Miliukov, the future leader of the Constitutional Democrats and a major force in Russian politics before November 1917, later a renowned historian following his emigration from Russia. On April 3, 1878, the meat packers of Okhotnyi Riad, a historical trader row in the heart of Moscow, assisted the police in the beatings of students who were peacefully demonstrating in a procession from the Kursk Railway Station in Moscow to demand freedom and better options for their education. After the brutal crackdown, Miliukov and five other students addressed Dostoevsky directly. They wanted to know whether the meatpackers' action was a legitimate response of the Russian people (henceforth *narod*) to the intelligentsia.[10]

Unexpectedly, in his response on April 18, 1878, Dostoevsky blames the victims, the beaten youths, for thinking with the brain of a European "Man-in-General" (*obshchechelovek*) (*PSS*, 30[1]:21–25), and for not recognizing the hand of the Russian people in the meatpackers who struck them (30[1]:23). Dostoevsky went as far as to brand the flogged students "les moutons de Panurge" (*Panurgovo stado*) (30[1]:22), implying that the demonstrators followed blindly towards their destruction after the first discarded sheep in their flock went overboard.[11] (Note that Dostoevsky is not dealing with a Schillerian "All-Man" (*vsechelovek*), but with a commonality, the "Man-in-General"). Miliukov and fellow students realized that their faith in

---

9   I discuss Dostoevsky within the contexts of Russian debates and polemics on education in his time and the important outlines of his views on education in his works of fiction in Inessa Medzhibovskaya, "Education," in *Dostoevsky-in-Context*, ed. Deborah Martinsen and Olga Maiorova (Cambridge: Cambridge University Press, 2015), 106–13. For reasons of space, in this chapter I limit to the necessary minimum the discussion of Dostoevsky's creative fiction.

10 The students' letter appeared in Fyodor Dostoevsky, *Pis'ma*, ed. and commentary A. S. Dolinin (Moscow: Gosizdat, 1928–59), 4:355–56.

11 See book 6, chaps. 6–8 of François Rabelais's *Gargantua and Pantagruel*, recounting the wrangling of Panurge and Dindenault over the ownership of the herd of sheep. When trickster Panurge throws one sheep into water, the rest of the herd blindly follows; see François Rabelais, *Gargantua and Pantagruel*, trans., ed., and intro. M. A. Screech (London: Penguin, 2006), 680–87.

Dostoevsky was misplaced, that they could not subscribe to the proposed idolatry of the ultraconservative, violent, and monarchist tendencies of Dostoevsky's God-bearers.[12]

In *Diary of a Writer* for 1873, Dostoevsky brings up Gogol's "Nevsky Prospect" ("Nevskii Prospekt," 1833–34), in which a frivolous Lieutenant Pirogov receives a hearty flogging from locksmith Schiller, a German operating his business in St. Petersburg, for chasing after his wife through the glittery mists and snow flurries of the wintry capital. For Dostoevsky, Gogol's fantastic anecdote is no laughing matter because he retells it to impress upon the reader that the thrashing received by Pirogov from Schiller should be taken seriously, as a "terrifying prophesy" into the future of Russia and its two-hundred-year habit of being "spat at in the face" by Europe (*PSS*, 21:124). The choice of names is not coincidental: in *Diary of a Writer* for 1876, Dostoevsky was arguing that another Schiller, the great Friedrich Schiller, not a locksmith but a surgeon by trade, was one great example of an All-Man, a cosmopolitan citizen of the universe (*vsechelovek*) who had left the impression of his trademark (*kleimo*) on the soul of Russia as a token of its readiness for life in world culture. It is good then that another historical prototype of Dostoevsky's drafts, field surgeon Nikolai Pirogov, hero of the Crimean campaign, later head of the Odessa and Kiev educational districts, was a flogger by conviction and in practice. It is not only that Dostoevsky defends Pirogov's doting authoritarianism from the liberal and democratic attacks and supports flogging (19:69, 268; 20:158–61).[13] In *Diary of a Writer* for December 1876, Dostoevsky responds to the coverage of a peaceful student demonstration in *Moskovskie Vedomosti* in which editor Mikhail Katkov dismissed the demonstration as a demarche of an "egged-on herd" (*nastegannoe stado*)—translated more literally, "a herd flogged so as to be induced into obeying an external ill will." Dostoevsky does not dispute the very use of the flogging metaphor, which implies underhandedly that the students

---

12 P. N. Miliukov, *Vospominaniia (1859–1917)*, 2 vols., ed. M. M. Karpovich and B. I. El'kin. (New York: Izdatel'stvo imeni Chekhova 1955), 1:62–63, 68. Writing his memoir years after the events, Miliukov remembers incorrectly the date of their address to Dostoevsky, which occurred in 1878, not 1876 (ibid., 62).

13 See Dostoevsky's "Bov and Pirogov," in his Notebook for 1860–62 (*PSS*, 20:162–68), and other notations in the same notebook regarding the Pirogov question (*PSS*, 20:153–56, 158–61) in response to Dobroliubov's "The Illusions of All-Russia Destroyed by Birch-Rods" ("Vserossiiskie illiuzii, razrushaemye rozgami," 1860).

misbehaved precisely because they were an "unflogged herd," spoiled by their complacent educators (24:50–54).

These episodes illustrate the direct connections that Dostoevsky makes among cultural borrowing, politics of native soil, traditions of national dignity, discipline, the leadership role of the shepherd, and his authority. He explains *pochvennichestvo* itself as a vehicle of his messianic educational project. Thus, he interprets the triumph of his famous "Pushkin Speech" (1880) as a "victory of our idea" [*pobeda nashei idei*], that is, the victory of the idea of *pochvennichestvo*.[14] In preparatory drafts for the speech and in the speech itself, Dostoevsky reflects on the homelessness of Aleko, the superfluous fugitive from the shackles of the Enlightenment in Pushkin's narrative poem "Gypsies": "He has no soil for support under his feet" (*u nego nikakoi pochvy*) (*PSS*, 26:143). To become a true Russian is to become universal (*vselenskii*), like Pushkin, "the great teacher" of the Russian nation, who was capable of responding to all humanity, and of absorbing lessons from the common Russian people (1880) (26:47; 151–53). Pushkin's note "On Popular Upbringing" ("O narodnom vospitanii," 1826) first appeared in print in 1872, and its resonance was great, coinciding with Dostoevsky's preoccupation with the question of whether popular education should be enforced.[15] In the note, submitted privately to Nicholas I after the suppression of the Decembrists, Pushkin insists on the advantages of the government's boundless might with respect to the application of top-down Enlightenment, but without coercion; he also protests against corporal punishment.

By following Pushkin, Dostoevsky chooses to overlook authoritarian violence. His chief goal is to illuminate the original sense of the Russian word "enlightenment" (*prosveshchenie*), which is the enlightening of the flock (*pouchenie pastvy*).[16] He responds effusively to the "toothless liberal skepticism" of historian Alexander Gradovsky: "You have uttered an important word: Enlightenment.

---

14   See Dostoevsky's letter to A. G. Dostoevskaya of June 8, 1880, *PSS*, 30(1):184–85.

15   See Pushkin, "On narodnom vospitanii," in A. S. Pushkin. *Polnoe sobranie sochinenii*, 19 vols.; reprint of A. S. Pushkin, *Bol'shoe akademicheskoe izdanie*, ed. D. D. Blagoi, S. M. Bondi, G. O. Vinokur et al. (Moscow-Leningrad: Izdanie Akademii Nauk SSSR, 1937; Moscow: Vozrozhdenie, 1994–97), 11:43–47.

16   It is in this sense that Pushkin commends enlightenment in his comments on the activity of Grigorii Konisky, the archbishop of Byelorussia under Catherine the Great; see Pushkin, *Polnoe sobranie sochinenii*, 12:14. See the definition of words "to enlighten" (*prosvetit'*), "the enlightener" (*prosvetitel'*) and "enlightenment" (*prosveshchenie*) in Vladimir Dal's famed Russian thesaurus, which came out in 1863–66; see V. I. Dal', *Tolkovyi slovar' velikarusskogo iazyka*

Allow me to ask how you mean: Western sciences, useful knowledge, professional handicrafts or spiritual Enlightenment?" (*PSS*, 26:150). In the latter sense, Dostoevsky is sure that "our *narod* was enlightened already a long time in the past, having embraced Christ and His teaching" (*Diary of a Writer*, 1880; 26:150). In the autobiographical sketch "Peasant Marey" published in his *Diary of a Writer*, Dostoevsky tells us an indirect parable about popular Russian enlightenment. The words "Je hais ces brigands!," about thieving Russian commoners led out for flogging and addressed to him in French in the barracks of the Siberian camp by an educated Pole, make Dostoevsky recall the words of kindness received by him, a fearful little boy, from peasant Marey. He encounters Marey in the fields during his panicked flight from imagined wolves. Patting the boy's face with his unwashed fingers soaked in black native soil—an important detail—and in a tone of unusual kindness, Marey tells him never to be frightened (February 1876; 22:46–50).

Alongside his recovery of the original Russian meaning of *prosveshchenie*, Dostoevsky pays equal attention to the importance of the other two Russian words, "education" proper (*obrazovanie*), and "upbringing" (*vospitanie*). These two also carry a considerable cultural-semantic weight that is crucial for understanding Dostoevsky's messianic program. The former connotes *prima facie* the process of "shaping" and "forming" rather than simply providing one with the knowledge and techniques of learning. Its semantic root is *obraz* ("image, face, shape"), which readily associates with religious aspects of holiness and beauty—and in that case may become synonymous with another Russian word, *lik*, a "saintly visage," "a face painted on an icon."[17] The word *vospitanie* connotes the condition of having received the nourishment (bodily and soulful) without which it is impossible to grow, and only then does it underscore the acquisition of secular forms of conduct and of social skills.[18] Yet again, Dostoevsky privileges the spiritual and moral content of both terms by claiming that anyone educated and with the right upbringing is not only capable of discriminating good from evil but is also well armed to confront evil. Such an understanding of these Russian words hearkens back to the ancient Greek *paideia* and its later Patristic overtones, underscoring the process and science of raising and *leading* children towards knowledge by training

---

Vladimira Dalia, 3rd ed., corrected by I. A. Baudouin de Courtenay (St. Petersburg-Moscow: Tovarishchestvo M. O. Vol'fa, 1907), 3:1327.

17 Dal', *Tolkovyi*, 2:1580–81.
18 Ibid., 1:610.

them the skills for life. By assuming that the traditional Russian Enlightenment leads the flock, Dostoevsky objects to the opinion of a conservative critic V. D. Skariatin that in its regular communal ways and even in its radical gestures the Russian nation resembles a herd (*PSS*, 20:70).[19] Even in its backwardness Russia was distinct. Despite the Russians so-called barbarism, the Genevan Franz Lefort, Peter's Westernizing mentor, decided to focus his great educational experiment on the young tsar and his nation (18:42).

Dostoevsky conceives of Peter the Great as the only modern Russian leader (*vozhàtai* [*sic*]) who had proved himself in the role of the conductor of the nation walking the road of secular enlightenment. Having walked to the end of this modernizing road of sheer borrowing, the *narod* has been left without shepherds (*bez vozhataev*). The new forms of life (*novye formy zhizni*) that resulted from the disorderly creativity of a leader-less *narod* are repellent, have lost their face (*bezobrazny*) (*PSS*, 18:36). Only the education rooted in the highly moral upbringing (*vysokonravstvennoe vospitanie*) of Russian Orthodoxy sponsored by the tsar and the government could restore the face (*obraz*) of the people (20:122). Therefore, in the 1870s Dostoevsky accepted in good faith Minister of Enlightenment Dmitry Tolstoy's policy of returning to the classical and deliberately antiprogressive education model: "We have still to educate ourselves much to be considered truly Russian" (ibid.). At the same time, Dostoevsky's messianic ideology overemphasized the preservation of *svoe* ("the native element") (20:21).

In his address to "fathers and teachers" in Alyosha Karamazov's notes of the same,[20] the elder Zosima uses the term "enlightenment" strictly in the original Patristic sense of the accomplished illumination of the flock in the "joys and heroic deeds of Enlightenment and charity" (*radosti v podvigakh prosveshcheniia i miloserdiia*) (*PSS*, 14:288). Untouched by the light of spiritual reality, the secular education of the "superfluous" and their science confirm at best what is

---

19 See Dostoevsky's responses and objections in *Vremia* (*PSS*, 20:59–70) to Slavophiles and Westernizers: "Two Theoretical Camps" ("Dva lageria teoretikov") and "On New Literary Organs and Theories" ("O novykh literaturnykh organakh i o novykh teoriiakh"), the latter of which includes his response to Skariatin's piece "On the Herd Qualities of Russian Man" ("O tabunnykh svoistvakh russkogo cheloveka").

20 As Dostoevsky's narrator puts it, he prefers to limit the discourses to the rendition based on the manuscript of "Aleksey Fedorovich Karamazov. It will be shorter, and not as tedious, although, and I must repeat this, much of it was taken by Alyosha from the previous discourses" and he "joined them into a harmony [*sovokupil vmeste*]" (*PSS*, 14:260).

already prompted by divine intuition (14:284–86). What has been lost in the "teaching of this world," which trains one only for the "freedom of sating one's demands" (14:284), must be restored through the power of the "brotherhood and integrity of the human beings" (*bratstvo i tselostnost' liudei*) who are educated (*obrazovany*) in the image of Christ (*obraz Khristov*) (14:284), well preserved in the people, the God-bearer (*narod-bogonosets*), and in the monasteries which spread Christ's teaching.

Like his Zosima, Dostoevsky is reluctant to dissociate the discussions of "the highest meanings of life" (*vysshii smyls zhizni*) from practical tasks (*prakticheskie zadachi*) (*PSS*, 24:50–52). He agrees that the "literate common folk" (*gramotnoe prostonarodie*) are the most reverent and judicious consumers of "the spiritual bread" of education (1861) (18:60–67), but he steers clear not only of utilitarian simplifications committed by civic critics like Dobroliubov and Chernyshevsky but also of the anarchic religiosity of Leo Tolstoy. Tolstoy is fine with peasant charges being taught by "pilgrims, clerics, soldiers."[21] Tolstoy's choice of educational roles in his 1874 essay on popular education—read by Dostoevsky in 1878 in the early stages of his drafting of Zosima—is an accurate and subversive recycling of the dramatis personae (pilgrims, clerics, soldiers) of Denis Fonvizin's immortal comedy *The Minor* (1782). The group consists of teachers to the unenlightened and slow-witted landowner son, Mitrofan Prostakov, the national symbol of gluttony, arrogance, and vice. Dostoevsky disagrees with Tolstoy's propositions regarding who should teach peasants by the proverbial "natural method." The method of this type would do little to arm the Russian populace with up-to-date knowledge ready to undertake the task of its theophanic liberation of the world. Minister Dmitry Tolstoy and Dostoevsky could agree, but Leo Tolstoy and Dostoevsky could not. In his first essay on popular education of the same name, written in 1862, Tolstoy (the writer) postulated his objection to the principles of autocratic pedagogy in the monarchy that maintained "not the shepherd for the flock, but the flock for the shepherd."[22]

How do we measure Dostoevsky's pedagogical messianism by comparison to his predecessors and contemporaries, on the one hand, and to some important later extensions, on the other? Was his messianism unique? It does not take long

---

21 L. N. Tolstoy, *Polnoe sobranie sochinenii*, Jubilee Edition in 90 vols., ed. V. G. Chertkov et al. (Moscow: Khudozhestvennaia literatura, 1928–58), 17:128.

22 Ibid., 8:4–25

to notice a multitude of resonances with other artists and thinkers who are as open as Dostoevsky to an authoritarian cultural borrowing in making the foreign (*chuzhoe*) become their own or, in the case of making the claim for national destiny, Russia's own (*svoe*) (*PSS*, 19:141).

The great Germans who furnished the ideas of *Bildung* to prepare the foundation of their national culture within the framework of modern humanism quite similarly claimed their exclusionary capacity among the enlightened folk (*Volk*, same as *narod*) for putting the principles of Greek *paideia* in their missionary employ.[23] It takes remembering Herder's categories of *Bildung* (logical, moral, political) to notice their imitation of the liberal arts concepts of *paideia* explained by Aristotle in *Nichomachean Ethics* (1337a–1338b).[24] In much the same manner, Dostoevsky claims that through the finest modification of the cultural treasures of its European teachers, Russia alone is destined for the role of their most deserving disciple. (In place of Dostoevsky's Pushkin, the Germans place Goethe, their version of a universal genius.) Even more striking are the similarities of Dostoevsky's nationalist education schemes with those of Fichte and Hegel. Recall Headmaster Hegel's address to a gymnasium audience at Nuremberg in 1809 and Fichte's speeches to the German nation under Napoleon in 1813.

Let Hegel be the first to speak:

> The spirit and purpose of our foundation is preparation for learned study, a
> preparation grounded on Greece and Rome. For more than a thousand years
> this has been *the soil* on which all civilization stood, from which it has sprung,

---

23 On this feature of German messianism, see Werner Jaeger, *Paideia: The Ideals of Greek Culture*, 2nd ed., trans and ed. Gilbert Highet (Oxford: Oxford University Press, 1973), 1:xxiii–xxix. The figure of an educator who leads and cultivates a harmonious human being is crucial for the focus on a connective link between the oneness of all and the multiplicity of the world, of ideas (*eidos*) and the images they generate (*eikones*). The modern German term *Bildung*, born during the days when Germany was seeking to become a unified nation, embraces the meanings of "formation," "shaping," "education," and "cultivation." It is thus a gathering into one word of the Greek *paideia* and the Latin *educatio*, which signifies cultivation alongside instruction, the leading and conducting of somebody's growth. The German adjective *gebildet*, according to Gadamer's classic analysis, is not being said of someone who is simply educated, but of someone who becomes "open to the universal sense"; Hans-Georg Gadamer, *Truth and Method*, 2nd rev. ed., trans. and revised Joel Weinsheimer and Donald D. Marshall (New York: Continuum, 1988), 17. For the historical changes of these basic distinctions in antiquity, see H. I. Marrou, *A History of Education in Antiquity*, trans. George Lamb (Madison: University of Wisconsin Press, 1956).

24 See Johann Gottfried von Herder, *Philosophical Writings*, trans. and ed. Michael N. Forster (Cambridge: Cambridge University Press, 2002), 22–27; and Aristotle, *Selections*, ed. W. D. Ross (New York: Charles Scribner's Sons, 1955), 318–23.

and with which it has been in continual connection … the fine arts and the sciences have grown up on that *soil*, and, while they have attained a self-subsistence of their own, they have not yet emancipated themselves from the recollection of that older culture. … But, however important the *preservation of this soil* is, the modification of the relation between antiquity and modern times is no less essential.[25] (my emphasis)

Instead of rejection and abolition, Hegel makes a case for modification and rework, or "digesting and transforming" the treasures of *paideia*, this "mother earth" of science and learning, through the vehicles of German language after a necessary phase of dialectical alienation and estrangement from both.[26] Recall Dostoevsky's "detachment from the soil" (*otorvannost' ot pochvy*) and his "do not imitate, but continue" (*PSS*, 19:114). Like Hegel, Dostoevsky therefore supports the liberal arts and does not protest the return of classical curricula and the study of Russian in place of science initiated by Minister Dmitry Tolstoy. In objection to the avatars of professional and specialist training, he observes that Aristotle would never have become a great thinker had he started with *techne* and technology. Thank God he had started with *The Iliad* (*Diary of a Writer*, 1873; 21:129). Dostoevsky's constant recourse to Hegel's principle of *Aufhebung* ("sublation"), or the lifting of contradictions (*sniatie protivorechii*) and reconciling contradictions dialectically, is remarkable in its intended messianic sense: "We have adopted into our soul the geniuses of other nations, with love and in a friendly spirit rather than with hatred—all together, without discriminating them by their tribe. We were capable of discriminating, lifting all contradictions, practically from the very first step and by way of instinct, to forgive and to reconcile differences" (*Diary of a Writer*, 1880; 26:147).[27]

Fichte's topical addresses structurally resemble Dostoevsky's answers to the enemies of Russia in his *Diary of a Writer* (this includes his answers to the anti-Russian militarism of Bismarck in 1877, which he blames on Luther's and

25 G. W. F. Hegel, *Early Theological Writings*, trans. T. M. Knox, with an introduction and fragments translated by Richard Kroner (Philadelphia: University of Pennsylvania Press, 1975), 321.
26 Ibid., 327.
27 See similar statements in Dostoevsky's chapter on Tolstoy's *Anna Karenina* (*Diary of a Writer*, July–August 1877): "Only Russian Spirit has been graced with universality [*vsemirnost'*], has been granted a mission to grasp and unite in the future the whole variety of nationalities, and to lift all of their contradictions" (*PSS*, 25:199).

Kant's spirit of criticism) (*PSS*, 25:151–54). Substantively, Fichte's ideas resonate powerfully with Dostoevsky's ideas discussed in the earlier parts of this
chapter. Fichte speaks about "thieving from the fruits of the soil" in the system
of national education because of its being "ungrounded in the nature of things."
So does Fichte's insistence that the new German education prepare its trademark citizens and human beings without the slackening of the reins of the
state.[28] Among the other drawbacks, Fichte names national and personal selfish-
ness, complacency in times of peace, pursuit of ranks and comforts with the
receipt of the sinecures afforded by specialty training, frivolous behavior and
detachment from the demands of real life, and indifference to religion and to the
historical mission of the land.[29] Like Hegel and Humboldt, Dostoevsky identifies the power of the nation with the power of its language. Dostoevsky's notion
of "language-nation" (*iazyk-narod*) (*Diary of a Writer*, June 1876; *PSS*, 23:80–
84) is a word-for-word borrowing of the phraseology of Herder and Humboldt
on "cultivated" and "uncultured" tongues and their role in the formation of
national languages, which define the success or failure of cultures. Humboldt is
especially important. The founder of the University of Berlin has a whole
chapter on the mental individuality of a people and the shape of its language
and several chapters on how the efficacy of an individual suffers from lack of
connection with the character of the people, disallowing each the achievement
of Absolute Identity.[30] Dostoevsky marches ahead of Humboldt by advancing
the idea of the superiority of Russian language, even at its as yet uncultured
stage, thanks to its alleged capacity for translating the universality of the absolute. "The deepest forms of the Spirit and thought of European languages," he
argues, translate well in Russian, as imperfect as it might be, whereas the refined
European languages and their best poets are unable to translate Russian artists.[31]
Despite these rather extreme pronouncements, they are a century-old remnant
of Herder's insistence on the superiority of local color, however crude, a sort of

---

28 Johann Gottlieb Fichte, *Addresses to the German Nation*, ed., intro., and notes Gregory Moore
    (Cambridge: Cambridge University Press, 2008), 14–15, 22–24, 36, 124, 130.

29 See ibid.

30 See Wilhelm von Humboldt, *On Language: On the Diversity of Human Language Construction
    and Its Influence on the Mental Development of the Human Species*, ed. Michael Losonsky, trans.
    Peter Heath (Cambridge: Cambridge University Press, 1999), passim.

31 Dostoevsky laughed at the first European translations of Gogol (*Diary of a Writer*, June 1876;
    PSS, 23:80–84).

messianism through imperfection. (Herder disputes Kant's arguments for teleo-
logical cosmopolitanism and the presence of international rather than only
German vocabulary in philosophical discourse.)[32]

Humboldt's idea that the university should be responsible for the task of
providing a well-rounded and well-grounded education to the nation in the
state of constant advancement brings us to Dostoevsky's ideal, his "All-Man"
(*vsechelovek*), a model endowed with philosophical, scientific, professional, and
artistic knowledge, who would implement this knowledge for the good of society
and whose motto is "to continue rather than imitate" (*Ne podrazhat', a prodolzhat'*)
(*PSS*, 19:114). However, Humboldt's persuasion that the university—or any
other institution, or the state itself, for that matter—should exercise restraint
when interfering in the affairs of education, limiting its solicitude to protecting
the pedagogical well-being of a tutee, does not agree with the view of Dostoevsky, who thinks it false to "defend student youth from the government"
(21:126).[33] Dostoevsky has been shown above to be a huge supporter of solici-
tous violence against charges of misbehaving—even though protested against
by Rousseau, Pestalozzi, Pushkin, Froebel, and most of other major thinkers
whom he otherwise admires. In the words of Pestalozzi, one of the initiators of
the prohibition of flogging, a young person, an individual, is a germ and a seed
of humanity deserving of kind tending in order to grow.[34]

Dostoevsky praises the "living and independent spirit" of Pestalozzi's
idea of the childhood garden and Froebel's idea of the kindergarten, but
educational innovations and various scientific conventions assembled apropos
are usually "rubbish," in his view (loose drafts for *Diary of a Writer*, *PSS*,

---

32 See the famous "paragraph 83" in support of cosmopolitanism, a form of maturity of
    humanity, its self-discipline in freedom, and the ultimate ends of humanity in history, in
    Immanuel Kant, *The Critique of Judgment*, trans. James Creed Meredith (Oxford: Oxford
    University Press, 1952), 92–97. Also on this score, see "The Idea for a Universal History with
    a Cosmopolitan Intent" (1784), in Immanuel Kant, *Perpetual Peace and Other Essays*, trans.
    Ted Humphrey (Indianapolis, IN: Hackett, 1983), 29–38. On Herder's objections, see "This
    Too a Philosophy of History for the Formation of Humanity," in J. G. von Herder, *Philosoph-
    ical Writings*, trans. and ed. Michael N. Forster (Cambridge: Cambridge University Press,
    2002), 272–358.
33 For a view opposite to Dostoevsky's, see Wilhelm von Humboldt, *The Limits of State Action*,
    ed. J. W. Burrow. (Indianapolis, IN: Liberty Fund, 1993), 46–52.
34 Heinrich Pestalozzi, *The Education of Man*, preface by William H. Kirkpatick; trans. Heinz
    and Ruth Norden (New York: Philosophical Library, 1951), 11–20, 57–64.

22:146, 148).[35] In his novels and journalism, Dostoevsky, like Rousseau, Pestalozzi, and Froebel, often juxtaposes adolescents and young adults to children, who arrive at the most powerful insights thanks to their unspoiled and healthy instincts about life (*Diary of a Writer*, May 1876; *PSS*, 23:22; and 8:58, which is pt. 1, ch. 9 of *The Idiot*). These ideas ring in strong accord with Rousseau and Pestalozzi (and with Schopenhauer and Nietzsche) in terms of Dostoevsky's concern for preserving independence from various commissions: "It is bad if [independence] turns into something purely institutional ... the beginning is naïve, and then there is an organization" (*Diary of a Writer*, drafts 1876; 22:146).

The question of institution as a form of authority is therefore important. Dostoevsky's solution is ultimately a losing one if judged by his messianic program's checklist for success. The national education of which he dreams is dependent on stable institutions and on what Hegel calls "incorporation" (*Einbildung*), the summit of upbringing in a strong national state. This is the absolute value of education, amounting to the "cultivation of the universality of thought" and the "incorporation of reason into reality which the whole of world history has worked to achieve."[36] So understood and implemented, the incorporation entails the rationalization of education and training that creates the bureaucracy of specialists, a privileged caste with aspirations for proper remuneration, who are not the same as the cultivated men reared in the ideas of messianism.

As Max Weber puts it, educational certificates do not create the conditions for democracy, but for professional meritocracy.[37] Dostoevsky's guardedness vis-à-vis the necessity of institutions (*uchrezhdeniia*) undermines his messianic project, which would otherwise have been like Hegel's, the sublimation or fulfillment of Russian (rather than Prussian) incorporation in world history. His guarded behavior around institutions is his fear of German barbarism, equivalent to Weber's fear of "the iron cage"—what Durkheim would

---

35 On Froebel's child-centered pedagogy in the kindergarten, see F. W. Froebel, *The Education of Man*, trans. W. N. Hailmann (New York: Dover, 2005), and R. B. Downs, *Friedrich Froebel* (Boston: Twayne, 1978).

36 G. W. F. Hegel, *Elements of the Philosophy of Right*, trans. H. B. Nisbet, ed. Allen W. Wood. (Cambridge: Cambridge University Press, 1991), 52, 294–95.

37 Max Weber, *From Max Weber: Essays on Sociology*, trans., ed., and intro. H. H. Gerth and C. Wright Mill (Oxford: Oxford University Press, 1975), 240–43.

juxtapose, as a case of the failure of German *Bildung*, to the healthy humanism derived by other national traditions and systems of education from organic pagan cultures, such as the Greeks and the Romans.[38] In the steady displays of his fear against state bureaucracy, which he shares with the Slavophiles, most notably K. S. Aksakov, Dostoevsky also displays his caring humanism, what Durkheim calls "Christian habits of the soul," which agrees with the tradition inherited from the Renaissance humanism of Rabelais and sentimentalist humanism of Rousseau.[39] Prophetic humility could be the reason why Dostoevsky, to confirm Bakhtin, prefers a loophole approach to sanctimonious preaching in pedagogical matters.[40]

Another aspect of the failing authority of Dostoevsky's messianism is disclosed in Hannah Arendt's explanation of the crises-laden approaches to education by the extreme "new ones." By "new ones" she means the newbies of modern civilization. (Arendt concentrates on the United States, but her explanation is perfectly applicable to Russia, whose construction of the modern educational project is also starting within the framework of the eighteenth century.) There is always a danger with the newbies, these disciples of Rousseau, as Arendt understands it, for confusing education with politics and for making education "an instrument of politics."[41] The result of this confusion is a disastrous failure of persuasion, which invites "dictatorial interference."[42] More directly on the same issue is what Gadamer has to say about authority, about the confusion of the question of the authority of the teacher based on knowledge, pedagogical skill, and intellectual integrity with authoritarianism. Russia and Germany of the twentieth century serve up an example of "Enlightened barbarianism" and totalitarian appropriation of the program

---

38 On the barbarism and failure of German *Bildung* built off Protestantism and moral rationalism, see Emile Durkheim, "The Social Bases of Education," in *Selected Writings*, ed. Anthony Giddens (Cambridge: Cambridge University Press, 1972), 203–18.

39 Ibid., 207.

40 On the topic of education, Dostoevsky was especially reluctant to speak "in essences" (*essentsiami*) (*Diary of a Writer* for 1873, "Riazhenyi"; *PSS*, 21:88), but in his preferred method of "words with a loophole" (ibid.)

41 Hannah Arendt, "The Crisis in Education," in *Between Past and Future*, intro. Jerome Kahn (New York: Penguin Classics, 1968), 170–93, esp. 173–77 and 186. The US crisis of failure, according to Arendt, is a conflict between its original principles of equality and democracy and the principles of meritocracy necessarily present in modern systems of education.

42 Ibid., 173.

that had started on more innocent notes of messianic superiority among the Aryan nations.[43]

This is a fruitful conflict that can help to penetrate Dostoevsky's messianism from yet another angle. By recovering the idea of the care of life as the care of self, Dostoevsky returns to principles of premodern Russian Christian learning, which concentrate on the building of the soul through the guidance obtained from shepherds and holy books. In this case, Dostoevsky complies with Durkheim's solution for perfect shepherding, in which a spiritual shepherd prepares the healthy sociological future for his nation.[44] By endorsing the healthy social bases of education originating from religion and spirituality—they stifle modern anomie in its cradle—Durkheim is notably excluding extreme nationalism, which he ascribes to the very controlling barbarism of Germany. In this regard, François Lyotard considers Martin Heidegger, the Nazi-appointed rector of Freiburg in 1933. A comparison suggested by Lyotard is useful: before embracing extreme nationalism, Heidegger had accepted that pedagogy is a form of relentless questioning of being. For the nationalistic Heidegger, as Lyotard aptly sums up, "the questioning of being becomes a conversation on the 'destiny' of historico-spiritual people."[45] Unsurprisingly, the Fichte of 1933 unfolds a threefold mission of the National Socialism–led *Bildung*, in which learning trails behind at a distant third position after military service and labor, allowing the nationalistic party "to assume direct control over the training of the 'people.'"[46]

Unlike his fiction, Dostoevsky's political program for education supplies the Russian state with a comparably dangerous narrative. Schiller was the first to warn against the conflation of pedagogical and political acts and the

---

43 Hans-Georg Gadamer, "Authority and Critical Freedom," in *The Enigma of Health. The Art of Healing in a Scientific Age*, trans. Jason Gaiger and Nicholas Walker (Stanford, CA: Stanford University Press, 1996), 117–24.

44 Durkheim, "Social Bases of Education," 217.

45 Jean-François Lyotard, *The Postmodern Condition: A Report on Knowledge*, trans. Geoff Bennington and Brian Massini, foreword by Fredric Jameson (Minneapolis: University of Minnesota Press, 1984), 37.

46 Ibid., 32. See Martin Heidegger, *German Existentialism*, trans. and intro. Dagobert D. Runes (New York: The Wisdom Library, 1965), 13–19. In this regard, it is meaningful that the turn-of-the-century and the early Weimar Republic German admirers of Dostoevsky—Musil, Mann, Hesse, Benjamin—all became political émigrés who had chosen not to live under Nazism.

application of artisanal violence to matter. Schiller distinguishes between barbarism (rationalistic and doctrinaire application of violence) and savagery (where the violent action springs from emotion and feeling).[47]

In the context of this conversation on shepherding as an attempt of forming, it is important to remember Martin Buber's idea of religious dialogue: "Man, the creature, who forms and transforms the creation, cannot create. But he, each man, can expose himself and others to the creative Spirit. And he can call upon the Creator to save and perfect His image."[48] Buber's is a preventive response to "shaping" the destiny of individual people and nations by means of casting them into nationalistic molds. Such programs do not bring a pupil face-to-face with God, nor is dialogue with the divine achieved by peeping through a Menippean loophole.

The possibility of truth is subject to cautious withholding for reasons other than polyphony. In the words of Karl Jaspers, education in the universities has forfeited its original purpose of being a "possible safeguard of truth against the reality of the state." By becoming the servants of nationalism, they betrayed their eternal idea: "The responsibility of the university as a Western, supranational and suprapolitical idea was lost."[49] For existentialists like Jaspers, forfeiting the authority of educational institutions only increases the value and responsibility of the behavior of lonely selves caught in the limits of life's situations. If the educational institution and the state cease to offer choices to the individual, the individual should nonetheless traverse the spaces of existence.

The spaces of postmodern existence extinguish grand narratives, the narratives which become delegitimized, along with institutions that supported it: be it nation states, permanent professions, historical traditions or iconic institutions, including the new messianism.[50] There is no hope for organic society in the reality of systems that regulate performativity in which language

---

47   See letter 3 in Friedrich Schiller, *On the Aesthetic Education of Man: In a Series of Letters*, ed. and trans. with an introduction and commentary by Elizabeth M. Wilkinson and L. A. Willoughby (Oxford: Clarendon, 1982), 10–15.

48   The quote comes from an address that Buber delivered on "the matter of education," "Rede über das Erzieherische," at the Third International Educational Conference held at Heidelberg in August 1925; see Martin Buber, *Between Man and Man*, trans. Ronald Gregor Smith (Boston: Beacon Press, 1961), 103.

49   Karl Jaspers, *Philosophy and the World: Selected Essays and Lectures* (Washington, DC: Regnery Gateway, 1963), 247.

50   Lyotard, *Postmodern Condition*, 15–17.

is a game of pragmatic means. Worst of all, a human being cannot be educated or developed, being "already positioned as the referent in the story recounted by those around him."[51] In the global age where we live today, what is the relevance for Dostoevsky's messianism? I see it as still relevant, both negatively and positively.

Negativity first. Let us look at the question of shepherding and authority from the perspective of youthful rebellion. The young Benjamin credits Dostoevsky with understanding the crux of the conflict in modern society, which is the generational face-off between the educators and the educated, the grown-up world and the world of radicalizing youth: "In pursuit of its goal, humanity continually gives birth to an enemy: its young generation, its children, the incarnation of its instinctual life, of its individual will, the properly animal part of its existence, its continually self-renewing past."[52] Hence, there is no more important task for humanity than to appropriate this youthful existence, to introduce it into the process of human development before it becomes a vehicle of terror. "This is the function of education," writes Benjamin.[53]

As much as he abhors radicalism, Dostoevsky enters into a contest with a generation of revolutionary-minded students of the 1860s and 1870s, telling them angrily that members of the Petrashevsky circle to which he had belonged had not only been better educated but also more determined to die for their ideals (*Diary of a Writer*, January 1877; *PSS*, 25:23–26).[54] In his response to Miliukov in 1878, Dostoevsky thinks of radical youth clearly as an enemy of the Russian Orthodox Christians: "Last winter, during the Kazan Railway affair, a throng of youth defiles the Temple of our Nation, smokes cigarettes in church, and instigates a scandal. Listen, I'd like to say to these Kazansky Railway marcher boys . . . you do not believe in God, this is your trouble, but why do you insult the *narod* and his Temple? And so the

---

51 Ibid.
52 Benjamin, "Dostoevsky's *The Idiot*," 40.
53 Ibid.
54 During his detention in the Peter and Paul Fortress, Dostoevsky claimed that the education of the fellow Petrashevsky circle members, steeped in the ideals of libertarian Enlightenment, posed no danger to the state (*PSS*, 18:120).

narod called them 'noble brats' and, worse than that, stigmatized them as 'students,' but truth be told, there were quite many Jews and Armenians in there (so it is proven, that the demonstration is political and arranged by external force)" (30[1]:23).

And now the positivity, in its plural senses. Regarding the question of enlightenment, Dostoevsky can be said to prefigure Foucault in *not* conflating enlightenment with humanism because—and despite his support of authoritarianism—he believed that correct methods of education are not expressed through discourses of power, but through the effort of the entire Russian nation. Enlightenment for both Dostoevsky and Foucault involves primarily a test of "problematization of being" and the following questions: "How are we constituted as subjects who exercise or submit to power relations? How are we constituted as moral subjects of our own actions?"[55] But whereas for Foucault the test that requires work on "our limits" is a "patient labor giving form to our impatience for liberty,"[56] the same would be for Dostoevsky a patient labor for God, since the proverbial "impatience for liberty" is the very problem he identifies with Western enlightenment.

It can be said that Dostoevsky's messianism leads to undesired results (undesired by him, that is). He did not design his Underground Man to be a warning against institutions. He wanted his paradoxalist to perpetuate his condemnation of the loss of Christian humility and an inability to achieve redemption by suffering with and for another. In the West, the type is none of the above: it is a postmodern emblem of ironic decentering and displacement in disguise, best summarized in Gilles Deleuze's concepts of pure difference and complex repetition. Deleuze thinks that in the times of the loss of history, the Underground Man teaches us to be untimely. At the risk of "playing the idiot, do so in the Russian manner: that of an underground man who recognizes himself no more in the subjective presuppositions of a natural capacity for thought than in the objective presuppositions of a culture of the times, and lacks the compass with which to make a circle. Such a one is Untimely, neither

---

55 Michel Foucault, "What Is Enlightenment?," in *The Essential Foucault*, ed. Paul Rabinow (New York: New Press, 1994), 56–57.

56 Ibid., 57.

temporal, nor eternal."[57] Thus Dostoevsky's messianic pursuit of "All-Knowl-edge" through constant reauthoring "with a difference" of what is borrowed is misappropriated in the intellectual mainstream of the West. Deleuze and other Western postmodernists take Dostoevsky's message for the warning against "overfull understanding,"[58] a means to protect one's subjectivity from *knowing all* and *knowing like all.*

A shepherd is judged in his art by "nothing else than how to provide what is best for that over which it is set," says the master of loophole wisdom, Socrates.[59] Was Dostoevsky a good shepherd or an evil prophet, the purveyor of Aristotle's *tokos* ("interest gained off offspring") or *chrematics* ("artificial, bad, mercantile mentoring")?[60] Did he gain a fair rate in receiving the interest off the offspring that was good?[61] From the doctrinal point of view of Russian Orthodoxy, a writer cannot be a shepherd. The institute of shepherds is not a mere branch of pedagogical leadership broadly understood, but a consecrated and ordained clerical duty.[62] Dosto-evsky's shepherd also bears no likeness to the sinister conductors and leaders of the twentieth century, whom he had predicted with horror in a whole gallery of characters, especially in the monstrous Verkhovensky. What is known for sure is that Dostoevsky's art spawns a generous offspring in the complex repetition of other big artists. In this regard, the effusive lyricism of Robert Musil's *Young Törless*, which echoes the confusions of Arkady Dolgoruky in Dostoevsky's *Adolescent*, reaffirms the existence of indwelling goodness in the native soil of world literature:

---

57 Gilles Deleuze, *Difference and Repetition*, trans. Paul Patton (New York: Columbia University Press, 1994), 130.

58 Ibid.

59 See *Republic* 345d (bk. 1), in Plato, *The Collected Dialogues*, ed. Edith Hamilton (Princeton, NJ: Princeton University Press, 1961), 595.

60 See Marc Shell, *The Economy of Literature* (Baltimore: Johns Hopkins University Press, 1978), 24, 46.

61 Plato, *Republic* 507a (bk. 4); 742.

62 See Metropolitan (Mitropolit) Antonii, *Uchenie o pastyre, pastyrstve i ob ispovedi*, intro. Archbishop Nikon (Ryklitsky) (New York: Izdatel'stvo Severo-Amerikanskoi i Kanadskoi Eparkhii, 1966). It will be recalled that Alyosha Karamazov leaves the monastery and does not attend the seminary after organizing his notes of Zosima's instructions. Dostoevsky believed seminaries to be training grounds for unthinking herd or future radicals, as reflected in his notebooks for 1875–77 (*PSS*, 24:67).

He had a longing for silence, for books. As though his soul was black earth, beneath which the seeds are stirring, and no one knows how they will break forth. The image of a gardener occurred to him, watering his flower-beds each morning, with even, expectant care. That image wouldn't let him go, its expectant certainty seemed to attract all his yearning to itself. ... All his reservations ... were swept aside by the conviction that he must stake everything on achieving that state of mind.[63]

"Man and plant blossom differently," says Humboldt.[64] Musil's hero, who—like his author—leaves the military academy to become a writer as a result of his contemplation about the black soil in the care of a good gardener, is only following in the footsteps of Fyodor Dostoevsky, graduate of the Academy for Military Engineering.

---

63 Robert Musil, *The Confusions of Young Törless*, trans. Shaun Whiteside, intro. J. M. Coetzee (London: Penguin, 2001), 146.

64 Humboldt, *Limits of State Action*, 13.

PART

5

Intercultural Connections

XIX

Achilles in *Crime and Punishment*

Donna Orwin

In part 6, chapter 6 of *Crime and Punishment*, Svidrigailov commits suicide in front of a horrified watchman[1]. This watchman is a Jew dressed in a grey soldier's overcoat and "a copper Achilles helmet." To emphasize the importance of this second detail in this very short but crucial episode, the narrator calls the watchman "Achilles" four times. The purpose of my study is to explore the significance of this appearance of Homer's hero in the novel.

The *Iliad* does not describe Achilles's helmet in detail, but it does have a plume, comb, or metal crest on its top, and Achilles is depicted with a helmet like this from antiquity onward on vases and other images. So far as I have been able to discover, no one has seriously investigated the reason the watchman in *Crime and Punishment* wears an Achilles helmet, and it is easy to speculate why. For one thing, this detail is disguised as part of the realistic setting in which the suicide occurs.[2] Svidrigailov catches sight of a "tall watch tower" and decides to

---

1 F. M. Dostoevsky, *Polnoe sobranie sochinenii v tridtsati tomakh* [*PSS*], 33 vols., ed. V. G. Bazanov et al. (Leningrad: Nauka, 1972–90), 6:394–95; hereafter cited as *PSS* by volume and page. I thank Arkadi Klioutchanski for his editing and comments on this chapter.

2 In the terms of Roman Jakobson's famous article on realism, it is an "unessential detail" (*nesushchestvennyi priznak*) characteristic of the mode; see Jakobson, "On Realism in Art," in *Language in Literature*, ed. Krystyna Pomorska and Stephen Rudy (Cambridge, MA: Harvard University Press, 1987), 19–27.

shoot himself near it so that there will be a witness to his suicide. He therefore turns onto Svezhinskaia Street, where he finds a man standing at the gates of "a large building with a watch tower" (and not on the tower itself). In mid-nineteenth-century Petersburg, towers called *kalanchi* were used for various purposes related to public safety, and especially for fires. They were part of large compounds containing stables, sheds, and barracks, and watchmen stood on them around the clock looking for suspicious smoke or flames. Though a soldier—note his military overcoat—the watchman is working in the fire department; therefore, he is wearing a brass helmet with a crest that was part of the uniform of firemen at that time. [3]

The watchman is a Jew with a heavy accent. This is plausible within realistic poetics because there were in fact many Jewish firemen in Petersburg at the time, and some Jewish soldiers were allowed to retire there. [4] Nonetheless, the watchman's Jewishness stands out because neither Dostoevsky nor his readers would associate Jews with the manly men who become soldiers or firefighters. Dostoevsky's Jewish watchman is a coward, a warrior in costume only: his eyes widen with fear when he realizes that Svidrigailov is about to shoot himself, and he does nothing to stop him. [5] On the face of it, the reference to Achilles therefore seems either merely coincidental, as might befit realist prose, or ironic, or even absurd. My investigation suggests that it is intended to be ironic, but also that it should be understood within a larger and self-conscious engagement by Dostoevsky with the *Iliad*.

---

3   See Rivosh N. Ya, "Odezhda obshchestvennogo i chastnogo obsluzhivaiushchego personala v dorevoliutsionnoi Rossii," in *Vremya i veshchi*, accessed November 15, 2014, http://lib. vkarp.com/2013/09/15/ривош-н-я-одежда-общественного-и-частн/. See also http:// www.cleper.ru/articles/description.php?n=310, accessed November 16, 2014. L. V. Karasev, in "O simvolakh Dostoevskogo," *Voprosy filosofii* 10 (1994): 102, accessed February 14, 2016, http://www.durov.com/study/file-602.htm, identifies the helmet as belonging to a fireman, but he focuses on its composition from brass rather than the Achilles connection.

4   See Yohanan Petrovsky-Shtern, *Jews in the Russian Army, 1827–1917: Drafted into Modernity* (Cambridge: Cambridge University Press, 2009), 71, 86n72; or Petrovskii-Shtern, *Evrei v russkoi armii, 1827–1914* (Moscow: Novoe literaturnoe obozrenie), 88–90.

5   For other speculations about the Jewish symbolism here, see David I. Goldstein, *Dostoyevsky and the Jews* (Austin: University of Texas Press, 1981) 51–54; and Elena M. Katz, *Neither with Them, nor without Them: The Russian Writer and the Jew in the Age of Realism* (Syracuse, NY: Syracuse University Press, 2008), 162–67. Katz also touches upon the possible role of Achilles in the scene (163–64).

Dostoevsky's earliest surviving comment about Homer is in a letter to his brother Mikhail, dated January 1, 1840:

> Homer (a legendary figure, perhaps, as Christ was, incarnated by God and sent to us) could be parallel only to Christ, and not to Goethe. Get into him, brother, understand the *Iliad*, read it well (you haven't read him? Admit it). In the *Iliad* Homer gave the entire ancient world the structure of both its spiritual and earthly life, and did it with the same power as Christ did for the new world. Now do you understand me? Victor Hugo as a lyric poet has a purely angelic character, a Christian, childlike direction in his poetry and no one is his equal in this ... Only Homer, with the very same unshakeable belief in his calling, with a childlike faith in the god of poetry, whom he serves, is like Victor Hugo in the direction of the source of his poetry, but only in his direction, not in his [Homer's] thought, which was given to him by nature, and which he expressed; I'm not talking about this last.[6]

Although Dostoevsky does not mention which translation of the *Iliad* he has read, it is certainly the one by N. I. Gnedich, originally published in 1829, but reissued and reviewed, by, among others, V. G. Belinsky, in 1839.[7] Dostoevsky's comments in the letter just cited seem to echo Gnedich's interpretation of Homer in his introduction to the translation, also republished in the 1839 edition:

> They [the poems of Homer] are like the books of the Bible, they are the seal and mirror of the age. And whoever loves to go back to the youth of mankind so as to view the bare charm of nature or to take nourishment from the lessons of bygone eras, before that person a whole world, earth and heaven, unwinds into a marvelous picture, bubbling with life and movement, the finest and most grand that the genius of man has ever created. ... From these beginnings there flow the grandest beauties of Homeric poetry, not including anything local, they are as universal and eternal as the nature and heart of man. Homer and nature are one and the same.[8]

---

6 *PSS*, 28(1):69–70. Unless otherwise stated, all translations from Russian are mine.

7 For the Belinsky review, see V. G. Belinsky, *Polnoe sobranie sochinenii* (Moscow: Izdatel'stvo Akademii Nauk SSSR, 1953–1959), 3:163, 307–9, accessed December 13, 2014, http:// www.vgbelinsky.ru/texts/books/13-3/articles-and-reviews/1839/. For polemics in the 1840s around the new translation, see A. N. Egunov, *Gomer v russkikh perevodakh XVIII– XIX vekov* (Moscow: Nauka, 1964), 345–53.

8 See http://az.lib.ru/g/gnedich_n_i/text_0080.shtml.

Like Gnedich in this passage, Dostoevsky perceives Homer as the primary "organizer" (in Dostoevsky's terms) of the Greek world and as the spokesman for nature. Like Gnedich, Dostoevsky takes a historical approach to the *Iliad* but also regards it as an expression of universal truths. Both Gnedich and Dostoevsky were Christians, and as part of their argument for the universal importance of Homer, both of them connect him to Christianity as an earlier but legitimate stage of religious consciousness.[9] Dostoevsky, in his letter to Mikhail, goes so far as to compare Homer to Christ, but Gnedich, in the eloquent introduction to his translation, equates Homeric to Old Testament times and Zeus to Jehovah:

> This simplicity of narrative, life, mores, expressed in the *Iliad*, and many special qualities of the poetry disclosed in it remind us forcefully of the deep antiquity of the East, and the poems of Homer are close, in a literary sense, to the writings of the Bible. ... Zeus himself, usually seated on Mount Ida amidst thunder and lightning, dispensing good to mankind in general in the ancient generation of the Dardans (Trojans), but often aiding one against the other, the tribe of Anchises against the successors of Priam, is the very same God of a family as was Jehovah in the history of the forefathers.[10]

Dostoevsky's reception of Homer in the letter to his brother, probably influenced by this passage by Gnedich, already provides clues about how to interpret the scene in *Crime and Punishment*. The combination of Greek and Jewish elements in the watchman could be a reference to the old, pre-Christian world.[11] The term *kalancha*, which is of Turkish origin and originally referred to Ottoman defensive towers, provides a third such reference that is pre-Christian in spirit if not in historical time. The hotel in which Svidrigailov spends his last night is the Adrianople, a reference to the Battle of Adrianople (or Hadrianopolis), and therefore a reference to the late Roman Empire and

---

9 On Gnedich's Christianized Homer, see Mariia Maiofis "'Ruka vremën,' 'Bozhestvennyi Platon' i gomerovskaya rifma v russkoi literature pervoi poloviny XIX veka: Kommentarii k neprochitannoi poeme N. I. Gnedicha," *Novoe literaturnoe obozrenie* 60 (2003): 145–70.

10 See http://az.lib.ru/g/gnedich_n_i/text_0080.shtml.

11 My interpretation of the scene as philosophical-historical rather than merely realistic is bolstered by the fact, noted by Katz (*Neither with Them*, 164), that, contrary to his usual practice, in this scene Dostoevsky uses the term *evrei* for the Jewish fireman soldier rather than *zhid*. Furthermore, the watchman's sorrowful expression (*vekovechnaya briuzglivaya skorb*; pt. 6, ch. 6; *PSS*, 6:394) connects him to the archetype of the Wandering Jew.

its decline.[12] In this episode, the pre-Christian world is presented as degraded and even negative. As in Gogol's "Overcoat," the watchman does not protect or attempt to save a man in trouble: he first tells Svidrigailov to move on, and then is paralyzed at the sight of his gun.

This parodic and negative version of the old world is not Dostoevsky's final word on it in *Crime and Punishment* or elsewhere, however. To follow the thread further, we turn to the article that Dostoevsky published in 1861 entitled "Mr. –bov and the Question of Art," in which he discusses the rejection by positivist writers, like N. A. Dobroliubov (the "–bov" of the title), of the great classics of past civilizations as irrelevant in the present day.[13] The *Iliad* is his example of such a text. Dostoevsky makes fun of the application of materialist standards to determine its value:

> And for that reason, how, for instance, would you define, measure, and weigh what use the *Iliad* has been to all humanity? Where, when, and in which circumstances was it useful, in what way, finally, precisely what influence has it had on which nations, in which moment of their development, and precisely how much was there of this influence (let's say in pounds, pouds, arshins, kilometres, degrees, and so on and so on)?[14]

Dostoevsky insists in this article that "beauty is always useful,"[15] but he defends the *Iliad* on more specific grounds. He claims that it is "useful"—the most important criterion for the utilitarian critics—precisely in addressing the most pressing issues of the day:

> Even now the *Iliad* sends a shiver through the soul. This is an epic of such powerful, full life, of such an elevated moment in the life of a nation, and, we note also, the life of such a great tribe, that in our time—a time of strivings, of struggles, of waverings and of faith (because our time is a time of faith), in a word, in our time of heightened life, the eternal harmony that is incarnated in the *Iliad* can act on the soul too decisively. Our spirit is now at its most receptive, the influence of beauty, harmony, and force can grandly and beneficially act on it, act *usefully*, infuse with energy, support our strengths. That

---

12 *PSS*, 6:388. The battle was part of the Gothic War (376–82) and "is often considered the start of the final collapse of the Western Roman Empire in the 5th century"; see http://en.wikipedia.org/wiki/Battle_of_Adrianople.

13 *PSS*, 18:269; "G-n –bov i vopros ob iskusstve."

14 *PSS*, 18:95.

15 *PSS*, 18:95.

which is powerful loves power; whoever believes, that one is strong, and we believe, and most importantly, we want to believe.[16]

In another article from the same year, Dostoevsky identifies Achilles as a Greek type and the *Iliad* in its entirety as "the national epic of ancient Greece."[17] As he sees it, Homeric times and the Russia of 1861 are both peak moments in the national lives of their respective peoples. As during the Trojan War, Russia in 1861 is characterized by striving, battle, fluctuations, and religious faith. The *Iliad* is powerful and alive, on the one hand, and characterized by "eternal harmony" on the other: "That which is powerful loves power." Because of the combined crisis and opportunity in Russian society brought about by the impending emancipation of the serfs, the Russian reader in 1861 is maximally open both to the power of Homer's epic and to what Dostoevsky calls its beauty and harmony. The "thrill" that the *Iliad* causes in the soul of the Russian reader is the effect of the release of energy directly from Homer into that reader. Hence, Dostoevsky says, Homeric energy can "support our forces" in a way that is "useful."

This dynamic is not present in the scene with Svidrigailov and the watchman, where all reeks of death and decay. It is worth keeping in mind, however, that although Svidrigailov is not "useful" for Russian society, he is a representative of its potential power. He is related to Stavrogin from *The Demons* in this respect, though Svidrigailov, unlike Stavrogin, does good *and* evil.

The scene of Svidrigailov's suicide needs to be compared to the scene in Siberia in the epilogue, in which Raskolnikov, now a convict, gazes across a "wide and empty river" at a pastoral landscape:

> Raskolnikov went out of the shed up to the bank, sat down on logs piled up near the shed, and started to gaze at the wide and empty river. From the high bank a broad landscape opened up. From the other bank, far away, came a faint sound of singing. There, in the immensity of the steppe, flooded with sunlight, the black yurts of the nomads were barely visible dots. Freedom was there, and other people lived there who were not at all those on this side of the river; there it was as though time had stopped, and the age of Abraham and his flocks had not yet passed. Raskolnikov sat on and he gazed motionlessly and

---

16   *PSS*, 18:95–96; emphasis in original.
17   *PSS*, 19:9. See "A Series of Articles on Russian Literature, No. IV. Book-learning and Literacy, Article Two" ["Riad statei o russkoi literature. IV. Knizhnost' i gramotnost'. Stat'ia vtoraia"].

without interruption; his mind had wandered into day-dreams; he thought of nothing, but an anguished longing disturbed and tormented him.[18]

The shed with the kiln from which Raskolnikov emerges is associated with hard labor and imprisonment. The river represents historical time flowing between Raskolnikov and the seemingly timeless but distant biblical setting. Raskolnikov is literally mesmerized in this scene: thought turns into vision and yearning. He is in that state of pure receptivity described in "Mr. –bov and the Question of Art," but he also feels utterly separate from what he sees: the people there are "not at all those on this side of the river."

In Svidrigailov's suicide, "Achilles" is first indifferent to Svidrigailov, and then tells him repeatedly that he is in the wrong place. When Sonya Marmeladova appears on the river bank and touches Raskolnikov, he falls before her and embraces her knees. Sonya reaches out to Raskolnikov to draw him back to life. In the first case, the symbols of antiquity jangle falsely and inappropriately. In the second one, the seemingly ancient scene pours energy into Raskolnikov's soul that expresses itself by "yearning" (*toska*) that Sonya's appearance and touch then catalyze into Christian resurrection.

The character in *Crime and Punishment* who marshals his energy for one grand deed is Raskolnikov. As is well understood and accepted, Svidrigailov is intended as one double of Raskolnikov—Svidrigailov is attracted to Raskolnikov and visits him while he is wrestling with the consequences of his deed. We recall Dostoevsky's caution in the passage from "Mr. –bov and the Question of Art" that the *Iliad* can "too decisively act on the soul."[19] Raskolnikov, in fact, is an example of a great-souled man, an Achilles who has been affected by a mixture of offended honor, moral indignation, and eternal standards of justice that can lead to terrible crimes.[20] I'm not suggesting that Raskolnikov has been reading

---

18 Epilogue, ch. 2; *PSS*, 6:421. Translations of *Crime and Punishment* are versions of the Jessie Coulson translation—*Crime and Punishment*, Norton Critical Edition, ed. George Gibian (New York: W. W. Norton, 1964)—which I have modified in a few places for clarity.

19 See *PSS*, 18:96, quoted above.

20 V. G. Belinsky reviewed Gnedich's translation in 1839, and Egunov, in *Gomer v russkikh perevodakh*, 295, points out that he interprets Achilles's weeping by the sea in book 1 as motivated by love of justice (*spravedlivost'*—a word that does not appear in the scene) rather than at his loss of Briseis. Dostoevsky may have read Belinsky's unsigned review, which appeared in *Notes of the Fatherland* in 1839 (vol. 6, no. 11, pt. 7, 146–48). For Belinsky's review, see Belinsky, *Polnoe sobranie sochinenii*, 3:307–9.

Homer, but I do believe that he conceives of himself, and he is intended by Dostoevsky, as a hero in the mold of an Achilles or Ajax. His first name and patronymic are meant to indicate this. "Rodion" is the Russian version of the name "Herodion," which is related to the Greek word for "hero," and the name "Roman" refers to a Roman citizen. In his reaction to the crisis of his times, Raskolnikov is caught between the standards and moral organization of Homer *or* Christ, between the rage and offended honor of an Achilles and the humility of a Sonya. His rage leads to murders that Dostoevsky describes with the surgical efficiency, brevity, and mention of body parts and motion characteristic of the depictions of death in battle in the *Iliad*.[21]

---

21 Here are the two murders as described in pt. 1, ch. 7 (*PSS*, 6:63, 65):

> Удар пришелся в самое темя, чему способствовал ее малый рост. Она вскрикнула, но очень слабо, и вдруг вся осела к полу, хотя и успела еще поднять обе руки к голове. В одной руке еще продолжала держать 'заклад.' Тут он изо всей силы ударил раз и другой, всё обухом и всё по темени. Кровь хлынула, как из опрокинутого стакана, и тело повалилось навзничь.

> Because she was so short the axe struck her full on the crown of the head. She cried out, but very feebly, and sank in a heap to the floor, still with enough strength left to raise both hands to her head. One of them still held the "pledge." Then he struck her again and yet again, with all his strength, always with the blunt side of the axe, and always on the crown of the head. Blood poured out as if from an overturned glass and the body toppled over on its back.

And,

> Она только чуть-чуть приподняла свою свободную левую руку, далеко не до лица, и медленно протянула ее к нему вперед, как бы отстраняя его. Удар пришелся прямо по черепу, острием, и сразу прорубил всю верхнюю часть лба, почти до темени. Она так и рухнулась."

> She only raised her free left hand a little and slowly stretched it out towards him as though she were trying to push him away. The blow fell on her skull, splitting it open from the top of the forehead almost to the crown of the head, and felling her instantly.

Compare these killings to two of the dozens of such deaths from Gnedich's translation. For the English, I use the Lattimore translation: *The Iliad of Homer*, ed. and trans. Richmond Lattimore (Chicago: University of Chicago Press, 1962).

(Antiloches kills the Trojan charioteer Mydon; *Iliad* 5.584–86)

> Прянул младой Антилох и мечом в висок его грянул;
> Он, тяжело воздохнувший, на прах с колесницы прекрасной
> Рухнулся вниз головой и, упавший на темя и плечи.

> Antilochos charging drove the sword into his temple,
> So that gasping he dropped from the carefully wrought chariot
> Headlong, driven deep in the dust his neck and shoulders;

In his conversation in book 6 with Raskolnikov, Svidrigailov characterizes him over and over again as an "idealist" in the Schillerian mold. In the same idealist vein, he calls him "a citizen and human being":

> I understand (but don't trouble yourself: don't say much if you don't want to). I understand what thoughts are on your mind: moral ones, are they? Questions of a citizen and a human being? But you should put them aside; what are they to you now? He-he! Is it that you are still a citizen and a human being?[22]

Raskolnikov's sister, Dunya, is of the same ilk. Had she been born in the early Christian era, according to Svidrigalov she could have been a Christian martyr or desert ascetic saint.[23] It is this Dunya whom Svidrigailov considers godlike[24] and whose assurance that she does not and cannot love him finally prompts him to choose suicide. Unlike Raskolnikov and his sister, Svidrigailov has no goal in life upon which to focus his enormous energy. He explains this in his conversation with Raskolnikov:

> Believe me, if only I were something—a landowner, say, or a father, an officer in the Lancers, a photographer, a journalist ... but I'm nothing. I have no profession. Sometimes it is almost boring.[25]

Hence Svidrigailov squanders his energy on sensual pleasure and depravity; hence the broadness of his nature that Dunya ascribes to him as he lurches from evil to good and back.[26] Because he is nonetheless himself human, he yearns for an ideal, and wants to possess the godlike Dunya.

(Hector kills Ajax's friend Lycophron; *Iliad* 15.433–35)

Гектор его, близ Аякса стоящего, в череп над ухом
Дротом ударил убийственным: в прах он, с кормы корабельной
Рухнувшись, навзничь пал, и его сокрушилася крепость.

Hektor struck him in the head above the ear with the sharp bronze
As he stood next to Aias, so that Lykophron sprawling
Dropped from the ship's stern to the ground, and his strength was broken.

22 Pt. 6, ch. 5; *PSS*, 6:373.
23 Pt. 6, ch. 4; *PSS*, 6:365.
24 Pt. 6, ch. 5; *PSS*, 6:377.
25 Pt. 6, ch. 3; *PSS*, 6:359.
26 Pt. 6, ch. 5; *PSS*, 6:378: "The minds of the Russian people in general are broad, Avdotya Romanovna, like their country, and extraordinarily inclined to the fantastic and the chaotic [...] You were always reproaching me with that breadth of mind."

If, as Edward Wasiolek asserts, Svidrigailov is a "bronze man,"[27] the Napoleon beyond good and evil whom Raskolnikov aspires to be, this Russian Napoleon indebted to literary predecessors, like Pushkin's Hermann (*The Queen of Spades*) and Lermontov's Pechorin (*Hero of Our Time*), has already moved beyond the dynamics of power that motivated Napoleon the historical actor.[28] Svidrigailov blames this condition on a lack of sacred traditions in Russia that would properly anchor the Russian soul:

> In our educated Russian society, Avdotya Romanovna, there are no sacred traditions: at most someone may possibly construct some for himself out of books … or deduce something from old chronicles. But such people are the more learned sort, and, you know, all more or less simpletons, so that a man of the world would think their procedures quite unbecoming to himself. However, you know my general opinions; I make it a rule to condemn absolutely nobody, since I myself am a do-nothing and I intend to remain one.[29]

Though he seeks goals or possessions that can galvanize his restless energy, Svidrigailov is too worldly to cook up new traditions out of old ones: hence his egotistical sensualism, hedonism, and moral relativism. In Dostoevsky's discussion in 1861 in "Mr. –bov and the Question of Art" about the criticism by utilitarian thinkers of practitioners of "pure art" who merely imitate ancient traditions, he goes on to agree that such imitators are "foul" (*gnusno*):

> Really, what is foul in the engagement with the *Iliad* and its imitation in art according to the opponents of pure art? It's that we, like dead men, like those who have lived ourselves out, or like cowards, who are afraid of our future life, finally—like indifferent traitors of those of us in whom there is still life force and who are surging ahead, like those who are enervated to the point of torpor, to not being able to understand that there is life among us—we throw ourselves into the epoch of the *Iliad* and in this way create for ourselves an artificial reality, life that we have not created and we have not lived, a dream, empty and tempting. And like base people, we borrow, we steal our lives from times long past and we turn sour in the enjoyment of art like useless imitators! You will agree yourself that the direction of utilitarians

---

27 Edward Wasiolek, *The Notebooks for "Crime and Punishment" by Fyodor Dostoevsky* (Chicago: University of Chicago Press, 1967), 8.

28 See pt. 3, ch. 5 (*PSS*, 6:204) for the reference to Russian Napoleons by Porfiry, and the suggestion by Zametov that an aspiring Napoleon killed the pawnbroker.

29 Pt. 6, ch. 5; *PSS*, 6:378.

from the point of view of such reproaches is to the highest degree noble and elevated. It's for this reason that we so sympathize with them; and for this reason we wish also to respect them.[30]

The aesthetes whom Dostoevsky describes here turn to the past in order to avoid the chaos of the present and the future. The "simpletons" whom Svidrigailov disdains do the same thing, and hence he calls them "dead men." Strangely enough, however, Svidrigailov seems like a dead man or walking corpse himself: his face is a mask, and his gaze, especially, is "too heavy [massive] and motionless."[31]

Crime and Punishment illustrates Dostoevsky's position as declared in his "Mr. –bov and the Question of Art": "That which is powerful loves power; whoever believes, that one is strong, and we believe, and most importantly, we want to believe." Strength to commit great deeds (rather than merely brutal self-serving ones) requires faith. In Dostoevsky's reading, a conventional nine-teenth-century one in this respect, Homer's Greeks were like today's Christians in their unshakable religiosity. The harmony and life-loving strength of their culture come from their belief in the gods and their obedience to them. There-fore only Christian believers can truly access that strength today. Since neither Svidrigailov nor Raskolnikov in the lead-up to and aftermath of each man's grand deed possesses faith, neither can be a Greek hero. Svidrigailov, like his successor Stavrogin, cannot overcome his deep cynicism, and his final descen-dant in Dostoevsky's prose is therefore Ivan Karamazov's devil, who also mocks powerful cultural symbols, and who sneers at Ivan for thinking like a citizen and a human being, when his idea could and perhaps should liberate him from such quaint idealistic notions. In the case of Raskolnikov—who like his descen-dant Ivan remains on the fence between good and evil, and whose future, like Ivan's, is uncertain—before he can access his hidden power, he must discover the link between power and love, the Greeks and Christianity, as he does in the scene in Siberia.

As for Svidrigailov, like those aesthetes who imitate Homer without imbibing Homeric energy needed to accomplish today's tasks, in his self-indulgent hedonism he has opted out of the turmoil of present-day Russia. He is an ironic bystander who snickers at its complexity and contradictions. He is a gentry parasite, a "do-nothing" who no longer plays any role in the shaping of

---

30 *PSS*, 18:96.
31 Pt. 6, ch. 3; *PSS*, 6:357.

society—and does not want to do so. His cynical outlook empties the most powerful symbols of the past—whether Greek, Old Testament, Ottoman, or Roman—of meaning. He associates one of the most beautiful cultural icons in Dostoevsky's pantheon—Raphael's *Sistine Madonna*—with the young girl to whom he is supposedly engaged and whom he might have raped and ruined had he not killed himself.[32] Icons of strength related to Homer and the Old Testament are linked with the only grand deed of which Svidrigailov is capable, his own suicide, but they appear in debased, ironic form.

---

32 Pt. 6, ch. 4; *PSS*, 6:369.

XX

Raskolnikov and the Aqedah (Isaac's Binding)

Olga Meerson

Many offensive quotes can be used to expose Dostoevsky's anti-Semitic prejudices. Like some anti-Semites, Dostoevsky tends to usurp the uniqueness of Jews' identity, experience, messianic missionism, and relationship with God, claiming these features as those of his own or of his own group. Unlike most anti-Semites, however, rather than merely appropriating them for his nation, the God-fearing Russians, he identifies with specific Jews, very personally. This makes him a Jew wanna-be much more than a Jew-hater—but some may still justly consider these to be two sides of the same coin.

This love–hate attitude points to an interesting notion in his poetics, and even his Christianity. His identification with the Jews is more poetically productive, and morally and theologically significant, than his hatred of them. Paradoxically, in some cases, the only key to interpreting both Dostoevsky's faith and his poetics is his personal identification with Jewish figures important for the Jews themselves. This identification might be a matter of life-and-death importance for the writer.

We may notice, for example, not only that Isai Fomich, in *Notes from a Dead House*, symbolically presides over a scene very much like the hierarchy of hell—to which the narrator Gorianchikov compares the bath-house with its shelves and tiers—but also that he symbolizes freedom, a very important motif in the

Notes as such. Isai Fomich is free to come and go from the territory of the Siberian prison because he is permitted to attend Jewish worship outside the territory. More importantly still, unbeknownst to the prejudiced and unsuspecting narrator, Isai Fomich cites a key Jewish song about liberation. According to the narrator Gorianchikov, Isai Fomich claims that the song was sung by all the Jews as they left Egypt. Gorianchikov himself, of course, hears merely gibberish—a meaningless "la-la-la-la." But if we assume the song could be meaningful, we may guess that it is "Dai-dayeinu" (די–דיינו), indeed sung during the Passover Seder by the Jews. The song says, in a rather apophatic manner, that each step God grants us (the Jews) on our way to liberation, even taken separately and not followed by the rest of the steps, would be "enough," "enough for us":

> Isai Fomich … starts to sing, in a high treble, for the whole barrack to hear: "La-la-la-la-la!"—a song without words, to some absurd and ridiculous tune, the only one he sang all the while he was in prison. Lately, when he became more closely acquainted with me, he assured me under oath that it was the same song and the same tune that all six hundred thousand Jews, big and small, sang as they crossed the Red Sea, and that every Jew was supposed to sing it at the moment of triumph and victory over his enemies.[1]

But even Gorianchikov is impressed by the liberating effect of Isai Fomich's prayer—ridiculous and ecstatic, it renders the Jew oblivious of all external observers, including the representatives of oppressive authorities. The hostile and prejudiced Gorianchikov, of course, believes that Isai Fomich is pretending and making a show of his prayer and that he follows a very precise script provided by his Jewish prayer book—specifying when to rejoice, when to feel upset, and when to make a noble face "shouting and grimacing."[2] What he describes to us, however, is the praying Jew's defiance of earthly authority, Egyptian or Russian. Once when the Jew prayed, the major came in. Isai Fomich continued to follow his prayer script by grimacing the major straight in the face, but when reminded of that by his admiring fellow inmates, the Jew was genuinely surprised:

—"What major?"

—"What do you mean what major? Didn't you see him?"

1 Fyodor Dostoevsky, *Notes from a Dead House*, trans. Richard Pevear and Larissa Volokhonsky (New York: Alfred Knopf, 2015), 117.
2 Ibid., 118.

—"No."

—"Why, he was standing two feet away, right in front of your face."

But Isai Fomich began to assure me in the most serious way that he had decidedly not seen any major and that while saying these prayers he falls into some sort of ecstasy, so that he no longer sees or hears anything that happens around him.[3]

Isai Fomich is not the main point of my investigation, but even this case demonstrates a feature of Dostoevsky's polyphony important to us: the described character is sincere, while the describing one, albeit a seemingly reliable narrator, mistrusts and disdains him. Gorianchikov is an unreliable narrator who seems reliable. He implicates us in believing Isai Fomich is insincere. Dostoevsky, on the other hand, implicates us in the *wrong* of that narrator's vision. Of course, we do see Isai Fomich through the anti-Semitic prism of Gorianchikov, but this does not make us or Gorianchikov see right. Dostoevsky himself, however, may or may not subscribe to his narrator's anti-Semitic prejudice. He shows us more than his narrator understands. The Jewish character symbolizes too many things important for Dostoevsky himself for us to believe that this character is a mere caricature.[4]

But, even if very significant for Dostoevsky, Isai Fomich is at most a complicated Jewish role model for the writer. In what follows, I will discuss a case of Dostoevsky's own real and complete identification with an important—and sacrificial—act of faith by a Jewish character.

Isaac and Raskolnikov—What Is at Stake for Dostoevsky?

The Aqedah: Isaac and Dostoevsky

Following his own mock execution, Dostoevsky completely identified with a mortal Jew—not merely with the immortal Christ—who survived his own death. The Jew was Isaac, Abraham's first-born son, from whom all Jews, including Jesus Christ, were to descend, after he had survived the experience of

---

3 Ibid., 117–18ff.

4 In my most recent book, *Personalizm kak poetika: Literaturnyi mir glazami ego obitatelei* (St. Petersburg: Pushkinskii dom, 2009), chap. 9, 330–49, I investigate the same split between the actual author—in that case, Nikolai Leskov—and his anti-Semitic narrator, in Leskov's long short story (his *povest'*) "The Bishop's Judgment" ("Vladychnyi sud").

his intended death. Like Isaac, Dostoevsky survived his own imminent death. Readers, admirers, and detractors have linked Dostoevsky's mock execution to the context of his discovery of Christ and His sacrifice. Although prefiguring Christ for Christians, including Dostoevsky, Isaac also matters as a role model on his own, for both Christians and Jews: Isaac was a mortal human, but, at the time of his imminent death, an innocent boy. For the Jews, the notion of him facing a sacrifical death was taboo, hence the "binding" (עקדה), not the "sacrifice" of Isaac.

As the biblical prototype of Dostoevsky's own survival of his mock execution, the episode of Isaac's binding (עקדה) has informed Dostoevsky's consciousness. It has also informed a very important subtext to at least one episode in Dostoevsky's fiction. To the best of my knowledge, Dostoevsky's readers have completely neglected this subtext. Yet in the case in question, the subtext provides an important clue to the meaning of both the episode and the whole novel it appears in: without this subtext, the novel's denouement appears somewhat puzzling. I mean the epilogue to *Crime and Punishment*. Dostoevsky, rather unexpectedly, likens Raskolnikov to Isaac, bound and about to be sacrificed by his father to God.[5]

The Aqedah: Isaac and Raskolnikov

Let us now examine this key episode in *Crime and Punishment* in the light of Gen. 22:1–13 as its subtext:

> Again it was a clear warm day. Early in the morning, at about six o'clock, [Raskolnikov] went to work in the shed on the riverbank, where gypsum was baked in a kiln and afterwards ground.[6] Only *three workers went there. One of them took a guard and went back* to the fortress to get *some tool;* the second began splitting firewood and *putting it into the kiln.*[7] Raskolnikov walked out of the shed and right to the bank, *sat down on some logs piled*

---

5 Admittedly, Christians call this episode, from Gen. 22, the "sacrifice of Isaac." The sacrificial elements of this episode and its symbolism matter very much, to us and to Dostoevsky, but the Jewish name for the episode—the "binding of Isaac" (עקדת יצחק)—is also important. After all, Isaac was never sacrificed. So the Jewish name emphasizes his *survival* of his own death.

6 In the original, "Where a kiln was *built/arranged* to bake gypsum and grind afterwards" (**устроена** была обжигательная печь).

7 Literally, "piling it up in the kiln" (накладывать в печь)—so the image, in Russian, is a pileup of logs.

near the shed, and began looking at the wide, desolate river. From the high bank a wide view of the surrounding countryside opened out. A barely audible song came from the far bank opposite. There, on the boundless sunbathed steppe, nomadic yurts could be seen, like barely visible black specks. There was freedom, there a different people lived, quite unlike those here, there time itself seemed to stop, *as if the centuries of Abraham and his flocks had not passed.*

Raskolnikov sat and stared fixedly, not tearing his eyes away; *his thought turned to reverie, to contemplation; he was not thinking of anything* but some anguish troubled and tormented him.

Suddenly Sonya was beside him. … *How it happened he himself did not know but suddenly* it was as if something had lifted him and flung him down at her feet. … They still had seven years more … but *he was risen and he knew it, he felt it fully with the whole of his renewed being.*[8] (all emphasis is mine)

The episode itself seems to bear no relation to the story of Raskolnikov's alleged repentance or conversion, or to anything about his inner life. Furthermore, no details of this episode "belong" in the context of the epilogue story itself. Yet they are numerous, and meticulously narrated. Such details include the mention of the following:

1. a kiln—an outdoor hearth situated on a high place, so that one needs to climb up to it, really, very much resembling an altar for burnt offerings, and a necessary but forgotten tool;
2. firewood logs piled up and prepared for burning in this outdoor contraption;
3. three people, besides the main protagonist, mounting the high, relatively faraway place with the outdoor hearth;
4. two of them coming back down, or sent away, after only one other and the protagonist continue to go/remain up above;
5. one other person remaining on top, or making it to the top, besides the protagonist, who piles up and prepares the firewood;
6. the protagonist situated on top of the pile of logs;

---

8 *Crime and Punishment*, trans. Richard Pevear and Larissa Volokhonsky, 549–50, Kindle ed. (New York: Vintage, 1992), 1099–1100. All the citations for the Russian edition of *Crime and Punishment* are according to *Polnoe sobranie sochinenii v tridtsati tomakh* [*PSS*], ed. V. G. Bazanov et al. (Leningrad: Nauka, 1972–1990); hereafter cited as *PSS* by volume and page.

7. the protagonist being unaware of the significance of his being situated there; and

8. the mention of Abraham's flocks and his "centuries" (века Авраама и стад его);

9. the protagonist's resulting resurrection

Beyond some vague sense of a workday dragging rather slowly, and Raskolnikov's—or the narrator's—equally vague nostalgia for the long-gone biblical era, this passage seems to have no purpose in Raskolnikov's "story." It is not well embedded in the context of the narration. All the more imperative it then becomes for us to understand why this story is here, complete with so many details. The less they belong to the context of the story, the more apparently they belong to its biblical subtext, Gen. 22: 1–13, the sacrifice, or rather binding, of Isaac. We may, therefore, safely assume that the subtext of Isaac's binding—that is, the protagonist's intended and annulled sacrifice—appears for one and only one purpose—instead of "making sense" in the context, it makes sense *out* of the context—providing a valid clue to Raskolnikov's internal development at that point in the epilogue.

To further understand the significance of this clue, let us first try to locate all the relevant elements of the Genesis passage as we find them in the previously quoted passage from the epilogue to *Crime and Punishment*. I use the numbers from the list of these details in the enumerated list above (verse numbers are superscripted):

Gen. 22:1–13:

1. And it came to pass after these things, that God did tempt Abraham, and said unto him, "Abraham": and he said, "Behold, here I am." 2 And he said, "Take now thy son, thine only son Isaac, whom thou lovest, and get thee into the land of Moriah; and offer him there for a burnt offering (1) upon one of the mountains (1) which I will tell thee of." 3 And Abraham (8) rose up early in the morning, and saddled his ass, and took two of his young men with him, and Isaac his son, (3) and clave the wood (2; 5) for the burnt offering (1), and rose up, and went unto the place (3) of which God had told him. 4 Then on the third day Abraham (8) lifted up his eyes, and saw the place afar off (3). 5 And Abraham (8) said unto his young men, "Abide ye here with the ass; and I and the lad (3; 4) will go yonder and worship, and come again to you." 6 And Abraham took the wood of the burnt offering (5), and laid it upon Isaac his son; and he took the fire in his hand, and a knife (1);

and they went both of them together (4). 7 And Isaac spake unto Abraham his father (8), and said, "My father": and he said, "Here am I, my son." And he said, "Behold the fire and the wood (1; 2): but where is the lamb for a burnt offering?" (7)

⁸And Abraham said, "My son, *God will provide himself a lamb for a burnt offering* (7): *so they went both of them together* (4). ⁹

And they came to the place which God had told him of; and Abraham *built* an altar there, and *laid the wood in order* (2; 5) and bound Isaac his son, and laid him on the altar *upon the wood* (6; 7). ¹⁰

And *Abraham* (8) stretched forth his hand, and took *the knife* (1) to slay his son. ¹¹

And the angel of the LORD called unto him out of heaven, and said, "*Abraham, Abraham*" (8): and he said, "*Here am I*" (8). ¹²

And He said, "*Lay not thine hand* (9) upon the lad, neither do thou any thing unto him: (9) for now I know that thou fearest God, seeing thou hast not withheld thy son, thine only son from Me." ¹³

And *Abraham* (8) lifted up his eyes, and looked, and behold behind him a ram caught in a thicket by his horns: and *Abraham* (8) went and took the ram, and offered him up for a burnt offering *in the stead of his son* (9). (KJV) (all emphasis is mine)

Verse 9 of Gen. 22:1–13 deserves a special mention for an interesting parallel between this verse, in the Russian synodal translation—which Dostoevsky was one of the first Russian writers to read and quote from,[9] and Dostoevsky's own text: "and Abraham *built* an altar there" (**устроил** жертвенник).[10] In the relevant passage in the epilogue, the narrator says about the arrangement for the kiln: "была **устроена** печь." Unfortunately, translators—not only Pevear and Volokhonsky—ignore the importance of conveying this rather marked participle invoking the equally marked verb "устроил" in the Russian synodal text of Gen 22:9. Of course, likening an outdoor kiln to an altar may seem a little far-fetched, but using a participle deriving from a rather marked verb for making an altar seals the parallel between that kiln and Abraham's altar.

---

9 Before it, the translation was not available, only the Church Slavonic text of the Bible, to be quoted in Russian. Russian writers, including Pushkin, read and referred to the Church Slavonic text alongside the French.

10 "и **устроил там Авраам жертвенник, разложил дрова** и, связав сына своего Исаака, положил его на жертвенник поверх дров."

Just as in verse 9, the word *there* (там) figures prominently in the relevant epilogue excerpt where the pronominal adverb is even repeated four times: "*There*, on the boundless sunbathed steppe, nomadic yurts could be seen, like barely visible black specks. *There* was freedom, **there** a different people lived, quite unlike those here, **there** time itself seemed to stop, as if the centuries of Abraham and his flocks had not passed."[11]

This repeated pronominal adverb там supports and reinforces the importance of the general tone invoking the Bible and its chronotope: the word points to a mystical realm.[12]

Back to Raskolnikov as Unrepentant Sinner: Why Isaac?

Having established the parallel between Gen. 22:1–13 and the relevant excerpt in the epilogue to *Crime and Punishment*, we can consider how this intertext clarifies the otherwise inexplicable aspects of the epilogue and of the novel as a whole. The epilogue indeed presents a stumbling block to even the friendliest and most supportive Dostoevsky reader. We all feel perplexed: Raskolnikov's repentance seems belated, in relation to his actual formal confession, unmotivated and therefore artificial and unconvincing. He formally admits to his crime but feels no repentance. In the epilogue, Raskolnikov remains unrepentant despite all the ordeals that he undergoes and Sonia undergoes on his behalf. The reader feels uncertain about how and why Raskolnikov, who has been impenitent up to now, suddenly repents. What is so special about that moment, with the kiln, the firewood, and all the rest?

The narrator provides no plausible psychological motivation. In fact, the narrator seems to deliberately present Raskolnikov's repentance as incomprehensible, both morally and psychologically. No words narrate it as a process of reason or anything logical. In the epilogue, Raskolnikov has nightmares

---

11 "**Там**, в облитой солнцем необозримой степи, чуть приметными точками чернелись кочевые юрты. **Там** была свобода и жили другие люди, совсем не похожие на здешних, **там** как бы самое время остановилось, точно не прошли еще века **Авраама** и стад его" (emphasis is mine).

12 A possible Hebrew etymology for the word "heaven," or "sky," or whatever was created in the beginning, matters. The word in Hebrew is "HaShammayim" (השמים), the dual for "sham" (שם), which means "there." The dual number, in Hebrew morphology, especially in the biblical Hebrew, is a way to form abstract nouns. In that case, the word "heaven" literally means "the there," or even "there-ness."

about ideas as viruses, remains an unrepentant nonbeliever, patiently yet dispassionately endures the ensuing justified disdain of his fellow inmates—the same ones who love Sonia!—and then, one day, goes to sit on a bunch of wood logs on a riverbank, and gets up a new person, full of love and pity for Sonia, repentant for his crime, and even his ideas, visibly redeemed, aware of being resurrected, and capable of a new life. This does not sound too plausible indeed.

Why does Dostoevsky make no other path to repentance available to Raskolnikov—besides his sitting on a bunch of logs mounted on a riverbank, contemplating the olden days of Abraham and his flocks? Why would no other way, besides situating Raskolnikov in the position of Isaac, work for his sincere repentance? Why would his identification with Isaac lead to his reform?

Well into his prison term and almost through the whole epilogue, Raskolnikov persists in the idea that his main failure was not ideological or moral but in the fact that he, personally, was unfit for the task, being incapable of what truly great men are capable of—of killing cold-bloodedly. In his dialectic ruminations within himself, he claims that his "conscience is at peace." He is even ready to pay for his violation of the law "with his own head," but at no point then does he feel any connection between "the letter of the law" and his own conscience.[13]

The whole novel dwells on the difference and discrepancy between Raskolnikov's conscience and the dictates of formal law, and, more importantly, on the difference between his seemingly impossible true repentance and his formal confession and subsequent punishment by Siberian exile. Instead of resolving this discrepancy, the epilogue, in fact, seems to exacerbate it. If, so late into the epilogue, Raskolnikov continues to insist, very consciously, that his conscience is at peace and all he is doing is serving term for violating a "mere" social law, the reader has difficulty believing that any sincere repentance is possible for such a person.

Until the Aqedah-like scene, Raskolnikov keeps reasoning. In this episode, however, he no longer reasons. The identification with Isaac's binding makes him feel, not think. Like Isaac, he experiences being prepared for sacrifice, not thinking about it. The reader also can only experience the events described in the episode, without consciously realizing their significance. Up until that moment, the narration was also that of reasoning—it was Raskolnikov-centric. So much

---

13   See *PSS*, 6:417.

has this narration implicated us in both condemning Raskolnikov and thinking like him that, in fact, we tend to mistrust or ignore any type of discourse the same narrator may now adopt in the same epilogue. Although this new discourse may in fact suggest a sincere repentance, to the reader it sounds artificial and unmotivated. But to what end, in this specific case, does the narrator implicate *us* in the idea that Raskolnikov is incapable of repentance? Perhaps the only possible answer to this question is the specific nature of repentance that a rationalizing ideologue like Raskolnikov himself would require. To counter the ideological nature of the protagonist's crime, his repentance should probably not be contained in words or ideas but should be much more existential, perhaps consist of a sensory experience less conscious than his life hitherto, or unconscious altogether. But since Dostoevsky continues to implicate his readers in his protagonist's world, this implies that, on a rational level, the relevant passage would also sound illogical and unmotivated to the reader.

After so much show of Raskolnikov's moral callousness, the reader has been desensitized to any signs of his possible repentance. No rational explanation would affect the reader by now, just as no rational argument would liberate the character from his own prison of ideological labyrinths. After all, "Dostoevsky's reader is an implicated reader."[14] In order to trust Raskolnikov's repentance as genuine, we also, like him, need to experience it rather than think about it. This river-bank passage, preceding rather than seeming to adequately explain Raskolnikov's repentance and regeneration, seems strange and inexplicable to the reader as much as, perhaps, to Raskolnikov himself. Such things can be narrated in one and only way—being shown rather than explained.

This passage, therefore, aims to affect our senses, not our intellect—aesthetically rather than ideologically. It is a sensory experience, rather than intellectual reasoning, which also leads the protagonist to repentance. To implicate us in the reality of sensory experience of Raskolnikov, an inveterate and self-manipulating intellectual, Dostoevsky models and narrates Raskolnikov's repentance on his own terms, namely, avoiding all notions inaccessible to his protagonist, or, in Bakhtin's terms, without "looking him in the back."[15] Inevitably,

---

14 Robin Feuer Miller, *The Brothers Karamazov: Worlds of the Novel* (Boston: Twaine, 1992), 4. The idea is very important to our mutual teacher, Robert L. Belknap.
15 See, for example, Bakhtin's *Problems of Dostoevsky's Creativity: Problemy tvorchestva Dostoevskogo* (Leningrad: Priboi, 1929), 101–2.

then, in order to model the protagonist's switch from the speculative mode to the intuitive, Dostoevsky also switches the reader's mode in the same way.

Besides the nature of this specific, ideological crime and what is therefore imperative about "undoing" it, the reason for the protagonist's uncharacteristically nonintellectual repentance is the nature of true repentance itself. A crime can be done on intellectual grounds, but repentance cannot. Apparently, the main difference between *a formal act* of confession or penitence and the *experience* of true repentance is that the former may result from a thought process—such as a dialectically constructed argument—while the latter results from raw experience alone. Raskolnikov's dialectic can lead him, as an ideological murderer, into claiming the necessity of his own crime, but this same dialectic is powerless about leading him out of that trap. His crime may be ideological, but a *non*ideology is necessary for true repentance and for true liberation. Either for intellectuals or simpletons, repentance is an experience.

To sum up:

1. True repentance may not come as a logical conclusion to a logical or dialectical argument. One can kill for ideological reasons, but one cannot—no matter how hard one tries—feel or experience repentance merely because one has come to a logical conclusion that repentance is good and right.
2. In Dostoevsky, true repentance cannot even be presented as a logical argument—hence the necessity of an allusion, a subtext.
3. Repentance may mark the failure or bankruptcy of an idea, but repentance itself cannot be an idea but only a raw experience, which is granted, rather than experiecned by one's own volition. Like faith, repentance is meta-dialectic. One can pray to the Granter of repentance for it, just as for Love, Faith, and Hope. But in order to do so, one has to believe in the Granter already.

There seems to be a vicious cycle: our protagonist is an intellectual who cannot feel anything unless he thinks it through. Moreover, the reader has been conditioned to perceive this intellectual protagonist in and on his own terms presented through dialectical reasoning. The only way to break this cycle for Dostoevsky, an Orthodox believer who read the Bible, is to introduce the world of the Bible as a subtext to the events described. The reader may recognize the experience of repentance as such—an experience—by analogy with another such experience in the Bible. Against the contrasting background of Dostoevsky's usual dialogic dialectics, this analogy tells by showing, not by proving or arguing. The biblical subtext in question concerns an intended sacrifice.

In *Crime and Punishment*, there are two versions of the motif of sacrifice and sacrificing for the sake of humanity, the male and the female. The male version purports to save humanity as a whole; it is motivated by the Napoleonic idea: to save all, a truly great man is entitled to killing some. The conversation between the student and the officer, which Raskolnikov finds so attuned to his ideas—about killing a useless society member for the sake of many others—represents this kind of sacrifice. The female version is exemplified by Sonia and Dunia, who sacrifice *themselves*, with the goal—perhaps not condoned by Dostoevsky himself—of saving their siblings. Although Dostoevsky does not approve this type of sacrifice either, he more explicitly condemns the male protagonists' version of sacrifice, which entails an allegedly great man sacrificing *another* person—not himself!—for a worthy cause. This Napoleonic sort of sacrifice motivates all of Raskolnikov's thoughts, temptations, and actions. The temptation of sacrificing another for a worthy cause seems purely cerebral in its origin. Although Raskolnikov's spontaneous actions are often exempt from this Napoleonic motivation, throughout the novel, the idea of sacrificing *another* for the sake of general good reigns supreme and possesses the protagonist's intellect and imagination first, then it informs his actions. Isaac undergoes the experience of being offered as a sacrifice *himself*—not as sacrificing anyone else. It is Isaac's experience that Raskolnikov undergoes, albeit unconsciously. As opposed to Raskolnikov, a seasoned sacrificer of others, this experience was not as novel to Dostoevsky himself. Thus, there are reasons to believe that his inclusion of the passage invoking that subtext was not random or accidental.

Self-sacrifice, however, is not a valid redemptive option for mortals: unlike Christ, the Son of God for Christians like Dostoevsky, we mortals may not offer ourselves up to slaughter voluntarily: that would be suicide. To the extent that Dostoevsky's female protagonists like Sonia or Dunia sacrifice themselves voluntarily, their sacrifice has that suicidal element, and that is as wrong as the idea of prostitution itself. What makes Sonia purer is that she is not conscious of sacrificing herself, she resembles someone led to the slaughter rather than one who goes voluntarily. As for the literally suicidal protagonists in *Crime and Punishment* and in Dostoevsky's works, in general, they are mostly, though not exclusively, male, and they often confuse the notion of self-sacrifice with legitimizing suicide. Dostoevsky, arguably, has more compassion for suicides than would be officially permitted by his faith. Yet, for our case, it matters that, with reference to the bindng of Isaac, Dostoevsky is not offering any apologia for suicides, precisely because the analogy goes only so far: when sacrificed, men may imitate some qualities of Christ but not the voluntary nature of His death. They must, therefore, be sacrificed by another and must not consciously wish to die. Isaac is such a character. He is a mortal man led to slaughter, and is not a suicide.

Much as in a Greek tragedy, the main drama of *Crime and Punishment* consists of the irreversibility of its events and temptations. The protagonist can argue himself into a deed, but he cannot argue himself out of it and into any repentance about it. Generally speaking, no reasoned argument, not even a formal confession, may undo a sin morally and symbolically, in the eyes of God. The core of Raskolnikov's specific cerebral temptation is the nature of the sacrifice it promotes—killing another for a cause, rather than dying yourself for it. To "undo" this specific sin by Raskolnikov in his own conscience, three conditions must obtain:

1. the sacrifice's main fallacy must be corrected, so the protagonist may experience it as an act of *self*-sacrifice;
2. the experience must be immediate, noncerebral, and perhaps even unconscious;
3. to learn the lesson, the protagonist must survive his own self-sacrifice.

These three conditions require a drastic change in the poetics of the whole novel. The crime is argued for and described dialectically, so the repentance for it must be cast in much more immediate, noncerebral terms. Hence the new mode of description, so unlike the one chosen for the history of the protagonist's temptation and sin that the reader may not even notice it. The only marker of this shift's deliberate nature—a very significant one, however—comes at the end of the fifth paragraph from the very end of the whole novel: "Instead of dialectics, there was life, and something completely different had to work itself out in his consciousness."[16]

The hardest problem is with the third condition: How can the ideological murderer experience his own sacrifice—which, in order to atone for his murdering another person, needs to be his own death!—yet survive it? Dostoevsky knew a precedent: Isaac bound and facing imminent death but surviving it. After his mock execution, Dostoevsky found himself in a unique position as an author—knowing, as Isaac, what it means to face and survive his own death, not as a possible risk or danger, the way we do on a battlefield or risking our lives otherwise, but an assured, sentenced, and scheduled death.

Dostoevsky's resulting views on capital punishment are known to us, through Prince Myshkin's philippic against it in *The Idiot*, most famously. What concerns us more here is Dostoevsky's view of such scheduled death as sacrifice— like the sentenced Crucifixion. However, in order to identify with Christ himself, or to identify another mortal man, albeit a character, with Him, he needed a mortal figure to mediate this identification—to avoid the self-sacrifice's distortion into a mere suicide. Hence Isaac. The link between the binding of Isaac and Christ's crucifixion figures very prominently, not only in the fifteen Old Testament readings during the Orthodox Holy Saturday liturgy, among other cases in the Church, but also, quite importatly, in the world of a very prominent Jewish artist—in at least one of Mark Chagall's many paintings of the Crucifix. Like Dostoevsky's case, Chagall's also concerns two very important questions: (1) To what extent does the artist identify with his or her characters' experience of genuine and sacrificial suffering, death, and resurrection? (2) To what extent does the artist identify with his or her own protagonists, mere mortal sinners?

Freedom: Back to the Jewish Leitmotif

Dostoevsky, who survived his execution and in its stead went to Siberian prison, was likely to consider his prison as his own liberation. This paradoxical association between outward prison and liberation from imminent death as inner

---

16 "Вместо диалектики наступила жизнь, и в сознании должно было выработаться что-то совершенно другое."

liberation is something Dostoevsky might have considered an important motif associated with the Jews. It is the Jew Isai Fomich who overtly draws a link between the Siberian prison and freedom—in his case, of speech, and perhaps even thought. Prisoners tease him: "Hey, Jew, you will get knout and go to Siberia." "I'm already in Siberia." "They'll send you further." "And is the Lord God there?" "That he is." "Well, so what, then . . . As long as there's God and money, it's good anywhere."[17]

This reply makes an unusual connection between God and money, which has historically been the main prejudice against the Jews among anti-Semites. But what seems interesting about the passage is that, given both these things, Isai Fomich is not afraid of prison or oppression. Albeit cast in terms of greed, his Jewish faith still liberates him from all fear of prison, exile, or oppression. Money or no money, the Jew is free inwardly. Like the prisoners around Isai Fomich, including the narrator Gorianchikov, Dostoevsky himself cannot help feeling fascinated by this Jew's sense of freedom amidst the Siberian prison.

Just as with Isai Fomich, who symbolizes freedom for Dostoevsky, the "other river bank," the "there" of it, also beacons Raskolnikov with a freedom that one may have while in prison yet may lack even when formally free: "*There was freedom*, there a different people lived, quite unlike those here, *there time itself seemed to stop*, as if the centuries of Abraham and his flocks had not passed." (*Crime and Punishment*, epilogue; my emphasis)

Raskolnikov's subjective and unconscious experience of the Aqedah takes him outside the this-worldly time and space (hence the "there"), thereby bringing him the liberation of the transcendent world. At least twice in his oeuvre, Dostoevsky casts this liberation in terms very relevant for the Jews—in *Notes from a Dead House*, using Isai Fomich to conjure up the imagery of the Passover, and in *Crime and Punishment*, with the Aqedah, by mentioning Abraham and his centuries, flocks, and, evidently, his bound son, who is liberated by God from his own imminent death.

---

17 *Notes from a Dead House*, 116–17.

Prince Myshkin's Night Journey: Chronotope as a Symptom

Marina Kostalevsky

Among the numerous scholarly works inspired by *The Idiot*, many of them address two crucial aspects of Dostoevsky's novel: (1) the themes and images associated with Christ and Christianity, and (2) the problem of time seen both as a philosophical subject of the novel and as the formative principle in the temporal structure of the text. In this chapter, I will focus on the question of time. However, I intend to address this question not solely within the context of Christian tradition but also to examine it against the background of a Koranic vision of time.

I would like to begin my analysis by establishing a connection between two vital issues presented in *The Idiot*. The first issue is Dostoevsky's preoccupation with the nature and meaning of time as it runs through the entire novel. The second issue has to do with a theme also frequently discussed by scholars of Dostoevsky: the Koranic motifs in his oeuvre and the author's implicit identification with the Prophet Muhammad as an epileptic.

There are three levels on which time functions in the novel. The lowest level is the ordinary flow of time, as we commonly understand it, in material reality. This time of, or rather within the narrative is, of course, an important matter since it serves as one of the novel's organizing principles. It is telling, for instance, that the entire action of part 1 takes place in the course of one day. The flow of time is linear: it is explicitly recorded, almost to the minute, from the moment when Prince Myshkin's train arrives at the St. Petersburg railroad station "around nine o'clock in the morning." Myshkin appears at General Epanchin's apartment "around eleven o'clock," he is invited to join Lizaveta Prokofyevna and her daughters for lunch "at half-past twelve," and so on. The narrative progresses in such a linear fashion until the end of the day (and end of part 1). The termination of such a display of linearity is marked by Prince Myshkin rushing headlong after the troika that carries away Nastasya Filippovna and Rogozhin.

The remainder of the novel, when the events begin to unravel out of control, is however, fraught with time gaps and increasingly destructured. In terms of space, the novel's overall framework is circular: it begins with Prince Myshkin arriving from Switzerland and ends with his return to Switzerland. But the need to emphasize the symbolic circular structure of narrative time in the novel is also strongly pronounced: the main character returns to the same condition he was in before his journey to Russia; that is to say, he has undergone no transformation despite intense interaction with a host of other characters over six hundred pages. By thwarting our expectations of psychological change in his main protagonist, Dostoevsky freezes time or, rather, makes it relapse to the zero point of his story.

The highest level on which time functions in the novel is eschatological, or we may call it "apocalyptic," referring to the temporal aspect in the book of Revelation rather than to the metaphysical meaning of the Last Judgment. This is oriented towards the end of time, when time will be no more. In a sense, it is the denial of time in its habitual and accepted form, and Dostoevsky embraces this denial. When the end (*eschaton*) comes, time ceases to matter. In the earthly sense, death is the ultimate end. The author is fully aware of the narrative possibilities hidden in the fictional representation of this moment. He is fascinated by the human being on the threshold of imminent death, that is to say, death that will come at a precise and predetermined moment. Take, for example, the condition of an individual sentenced to execution. This was, of course, a major event in Dostoevsky's own life. Shattered by it, he makes Prince Myshkin equally fascinated with the phenomenon of a looming execution. Myshkin repeatedly returns to the description of such an event and his own response to it. Initiating his first conversation in the novel, he addresses the question of the human condition as magnified through the lens of the impending execution: "The strongest pain may not be in the wounds, but in knowing for certain that in an hour, then in ten minutes, then in half a minute, then now, this second—your soul will fly out of your body and you will no longer be a man."[1] We must note that Prince Myshkin returns to the same haunting image "about an hour and a half" later when he proposes a subject for Adelaida's picture: a portrait of "a condemned man a minute before the stroke of the guillotine, when he's still standing on the scaffold, before he lies down on the plank."[2] Another variation on the same theme is presented by Lebedev, who prays for "the repose of the soul of the countess Du Barry" and justifies this rather extravagant move by emphasizing the countess's alleged last words before the execution: "*Encore un moment, monsieur le bourreau, encore un moment!*" ("Минуточку одну еще повремените, господин буро, всего одну!").[3] There is little doubt that Lebedev's obsessive interest in the final book of the New Testament underlines a pivotal connection between the image of the last moment of the condemned human being and the apocalyptical notion of time that runs through the entire novel. The predicament of death's imminence confronts Dostoevsky's characters and the reader with the challenge of comparing "historical," or "ordinary," time and eschatological time. After all, if the afterlife means eternity, then *eschaton* signifies the beginning of existence beyond death where time is irrelevant. Consequently, any near-death condition may—or may not—signify, in Dostoevsky's artistic reality, a presentation of time in its various forms. Ippolit, for example, exemplifies such variation: he undergoes his own personal apocalypse that involves a catastrophe and judgment, but it does not result in the *eschaton*. This same limitation is put into relief in the famous scene where Myshkin contemplates and then comments on the copy of Holbein's *The Body of the Dead Christ in the Tomb*, which he observes at Rogozhin's house. The prince utters in desperation that this dead and hopeless body may destroy one's faith. The fact remains, however, that neither his nor the author's faith is thus destroyed, because—unlike Ippolit or Rogozhin—they both knew (and not simply intuited) that Christ had

---

1 Fyodor Dostoevsky, *The Idiot*, trans. Richard Pevear and Larissa Volokhonsky (New York: Vintage Classics, 2001), 23.

2 Ibid., 63.

3 Ibid., 197. It is worth noting that Dostoevsky uses here a particular verb, "повремените," which is related to "время": "Минуточку одну еще повремените, господин буро, всего одну!" ("Just one moment more, Mr. Executioner, just a small moment!")

existed and died only within limited, historical, ordinary time, and not in the timeless eschatological realm where he continues to exist. The question remains, however: How did they know?

At one point Myshkin says, "My time is all my own." Though it is pronounced casually, the novel's reader may be able to figure out that this phrase means that Myshkin exists outside of time as we know it. However, Myshkin's statement does not point toward some kind of philosophical solipsism but, rather, refers to his experience of time that may be called "epileptic" (as in comparison to "apocalyptic"). Phonological similarity aside, this epileptic time is shared by both the novel's main character and its author. Myshkin speaks of his epilepsy (known for centuries as a "sacred illness," *morbus sacer*) on several occasions, but perhaps the clearest depiction of the transformation of time is given when Myshkin reflects upon it shortly before he suffers his first seizure in the novel:

> He fell to thinking, among other things, about his epileptic condition, that there was a stage in it just before the fit itself … when suddenly, amidst the sadness, the darkness of soul, the pressure, his brain would momentarily catch fire, as it were, and all his life's forces would be strained at once in an extraordinary impulse. The sense of life, of self-awareness, increased nearly tenfold in these moments, which flashed by like lightning. His mind, his heart were lit up with an extraordinary light; all his agitations, all his doubts, all his worries were as if placated at once, resolved in a sort of sublime tranquility, filled with serene, harmonious joy, and hope, filled with reason and ultimate cause.[4]

This passage continues with Myshkin's narrating his epileptic experience in the first person: "'At that moment,' as he had once said to Rogozhin in Moscow, when they got together there, 'at that moment, I was somehow able to understand the extraordinary phrase that "time shall be no more."'"[5] For Dostoevsky himself, to judge from recollections of several memoirists and particularly of Sofia Kovalevskaya, a similar experience proved to be one of the dramatic affirmations of his own faith: "'I felt,' said Fyodor Mikhailovich, 'that Heaven descended to earth and swallowed me.' 'Yes, God exists!' I cried. 'And I recall no more.'"[6] One might expect, given Dostoevsky's passionate adherence to the Orthodox faith, that in elaborating on his epileptic condition he would portray

---

4 Ibid., 225.
5 Ibid., 227.
6 S. V. Kovalevskaia, *Vospominaniia detstva: Nigilistka* (Moscow: Sovetskaia Rossiia, 1989), 117.

it, as so many Christian mystics did, as his soul's ultimate union with Christ. Instead, rather remarkably, he makes a connection not to Christ but to the Prophet Muhammad:

> "All of you, healthy people," Dostoevsky continued, "don't even suspect what happiness is, that happiness which we epileptics experience for a second before an attack. Muhammad avows in his Koran that he saw Paradise and was in it. All the wise folks are convinced that he is simply a liar and deceiver. But no! He does not lie! He actually was in Paradise during an attack of epilepsy, from which he suffered just as I do. I don't know whether that blessedness lasts seconds or hours or months, but trust my word, all the joys which life can give I would not take in exchange for it!"[7]

Similarly, Dostoevsky makes Prince Myshkin describe the epileptic fit with a Koranic reference: "'Probably,' he added, smiling, 'it's the same second in which the jug of water overturned by the epileptic Muhammad did not have time to spill, while he had time during the same second to survey all the dwellings of Allah.'"[8] The allusion is of great significance, because it demonstrates that this particular Koranic motif is highly relevant to Dostoevsky's perception of time and, therefore, should be relevant to our understanding of the novel's design.

Dostoevsky's relationship to Islam, and specifically his view of the Prophet Muhammad, has been addressed a number of times, for example, in James Rice's *Dostoevsky and the Healing Art*, which provides both medical and literary examination of Dostoevsky's life and work. There is also a more recent exploration of the topic in an insightful essay, "On the Koranic Motif in *The Idiot* and *Demons*," by the late Diane Thompson.[9] The episode discussed in *The Idiot*, the Prophet's night journey, in which he ascends to heaven, is only briefly mentioned in the Koran (which, as we know, Dostoevsky had perused in French and Russian translations). Its rendition in English reads, "Glory be to Him who took His servant on a night journey from the sacred place of prayer to the furthest place of prayer upon which We have sent our blessing that We might show him some of our signs. He is the all-hearing, the all-seeing."[10]

---

7 Ibid.
8 Dostoevsky, *The Idiot*, 227.
9 Diane Denning Thompson, "On the Koranic Motif in *The Idiot* and *The Demons*," in Robert Reid and Joe Andrew, eds., *Aspects of Dostoevskii: Art, Ethics and Faith* (Amsterdam: Rodopi, 2012), 115–34.
10 *Quran*, chap. 17, Surah Al-Isra' ("The Journey by Night").

It is important to note that the episode was further orchestrated and given multiple details in the Hadith literature. In addition to reading the Koran, Dostoevsky must have learned about Muhammad from Washington Irving's *Life of Mohammed*, translated into Russian by Pyotr Kireevsky in 1857. Irving's version of the legend says that the Prophet had been woken one night by the Archangel Gabriel and under his guidance ascended to seven heavens, traveling on the miraculous animal called Al-Buraq. Irving also conveys that, according to some Islamic accounts of the night journey, Muhammad, upon his awakening by Gabriel, knocked over a jug of water and that, after having seen all the glories of Allah's universe, at the moment of his descent he observed that the water continued to spill.[11] This detail, emphasized by Myshkin in his conversation with Rogozhin, finds its way into the climactic scene during the "evening gathering at the Epanchins' dacha. The prince, at the end of his "feverish speech," knocks over the "beautiful Chinese vase." This happens just a few moments before his second epileptic fit and creates an echo with the jug of water knocked over by Muhammad on his legendary departure to paradise. The episode of the water jug in Muhammad's epileptic experience also illustrates Myshkin's own memory of "epileptic time." Like the Islamic prophet or Dostoevsky, who insisted that Muhammad "actually was in Paradise during an attack of epilepsy," the novel's protagonist "could not doubt nor could he admit any doubts" that this was "the highest synthesis of life."[12]

The nature of what, in the context of this article, I call "epileptic time" can be further elucidated with the use of the *kairos* concept. In Greek, it signifies the right, or opportune, or supreme moment for something to happen. *Chronos* means "ordinary" sequential time, *kairos* implies its indeterminacy; *chronos* is quantitative, but *kairos* has a qualitative nature. In the New Testament, *kairos* means "the appointed time in the purpose of God," the time when God acts (e.g., Mark 1:15). As used in the Eastern Orthodox liturgy, the word indicates the time when it intersects with eternity. In *The Idiot*, Prince Myshkin's epileptic seizure serves precisely as *kairos*, transporting him into "epileptic time," which makes him experience, appreciate, and realize what eschatological, or apocalyptic, time— eternity—is like. Furthermore, this epileptic *kairos* (being, in medical terms,

---

11 See Washington Irving, *Mahomet and His Successors* (Honolulu: University Press of the Pacific, 2003).

12 Dostoevsky, *The Idiot*, 226.

a symptom of this disease) functions as an element of Dostoevsky's chronotope: the most essential moment within the novel's time-space. In other words, physiological dysfunction evolves into a literary form. Of the three time representations perceptible in the novel, traditional, "ordinary" time is finite as regards an individual human being—it ends with the end of his or her life. The eschatological time consists of the finite and the infinite stages. Its finite stage, up to the point of *eschaton*, denotes an end, but it is also infinite, by the very fact of its disappearance. In other words, Dostoevsky's eternity, in accordance with the apocalypse, is apophatic. It is described in terms of negation, when "time shall be no more." What is represented as "epileptic" time is also finite and infinite, but in a different sense: it is finite, since it has a beginning and an end at the brief moment prior to the actual fit. Yet it is also infinite, since at that point, as at the moment of the *eschaton*, it transforms to time that is "no more." The function of "epileptic" time is to mediate between the other two. It is rooted in the "ordinary" world for the very reason of its occurrence amidst ordinary temporal circumstances. And it pertains to the eschatological realm because it allows an immediate breakthrough into timelessness. One recalls that in the Islamic tradition, the Prophet Muhammad's role is likewise that of a mediator between Allah and his people. With this in mind, one may describe the Christian eschatological time model in *The Idiot* as inclusive of the "epileptic" form of time taken from the Islamic tradition of the Prophet's miraculous night journey to heaven.

Furthermore, the same legend shapes an artistic paradigm that looms over the whole time–space framework of *The Idiot*. Prince Myshkin's journey from Switzerland to Russia ends exactly where it begins, in the sanatorium for the mentally ill. What is more important is that despite—or because of—all the events that have occurred in between, he returns in the same "idiotic" condition, that is, as if nothing has happened at all.

On several occasions in the novel, Prince Myshkin evokes a beautiful landscape in Switzerland. At the beginning of the *vokzal* scene in Pavlovsk we read,

> Sometimes he imagined the mountains and precisely one familiar spot in the mountains that he always liked to remember and where he had liked to walk when he still lived there, and to look down from there on the village, on the white thread of the waterfall barely glittering below, on the white clouds, on the abandoned old castle. Oh, how he wanted to be there now and to think about one thing—oh! All his life only about that—it would be enough for a thousand years! Oh, it was even necessary, even better, that they not know

him at all, and that this whole vision be nothing but a dream. And wasn't it all the same whether it was a dream or a reality?"[13]

And about hundred pages later we again witness the prince immersed in his memory:

> It was in Switzerland, during the first year of his treatment. He was still quite like an idiot then, and could not even speak properly, and sometimes did not understand what was required of him. Once he went into the mountains on a clear, sunny day, and wandered about for a long time with a tormenting thought that refused to take shape. He remembered now how he had stretched out his arms to that bright, infinite blue and wept. What had tormented him was that he was a total stranger to it all. Every morning the same bright sun rises; every morning there is a rainbow over the waterfall; every evening the highest snowcapped mountain, there, far away, at the edge of the sky, burns with a crimson flame; every little blade of grass grows and is happy! … only he knows nothing, understands nothing, neither people nor sounds, a stranger to everything and a castaway.[14]

It is not by accident that in the final scene we see Prince Myshkin in his "preexisting" condition back in Switzerland on the "familiar spot in the mountains" looking at the white thread of the waterfall. What we readers observe is not merely a "circular composition," a well-known literary device, but something deeper. It is the realization or, rather, the filling out of the time metaphor within the novel's narrative fabric. Time relapses to the zero point of the story about "the night journey" of "a positively beautiful person." And the water continues to spill.

---

13 Ibid., 347.
14 Ibid., 423.

Index

Lightning Source UK Ltd.
Milton Keynes UK
UKHW021704110219
337114UK00003B/166/P